Telecinematic Stylistics

Advances in Stylistics

Series Editors: Dan McIntyre, University of Huddersfield, UK and
Louise Nuttall, University of Huddersfield, UK

Editorial Board:
Jean Boase-Beier, University of East Anglia, UK
Beatrix Busse, University of Heidelberg, Germany
Szilvia Csábi, Independent Scholar
Yaxiao Cui, University of Nottingham, UK
Manuel Jobert, Jean Moulin University, Lyon 3, France
Lorenzo Mastopierro, University of Nottingham, UK
Eric Rundquist, Pontifica Universidad Católica de Chile, Chile
Larry Stewart, College of Wooster, USA
Odette Vassallo, University of Malta, Malta
Peter Verdonk, University of Amsterdam (Emeritus), The Netherlands
Chantelle Warner, University of Arizona, USA

Titles in the series:
Chick Lit: The Stylistics of Cappuccino Fiction, Rocío Montoro
Corpus Stylistics in Principles and Practice, Yufang Ho
Crime Fiction Migration, Christiana Gregoriou
D. H. Lawrence and Narrative Viewpoint, Violeta Sotirova
I.A. Richards and the Rise of Cognitive Stylistics, David West
Mind Style and Cognitive Grammar, Louise Nuttall
Opposition in Discourse, Lesley Jeffries
Oppositions and Ideology in News Discourse, Matt Davies
Pedagogical Stylistics, Michael Burke, Szilvia Csábi, Lara Week and Judit Zerkowitz
Style in the Renaissance, Patricia Canning
Stylistic Manipulation of the Reader in Contemporary Fiction, Sandrine Sorlin
Stylistics and Shakespeare's Language, Mireille Ravassat
Sylvia Plath and the Language of Affective States, Zsófia Demjén
Text World Theory and Keats' Poetry, Marcello Giovanelli
The Discourse of Italian Cinema and Beyond, Roberta Piazza
The Stylistics of Poetry, Peter Verdonk
World Building, Joanna Gavins and Ernestine Lahey
World Building in Spanish and English Spoken Narratives, Jane Lugea

Telecinematic Stylistics

Edited by Christian Hoffmann and
Monika Kirner-Ludwig

BLOOMSBURY ACADEMIC
LONDON • NEW YORK • OXFORD • NEW DELHI • SYDNEY

BLOOMSBURY ACADEMIC
Bloomsbury Publishing Plc
50 Bedford Square, London, WC1B 3DP, UK
1385 Broadway, New York, NY 10018, USA
29 Earlsfort Terrace, Dublin 2, Ireland

BLOOMSBURY, BLOOMSBURY ACADEMIC and the Diana logo are
trademarks of Bloomsbury Publishing Plc

First published in Great Britain 2020
This paperback edition published in 2021

Copyright © Christian Hoffmann, Monika Kirner-Ludwig and Contributors, 2020

Christian Hoffmann and Monika Kirner-Ludwig have asserted their right under the
Copyright, Designs and Patents Act, 1988, to be identified as Editor of this work.

For legal purposes the Acknowledgements on p. xii constitute an extension
of this copyright page.

Cover design: Ben Anslow

All rights reserved. No part of this publication may be reproduced or transmitted
in any form or by any means, electronic or mechanical, including photocopying,
recording, or any information storage or retrieval system, without prior
permission in writing from the publishers.

Bloomsbury Publishing Plc does not have any control over, or responsibility for,
any third-party websites referred to or in this book. All internet addresses given in
this book were correct at the time of going to press. The author and publisher regret
any inconvenience caused if addresses have changed or sites have ceased to exist,
but can accept no responsibility for any such changes.

A catalogue record for this book is available from the British Library.

A catalog record for this book is available from the Library of Congress.

ISBN: HB: 978-1-3500-4285-8
PB: 978-1-3502-9452-3
ePDF: 978-1-3500-4287-2
eBook: 978-1-3500-4286-5

Series: Advances in Stylistics

Typeset by Deanta Global Publishing Services, Chennai, India

To find out more about our authors and books visit www.bloomsbury.com
and sign up for our newsletters.

Contents

List of illustrations	vi
Notes on contributors	ix
Acknowledgements	xii
Introduction *Christian Hoffmann*	1
1 'I shouldn't have let this happen': Demonstratives in film dialogue and film representation *Maria Pavesi*	19
2 On the usefulness of the Sydney Corpus of Television Dialogue as a reference point for corpus stylistic analyses of TV series *Monika Bednarek*	39
3 'Drucilla, we need to talk': The formulaic nature of problem-oriented talk in soap operas *Sabine Jautz and Verena Minow*	63
4 Repetition in sitcom humour *Thomas C. Messerli*	87
5 Ideology in the multimodal discourse of television documentaries on Irish travellers' and gypsies' communities in the UK *Roberta Piazza*	113
6 Voice-over and presenter narration in TV documentaries *Jan Chovanec*	141
7 A mixed-method analysis of autism spectrum disorder representation in fictional television *Susan Reichelt*	165
8 The visual discourse of shots and cuts: Applying the cooperative principle to horror film cinematography *Christoph Schubert*	183
9 Effectful advertising? Film trailers and their relevance for prospective audiences *Heike Krebs*	205
10 Adapting scripture to (trans)script: A cognitive-pragmatic approach to cinematic strategies of evoking pseudo-medieval frames *Monika Kirner-Ludwig*	223
11 How comics communicate on the screen: Telecinematic discourse in comic-to-film adaptations *Christina Sanchez-Stockhammer*	263
12 'Subtitles have to become my ears not my eyes': Pragmatic-stylistic choices behind Closed Captions for the deaf and hard of hearing: the example of *Breaking Bad* *Annie Dahne and Roberta Piazza*	285
13 Metapragmatic awareness in cinematic discourse: Cohesive devices in *Notorious* (Hitchcock, 1946) *Adriana Gordejuela*	309
Index	323

Illustrations

Figures

2.1	Situating the case studies	45
2.2	Combined raw frequencies of thirteen word types ending in [In] or [Ing] in SydTV	51
2.3	Raw frequencies of *gonna/going to* in SydTV (where to ≠ preposition)	51
2.4	Raw frequencies of *wanna/want to* in SydTV	52
2.5	Raw frequencies of *'cause/because* in SydTV	52
2.6	Raw frequencies of *ain't/isn't/is not* in SydTV	53
2.7	Raw frequencies of *gotta/got to/has to/have to* in SydTV (where ... *got to* is replaceable by *gotta*)	53
5.1	*TT*'s reporter and VO using a hidden camera. 'The Town the Travellers Took Over' © Channel 5 2013	121
5.2	Tammy answers questions in close-up. 'My Life: Children of the Road' © BBC1 2011	129
5.3	Protesters at Dale Farm. 'Gypsy Eviction: The Fight for Dale Farm' © Channel 4 2011	133
5.4	Feisty Mary. 'Gypsy Eviction: The Fight for Dale Farm' © Channel 4 2011	133
5.5	Young girls and prams in Dale Farm. 'Gypsy Eviction: The Fight for Dale Farm' © Channel 4 2011	134
5.6	Grim ordinariness in Rathkeale. 'The Town the Travellers Took Over' © Channel 5	135
6.1	Humorous displacement between non-diegetic voice-over ('a new way of life') and the visual track. 'How Britain Worked' © Channel 4 2012	148
7.1	Pragmatic marker *you know*, per 1,000 words	172
7.2	Pragmatic marker *I mean*, per 1,000 words	173
7.3	Hedge *kind of*, per 1,000 words	174
8.1	Screenshot from *The Shining* (minute 00:26:31). 'The Shining' directed by Stanley Kubrick © Warner Brothers. 1980. All rights reserved	190
8.2	Screenshot from *Signs* (minute 00:57:57). 'Signs' directed by M. Night Shyamalan © Touchstone Pictures. 2002. All rights reserved	192
8.3	Screenshot from *Signs* (minute 00:27:03). 'Signs' directed by M. Night Shyamalan © Touchstone Pictures. 2002. All rights reserved	193
8.4	Screenshot from *The Shining* (minute 00:26:40). 'The Shining' directed by Stanley Kubrick © Warner Brothers. 1980. All rights reserved	199
10.1	(http://io9.gizmodo.com/ye-olde-is-fake-old-english-and-youre-mispronouncing-1679780566)	237
10.2	(https://boardgamegeek.com/thread/570408/how-speak-knights-worthy-sitting-round-table)	237

11.1	Spoken-language features in *Tintin* (*The Secret of the Unicorn*: 45) © Hergé/Moulinsart 2019	265
11.2	Correspondences between the use of language in comics versus films	268
11.3	The main cast of *Tintin*	273
11.4	The scroll (*The Secret of the Unicorn*: 11) © Hergé/Moulinsart 2019	277
12.1	A relevance model of character impression formation for both hearing and deaf audiences	288
13.1–13.3	'Tunnel shots'. 'Notorious' directed by Alfred Hitchcock © RKO Radio Pictures. 1946. All rights reserved [01:10:38]	313
13.4 and 13.5	Devlin observes Alicia and Alex Sebastian's reencounter. 'Notorious' directed by Alfred Hitchcock © RKO Radio Pictures. 1946. All rights reserved	314
13.6 and 13.7	'Tunnel shot'. 'Marnie' directed by Alfred Hitchcock © Universal Pictures. 1964. All rights reserved	314
13.8 and 13.9	Alicia's ascent and descent. 'Notorious' directed by Alfred Hitchcock © RKO Radio Pictures. 1946. All rights reserved	315
13.10–13.13	Evil characters up and down the stairs in Notorious (1946) and Suspicion (1941). 'Notorious' directed by Alfred Hitchcock © RKO Radio Pictures. 1946. All rights reserved. 'Suspicion' directed by Alfred Hitchcock © RKO Radio Pictures. 1941. All rights reserved	316
13.14–13.17	Drinks of an uncertain nature. 'Notorious' directed by Alfred Hitchcock © RKO Radio Pictures. 1946. All rights reserved	317
13.18 and 13.19	'Tunnel shots' in Shadow of a Doubt (1943) and North by Northwest (1959). 'Shadow of a Doubt' directed by Alfred Hitchcock © Universal Pictures. 1943. All rights reserved. 'North by Northwest' directed by Alfred Hitchcock © Metro-Goldwyn-Mayer. 1959. All rights reserved	318
13.20 and 13.21	Parallelism between Notorious (1946) and Suspicion (1941). 'Notorious' directed by Alfred Hitchcock © RKO Radio Pictures. 1946. All rights reserved. 'Suspicion' directed by Alfred Hitchcock © RKO Radio Pictures. 1941. All rights reserved	319

Tables

0.1	Aural and Visual Modalities (Bednarek 2015: 66)	4
1.1	Demonstrative Pronouns in the Pavia Corpus of Film Dialogue	23
1.2	Demonstrative Pronouns in the Pavia Corpus of Film Dialogue (Exophoric vs. Endophoric Use)	24
1.3	Gestural and Symbolic Exophoric Demonstrative Pronouns in Four Films	29
1.4	Sample Concordances of Symbolic *this* in the Four Films of the PCFD	32

1.5	Sample Concordances of Symbolic *that* in the Four Films of the PCFD	34
2.1	A comparison of *Gilmore Girls* and SydTV	47
2.2	Character keywords/n-grams from Bednarek (2010, 2012b)	48
2.3	Selected variants in SydTV	50
2.4	A comparison of *ain't* in SydTV and COCA/S	54
2.5	A comparison of *ain't* in SydTV and SOAP	54
3.1	Overview of (Excluded) Hits	74
3.2	Number of Hits for **[np1] , we need to talk** . across Soaps	75
3.3	Frequencies of Occurrence of Different Response Categories	77
3.4	Gender of Speakers and Addressees	80
3.5	Composition of the SOAP Corpus (Davies 2011–): Number of Words per Soap and Year	81
4.1	Types of Repetition in Episode 1 of *Better with You*	96
7.1	Word Count for Characters in *Parenthood* by Number of Episodes	168
7.2	The Hospital Scene	176
8.1	Survey of Horror Films in the Dataset	187
9.1	Double Usage Structure of Trailers	217
10.1	The Medieval Film Corpus	229
10.2	Time and Setting of Movies in the Film Corpus Sample	230
10.3	Script and Screenplay Writers of the Samples	232
10.4	Medieval Topical Components Featured in the Movie Samples	236
10.5	Wordlist of Most Frequent Types and Tokens in the Corpus	236
10.6	Checklist of Pseudo-Archaic Features in the Movie Corpus	239
10.7	The Distribution of *Thou, Thee, Ye* and *You* in the Corpus	242
10.8	Keywords in the Corpus	248
10.9	Distribution of *Sir* and *Sire* across the Corpus	249
10.10	Words with Negative Keyness in the Corpus	250
10.11	Anachronistic Reference Types	252
11.1	Code parlé, écrit, phonique and orthographique	264
11.2	Comparison of the Dialogue in the Comic Book *The Secret of the Unicorn* (23) and the Spielberg Film *The Adventures of Tintin* (2011)	272
12.1	Exhalations and Inhalations in Scene 4	292
12.2	Properties of the High-Pitched Sound Effect in Scenes 1–4	294
12.3	Identifying Speakers 1	295
12.4	Identifying Speakers 2	295
12.5	Missed '*You Know*'	296
12.6	From Embedded to Explicit Directives	297
12.7	Omissions in the CC Text	297
12.8	Identifying Point of Identity Change 1	299
12.9	Identifying Point of Identity Change 2	300
12.10	Clear Visuals	302

Contributors

Monika Bednarek is Associate Professor in Linguistics at the University of Sydney, Australia. She is a corpus-based discourse analyst who works on language use in the mass media (media linguistics) and on the connection between language and emotion/attitude. She is the author of six books, including *Language and Television Series: A Linguistic Approach to TV Dialogue* (2018, www.syd-tv.com) and *The Discourse of News Values* (2017, with Helen Caple, www.newsvaluesanalysis.com). Most recently, she has published a collection of interviews with Hollywood screenwriters, *Creating Dialogue for TV: Screenwriters Talk Television* (2019). She tweets @corpusling.

Jan Chovanec is Associate Professor of English Linguistics in the Department of English and American Studies, Masaryk University, Brno, Czech Republic. He specializes in media discourse analysis, pragmatics and sociolinguistics. He has published on various genres of written and spoken media communication, including online news, live text commentary, sports broadcasting and, most recently, unscripted broadcast programmes and TV documentaries. He is the author of *The Pragmatics of Tense and Time in News* (2015), *The Discourse of Online Sportscasting* (2018) and co-editor of several volumes, including *The Dynamics of Interactional Humor* (2018, with Villy Tsakona).

Annie Dahne graduated from the University of Sussex with First Class Honours in BA English Language and Linguistics. She currently works in Hong Kong as a development analyst for a non-profit education organization called Room to Read, which provides literacy programmes and publishes children's books in local languages for students in low-income communities throughout Asia and Africa.

Adriana Gordejuela is a junior researcher at the Institute for Culture and Society of the University of Navarra (Spain). Her doctoral dissertation dealt with the cognitive dimension of film flashbacks and developed a model of analysis that accounts for the viewers' understanding of such devices. She is interested in different issues regarding cinematic cognition and pragmatics, such as the comprehension of cinematic transitions in general, embodiment in film and the emotional dimensions of film cognition.

Christian Hoffmann is a senior lecturer in English Linguistics at the University of Augsburg, Germany. He has worked on narratives in old and new media (*Narratives revisited*, 2011) as well as on online discourse (*Meaning and Interaction in Blogs, 2013*). More recently, Christian Hoffmann has co-edited de Gruyter's eleventh instalment of the Handbook of Pragmatics Series (*The Pragmatics of Social Media*, 2017), and co-written an introduction of Pragmatics (Englische Pragmatik 2019). His research efforts are currently devoted to compiling a comprehensive large-scale, cross-generic corpus of annotated television scripts, while writing a monograph on the pragmatics of film genres.

Sabine Jautz works as a lecturer for English and applied linguistics at the University of Siegen, Germany. Her research interests include variational pragmatics, corpus linguistic as well as conversation analytic approaches to discourse in mass media such as radio and television and, most recently, communicative practices in coaching and other helping professions.

Monika Kirner-Ludwig is Assistant Professor of English Linguistics at the University of Innsbruck, Austria, and Research Affiliate of both the National Research Tomsk State University, Russia, and the University at Albany, State University of New York, USA. Her research interests cut across the rich areas of Sociolinguistics, Multilingualism and Intercultural Pragmatics, all of which she approaches from both synchronic and historical as well as interdisciplinary and cross-linguistic viewpoints. Her most recent publications include single- and co-authored papers in the *Journal of Pragmatics* (2018, 2019) and the *Journal of Corpus Pragmatics* (2017, with Istvan Kecskés).

Heike Krebs is a Research Assistant and PhD candidate in the field of English linguistics at the University of Augsburg, Germany. In her research she focuses on media studies, multimodality, pragmatics and film theory, as well as gender and diversity in educational settings.

Thomas C. Messerli is a research and teaching assistant at the University of Basel, Switzerland, where he is writing his doctoral thesis on repetition and humour in telecinematic discourse. He has an M.A. in Linguistics from the University of Zürich (thesis on the dubbing of humour in the sitcom *The Big Bang Theory* from English to German), and an M.A. in Film Studies from the Réseau Cinéma CH (Universities of Zürich and Lausanne, thesis on Hollywood Adaptations of Japanese horror films). His current research interests are in telecinematic discourse and in humour research – with a particular focus on the interface between humour and repetition.

Verena Minow is Senior Lecturer in English Language and Linguistics at Ruhr University Bochum, Germany. Her research and teaching focuses on World Englishes, (variational) pragmatics, audiovisual translation and language on social media. Her most recent publication is 'Royal Vowels: The Use of Received Pronunciation among Members of the Royal Family' (2017).

Maria Pavesi is Professor of English Language and Linguistics at the Department of Humanities at the University of Pavia. Her current research has addressed several topics in English applied linguistics, including audiovisual translation, the language of dubbing, corpus-based translation studies and second language acquisition. She was recently member of the core team of the international project Tapping the Power of Foreign Films – Audiovisual Translation as Cross-cultural Mediation, funded by the UK Arts and Humanities Research Council. Her most recent publications include 'Reappraising Verbal Language in Audiovisual Translation: From Description to Application' (2018) and 'Corpus-Based Audiovisual Translation Studies: Ample Room for Development' and 'Dubbing' (2019).

Roberta Piazza is Reader in English Language & Linguistics at the University of Sussex, UK. Her interests range from ethnographic linguistic studies of identity, as she explores in her edited volume *Discourses of Identity in Liminal Places and Spaces* (2019) and the co-edited book with A. Fasulo *Marked Identities* (2014), to pragmatics and media discourse, which she investigates in *The Discourse of Italian Cinema and Beyond* (2011), *Telecinematic Discourse* (2011 co-edited with M. Bednarek and F. Rossi) and *Values and Choices in Television Discourse* (2015 co-edited with L. Haarman and A. Caborn). She has published widely in international refereed journals.

Susan Reichelt is a Lecturer for English linguistics at the University of Greifswald in Germany. Her research interests lie with the linguistic construction of diverse characters in television series. This was also the focus of her doctoral dissertation, which she completed at Cardiff University in 2018. She has since worked on current developments in discourse-pragmatic variation in British English and big data corpus compilation for sociolinguistics.

Christina Sanchez-Stockhammer is Senior Lecturer in Modern English Linguistics at LMU Munich. She has published on a large variety of topics, such as the word-family integration of the English lexicon (*Consociation and Dissociation*, 2008), interdisciplinary semiotics, the language of comics, hybridization in language, punctuation as an indication of register, the corpus-based translation equivalents of the times of day in English and German and the question of whether one can predict linguistic change. Her most recent book is *English Compounds and Their Spelling* (2018). For further information, see www.christina-sanchez.de

Christoph Schubert is Full Professor of English Linguistics at the University of Vechta, Germany. He has published mainly in the areas of discourse studies, stylistics, pragmatics and text linguistics. He is author of a book-length introduction to English text linguistics (2nd ed. 2012), co-editor of a special issue of the *Journal of Language and Politics* entitled 'Cognitive Perspectives on Political Discourse' (2014), co-editor of the collections *Variational Text Linguistics* (2016) and *Pragmatic Perspectives on Postcolonial Discourse* (2016), as well as co-author of the new edition of *Introduction to Discourse Studies* (2018).

Acknowledgements

In the process of editing this volume, we have received generous assistance, which we are pleased to acknowledge here. First, we would like to thank the series editor, Dan McIntyre, for his enduring support and guidance during the production of this book. In a similar vein, we owe a great debt of gratitude to the various reviewers. Their constructive feedback has helped us considerably in increasing the overall quality and substance of the book. In addition, many of our colleagues and friends have helped shape our vision associated with this volume. Many a discussion has enhanced our understanding of what telecinematic stylistics is and what it has to offer.

We are also grateful to the International Pragmatics Association (IPrA) for enabling us to chair a workshop at the IPrA conference in Antwerp, Belgium, in 2015, where many of our ideas picked up pace. At the time, the workshop proved the incredible potential of telecinematic research for linguists. It has thus been a major stepping-stone on our way towards publishing a volume on telecinematic stylistics some five years later.

We are particularly indebted to the various contributors of this volume for their patience as well as loyal and unwavering commitment to our project. In terms of production, we would like to pay tribute to the many helping hands at Bloomsbury, who have actively contributed to getting the book 'into shape', most notably perhaps Andrew Wardell, Becky Holland, Leeladevi Ulaganathan and Dhanuja Ravi. The same naturally applies to the many helpers at the University of Augsburg, Germany, and the University of Innsbruck, Austria, who helped us tremendously during the formatting phases of the book. To this end, we would like to show our heartfelt appreciation to Julia Heiss, Viktoria Kruckenhauser, Carolina Vasconsellos Billio Manhaes de Azevedo, Lena Scharrer and Elena Mayer.

Christian Hoffmann & Monika Kirner-Ludwig, Augsburg/Innsbruck, December 2019

Television series

(in order of appearance)
'The Town the Travellers Took Over' © Channel 5 2013
'My Life: Children of the Road' © BBC1 2011
'Gypsy Eviction: The Fight for Dale Farm' © Channel 4 2011
'How Britain Worked' © Channel 4 2012
'Parenthood' © NBC 2010-2015
'Breaking Bad' © AMC 2008-2013

Feature films

'The Shining' directed by Stanley Kubrick © Warner Brothers. 1980. All rights reserved.

'Signs' directed by M. Night Shyamalan © Touchstone Pictures. 2002. All rights reserved.

'The Adventures of Tintin' directed by Steven Spielberg© Columbia Pictures and Paramount Pictures. 2011. All rights reserved.

'Notorious' directed by Alfred Hitchcock © RKO Radio Pictures. 1946. All rights reserved.

'Suspicion' directed by Alfred Hitchcock © RKO Radio Pictures. 1941. All rights reserved.

'Shadow of a Doubt' directed by Alfred Hitchcock © Universal Pictures. 1943. All rights reserved.

'Marnie' directed by Alfred Hitchcock © Universal Pictures. 1964. All rights reserved.

'North by Northwest' directed by Alfred Hitchcock © Metro-Goldwyn-Mayer. 2959. All rights reserved.

Introduction

Christian Hoffmann

The term *motion picture* is a well-known synonym for *feature film*. It speaks to the classic idea of film making as an artful sequential assemblage of film shots which tricks audiences into believing that the projected images on screen come alive in front of their eyes. Film, regarded as a purely visual medium, we might infer, could easily fare without spoken or written language (cf. Jaeckle 2013: 14), and, following this rationale, great film directors in the past have often preferred to tell their stories through visual rather than verbal means of expression (Toolan 2014: 455, cf. Kozloff 2000: 26; Bednarek 2018: 3). This notwithstanding, film directors today are likely to question the idea that films are purely visual art forms. More likely, they will point out, instead, how sound can change the overall film experience. For instance, Bordwell (2014: n.p.) holds that, historically, visual storytelling has never been 'purely visual [and i]n film [...] needs concepts and music and noises and even dialogue to work most fully' (cf. Chion 2019). The contemporary film and television experience is only partly driven by a quick series of pictures we perceive as movement on the silver screen. More than that, today's film is additionally fuelled by sounds and voices emanating from a complex array of loudspeakers, which envelop the film audience with carefully crafted soundscapes. The mélange of sound and vision turns film interpretation into a complex business, one in which the audience needs to combine what they see with what they hear (and what they know and expect):

> I work with actors through my ear. Prior to making television films and films for the cinema, I spent twenty years as a stage director. Inevitably, during our rehearsals [with actors], I would be looking down, with my head in my hands, and the actors would complain I wasn't looking at them. I would reply that I can see them better when I'm looking down because I hear the mistakes that they are making. I can hear how they are acting. (Director Michael Haneke in Film Society of Lincoln Center 2009)

What such quotes illuminate is, on the one hand, the complex multimodal nature of film and television discourse and, on the other hand, the deeply interwoven nature of sound and pictures in cinematic storytelling. Today, cinematic sound has much to contribute not only during audience reception but likewise in film production. As a result, any serious analysis of film and television needs to pay attention to (at least) two different strands of cinematic expression: one that focuses on the choice, set-up and arrangement of film (photographic) pictures and another one that centres on the use of *cinematic sound* (music, sound design, spoken and written language).

Janney (2012: 86) acknowledges this fundamental expressive division between the visual and the verbal in film by distinguishing the concepts of *cinematic discourse* and *film discourse*. While the former embraces 'the discourse of mise-en-scène, cinematography, montage, [etc.]', the latter refers to the 'scripted conversation in fictional interaction' (Janney 2012: 86).[1] Similarly, Toolan (2001: 104) encourages us to systematically probe spoken language in films but equally insists that, in the realm of cinema, the exploration of language must be linked to what he describes as a 'blend of several modalities' (Toolan 2001: 104). In fact, film stylistics, he claims, can

> show how the subjective impressions and intuitive responses of reasonably acculturated filmgoers are sourced in a range of foregrounded or patterned effects and techniques carefully achieved by the film-making team, and to underpin its account with arguments, evidence and texts. (Toolan 2014: 449)

Toolan's insight has certainly not escaped the attention of stylisticians who have begun to chart the stylistic landscape of film language since the early 1980s (e.g. Scannell and Cardiff 1991; Tolson 2005; Stokoe 2008; McIntyre 2008, 2012; Bednarek 2010; Bousfield and McIntyre 2011). Stylistic studies on film and television seem to have been gaining special momentum since the turn of the century, including new and original work on film and television characters, genre properties, narrative styles and audience effects (Montgomery 2007; Richardson 2010; Heritage and Clayman 2011; Hodson 2014; Thornborrow 2014; Bednarek 2008, 2018).[2] As a result, this book contributes to what has by now grown into a veritable field of stylistic research in its own right, that is, 'telecinematic stylistics'.[3] This book aims to retrace some of its more recent trends, showcasing the rich confection of theoretical and methodological approaches which find broad application in the field. To us, it appears that these trends can be linked to five key developments which stylistic film studies have undergone in the last two decades:

1. An investigation of different film and television genres, subgenres and hybrid genres, including the expansion of stylistic studies to non- and semi-fictional film genres, for example, documentaries or news shows. This trend allows, over time, for ever more 'vertical' readings of compatible film and television shows, exploring the verbal landscapes of film and television genres in greater detail. The aim of such research clearly is to accumulate more reliable, empirically based findings of film and television genres, their norms and expectations, deviations and differences linked to recurring formal or functional properties.
2. A more diverse use of different types and formats of film discourse on which analysts draw to engage with films and television. Such types can range from (blends of) dialogues and monologues, narrators and characters, on-screen or off-screen, diegetic and non-diegetic sounds to the cinematic exploitation of written language both on-screen and in screenplays.

3. A broadening of quantitative and qualitative methods from a wide array of linguistic disciplines to explore the shades of spoken and written language in film and television (including critical discourse studies, systemic-functional linguistics, conversation analysis, ethnomethodology or corpus linguistics and qualitative and quantitative sociolinguistics).
4. The gradual move from (monomodal) studies on the language used in film and television to more elaborate examinations of the multimodal resources which collectively yield the audiovisual experience of cinematic discourse, thereby incorporating other forms of cinematic expressions, for example, sound, music, editing techniques, shot lengths, body language (O' Halloran 2004; Tseng and Bateman 2012).
5. A change from studies which focus on the 'naturalness', 'authenticity' or 'reality' of scripted film dialogues to the examination of cinematic language as a cultural object of study in its own right, fit to unearth social beliefs, values and ideologies in popular media (cf. Androutsopoulos 2012; Queen 2015).

All chapters of this volume revolve around these five general trends, although they may attend to different audiovisual patterns of cinematic discourse and be based on varying theories and methods to describe quite distinct verbal and visual patterns and meanings. To draw out the commonalities and differences between the studies in this book, we feel it is necessary to consider first what we mean by the notion of *telecinematic discourse*. We shall then address the main challenges and opportunities that come with studying telecinematic discourse from a stylistic vantage point, and recapitulate what telecinematic research has treated so far. Finally, we will round off the chapter with a look at each contribution, unpacking the topical links that turn the chapters into a meaningful whole.

1 What is telecinematic discourse?

To understand the scope and nature of this volume, it is important to comprehend its central concept 'telecinematic discourse'. In this section, we will sketch out what it means and how this meaning is related to similar notions as used in the field today, such as *telecinematic dialogue, film dialogue, film language*. The term itself was arguably first coined by Piazza, Bednarek and Rossi (2011: 1), who used it as a cover term for all linguistic investigations into the nature of film and television. More precisely, they describe telecinematic discourse as

> an exploration of <u>spoken and written language used in fictional/narrative film and television</u> from various perspectives and discussing different kinds of data. [... It] attempts to understand, describe and define such language in its relation to real life and in consideration of its functions within the fictional narrative: how special if at all is <u>the language of cinema and television</u>. (Piazza, Bednarek and Rossi 2011: 1, my emphasis)

We share the implicit view that film and television are two very similar types of audiovisual media,[4] which aligns with Androutsopoulos (2012) convergence assumption of film and television. The latter (Androutsopoulos 2012: 149) contends that

> assuming clear-cut boundaries between [television and cinema] is in my view empirically futile and theoretically unproductive in the context of contemporary transmedia flows, where films are screened on television, TV serial productions adopt film narratives and visual aesthetics, and all of the above is increasingly transferred to the Internet.

Our own reading of telecinematic discourse, however, departs from Piazza, Bednarek and Rossi's classic description in three essential ways to be discussed in the following:

First, we feel that the notion of 'language' in the original definition needs some further specification. The language of cinema and television comprises more than just television or movie monologue or dialogue. Following Janney (2012); Bateman and Schmidt (2013) and McIntyre (2008), we advocate a broader vision of telecinematic discourse, which includes all types of cinematographic and semiotic resources which take part in the meaning-making process of film and television production. To be sure, these resources either fall into the realm of verbal *film discourse* (film and television monologue and dialogue) or align with Janney's class of visual *cinematic discourse* (cinematographic techniques – for example, framing, editing, lighting, colours, montage). Such a distinction also reverberates in classification schemes offered by other film scholars. Bednarek (2015: 66), for instance, likewise splits the film experience into visual and aural modes of expression (see Table 0.1), which underscore the keyness of the conceptual cut between the aural and the visual as two primary semiotic dimensions of telecinematic expression.

Second, Piazza, Bednarek and Rossi (2011) share a rather restrictive view of the concept telecinematic discourse. They deliberately constrain it to the study of 'fictional/narrative film and television' (1). In contrast, we would like to use the term in a much broader sense. For us, the notion additionally expands to all types and forms of non- or semi-fictional film and television genres, including documentaries, talk or news shows. Since the conceptual boundary between fictional and non–fictional representation in film and television is inherently fuzzy and hard to delineate, we aim for such an inclusive, prototypical reading of (non-)fictional film discourse, which encapsulates

Table 0.1 Aural and Visual Modalities (Bednarek 2015: 66)

Film and TV narratives as multimodal and multisemiotic texts		
Modalities	**'Aural' (what we can hear)**	**'Visual' (what we can see)**
Semiotic systems (incomplete inventory)	Musical scoring, sound effects, dialogue (the three subsets of the film soundtrack, Kozloff 2000: 117) or music, noise, speech (Bordwell and Thompson 2008: 268)	Moving images (angle, colour, brightness, etc.); transitions (cuts, fades, wipes, etc.); written language; gesture, posture, facial expression; and so on

overtly dramatized fictional discourse (e.g. romantic comedies), more covertly semi-objective forms of film making (e.g. docufiction), to clearly and openly non-fictional film and television formats (e.g. documentaries). We must admit that feature films and television are different media which come equipped with their own areas of specialization. Concurrently, some non- or semi-fictional television programmes will probably never find their way onto the silver screen, for example, cooking shows and news shows. Other (fictional) television series do. It is thus fair to say that, despite their differences, feature films and television shows have converged considerably throughout the last three decades, not only in their respective use of cinematography, production and technology. A growing number of feature films has recently even been co-released and cross-marketed in film theatres and on (online) television streaming services alike. Today, news shows readily apply cinematic and linguistic effects of the classic Hollywood cinema, while fictional television series may choose to adopt the cinematography from classic film documentaries (Montgomery 2007: 89f.). We have thus no reason to preclude film from television, nor can we clearly contrast non-fictional discourse from dramatized fictional discourse per se. They have moved closer and have more in common today than separates them. Such similarities (between feature film and television) might be most tangible in *dramatized fictional discourse* recorded in audiovisual form. It is thus unsurprising that most of this volume's contributions focus on this type of discourse bar two papers which take a critical look at the dramatization of (non-fictional) documentaries (cf. Piazza, Chovanec).[5]

Third, Piazza, Bednarek and Rossi (2011) almost exclusively present studies that deal with scripted fictional talk in film and television.[6] However, film discourse does not only comprise dialogues but also monologues, spoken by primary or secondary characters on- or off-screen (diegetic) or by one or many different narrators from off-screen (non-diegetic) positions. This raises the level of communicative complexity for film analysts in considerable ways. So, telecinematic voices do not only find expression in film dialogues but may take the shape of a wide array of aural (re-)presentations, for example, in music scores, songs and sounds.

Our three central differences thus give rise to a new, arguably more nuanced, definition of telecinematic discourse which we have tried to capture here:

> Telecinematic discourse refers to the use (and interplay) of both (aural) film discourse and (visual) cinematic discourse. While film discourse refers to the use of verbal language in all of its possible forms, shapes and shades of expression (spoken and written, monologue and dialogue, diegetic and non-diegetic), cinematic discourse describes the manifold (visual) techniques and semiotic resources (apart from aural language) which directors strategically apply to create comprehensive, complex telecinematic experiences for a given audience at home or in cinemas.

While we have now set out our position on telecinematic discourse, the next section will address some of the major challenges and problems film analysts face when they confront this specialized type of discourse. As we shall see, most issues are of a methodological nature and commonly appear as three basic types, which we would like to call the *complexity problem*, the *transcription issue* and the *participation complex*. Each one of these issues will be introduced and discussed in the following in more detail, providing new insight into the overall structure and coherence of all contributions in this book.

2 How to analyse telecinematic discourse

Film and television are media which are notoriously difficult to capture and study in any comprehensive fashion since the cultural artefacts they produce constitute semiotically rich, technically advanced products which are hard to unpack and difficult to process. Usually, the expressive modes, which collate to build up the audiovisual cinematic experience, operate simultaneously on various layers of multimodal meaning in a given film shot or scene. Film art is thus about knowing how to orchestrate the different visual and aural resources which are invested in this experience, for example, spoken and written language, gesture and mimics, sound effects and music.

Understandably, describing how all of these cinematic 'ingredients' are mixed is intricate, and often difficult to expose in linear academic writing, and we may call this the *complexity problem*. It forces us to select, and consequently foreground, particular expressive modes which usually serve the analyst's own objectives or scholarly interest. The selection, however, comes at the expense of losing the cinematic 'voice' of other semiotic resources, which play into the dynamics of the final film, but remain analytically suppressed in a study at hand. Analytical 'condensation' of this kind, however, must be justified on (at least) three grounds:

1. The fact that the basic research interest, tradition and orientation of the scholar necessitates such choices to make studies tangible and comprehensible to specialized research communities. For instance, linguists are more inclined to study language use in films than film historians.
2. The relative salience (size, volume, positioning) of expressive modes in a series of film shots, scenes or episodes might make them perceptually more important than others; for example, the character dialogue and camera framing may be more prominent in given scene than the lighting or the score.
3. The focus on the semiotic interplay of a *limited* set of semiotic resources naturally depends on the technical exigencies of each resource within a given film shot or scene. Film dialogue and film edits might contribute more important meaning facets in a given shot than other audiovisual resources.

In light of these reflections, the studies in this volume are arguably lodged in a linguistic tradition, which makes them privilege the analysis of spoken and written language. We believe that this 'logocentric' orientation is acceptable, since our knowledge of language use both within and across different film and television genres is still piecemeal. While all studies in this book thus begin with some type of analysis of film or television language, most deliberately expand their analytical reach beyond the spoken or written word. They explore how spoken language in telecinematic discourse unfolds and how it is aligned and combined with additional semiotic building blocks. All studies, in one way or another, however, will rely on a corpus, usually a transcription of the audiovisual film artefact, so that the expressive modes can be explored systematically. This requires the symphony of audiovisual modes to be split up and broken down into a 'readable' verbal format, into some sort of document. Such a 'document' or script only approximates the actual film product, which it is designed to mirror. To this effect, every film transcription process already involves a number of (subjective) judgement calls, that is, coding choices and interpretations on the part of the transcriber, which might impose on the results and interpretation of the study in the end. This problem, that is, the practical decomposition of the overall film experience into some tangible form, is what we call *the transcription problem*.

According to Bednarek (2015: 69), there are four different strategies to resolve this problem. She proposes four different strategies for using corpora for television research. The first would be to draw on existing corpora of film and television discourse, such as the Corpus of American Soap Operas, the television corpus or the movie corpus (SOAP, TV Corpus, Movie Corpus, Davies 2012). The second strategy would be the automatic extraction of subtitles, which would provide you with dialogue data but insufficient information on character names, screen directions, and so on. The third strategy would be to build a corpus based on existing screenplays or scripts accessible on the internet, with the caveat that actor performances might deviate from initial screenplays in the film product. The final strategy, Bednarek recommends, is the compilation of a corpus of film and television language from scratch: an option which, for most, is probably too time-consuming but may be the right choice for analysts who wish to examine specific scenes or sequences exclusively.

In addition to these four strategies, we hold that three central features determine the usability of scripts found, selected or compiled offline or online: *production time*, *transcription quality* and *accessibility*. In terms of production time, scripts can be created before, during or after the production of a film or television series. Scripts written before or during film production are typically labelled *screenplays* and may come in different drafts, reflecting different temporal stages in the preproduction process of a film. When scripts are written (commonly by fans) after the official release of a film or television series, they are called 'transcripts' (Bednarek 2015: 63). These transcripts, though similar to screenplays, are often written and composed by non-professional authors, with different purposes and audiences in mind. Differences usually surface in transcription consistency, level of detail and transcription accuracy (e.g. excluding screen directions, camera movements, frame positions). Naturally, each type of script – that is, screenplay, script, transcript – has its own upshots and downsides. Screenplays may be very precise and complete but can differ from the final film shown on screen because directors chose to omit a shot sequence altogether. Some actors may also be more 'flexible' with screenplays and alter dialogue parts during the shoot of a scene. In contrast, transcripts may be able to capture these final changes to the screenplay, but instead their quality may be poor.

So, when you read through the studies in this book, bear in mind that the chapters might draw on different types of scripts. Some studies may use screenplays, others fan scripts and still others self-compiled multimodal transcripts of the final film. The respective corpus choice and individual corpus design is always dovetailed to the studies seek to find.

Sometimes, however, analytical choices are restricted, for instance by the scarcity or limited accessibly of screenplays and scripts. To this end, some screenplays might be accessible gratuitous on the internet in acceptable quality, but others may be harder to come by, could be copyright-protected and have to be purchased in advance.

The final problem we need to address when working with telecinematic discourse is what we have chosen to call the *participation complex*. It addresses the fact that film and television discourse have always been subject to complex levels of communication, involving a large collection of creators (e.g. directors, actors, screenwriters, editors, directors of photography) as well as recipients (e.g. characters/actors, third party actors, target audience, secondary, unaddressed audience). What Scannell and Cardiff (1991) called *dual articulation* consists of at least two different communicative frames: one in which the diegetic story characters communicate through scripted dialogues, and a second one in which the creative team of film makers ('the collective sender', Dynel 2015: 5) addresses the film audience. The first communicative plane already unfolds a communicative dynamic with one (primary) story character talking to another (primary) character, or indeed a group of characters, while other (secondary) characters remain unaddressed by the first character although the film shot clearly shows them to be present and attentive to the ongoing talk.

Goffman (1981) and Levinson (1988) have described speaker's audience design (their awareness of who is addressed and who is listening) and both have developed quite distinctive frameworks for the specification of production and reception roles in different communicative contexts.[7]

If we move to the second plane of communication, the communication framework becomes even more complex. Brock (2015), for instance, has shown how different television genres make use of various communicative constellations between participants on both levels of communication and exploit it for various (narrative, social, humorous) effects. In comedy shows or news shows, for example, characters address the television audience directly or address characters and (a specific group of) the viewing audience at the same time. Screenwriters can also choose to make audiences (more or less) aware of character flaws to anticipate future conflicts and increase the suspense of story events as they unfold over time. To this end, acknowledging the value of audience design in studying telecinematic discourse turns out to be extremely important since it can influence the plot development, the language and style of characters, their sociolinguistic patterns, for example, dialects, accents, code switching, grammatical and lexical choice, degree of formality, and so on (Bubel and Spitz 2006; Taylor 2006; Bucholtz and Lopez 2011; Walshe 2011; Bleichenbacher 2008).

All contributions featured in this volume relate and differ from each other in view of these three key methodological issues in telecinematic stylistics, that is, the complexity problem, the transcription issue and the participation complex. Knowing which film resources they focus on (monomodal, verbal studies vs. multimodal investigations), which scripts they use (screenplays, fan scripts, subtitles, self-compiled scripts) and which films, scenes and target audiences they address will help you understand what unites their approaches and what tells them apart. What is more, you will be able to appreciate and assess the chapters to come much better once you consider how they dealt with the problems discussed before.

3 Previous research

Before we introduce the individual chapters and their topical coherence in more detail, we would like to acknowledge the exceptional work on film and cinematic discourse that has shaped how we approach the study of telecinematic stylistics today. Praise is certainly due to early work on cinematic dialogue by a range of eminent film sound scholars, such as Weis (1982), Silverman (1988), Chion (1994, 1999), Kozloff (2000) or Jaeckle (2013) who each contributed genuine insights to the 'gendered, ideological and epistemological implications of the voice in cinema' (Jaeckle 2013: 14). Without these studies, and their theoretical and practical considerations of cinematic voices and sounds, linguistic explorations of film discourse seem unthinkable.

With a view to cinematic discourse, classic introductions to the cinematography and 'visual grammar' of film come to mind, including but not restricted to Lacey (1998), Prince (2007), Monaco (2009), Bordwell and Thompson (2008), van Leeuwen (1999), Nichols (2010), Janney (2010, 2012). Corpus-linguistic approaches to the study of film and television have likewise had a profound impact of telecinematic stylistics, using keywords, collocations, concordances to determine language patterns across larger sets of films and television series. A different strand of film and (mostly) television research centres on the organization of talk-in-interaction and includes the notable insights of ethnomethodological conversation analysis (Hutchby 2005; Thornborrow 2017; Montgomery 2007; Lorenzo-Dus 2009; Lorenzo-Dus and Garcés-Conejos Blitvitch 2013; Stokoe 2008).

Other linguistic studies have engaged in 'fidelity checks' (Androutsopoulos 2012: 145), examining the general properties of film talk comparing it natural-occurring conversations (Quaglio 2009; Rodríguez Martín 2010; Bednarek 2010, 2011a, 2012b; Forchini 2012; McIntyre 2012). Stylistic studies on film and television have largely focused on characterization (Piazza 2010, 2011, 2012; Piazza, Haarman and Caborn 2015; Toolan 2011; Mahlberg and McIntyre 2011; Bednarek 2010, 2011a, 2012, 2015; Schubert 2017; Reichelt and Durham 2017) or the telecinematic construction of mind style and metaphor (Montoro 2009; Forceville 2007, 2014). More recently, multimodal studies of cinematic composition, argumentation, cohesion and coherence have seen the light of day, encouraging stylisticians to expand their examination of film discourse to cinematic discourse in a way we have advocated before (Bateman and Schmidt 2013; Tseng 2013; Tseng and Bateman 2010; Wildfeuer and Bateman 2016; Bateman, Wildfeuer and Hiippala 2017). Still other studies have explored the styles of dialogues and monologues, using qualitative approaches to uncover hidden scripted ideologies in news and sports broadcasting (Chovanec 2015, 2019), interactional humour (Dynel 2011: 1, 2012; Chovanec 2017; Schubert 2018), the coherence and comprehension of television dialogue (Toolan 2011; Wildfeuer) or the manifold effects of telecinematic audience design (cf. Dynel and Chovanec 2015). A field of research which seems particularly amenable to the analysis of film discourse is pragmatic literary stylistics

(Chapman and Clark 2014; Clark 2015; Chapman 2015; Wildfeuer 2017) and, more recently, sociolinguistics, which includes gender, dialect and ethnicity (Rey 2001; Baker 2005; McIntyre and Walker 2010; Richardson 2010; McIntyre 2012; Buscombe 2013; Bednarek 2011b, 2015; Planchenault 2017).

All of these strands of film research have built the groundwork for this volume, and the chapters you are about to read will reflect their rich scholarly heritage. It is on this basis that we now move to the overview of chapters in this book. The great range of topics and approaches unites different contributions in multiple, often-overlapping ways. While we have attempted to structure them in four general groups, to maintain a suitable level of topical coherence throughout the volume, fuzzy boundaries are unavoidable. Therefore, the next section introduces each chapter in more detail, for example, its object of study, research objective and methodology, revealing the general topical and methodological links that hold between them.

4 Overview of the volume

To give overall structure and coherence to the book, we decided to cluster all contributions around three key areas of interest in telecinematic stylistics, that is, *film discourse, cinematic discourse* and *intertextuality/intermediality*. They will be explained in more detail presently, alongside short previews of the contributions. While some approaches use quantitative, corpus-linguistic methods (Bednarek; Jautz and Minow; Reichelt; Pavesi) other take a qualitative (or mixed-method) approach (Schubert; Piazza; Piazza and Dahne; Sanchez-Stockhammer; Gordejuela). All chapters shall now be introduced in chronological order. We start by taking a closer look at the first part, that is, film discourse.

The first part of this volume (film discourse) joins contributions that focus exclusively on particular *language patterns and their meanings* in the scripted fictional talk of film and television characters. This section of the book contains studies by Pavesi; Bednarek; Minow and Jautz; and Messerli. In Chapter 1, Pavesi examines the use and meaning of demonstratives in feature films. Expounding the manifold pragma-stylistic dimensions of demonstratives in feature films, she uses a corpus-based approach to show how screenwriters employ this paramount linguistic feature to gear the audience's perception to important visual stimuli and control the narrative texture and flow of telecinematic discourse. Drawing on the *Pavia Corpus of Film Dialogue*, Pavesi likewise illustrates how demonstratives establish and negotiate common ground that unfolds over time between the characters on-screen and the film audience. Demonstratives thus constitute an important narrative device, evoking audience expectations and triggering conversational implicatures about the story's characters and potential plot development (Caink and Clark 2012; Pavesi 2015). In the second chapter, Bednarek equally focuses on ways to explore scripted film and television dialogues but exposes the methodological opportunities of a new, genre-balanced reference corpus of television language (*Sydney Corpus of Television Dialogue, SydTV*). Applying keyword analysis and concordances, the author introduces this television corpus as a benchmark for studies that wish to find out if the level of regional or social variation in the television show they investigate deviates from the SydTV 'standard'. More specifically, she explains how the reference corpus can be fruitfully applied to expose non-standard pronunciation variants or linguistic 'personality traits' of film characters (n-grams, keywords, etc.) in film and television. Also based on a corpus-driven approach, Jautz and Minow discuss the use of problem-oriented talk in soap operas in Chapter 3. They expect conflict talk to surface through recurring formulaic utterances in the scripted talk in the Corpus of American Soap Operas (Davies 2012). Focusing on the recurring expression '[Name], we need to talk', they manage to reveal striking quantitative and qualitative differences in the use of the expression as an indicator of conflict talk in different soap subgenres and different corpora of American English (e.g. COCA, SOAP). They likewise use their corpus analysis of the formulaic expression to dive deeper into the systematics of response strategies used by television characters when confronted with a request to engage in conflict talk. The study shows how corpus linguistics can also serve as a methodological springboard for studies which wish to capture the conversational dynamics of conflict talk in film and television.

Chapter 4 sees Messerli exploring the pragmatics of humour through various means of repetition in television sitcoms. He first describes the various types and functions of linguistic and multimodal repetitions which cue and (re-)activate narrative frames to create humorous effects for the recipient. By analysing how humour is constructed through repetition in the ABC sitcom *Better with You* (2010–1), the author relies on Suls's Incongruity-Resolution model (1972), which defines humour as the result of a 'clash' between a narrative frame and a surprising new linguistic stimulus breaking with that very frame. In his approach, Messerli already moves his analysis from the verbal to the visual, classifying verbal and visual repetitions as trigger mechanisms for telecinematic humour. As such, Chapter 4 acts as a bridging section between the first and second part of the book, leading the analysis of verbal patterns in telecinematic discourse to the description of audiovisual patterns in its second part.

The second part of this volume deals with cinematic discourse, that is, the manifold (visual) techniques and semiotic resources (apart from language) which directors strategically apply to create a comprehensive, complex telecinematic experience. Furthermore, it presents pragma-stylistic and multimodal investigations of the audiovisual texture of various film and television genres, for example, documentaries (Piazza; Chovanec), comedy/drama (Reichelt), horror films (Schubert), film trailers (Krebs). The following contributions by Piazza; Chovanec; Reichelt; Schubert; and Krebs all align with this second major topical theme of the volume.

In Chapter 5, Piazza looks at the audiovisual strategies used in different television documentaries to present and characterize Irish travellers and gipsy communities in the UK. Adopting analytical tool kits from critical discourse analysis, she first studies the voice and style of the narrator as well as the number and type of interviewer questions. She then analyses the film trailers of the documentaries under investigation. More specifically, she identifies multimodal patterns in the visual staging of shot sequences, including framing, mise en scène, transitions, and so on. The method of analysis Piazza has chosen enables her to uncover the subtle ideologies which lie dormant in the skilful multimodal orchestration of the documentary, disguising what is shown as 'factual and objective reality'.

Chapter 6 by Chovanec equally reflects on the 'quasi-authentic' nature of documentaries in a critical manner. However, he investigates their participation framework. The aim of the chapter is to underscore the ways in which diegetic and non-diegetic voices interact and collaborate to create narrative continuity, while tacitly instilling the allegedly 'objective' visual representations with distinct moral, verbal evaluations. To show this effect, Chovanec draws on data from the documentary series *How Britain Worked*, where he manages to demonstrate the reoccurring principles and strategies that are systematically employed to establish coherence and relevance for the audience.

In Reichelt's chapter, Chapter 7, the autism spectrum disorder of a television character in the television series 'The Bravermans' becomes the focus of attention. Using a mixed methods approach, the author first probes the character's 'apparent lack of social cues' which become manifest in the character's recurrent verbal repertoire. On this basis, she determines how the director makes use of specific cinematic discourse strategies (using a shot-by-shot analysis of visual depiction and verbal dialogue) to present one of the main protagonists, Max Braverman, as an unusual, deviant, strangely isolated character.

In Chapter 8, Schubert expands Grice's Cooperative Principle to the study of visual communication, detecting 'visual' implicatures in audiovisual film scenes (cf. Grice 1975). To this end, Schubert contends that the notion of *communicative* maxims (as a multimodal extension of conversational maxims) can be applied to the multimodal framework of film analysis. He demonstrates his claim by analysing implicatures and their cinematic effects in different samples from the horror film genre.

Taking an in-depth look at the understudied genre of film trailers, Krebs presents a new pragma-stylistic framework for the investigation of trailers in Chapter 9. She discusses Sperber and Wilson's notion of 'ostension' to watching a trailer, arguing 'the trailer can be seen as a multilevel utterance representing the film (thought)'. While offering a detailed analysis of various interacting modes, Krebs illustrates how their interaction can affect their relevance for a given audience (Sperber and Wilson 1986).

The final part of the volume deals with what Bateman, Wildfeuer and Hiippala (2017) fittingly called 'transcoding' (transmodal translation), that is, the process of semiotic adaptation between different semiotic resources or media. Transcoding is a necessary practice whenever documents or artefacts are moved from one semiotic code to the next or one medium to the other – for example, comic to film, film to written text, written text to spoken language. The last section of this book thus collates contributions which deal with related issues of intertextuality or intermediality (cf. Bolter and Grusin 2000). They usually contrast and compare the use, dispersion and function of semiotic resources across different publication formats – for example, one from film or text to the next, from one medium to another.

In Chapter 10, Kirner-Ludwig explores the use of language in historical drama. More precisely, she captures the linguistic strategies contemporary screenplay writers adopt in film dialogues to construe effects of 'pseudo-authenticity'. Analysing twelve different film scripts released between 1963 and 2015, Kirner-Ludwig suggests that pseudo-archaic linguistic features are neither primarily nor consistently used to establish the cognitive and cultural frames of medieval life. Instead, they take on a marginal role, supporting and enhancing the cinematic stylizations of historical times.

In Chapter 11, Dahne and Piazza identify transcoding issues related to two different semiotic resources (the spoken language: film dialogue and the written word: film captions). The authors manage to reveal the ways in which television series are subtitled for deaf recipients. Using a relevance-based framework, they combine insights from both translation studies and pragmatics to gain a better understanding of captioners' rendering strategies and decisions. Based on the analysis of the television show 'Breaking Bad', Dahne and Piazza study if technical and linguistic differences that hold between sound track and subtitles may affect the cinematic and narrative experience of deaf recipients in specific ways.

Chapter 12 features a study by Sanchez-Stockhammer who provides a fresh pragmatic perspective on the cross-modal links between the Belgian comic book classic 'Tintin' and its more recent Hollywood film adaptation by Steven Spielberg. Sanchez-Stockhammer explains how the visual code of comic books makes its way on to the silver screen, revealing how different semiotic resources are transcoded and adapted to appeal to the audience in a new medium.

Finally, in Chapter 13, Gordejuela demonstrates the surplus value of applying analytical tools from discourse analysis and pragmatics to study the intertextual dimension of cinematic discourse. Her analysis focuses on metatextual devices and the cohesive and intertextual references they establish over time in various Hitchcock films, paying tribute to his classic feature film *Notorious* (1946).

Shedding light on these three research topics in telecinematic stylistics, that is, film discourse, cinematic discourse and intertextuality/intermediality, we invite further stylistic explorations in this incipient field of research. We equally hope to show that its object of study – that is, telecinematic discourse – is ripe with opportunities for stylistic analysis that come in different theoretical and methodological shapes. Future research will surely expand to ever new fields of stylistics, ranging from cognitive stylistics and corpus stylistics to multimodal and pragma-stylistics. In many ways, the best is yet to come.

Notes

1 Bateman, Wildfeuer and Hiippala (2017: 328) call the analytical leap from film discourse to cinematic discourse 'the primary multimodal challenge presented by film [… which] lies in the extreme degree of orchestration and integration of very diverse forms of expression'.
2 Please consult Bednarek and Zago (2019) for a very extensive, thematically sectioned bibliography of linguistic research on film and television series.
3 Such a field, we believe, should not only examine the language in and of feature films but likewise explore language use in and through television series. We thereby acknowledge the new popular and scholarly acclaim and interest in television which has increased with the advent of new online streaming services, such as Amazon Prime Television, HBO Now or Netflix (Jenner 2018: 4).

4 See Bednarek (2010: 20) for a more extensive discussion of the formal similarities and differences that hold between cinema and television, and arguments for a collective view of both types of mass media.
5 We would like to thank the anonymous reviewer of our manuscript for pointing out the conceptual tension between non-fictional and dramatized fictional discourse and their different use and function in feature films and television.
6 Bednarek (2018) even prefers to talk of 'telecinematic dialogue' rather than 'telecinematic discourse', which epitomizes the reductive move from a broader reading of discourse to a more constrained meaning of spoken dialogue.
7 For an extensive discussion of further communication frameworks in linguistics and film studies, please consult Dynel and Chovanec 2015: 2f.).

References

Androutsopoulos, J. (2012), 'Introduction: Language and society in cinematic discourse', *Multilingua*, 31 (2–3) [Special issue on language and society in cinematic discourse]: 139–54.
Baker, P. (2005), *Public Discourses of Gay Men*, London: Routledge.
Bateman, J. and Schmidt, K. H. (2013), *Multimodal Film Analysis: How Films Mean*, London: Routledge.
Bateman, J., Wildfeuer, J. and Hiippala, T. (2017), *Multimodality: Foundations, Research and Analysis–A Problem-Oriented Introduction*, Berlin: Walter de Gruyter.
Bednarek, M. (2008), '"What the hell is wrong with you?" A corpus perspective on evaluation and emotion in contemporary American pop culture', in A. Mahboob and N. Knight (eds), *Questioning Linguistics*, 95–126, Newcastle: Cambridge Scholars Press.
Bednarek, M. (2010), *The Language of Fictional Television: Drama and Identity*, London and New York: Continuum.
Bednarek, M. (2011a), 'Expressivity and televisual characterisation', *Language and Literature*, 20 (1): 3–21.
Bednarek, M. (2011b), 'The language of fictional television: A case study of the "dramedy" Gilmore Girls', *English Text Construction*, 4 (1): 54–83.
Bednarek, M. (2012a), '"Get us the hell out of here": Key words and trigrams in fictional television series', *International Journal of Corpus Linguistics*, 17 (1): 35–63.
Bednarek, M. (2012b), 'Construing "nerdiness": Characterisation in The Big Bang Theory', *Multilingua*, 31: 199–229.
Bednarek, M. (2015), 'Corpus-assisted multimodal discourse analysis of television and film narratives', in P. Baker and T. McEnery (eds), *Corpora and Discourse Studies*, 63–87, Basingstoke and New York: Palgrave Macmillan.
Bednarek, M. (2018), *Language and Television Series: A Linguistic Approach to TV Dialogue*, Cambridge: Cambridge University Press.
Bednarek, M. and Zago, R. (2017), *Bibliography of Linguistic Research on Fictional (Narrative, Scripted) Television Series and Films/Movies*, version 1 (January 2017). Available at: http://unipv.academia.edu/RaffaeleZago (accessed 21 June 2017).
Bednarek, M. and Zago, R. (2019), *Bibliography of Linguistic Research on Fictional (Narrative, Scripted) Television Series and Films/Movies*, version 3 (May 2019). Available at: https://www.academia.edu/30703199/Bednarek_M._and_Zago_R._2019._Bibliography_of_linguistic_research_on_fictional_narrative_scripted_television_series_and_films_movies_version_3_May_2019_ (accessed 06 December 2019).

Bleichenbacher, L. (2008), *Multilingualism in the Movies: Hollywood Characters and their Linguistic Choices*, Tübingen: Francke.

Bolter, J. D. and Grusin, R. (2000), *Remediation: Understanding New Media*, Cambridge, MA: MIT Press.

Bordwell, D. (2014), 'Visual storytelling: Is that all?' [Blog post]. Available at: http://www.davidbordwell.net/blog/2014/12/07/visual-storytelling-is-that-all/.

Bordwell, D. and Thompson, K. (2008). *Film Art*, New York: McGraw-Hill Higher Education.

Bousfield, D. and McIntyre, D. (2011), 'Emotion and empathy in Martin Scorsese's Goodfellas: A case study of the "funny guy" scene', in R. Piazza, M. Bednarek and F. Rossi (eds), *Telecinematic Discourse: Approaches to the Language of Films and Television Series*, 105–23, Amsterdam: Benjamins.

Brock, A. (2015), 'Participation frameworks and participation in televised sitcom, candid camera and stand-up comedy', in M. Dynel and J. Chovanec (eds), *Participation in Public and Social Media Interactions*, 27–47, Amsterdam: Benjamins,

Bubel, C. and Spitz A. (2006), '"One of the last vestiges of gender bias": The characterization of women through the telling of dirty jokes in Ally McBeal', *Humor*, 19 (1): 71–104.

Buchholtz, M. and Lopez, Q. (2011), 'Performing blackness, forming whiteness: Linguistic minstrelsy in Hollywood film', *Journal of Sociolinguistics*, 15 (5): 680–706.

Buscombe, E. (2013), '"They will speak in our language": Indian speech in western movies. Indian speech in western movies', in J. Jaeckle (ed.), *Film Dialogue*, 157–71, New York: Columbia University Press.

Caink, A. and Clark, B. (2012), 'Special issue on inference and implicature in literary interpretation', *Journal of Literary Semantics*, 41 (2): 99–103.

Chapman, S. (2015), *Pragmatics and Stylistics: The Bloomsbury Companion to Stylistics*, London: Bloomsbury.

Chapman, S. and Clark, B., eds (2014), *Pragmatic Literary Stylistics*, Berlin: Springer.

Chion, M. (1994), *Audio-Vision: Sound on Screen*, trans. Claudia Gorbman, New York: Columbia University Press.

Chion, M. (1999), *The Voice in Cinema*, New York: Columbia University Press.

Chion, M. (2019), *Audio-Vision: Sound on Screen*, New York: Columbia University Press.

Chovanec, J. (2015), 'Participant roles and embedded interactions in online sports broadcasts', in M. Dynel and J. Chovanec (eds), *Participation in Public and Social Media Interactions*, 67–95, Amsterdam: Benjamins.

Chovanec, J. (2017), 'Participating with media: Exploring online media activity', in C. Cotter and D. Perrin (eds), *The Routledge Handbook of Language and Media*, 505–22, London: Routledge.

Chovanec, J. (2019), 'Multimodal storytelling in the news: Sequenced images as ideological scripts of othering', *Discourse, Context & Media*, 28: 8–18.

Clark, B. (2015), '"What do you want me to tell?" The inferential texture of Alice Munro's "Postcard"', *Etudes de Stylistique Anglaise*, 8: 99–120.

Davies, M. (2012), *The Corpus of American Soap Operas*. Available at: https://www.english-corpora.org/soap/ (accessed 20 June 2017).

Dynel, M. (2011), '"You talking to me?" The viewer as a ratified listener to film discourse', *Journal of Pragmatics*, 43: 1628–44.

Dynel, M. (2012), 'Setting our House in order: The workings of impoliteness in multi-party film discourse', *Journal of Politeness Research*, 8: 161–94.

Dynel, M. and Chovanec, J., eds (2015), *Participation in Public and Social Media Interactions*, Amsterdam: Benjamins.

Forceville, C. (2007), 'Multimodal metaphor in ten Dutch TV commercials', *Public Journal of Semiotics*, 1 (1): 19–51.

Forceville, C. (2014), 'Pictorial and multimodal metaphor in commercials', in E. McQuarrie and B. Phillips (eds), *Go Figure! New Directions in Advertising Rhetoric*, 184–210, London: Routledge.

Forchini, P. (2012), *Movie Language Revisited: Evidence from Multi-dimensional Analysis and Corpora*, Berlin: Peter Lang.

Goffman, E. (1981), *Forms of Talk*, Philadelphia: University of Pennsylvania Press.

Grice, H. Paul (1975), 'Logic and conversation', in: P. Cole and J. Morgan (eds), *Syntax and Semantics*, 41–58, New York: Academic Press.

Heritage, J. and Clayman, S. (2011), *Talk in Action: Interactions, Identities, and Institutions*, Oxford: John Wiley & Sons.

Hodson, J. (2014), *Dialect in Film and Literature*, Basingstoke and New York: Palgrave McMillan.

Hutchby, I. (2005), *Media talk: Conversation Analysis and the Study of Broadcasting*, London: McGraw-Hill Education.

Jaeckle, J., ed. (2013), *Film Dialogue*, New York: Columbia University Press.

Jenner, M. (2018), *Netflix and the Re-Invention of Television*, Berlin: Springer.

Janney, R. (2012), 'Pragmatics and cinematic discourse', *Lodz Papers in Pragmatics*, 8 (1): 85–113.

Janney, R. W. (2010), 'Film discourse cohesion', in C. Hoffmann (ed.), *Narrative Revisited: Telling a Story in the Age of New Media*, 245–66, Amsterdam: Benjamins.

Kozloff, S. (2000), *Overhearing Film Dialogue*, Berkeley, Los Angeles and London: University of California Press.

Lacey, N. (1998), *Image and Representation: Key Concepts in Media Studies*, Basingstoke and New York: Palgrave Macmillan.

Van Leeuwen, T. (1999), *Speech, Music, Sound*, London: Macmillan International Higher Education.

Levinson S. C. (1988), 'Putting linguistics on a proper footing: Explorations in Goffman's participation framework', in P. Drew and A. Wootton (eds), *Goffman: Exploring the Interaction Order*, 161–227, Oxford: Polity Press.

Lorenzo-Dus, N. (2009), *Television Discourse: Analysing Language in the Media*, Basingstoke and New York: Palgrave Macmillan.

Lorenzo-Dus, N. and Blitvich, P. G.-C., eds (2013), *Real Talk: Reality Television and Discourse Analysis in Action*, Basingstoke: Palgrave Macmillan.

Mahlberg, M. and McIntyre, D. (2011), 'A case for corpus stylistics: Analysing Ian Fleming's Casino Royale', *English Text Construction* 4 (2): 204–27.

McIntyre, D. (2008), 'Integrating multimodal analysis and the stylistics of drama: A multimodal perspective on Ian McKellen's Richard III', *Language and Literature*, 17 (4): 309–34.

McIntyre, D. (2012), 'Prototypical characteristics of blockbuster movie dialogue: A corpus stylistic analysis', *Texas Studies in Literature and Language*, 54 (3): 402–25.

McIntyre, D. and Walker, B. (2010), 'How can corpora be used to explore the language of poetry and drama?', in A. O'Keeffe and M. McCarthy (eds), *The Routledge Handbook of Corpus Linguistics*, 544–58, London: Routledge.

Monaco, J. (2009), *How to Read a Film: Movies, Media, and Beyond*, Oxford: Oxford University Press.

Montgomery, M. (2007), *The Discourse of Broadcast News: A Linguistic Approach*, London: Routledge.

Montoro, R. (2009), 'A multimodal approach to mind style: Semiotic metaphor vs. multimodal conceptual metaphor', in R. Page (ed.), *New Perspectives on Narrative and Multimodality*, 45–63, London: Routledge.

Nichols, B. (2010), *Engaging Cinema: An Introduction to Film Studies*, New York: WW Norton & Company.

O'Halloran, K. (2004), 'Visual semiosis in film', in K. O'Halloran (ed.), *Multimodal Discourse Analysis: Systemic-Functional Perspectives*, 109–30, London and New York: Continuum.

Pavesi, M. (2015), 'The translation of conversation and film dubbing as a discovery procedure: Evidence from demonstratives', in E. Miola and P. Ramat (eds), *Language across Languages: New Perspectives on Translation*, 143–71, Newcastle upon Tyne: Cambridge Scholars Publishing.

Piazza, R. (2010), 'Voice-over and self-narrative in film: A multimodal analysis of Antonioni's when love fails (Tentato Suicidio)', *Language and Literature*, 19 (2): 173–95.

Piazza, R. (2011), 'Pragmatic deviance in realist horror films: A look at films by Argento and Fincher', in R. Piazza, M. Bednarek and F. Rossi (eds), *Telecinematic Discourse: Approaches to the Language of Films and Television Series*, 85–104, Amsterdam: Benjamins.

Piazza, R. (2012), 'Voice-over and self-narrative in film: A multimodal analysis of Antonioni's when love fails (Tentato Suicidio)', *Language and Literature*, 19 (2): 173–95.

Piazza, R., Bednarek, M. and Rossi, F., eds (2011), *Telecinematic Discourse: Approaches to the Language of Films and Television Series*, Amsterdam: Benjamins.

Piazza, R., Haarman, L. and Caborn, A., eds (2015), *Values and Choices in Television Discourse: A View from Both Sides of the Screen*, London: Palgrave Macmillan.

Planchenault, G. (2017), 'Doing dialects in dialogues: Regional, social and ethnic variation in fiction', in A. H. Jucker and M. Locher (eds), *The Pragmatics of Fiction* [Handbook of Pragmatics, HOPS 12], 265–97, Berlin: Mouton de Gruyter.

Prince, S., ed. (2007). *American Cinema of the 1980s: Themes and Variations*, New Brunswick: Rutgers University Press.

Quaglio, P. (2009), *Television Dialogue: The Sitcom Friends vs. Natural Conversation*, Amsterdam: Benjamins.

Queen, R. (2015), *Vox Popular: The Surprising Life of Language in the Media*, Chichester: Wiley-Blackwell.

Reichelt, S. and Durham, M. (2017), 'Adjective intensification as a means of characterization portraying in-group membership and Britishness in Buffy the Vampire Slayer', *Journal of English Linguistics*, 45 (1): 60–87.

Rey, J. M. (2001), 'Changing gender roles in popular culture: Dialogue in Star Trek episodes from 1966 to 1993', in D. Biber and S. Conrad (eds), *Variation in English: Multi-dimensional Studies*, 138–56, London: Longman.

Richardson, K. (2010), *Television Dramatic Dialogue: A Sociolinguistic Study*, Oxford: Oxford University Press.

Rodríguez Martín, M. E. (2010), 'Comparing conversational processes in the BNC and a micro-corpus of movies: Is film language the "real thing"?', *Language Forum*, 36 (1–2): 35–48.

Scannell, P. and Cardiff, D. (1991) *A Social History of British Broadcasting 1. 1922–1939, Serving the Nation*, Oxford: Blackwell.

Schubert, C. (2017), 'Constructing the antihero: Linguistic characterisation in current American television series', *Journal of Literary Semantics*, 46 (1): 25–46.

Schubert, C. (2018), 'Mexicans on the American screen: The discursive construction of ethnic stereotypes in contemporary film and television', in C. Rosenthal, L. Volkmann and U. Zagratzki (eds), *Disrespected Neighbo(u)rs: Cultural Stereotypes in Literature and Film*, 2–22, Newcastle: Cambridge Scholars.

Silverman, K. (1988), *The Acoustic Mirror: The Female Voice in Psychoanalysis and Cinema*, Bloomington: Indiana University Press.

Sperber, D. and Wilson, D. (1986), *Relevance: Communication and Cognition*, Cambridge, MA: Harvard University Press.

Stokoe, E. (2008), 'Dispreferred actions and other interactional breaches as devices occasioning audience laughter in television "sitcoms"', *Social Semiotics*, 18 (3): 289–307.

Suls, J. M. (1972), 'A two stage model for the appreciation of Jokes and Cartoons: An information-processing analysis', in J. H. Goldstein and P. E. McGhee (eds), *The Psychology of Humor*, New York: Academic Press.

Taylor, C. (2006), 'The Translation of Regional Variety in the Films of Ken Loach', in N. Armstrong and F. M. Federici (eds), *Translating Voices, Translating Regions*, 37–52, Rome: Aracnee Editrice.

Thornborrow, J. (2014), *The Discourse of Public Participation Media: From Talk Show to Twitter*, London: Routledge.

Thornborrow, J. (2017), 'Styling the "ordinary": Tele-factual genres and participant identities', in J. Mortensen, N. Coupland and J. Thøgersen (eds), *Style, Mediation, and Change: Sociolinguistic Perspectives on Talking Media*, 143–65, Oxford: Oxford University Press.

Tolson, A. (2005), *Media Talk*, Edinburgh: Edinburgh University Press.

Toolan, M. (2001), *Narrative: A Critical Linguistic Introduction*, London: Routledge.

Toolan, M. (2011), 'I don't know what they're saying half the time, but I'm hooked on the series: Incomprehensible dialogue and integrated multimodal characterisation in The Wire', in R. Piazza, M. Bednarek and F. Rossi (eds), *Telecinematic Discourse: Approaches to the Language of Films and Television Series*, 161–83, Amsterdam: Benjamins.

Toolan, M. (2014), 'Stylistics and film', in M. Burke (ed.), *The Routledge Handbook of Stylistics*, 455–70, London: Routledge.

Tseng, C. (2013), *Cohesion in Film: Tracking Film Elements*, Berlin: Springer.

Tseng, C. and Bateman, J. A. (2010), 'Chain and choice in filmic narrative: An analysis of multimodal narrative construction in "The Fountain"', in C. Hoffmann (ed.), *Narrative Revisited: Telling a Story in the Age of New Media*, 213–44, Amsterdam: Benjamins.

Tseng, C. and Bateman, J. A. (2012), 'Multimodal narrative construction in Christopher Nolan's Memento: A description of analytic method', *Visual Communication*, 11 (3): 91–119.

Walshe, S. (2011), '"Normal people like us don't use that type of language. Remember this is the real world." The language of Father Ted: Representations of Irish English in a fictional world', *Sociolinguistic Studies*, 5 (1): 127–48.

Weis, E. (1982), *The Silent Scream: Alfred Hitchcock's Sound Track*, Madison: Fairleigh Dickinson University Press.

Wildfeuer, J. (2017), 'From text to recipient: Pragmatic insights for filmic meaning construction', in J. Wildfeuer and J. Bateman (eds), *Film Text Analysis: New Perspectives on the Analysis of Filmic Meaning*, 118–40, New York: Routledge.

Wildfeuer, J. and Bateman, J. A., eds (2016), *Film Text Analysis: New Perspectives on the Analysis of Filmic Meaning*, London: Routledge.

Online video sources

Film Society of Lincoln Center (2009), HBO Directors Dialogues: Michael Haneke & Darren Aranofsky. Available at: https://www.youtube.com/watch?v=T_8XEXROjGA (accessed 14 March 2019).

1

'I shouldn't have let this happen'

Demonstratives in film dialogue and film representation

Maria Pavesi

1 Introduction

Film, compared to other forms of representation and narration, shows more than it tells. Verbal language, however, is there, performing several functions among which relating what we hear with what we see. As in real life, deictic features in film evoke the space where interaction occurs together with the entities that populate it. They identify the objects and people involved in the interactional exchange, set the time of the event and refer to discourse itself. Yet, unlike real life, deixis in film works along two distinct dimensions: at the diegetic level, it appeals to the characters and tightens up their turns in the fictional world's spoken interactions; at the extra-diegetic level, it guides viewers to the scene and the represented events by linking what they hear in the dialogue with what they watch on-screen. Among the various deictic devices, demonstratives deserve special attention in fictional dialogue as they point to some segments of the extralinguistic reality or current discourse and, prototypically, to the physical and visual context surrounding participants. Here, verbal language refers ostensibly to entities perceivable in the scene but can also symbolically evoke wider situations belonging to the narrative.

Two major referential uses of demonstratives are recognized in general language: exophoric and endophoric (Halliday and Hasan 1976; Diessel 1999). Exophoric demonstratives are prototypical deictics directing the interlocutors' attention onto items in the non-verbal context. The entities referred to by the demonstrative can only be understood by drawing on the awareness and knowledge of the context of situation, that is, the set of extralinguistic circumstances of use that affect the linguistic form of an utterance, including physical and social setting, social relationships, the task at hand, the medium and the topic of discourse (cf. Halliday and Hasan 1985). Hence demonstrative pronouns can refer to physical objects, as well as – by extension – to more abstract situations, conditions and states of mind populating the environment in which the utterance is placed. By contrast, endophoric demonstratives point to elements, whole segments and propositions within the verbal text. Overall 'demonstrative pronouns [...] may have referents of all ontological types: first-order (individuals, physical objects), second-order (situations), third-order (concepts and prepositions) and [...] fourth-order entities (illocutionary forces)' (Cornish 2007: 150). The different types of reference are significant in films because, on the one hand, demonstratives have a cohesive role that serves an interactional function by linking up audiovisual dialogue turns together. Exophoric demonstratives, on the other hand, take viewers away from the verbal exchange and bring them to the local or global situation by shifting interlocutors' and viewers' attention onto the sensorial input and the fictional events unravelling on-screen.

Corpora studies show that demonstratives are more frequent in speech than in writing, both as pronouns and determiners and as all reference types (Biber et al. 1999; Botley and McEnery 2001; also Diessel 2014). This means that locutors in speech use more demonstratives than in writing to pick up portions of text as well as concrete and abstract entities in the context of situation. The frequent use of these deictic features in speech is due to a variety of factors, starting with the immediacy of the relationship between situation and discourse in face-to-face interaction, where speakers are usually involved in joint activities and experience the extralinguistic reality together and at the same time (Botley and McEnery 2001; Carter and McCarthy 2006: 178). In addition, demonstratives require less processing to pick up entities than more elaborated noun phrases and are thus more amenable to the communicative constraints of online verbal planning. Moreover, these devices do not impose a definite interpretation of referents, but rather contribute to the casualness of talk and promote face-to-face politeness, especially in face-threatening acts (e.g. Margutti, Traverso and Pugliese 2016). The emotional and interactional involvement frequently associated with demonstratives likewise increases their frequency in spoken discourse, a privileged locus for its expression (see Quaglio and Biber 2006). Demomstratives' attributes of immediacy, compactness, casualness and interactivity are highly relevant for telecinematic discourse, where spokenness is represented and the mechanisms underlying spontaneous conversation can be exploited for the specific goals of film.

The centrality of demonstratives in the staging of fictional worlds calls for an in-depth exploration of their frequency, uses and functions with reference to spontaneous conversation, the multimodal context of film representation and the double-layeredness of audiovisual communication. The present study hence aims to investigate the roles of demonstratives in audiovisual orality. It focuses on how they highlight the iconicity of film texts and offer a given perspective on narration. As a background to the ensuing corpus-based investigation, the next section provides a brief description and conceptual definitions of demonstratives in English.

2 A look at demonstrative deixis in English

In English demonstratives are traditionally distinguished into proximal and distal ones, depending on the relative proximity (*this/these*) or distance (*that/those*) of the reference object in relation to the speaker or the speaker and hearer. However, starting with Lakoff (1974) and Lyons (1977), the conceptualization of relative distance has been shown to be influenced by several different factors beyond the seemingly clear-cut spatial differentiation between demonstratives. By calling attention to the dynamicity of demonstrative reference, distance has actually been questioned as the main variable defining demonstratives, with their use being posited to draw mainly on interactional, discoursal, cognitive and affective principles (Lakoff 1974; Kirsner 1979; Strauss 1993, 2002; Cheshire 1996; Biber et al. 1999; Carter and McCarthy 2006; Piwek, Beun and Cremers 2008). More specifically, an alternative approach conceptualizes deixis as the speaker's intensity in directing the listener to look for an entity in context, or as 'the force with which the hearer is instructed to find the referent' (Strauss 1993: 404, 2002: 134). In this framework, demonstratives are analysed in terms of their highlighting functions. Entities identified by a demonstrative pronoun – compared with other referential means such as the third-person pronoun *it* – stand out more and bind the interlocutor to the speech event and the situational context. High focus or high deixis is attributed to proximal demonstratives, medium focus or low deixis to distal demonstratives, depending on the noteworthiness, givenness and foregrounding of the entities talked about (Kirsner 1979: 360; Strauss 1993: 404, 2002; cf. also Piwek, Beun and Cremers 2008). *This* is more powerful as it typically introduces information associated with the here and now, while strongly bringing a new referent into the hearer's consciousness; *that* is less emphatic as it is used to refer to entities more accessible to the hearer, thus conveying a commonality of interests and goals between interlocutors.

More generally, Diessel (2006, 2014) identifies demonstratives as the means that prototypically and universally index a 'joint focus of attention', a notion 'used to characterize triadic situations in which speaker and addressee share their attention on a particular referent. […] In order to communicate, speaker and hearer must share their attention, i.e., they must be focussed on the same entity or situation, which presupposes the ability to understand other people as "mental" or "intentional agents"' (Diessel 2014: 125). According to Diessel, the traditional, distance-oriented view can be reconciled with the alternative, focus-oriented model of deixis. Demonstratives – which are placed in the semantics-pragmatics interface – are accordingly recognized as fulfilling two, interrelated functions. The first one is to locate the referent relatively to the deictic centre; the second one is 'to coordinate the interlocutors' joint attentional focus' (p. 469). As for English, however, it is suggested that the semantic meaning of distance versus proximity to the speaker becomes relevant mostly in contexts of contrast, whereas the pragmatic meanings would prevail in the remaining cases (Diessel 2012: 12). Following Levinson (2004), Diessel argues that the demonstrative *that* is semantically unmarked for distance, that is, it does not carry a specific distal meaning and is consequently more frequent in speech when no emphasis on the spatiality of the entity is intended (cf. in particular Cheshire 1996).

By giving primacy to the cognitive-interactive dimension, Cornish (2001) also re-examines and challenges the standard view of deixis. He sees the use of English demonstratives as being governed by two principles involving the speaker's attitude towards the referent and his or her stance towards the addressee. The choice of demonstrative is interpreted as 'a creative act, manifesting different types of sociodiscoursal relationships between speaker and addressee, as well as the viewpoint from which the referent is envisaged. Such a use is both a function of the pre-existing context and serves to change it at the same time' (Cornish 2001: 298). According to Cornish, with the demonstrative pronoun *this* the speaker sets up the referent as cognitively within his or her discourse sphere: the referent occurs in the situation of utterance and relatively near the speaker's location, hereby expressing a strong personal involvement with it. Through *this*, moreover, referents are brought in forcefully into spoken interaction and are staged as going to acquire importance in the discourse (Cornish 2001: 312). With *that*, on the other hand, 'the speaker is signalling that the intended referent is not cognitively or subjectively within his/her discourse sphere, though this use may well indicate that s/he is aligning her/himself with the addressee' (Cornish 2001: 313).

The highlighting, interactional and creative functions of demonstratives are highly relevant for filmic discourse as these deictic features dynamically contribute to the creation of context on-screen. Moreover, as a variety of language 'written to be spoken as if not written' (Gregory 1967: 191–2), film dialogue is mostly constructed in such a way as to stage orality, hence the importance of comparing it to spontaneous spoken language. In what follows, I will empirically investigate the roles of demonstratives in audiovisual orality, at first comparing the frequency and major pragmatic functions of the pronouns in film language to conversational English. Secondly, I will concentrate on exophora, capitalizing on the distinction between gestural and symbolic deixis to explore how demonstratives discursively point to the represented situation in terms of both the multimodal perceivable context and the overall diegetic circumstances while involving the viewers in the staged situation. The analysis will later draw attention to the symbolic uses of *this*, the demonstrative that conveys the higher focus and in film specializes in exophoric deixis. In the concluding section, the major results of the analysis will be summarized with reference to the role demonstrative pronouns have in filmic narration and viewers' involvement.

The empirical basis of the study is provided by twelve American and British film dialogues belonging to the English component of the Pavia Corpus of Film Dialogue containing a total of about 112,000 running words (PCFD; cf. Freddi and Pavesi 2009; Pavesi 2014). The film dialogues were manually transcribed and each demonstrative pronoun in the twelve film dialogues was tagged for syntactic role and pragmatic function – endophoric or exophoric (Pavesi 2013); for the purposes of the present study the exophoric pronouns of a subset of four films were further categorized into gestural and symbolic demonstratives.

3 A corpus-based study of demonstrative pronouns in film

3.1 Frequencies of demonstratives and their function in spoken language and in film dialogue

As the aim of the present investigation is to explore the role of demonstratives in film dialogue, their frequency is the first aspect to consider in the comparison between film language and spontaneous spoken language. A first count of demonstratives in English and American films of the PCFD (Table 1.1) shows that their frequency is high and

Table 1.1 Demonstrative Pronouns in the Pavia Corpus of Film Dialogue*

	Films	Biber et al. (1999)	Strauss (2002)
Proximal pronouns	449	200	324
Distal pronouns	973	1,150	1,017
Total	1,422	1,350	1,341

*Normalized frequencies per 100,000 words.

compares closely with the frequency of demonstratives in spontaneous spoken English as reported by both Biber et al. (1999) and Strauss (2002). These findings firstly confirm the similarity between film language and conversational language with reference to contextual embeddedness and interactivity as already highlighted by Quaglio (2009) and Forchini (2012) in their corpus-based investigations of English telecinematic language.

However, proximal pronouns appear to be relatively more frequent in films than they are in spontaneous spoken English.[1] Film language is thus likely to display greater intensity in highlighting discourse entities and drawing them closer to the viewers, owing to the 'heightened emotivity and subjectivity [conveyed by *this*] in referring to object, propositions or situations in which the speaker is closely involved personally' (Cornish 2001: 305). In this way, demonstrative deixis verbally supports the focusing functions of the camera eye and the amplifying modality of film representation. In the following extract, *this* is reiterated five times with reference to the place where Roisin and Casim are standing: the room where Casim is finally planning to build his club. Meaningfully, both speakers' choice has fallen on a deictic device pointing to new and important information within the speaker's sphere of discourse:

(1)

[At Casim's club-to-be]
ROISIN: Is **this** it?
CASIM: **This** is it!
ROISIN: ((laughter)) Okay.
CASIM: Is **this** it? **This** is it. **This** is my place.
(*Ae Fond Kiss*, Ken Loach, 2004)

It should be further pointed out that in spoken language greater reliance on context does not automatically mean that exophoric demonstratives are more common than endophoric ones. On the contrary, Strauss (2002) has shown that in her spoken corpus endophoric or textual uses of English demonstratives are in fact more frequent than exophoric and non-phoric ones. The prevalence of endophora over exophora in spoken English is confirmed by Botley and McEnery's (2001) corpus study of different genres of written and spoken English including parliamentary debates. Interestingly, the analysis of the two functions of pronouns in the PCFD reveals a different distribution of demonstratives as endophoric and exophoric references have equal share in films (Pavesi 2013: 122). Here the pronouns create more frequent links to the extralinguistic situation than they do in spontaneous spoken English. Film dialogue may thus be expected to latch more onto the sensorial and narrative context[2] than onto the verbal co-text as a result of the intrinsic multimodality of the medium. In this way exophoric demonstratives in dialogue bring about an emphasis on the non-verbal dimension of cinema and help to instantiate the iconicity of the medium.

A closer look at the functions of the individual demonstratives (Table 1.2) reveals that distal pronouns mostly serve an endophoric function, with twice as many *that-those* pronouns referring to verbal discourse than to the extralinguistic situation. Conversely, the great majority of proximal pronouns are exophoric and identify objects, facts, events and situations in the immediate or extended context of situation.

3.2 Focusing on exophoric demonstratives

Given the relevance of the multimodal and narrative dimension of film, it is worth having a closer look at the exophoric uses of *this* and *that* by exploring their gestural and symbolic usages. This distinction within exophora concerns the amount and the type of information required to identify the referent by means of a demonstrative (Fillmore [1971] 1975, 1997: 62–4; Levinson 1983: 65–6). In previous discussions, gestural deictics have been understood as relying on the perceivable, physical setting of the speech event. When a gestural deictic expression is used, participants must refer to visual, auditory, tactile and olfactory coordinates in order to interpret the speaker's message appropriately and locate the referent in the sensory context. As a result, gestural deictics are typically accompanied by non-verbal indexes such as pointing, eye-contact and eye-fixation, head nodding and sounds. At the same time, they often co-occur with other attention-seeking words, such as the imperative verb forms *see, look, listen*, vocatives and interjections: for example, '*Lucien*, you should *see* this'; '*Ooh look* at this. This is a great shot!"; '*Hey, Dan!* Take a *look* at this!' (all examples from the PCFD).

In contrast, symbolic usages draw on the wider spatial and temporal context in which the speech event is embedded. According to Levinson (1983: 65), 'symbolic usages of deictic terms require for their interpretation only knowledge of (in particular) the basic spatio-temporal parameters of the speech event (but also, on occasion, participants-role and discourse and social parameter)'. Thus to interpret 'This city is really beautiful' (p. 65), we just need to know the general location of the participants, or to know 'certain aspects of the speech situation, whether this knowledge comes by current perception or not' (Fillmore [1971] 1975: [40] 259).

Looking at it from a complementary perspective, the difference between gestural and symbolic deixis thus appears to be related to the degree of specificity and concreteness

Table 1.2 Demonstrative Pronouns in the Pavia Corpus of Film Dialogue (Exophoric vs. Endophoric Use)

	Exophoric pronouns	Endophoric pronouns	Total
This/these	444	86	530
That/those	383	765	1,148
Total	827	851	1,678

versus the generality and abstractness of the referent picked up by the demonstrative (Cornish 2001). As a hard and fast rule, gestural demonstratives require for their interpretation a deictic gesture that points to the immediate perceptual environment (Levinson 1983), whereas without a gesture a deictic word indicates 'nothing more than a sphere, "a geometric place"' (Bühler [1934/1982] 2011: 128).

In film, however, the context evoked by the demonstrative in all cases explicitly pertains to the diegetic dimension only, in that gestural and symbolic deictics typically refer to concrete and abstract entities pointed at or referred to by the characters talking to each other in their fictive setting. That is, differently from direct-address audiovisual genres such as cooking programmes, speakers in films do not as a rule address the viewers directly, voice-over being one noticeable exception. In the opening of the film *Notting Hill* (Roger Michell, 1999), for example, William's voice-over speaks to the audience, while the locations referred to are symbolically presented to the audience by long shots and extreme long shots of the neighbourhood through which William is walking.

(2)

WILLIAM's voice: And so, **this** is where I spend my days and years, in **this** small village in the middle of the city, in a house with a blue door that my wife and I bought together, before she left me for a man who looked exactly like Harrison Ford.
(*Notting Hill*, Roger Mitchell, 1999)

3.2.1 *Gestural demonstratives in film*

As mentioned in Section 3.2, with gestural demonstratives the viewers' attention may be directed onto given entities or locations by means of gestures, pointing and gazes focused on by the camera. But in film it can also be ingeniously guided by a variety of visual and acoustic cues made available by the richness of cinematic affordances. By mirroring real life, a full shot of Stuart in extract (3) shows the character looking around the photography shop, hand-pointing to different locations in the room. More innovatively, the pronoun *this* in extract (4) is uttered while Rukhsana is flashing the headlights of her car onto the building where she lives with her family.

(3)

[At the photography shop]
STUART: Look at all *this*! What're you doing? It's lost its style, Maurice!
((points to the place with his arms))
(*Secrets and Lies*, Mike Leigh, 1996)

(4)

RUKHSANA: Ehm, *this* is our house, ehm ... ((flashes the headlights of her car))
(*Ae Fond Kiss*, Ken Loach, 2004)

Gestural demonstratives in films also exploit the dynamicity of the medium to portray changes of perspective. They may be used in tours which viewers join as silent, disembodied participants watching the scene through the camera eye. At the beginning of the birthday-party scene in *Secrets and Lies* (Mike Leigh 1996), Monica shows her house to her guests Jane and Cynthia. While she leads the walking tour, rooms and concrete objects come in turn into visual focus highlighted by the interaction between camera takes, characters' kinesics and the dialogue. Not surprisingly Monica, the house-owner, almost exclusively accompanies her gestures, postures and gazes with the proximal demonstrative *this*: 'This is the downstairs toilet', '*This* is the garage' 'and *this* is the master bedroom'. The pronoun elicits an interpretation of space as falling within Monica's discourse sphere and powerfully brings listeners' attention to the selected locations and entities. Conversely, the other, nondominant characters mostly resort to *that*, thus marking the referents as shared referential ground including both speaker and hearer. It should be noticed that Monica turns to the distal pronoun when responding to the interlocutor's prompts – Cynthia: 'Is *that* a new car?' ⟶ Monica: 'Yes, *that*'s my car'.

(5)

MONICA:	And **this** is the … oops!
CYNTHIA:	Oh, **that**'s a big lavatory!
MONICA:	**This** is the downstairs toilet.
JANE:	Oh, **that**'s handy, isn't it, 'cos if you're in the garden … […]
MONICA:	**This** is the garage.
JANE:	((laughter)) I thought it was the cupboard!
CYNTHIA:	Is **that** a new car?
MONICA:	Yes, **that**'s my car.
CYNTHIA:	What was the matter with your other one?
MONICA:	Nothing! I'll show you upstairs … ((sigh)) we'll start with **this**.
JANE:	Oh.
CYNTHIA:	There's the tank.
MONICA:	**That**'s where I keep my towels and bed-linen.
JANE:	**That**'s your airing cupboard.
MONICA:	Mhm. It's not very capacious. And **this** is Maurice's bathroom.
JANE:	It's green! matches your tank!
CYNTHIA TO MONICA:	**These** all new carpets, are they, sweetheart?
MONICA:	Oh, yes! And **this** is the master bedroom.
	(*Secrets and Lies*, Mike Leigh, 1996)

3.2.2 Symbolic demonstratives in film

If gestural pronouns identify perceivable and concrete entities and places, symbolic demonstrative pronouns abstractly focus on the wider situational context, while extending their reference to facts, events and situations. The wider context where such abstract and boundless entities are set typically originates from previous events or arises out of the interaction between the dialogue and the general situation depicted on-screen. For instance, in the film *Bend It Like Beckham*, the character Mrs Bhamara is reproaching her husband for the permissive attitude he holds with their daughter. To be correctly interpreted, the deictic element must be set within the cultural, ethnic, religious and family setting that has been assembled in the film up to the moment of speaking. The narrative import is obvious here since the demonstrative focuses on situations dynamically constructed on-screen, that is, through the events that have been represented visually and verbally in sequences of scenes and in the succession of turns. Without a gesture, *this* can acquire meaning in context only if interlocutors share specific knowledge and assumptions.

(6)

MRS BHAMRA: Dad [Punjabi]. No! **This** is where you spoil her!
(*Bend It Like Beckham*, Gurinder Chada, 2002)

In another crucial scene of *Secrets and Lies*, Jenny is the social worker who Hortense has come to see as she is searching for her biological mother. During their first encounter at the adoption office, Jenny enquires about the reasons that have led Hortense to her resolution. It is by using *this* in her question 'Are you sharing *this* with your parents?' that the social worker isolates the relevant state of affairs that has been building up in the whole narrative up to that moment: Hortense's need to uncover and understand her past and her decision to take an official move to find her biological mother. This complex web of cognitive and affective meanings is encapsulated in the demonstrative pronoun that is diegetically rooted in a spatio-temporal sphere equally accessible to both interlocutors on-screen. Extra-diegetically, it refers backwards to everything shown to the audience up to that moment.

(7)

[At the adoption office]
JENNY: ((laughter)) right, Hortense. Let's talk a little bit about you, shall we. Now, obviously, you've been giving a great deal of thought to things, and you've come to a decision, which is good, but, for me, the question is why now?
[...]
JENNY: [...] Are you sharing **this** with your parents? Do they know that you're here today? How do they feel about it?
(*Secrets and Lies*, Mike Leigh, 1996)

The same pronoun can refer to different aspects of narration as made relevant by the position of the pronoun in the dialogue and by the wording of the exchanges that summon different scenarios in contiguous turns. In the following extract from *Ae Fond Kiss* (Ken Loach, 2004), we find two symbolic pronouns. In the first instance – 'what the fuck is *this*?' – reference is made to the interethnic love relationship between the two protagonists who are seeing each other against the will of the young man's Muslim family and in defiance of the local Catholic Church. In the second instance – I don't believe *this*! – the pronoun latches onto the specific situation that has just been locally defined: the two lovers are spending a passionate and carefree weekend together when Casim announces to Roisin that he is soon to marry another woman, a Muslim cousin of his. In each case a separate context becomes relevant for interpretation and a distinct time span is profiled. Whereas for the first *this*, the whole film narrative centred on the love story between Roisin and Casim is evoked, the second *this* draws on the specific location and the news just been disclosed.

(8)

[at a hotel room]
Roisin: Hello! You're up early.
Casim: Couldn't sleep. There's something I've got to tell you. I'm due to marry my first cousin Jasmine in nine weeks.
Roisin: ((laughter)) Very funny.
Casim: Honestly.
Roisin: ((laughing)) I don't believe you.
Casim: Eleven words. Couldn't get them out.
Roisin: So, what the fuck is **this**? Hmm? ((crying)) Is it like some last-minute fling before you settle down to married life or … ?
Casim: No, no.
Roisin: ((crying)) No? And what the fuck am I? Some cheap fucking tart at a stag party? Jesus Christ! I don't believe **this**! Eleven little words, was it? Well, here's another two for you, fuck off! I mean, why couldn't you tell me before we got on the plane?
(*Ae Fond Kiss*, Ken Loach, 2004)

Thanks to their focusing and context-evoking function, symbolic demonstratives are also excellent means to stage major events in the story and create expectations in the audience. In the following extract, the highly charged questions 'What was it about William Yorkin that upset you so? I mean, what did he do to provoke all of ***this***?' are uttered at the beginning of ***One Hour Photo*** (Mark Romanek, 2002), when Sy Parrish, the protagonist, is framed sitting in a police station where he is going to be interrogated. The pictures the detective carries with him when he enters the interrogation room trigger the context the two characters need to activate in order to understand the reference of ***this***. The uninformed audience, in contrast, will be able to access the facts to which ***this*** refers only by watching the rest of the film. The film thus creates an anticipation in the viewers, who act as the unratified yet real addressees of Detective van Der Zee's questions.

(9)

[Detective van Der Zee enters the interrogation room with some pictures]
Sy Parrish: Can I see them?
Detective van Der Zee: That's not a courtesy, Mister Parrish. This is evidence.
[…]
Detective van Der Zee: […] Your legal aid should be here within thirty minutes or so. Now you understand, you don't have to talk to me until she gets here if you don't want to. You know that, Sy?

Sy Parrish:	Mm mm.
Detective van Der Zee:	Good ... Sy, can I ask you one question?
Sy Parrish:	Sure.
Detective van Der Zee:	What was it about William Yorkin that upset you so? I mean, what did he do to provoke all of **this**?

(*One Hour Photo*, Mark Romanek, 2002)

The last three extracts have underscored the narrative significance of symbolic demonstratives in film where they can direct the participants' attention backwards or forwards by isolating varying time spans and conjuring up different contexts of situation. Although overtly uttered by and for the on-screen characters, symbolic demonstratives perform a key role extradiegetically in packaging portions of the narrated story for the benefit of the viewers as well as alerting them about upcoming events.

3.3 A closer analysis

In order to investigate the role of demonstrative deictics more closely, four films taken from the PCFD have been analysed more in detail: *Ae Fond Kiss* (Ken Loach, 2004), *Billy Elliot* (Stephen Daldry, 2001), *Bend It Like Beckham* (Gurinder Chadha, 2002) and *Secrets and Lies* (Mike Leigh, 1996). In order to do so, all exophoric demonstrative pronouns in the four films have been tagged as gestural or symbolic drawing both on the verbal and the multisemiotic context, that is, by watching the individual scenes in which the demonstrative was embedded and considering all semiotic codes co-deployed with the verbal message. As can be seen from Table 1.3, of the 308 exophoric demonstratives in the four films, most (217) are gestural – a fact that confirms the immediacy of film language and its rooting in the perceptual world portrayed on-screen (Quaglio 2009; Forchini 2012). More specifically, there are 156 gestural distal pronouns vis-à-vis 61 gestural proximal pronouns: hence *that* is overwhelmingly gestural and more often than *this* it is used to refer to 'all of what is accessible to the participants by means of sensory perception' (Hausendorf 2003: 250).

Distance from the speaker's origo is not always relevant, with many distal pronouns being used to identify objects close to the speaker, in agreement with the unmarked status of the pronoun in English where the spatial dimension of the demonstratives is

Table 1.3 Gestural and Symbolic Exophoric Demonstrative Pronouns in Four Films*

	Gestural	Symbolic	Total
This	61	65	126
That	156	26	182
	217	91	308

*Ae Fond Kiss, Bend It like Beckham, Billy Elliot, Secrets and Lies.

'virtually always neutralised' (Cheshire 1996: 372; cf. also Levinson 1983; Strauss 1993). Overall, *that* is posited to perform a weaker-focused, listener-oriented purpose which may result in apparently opposite outcomes. On the one hand, by resorting to a distal pronoun 'the speaker is tacitly instructing the addressee to place the referent outside his/her (i.e., the speaker's) discourse-cognitive sphere' (Cornish 2001: 304), while stepping back from the entity and the people connected with that entity. On the other hand, *that* pronouns may suggest that the speaker takes the listener's point of view, empathizes with him or her and experiences a feeling of complicity with the interactant (Lakoff 1974; Strauss 1993; Cheshire 1996; Cornish 2001). In the first of the following two examples taken from *Billy Elliot* (Stephen Daldry, 2000), Billy's father is somehow complaining because Billy is dancing his way along the road instead of walking properly. *That* in this case marks the distance the father experiences between himself and his son. In (11) by contrast *that* conveys a meaning of emotional participation when Billy's ballet teacher asks him about a letter the boy has brought to class as she senses the meaningfulness of the object.

(10)

DAD: Is **that** absolutely necessary? Walk normal, will you?
(*Billy Elliot*, Stephen Daldry, 2000)

(11)

MRS WILKINSON:	Brought your things?
BILLY:	I don't know if they're right, miss.
MRS WILKINSON:	If they're special to you, they're right.
BILLY:	What are they for?
MRS WILKINSON:	To give us some ideas for a dance. Come on, then! Let's see them! … What's **that**?
BILLY:	It's a letter.

(*Billy Elliot*, Stephen Daldry, 2000)

In spite of the different emotional stance, the two instances of the distal pronoun have as a common denominator the listener's perspective on the state of affairs at hand coupled with an emphasis on shared knowledge between interlocutors. By means of its low focus, *that* performs a strong interactional function, unlike *this*, which is centred on the speaker's high intensity involvement. In the four films analysed the latter pronoun occurs with a similar frequency in gestural and symbolic usages; however, given the significance symbolic *this* acquires in film, in the next section our attention will shift to those uses of the proximal demonstrative.

3.3.1 Symbolic this

As previously pointed out, we consider demonstratives not so much in terms of the physical distance of the reference object from the origo but rather as regarding the interactional functions and the sociocognitive meanings they activate in the communicative setting (Strauss 2002: 135; Cornish 2001). The analysis of the corpus shows that symbolic functions in films are coded more often by *this* (Table 1.3), the pronoun that prototypically relies on the wider spatio-temporal context and potentially fulfils a narrative function. It has been argued that proximal demonstratives are used when greater importance is assigned to the referent or when the referent is new (Strauss 1993, 2002; Cornish 2001). As opposed to distal demonstratives that tend to imply alignment between interlocutors, proximal demonstratives thus impose the speaker's point of view while highlighting the situation represented on-screen.

But is symbolic *this* neutral in its affective meaning or does it carry an evaluative colouring? Does it express a stance? A closer look at the individual occurrences of *this* in the four films investigated reveals that with the pronoun events and facts are extracted from the flow of narration to be turned into objects of reflection; as such, they may also become objects of evaluation. In (12) the pronoun *this* is embedded in a pragmatic question: 'How could you do *this*, sweetheart?', which is not asked to seek information but has a rhetorical nature as it rather performs an indirect speech act of reproaching. Mrs Paxton is addressing her daughter, Jules, who she believes is a lesbian. In her rebuke, the strongly subjective *this* has a vague reference like many of these symbolic uses and presumably refers to behaviours the mother associates with Jules's homosexuality. The fact that the state-of-affair activated by the symbolic pronoun needs to be shared and negotiated among characters as interlocutors is highlighted in Jules's following turn. Her question 'What are you talking about?', uttered in bewilderment, shows that her mother's deictic reference was obscure and that she could not understand the reason of the reproach directed against her.

(12)

MRS PAXTON TO JULES	How could you do **this**, sweetheart?
JULES TO PINKY	Sorry.
JULES	Get in the car. What is wrong with you?! What are you talking about? ((they leave))
	(*Bend It Like Beckham*, Gurinder Chada, 2002)

It is true that in the multimodal environment of film where the verbal code interacts with the other signifying codes, evaluative colouring is often derived from parallel paralinguistic and non-verbal information. Confrontational physical postures, defying looks or charged gesticulation together with shouting or crying do in fact represent frequently co-occurring signs that contribute to the local meaning of *this*. However, even in such multimodal environments, evaluative meanings may also arise from the linguistic contour that comes with *this* (cf. Xiao and McEnery 2006). We may thus hypothesize that the symbolic pronoun has a given semantic prosody, that is, 'a consistent aura of meaning with which a form is imbued by its collocates' (Louw 1993: 157). More precisely, borrowing Partington's (2015: 292) words, the pronoun will 'carry with it prosodic suggestions (or primings) on how to use it when realized in discourse, that is, on the evaluative – favourable or unfavourable – force it is likely to contribute to discourse'. The inspection of the concordance of symbolic *this* in the four film dialogues does reveal recurrent patterns of lexico-semantic, syntactic and pragmatic co-occurrences that consistently point to an unfavourable prosody of the symbolic pronoun. *This* collocates with negatively connoted verbs, such as *happen*, *spoil*, *burge on* and *destroyed*, negatively connoted adjectives including *difficult*, *ridiculous*, odd, stupid and nerve-racking and the negatively connoted nouns mistake and shock. It is also repeatedly found in the company of swear words: 'What the fuck is *this*?', 'Fucking great Christmas this has been!', 'Is *this* some kind of fucking joke?'. Elsewhere, we find it embedded in negative clauses, such as 'I don't believe *this*', 'You can't do *this*', 'I know *this* isn't very nice', and within questions conveying face-threatening speech acts such as complaints or challenges: 'Why are you doing *this* to me, Joe?', 'Excuse me. *This* is not for my gratification', 'Is *this* why we got you educated?', 'So what is *this*? You're just gonna leave me sitting here like some fucking idiot and rub it in my face?'. The pronoun comes with hedges and apologies: 'I'm afraid *this* is your last day', 'I'm sorry, I know *this* must be a shock to you', 'I'm sorry to barge on you like *this*'.

Table 1.4 Sample Concordances of Symbolic *this* in the Four Films of the PCFD

```
 1  e come to see you, I suppose, ehm, you must think this is very odd, but basically I feel that I had to
 2  s sake, wee man! I'm gonna part your stains after this, Casim. He told us we were shifting a dresser,
 3  Couldn't get them out. So, what the fuck is this? Hmm? ((crying)) Is it like some last-minute fling
 4  at a stag party? Jesus Christ! I don't believe this! Eleven little words, was it? Well, here's anoth
 5  You're right, Roisin. I shouldn't have let this happen. I should have foreseen the hurt. Should,
 6  , right? Take it away! Enough is enough! Is this why we got you educated? That this day had to
 7  Look at me! ((crying)) I'll never forgive you for this. [Punjabi: I'm here for you.] You're only upset,
 8  our business! None of my business? I'm sorry, but this is my life you're talking about! It's-it's my
 9  live, what our family's like. Can't you see that this'll all be destroyed if … I was told that the we
10  I don't know. She's gone. I can't fucking believe this! What's going on here? She's gone. Listen!
11  hsana, take your mom inside! [Punjabi] Listen! Is this some sort of fucking joke? I may not be
12  ck are you? I think we better go inside. I know this might be difficult for you, but, today, Billy mi
13  a right twat for your gratification. Excuse me. This is not for my gratification. What goods it gonn
14  ll. Go on, then. Let's see this fucking dancing. This is ridiculous! If you're a fucking ballet dancer
15  the way, oh, what fun'. Fucking great Christmas this has been. Go on, have some. Where'd you get it?
16  's give the boy a fucking chance! Please don't do this to me, Dad. We'll find him some money. We'll fin
17  u understand? I realize we shall have to consider this very seriously … and it will be bound to affect
18  miss you, Miss. No, you won't. I will. Honest. This is when you go out and find life, and all those
19  ust in the park. Nothing as serious as this. This serious? It'll do for now. I want to play profes
20  Thanks, Jess. I'm sorry to barge in on you like this Mr and Mrs Bhamra, but I wanted to talk to you
21  Jess. Good luck. [German] Go on, Jess. You can do this! Yeah, mum, I'm fine. Pinky's fine. We're all
22  let you play? They want to protect me. From what? This is taking me away from everything they know.
23  mother can stand by and watch her son go through this. Well, our Pinky, she didn't come out of her
24  whole time! Yes? I'm sorry to bother you like this. I don't have anything to say to you, okay? I ap
25  atch out Move on up Move on up Move on up! Yes! This is not possible. No, no, no. Oh yes, yes!
26  to go. I'm on an emergency case. Yes, but could this be a mistake? I very much doubt it. Look, give
27  e Avenue, Sutton, Surrey. Look, I'm sorry, I know this must be a shock to you … Listen, darling, wha
28  G6. It ain't fair! Is this your signature? This is stupid. I don't understand it. I mean, I can'
29  Right, Cynthia again. Thank you, Maurice. Cor, This is living, ain't it? Mm. Yeah! Thank you!
30  e, sweetheart. It wasn't supposed to happen like this. Yeah, well it has, ain' it? So you tell them, g
31  ving a go at her next, I expect! I'm sorry about this, Hortense. Have you finished there, Jane? Why do
32  you talking about now? You wouldn't have none of this if I hadn't given Maurice the money to start
```

Following Xiao and McEnery (2006), a manual analysis was carried out of the sixty-five concordances of symbolic *this*,[3] distinguishing negative, positive and neutral prosodies for each instance of the pronoun (see Table 1.4 for a sample of the concordances in the four films). The results confirm an overwhelming unfavourable colouring of *this*, which exhibits a negative semantic prosody 71 per cent of the times it occurs in the four films analysed. As for the rest, in 18 per cent of the cases *this* shows a neutral prosody ('I'll handle *this* myself'), whereas only in 11 per cent of all the occurrences it has a positive prosody (e.g. 'Go on, Jess. You can do *this*!').

It should be pointed out that, irrespective of its semantic prosody, *this* repeatedly occurs at moments of conflict, contrast and disagreement. In consonance with the observed self-imposing function of the pronoun, by using *this*, the speaker stages his or her point of view or stance, often contrasting with that of the interlocutor. In a crucial scene of *Bend It Like Beckham* (Gurinder Chada, 2002), the two sisters Pinky and Jess are talking at the end of Pinky's wedding, commenting on the same state of affairs and putting in relief opposite stances. But the same proximal pronoun is used by the two sisters in turn to express a positive or a negative assessment of the same life goals. One sister attributes utmost significance to a beautiful wedding and a traditional marriage ('Don't you want all of *this*?'); the other sister states that these achievements are not fulfilling enough for her ('I want more than *this*'). Pinky values getting married with the man she loves, having a great wedding party and being cherished by the whole family; by contrast, Jess claims that she aspires to more than what her sister treasures so highly: she wants to play football and go to the States.

(13)

PINKY	Jess, don't you want all of **this**? This is the best day of your life, innit?
JESS	I want more than **this**. They've offered me and Jules a scholarship to go to America.

(*Bend It Like Beckham*, Gurinder Chada, 2002)

On the basis of the present analysis, we may hypothesize that the relatively higher frequency of *this* in film dialogue vis-à-vis spontaneous spoken language is partly due to the symbolic uses of the pronoun highlighting key events and situations in the filmic narrative.[4] In particular symbolic *this* occurs in the conflictual and adversarial exchanges that are characteristic of audiovisual language, where they foster narrative advancement (Freddi 2011; Bednarek 2012). In extract (14) the two characters are putting forward their diverging and conflictual needs:

(14)

CASIM:	Roisin, I need to go. It's important to me.
ROISIN:	And **this** is important to me! Look, I've tried to understand your sister, Casim, I really have, I've tried to understand your whole family in fact. If your dad's such a great guy, I don't see why he can't start treating me like a human being!

(*Ae Fond Kiss*, Ken Loach, 2004)

Table 1.5 Sample Concordances of Symbolic *that* in the Four Films of the PCFD

1 I think I owe you a new guitar, Miss Hanlon. **That**'s very thoughtful of you! What do you want me to
2 God! Eh, you bastard you! Eh! Oh God, you do **that** for them! Bastard! Bastard! ((breaks windows))
3 you coming to classes. It's not his fault, Miss. **That**'s all right with you, is it? I suppose so. You
4 up to him. You don't know what he's like. Well, **that** blows it. Blows what, Miss? Debbie. I've hea
5 me mom's. No. You all right? What are you doing **that** for? I'm just trying it on Christ. Come here.
6 you're a failure! Don't you dare talk to me like **that**. You don't even have a proper dancing school.
7 when you were young, huh? You've played enough. **That**'s not fair! He selected me! He?! She said
8 Not tonight I'm not that type of girl (I'm sorry). **That** was so brilliant the way you came to my house.
9 PSD5's all there is to it! You've betrayed me! So **that**'s it? Yeah, that's it. Bye! Goodbye, Mrs Pa
10 violent conduct towards a player. No! You can't do **that**! You haven't seen any of it, have ya? It's
11 Bhamra? I don't ever want to see anything like **that** from you ever again, do you hear me?! ((yelling)
12 e down the offices. You wanna get down there, get **that** sorted. That's someone having a joke. I do
13 You wanna get down there, get that sorted. **That**'s someone having a joke. I don't think so. Let
14 fteen, twenty grand. I don't know what I'd do if **that** happened to me. I'd kill myself. Hello. Hiya!
15 birthday! There you go! Oh, you didn't have to do **that**, sweetheart! That's okay! That's Paul,

3.3.2 Symbolic **that**

A comparison with the twenty-six concordances of the less frequent symbolic *that* (see Table 1.5) shows that the two demonstrative pronouns share a tendency towards a negative prosody, although less markedly so for the distal pronoun. *That* collocates with some negatively connoted verbs – for example, *dare*, *happen* and *betrayed* –; it is often embedded in negative clauses such as 'That's not fair', 'Don't start all *that* again', 'You didn't have to do *that*' and may come with swear words: 'Oh God! Eh, you bastard you! Eh! Oh God, you do *that* for them! Bastard! Bastard!' The similar behaviour of the two pronouns is hardly surprising given the fact that an implication of contrast is a distinctive property of demonstratives in general (Cornish 2001: 304).

Despite the similarities between the two symbolic pronouns, however, with *that* speakers signal that the referent does not fall inside their sphere cognitively or subjectively (Cornish 2001: 303), whereas with *this* they signal that they are concentrating on their personal vantage point. In the following extracts, two distinct situations are similarly evaluated as being unfair: 'It ain't fair' and 'That's not fair'. But in one case, (15), the use of *this* evokes the speaker's primary deictic domain – as if she was talking to herself, almost oblivious of her interlocutor – while in the other case *that* shifts the referent domain onto the addressee, who is thus to blame.

(15)

CYNTHIA: Yeah. I ain't never been in here before. They shouldn't go raising your hopes like that, it ain't fair!
HORTENSE: Is this your signature?
CYNTHIA: **This** is stupid! I don't understand it! I mean, I can't be your mother, can I!
(*Secrets and Lies*, Mike Leigh, 1996)

(16)

CASIM TO HAMID:	=((hearing Hamid blowing his horn)) I'm fucking coming! Wait! Wait!
ROISIN TO CASIM	That's not fair, Casim. It's not my fault!
CASIM:	And it's not my family's fault if they're treated like Paki foreigners! Not quite up to the mark! I need to go, Roisin. It's really important I meet them. (*Ae Fond Kiss*, Ken Loach, 2004)

4 Conclusions

As prototypical means that coordinate interlocutors' attention, demonstrative pronouns have been shown to be very frequent in filmic discourse. They perform specific exophoric functions including foregrounding objects and relevant narrative moments as well as representing both the speaker's and hearer's personal spheres and perspectives. When a gestural demonstrative expression is used in dialogue, participants are called on to identify the entity in focus by paying attention to the specific shot. In contrast, a symbolic demonstrative requires interlocutors to ascertain the intended referent by drawing on the general context. In both cases, the fictional interaction among characters is constructed in such a way as to include the audience as interactive participants, whose centre of attention must converge on a given entity in the scene or portion of the narrated story. This is a natural consequence of the double-layeredness of filmic communication (Bubel 2008; Bednarek 2010; Messerli 2017 among many). Through the use of gestural and symbolic demonstratives, viewers are thus enticed to become involved in the fictional world portrayed on-screen and identify, empathize and engage with the characters' viewpoints and personal stories (cf. Green, Brock and Kaufman 2004; Wissmath, Weibel and Groner 2009).

The analysis of the PCFD has further suggested that proximal demonstratives are more frequent in audiovisual dialogue as opposed to other spoken varieties of English. Due to its high focus, *this* is particularly apt to amplify the attention on selected items and special moments in film representation, this way intensifying the engagement of viewers with the displayed situation and the unfolding of events. It is this narrative function of symbolic deixis that is especially relevant in film where demonstratives can foreground whole event sequences, recapitulate them or make them objects of both the viewers' and characters' individual or shared assessment. Indeed, demonstrative pronouns belong to the repertoire of verbal devices that can express stance and stage conflict on-screen where they mostly contribute to the negative overtone of the turn in which they are embedded. Overall, by participating in the iconicity of the medium and in its modality of heightened expression, demonstrative pronouns ultimately qualify as verbal resources available in film to show rather than tell. They foreground one entity after another in the superimposed pictures and in so doing are likely to capture viewers in the flow of the shifting situations and represented events.

Notes

1. Whereas in speech, proximal pronouns are no more than one-third of distal ones, in films *this* and *these* pronouns represent almost half of *that* and *those* pronouns.
2. With sensorial context we refer to what is directly accessibile to viewers through their senses of vision and hearing such as physical objects (e.g. a photograph, a bottle of wine) and sounds (e.g. a thump, the ringing of the telephone), while narrative context refers to the whole story or relevant sections of it being narrated on-screen. These sections may be made of sequences of connected events or by wider situations that become relevant to the unfolding deigetic whole (e.g. an uncovered betrayal, a love relationship). The verbal co-text is the immediate dialogue in which the referring expression is embedded.
3. The data were processed with *AntConc*. Information and download instructions available at: http://www.antlab.sci.waseda.ac.jp/.
4. Inversely, this finding might also be retraced to the absence in present-day English corpora of particular types of spoken discourse that are hard to come by because of ethical and legal constraints, for example, conflict talk, casual or private conversations about problematic issues. These conflictive issues – which by contrast are usually at the centre of fictional storytelling – could result in contrastive, confrontational symbolic uses of *this* in non-fictional spoken discourse as well. I would like to thank the editor Christian Hoffmann for bringing this point to my attention.

References

Bednarek, M. (2010), *The Language of Fictional Television: Drama and Identity*, London: Continuum.

Bednarek, M. (2012), '"Get us the hell out of here": Key words and trigrams in fictional television series', *International Journal of Corpus Linguistics*, 17 (1): 35–63.

Biber, D., Johansson, S., Leech, G., Conrad, S. and Finegan, E. (1999), *Longman Grammar of Spoken and Written English*, London: Longman.

Botley, S. and McEnery, T. (2001), 'Demonstratives in English: A corpus-based study', *Journal of English Linguistics*, 29 (1): 7–33.

Bubel, C. M. (2008), 'Film audience as overhearers', *Journal of Pragmatics*, 40 (1): 55–71.

Bühler, K. (2011), *Theory of Language: The Representational Function of Language*. [*Translation of Sprachtheorie* (1934/1982), translation by Donald, Fraser Goodwin, in collaboration with A. Eschbach], Amsterdam: John Benjamins.

Carter, R. and McCarthy, M. (2006), *Cambridge Grammar of English. A Comprehensive Guide: Spoken and Written English Grammar and Usage*, Cambridge: Cambridge University Press.

Cheshire, J. (1996), 'That Jacksprat: An interactional perspective on English *That*', *Journal of Pragmatics*, 25 (3): 369–93.

Cornish, F. (2001), '"Modal" *That* as Determiner and Pronoun: The primacy of the cognitive-interactive dimension', *English Language and Linguistics*, 5 (2): 297–315.

Cornish, F. (2007), 'English demonstratives: Discourse deixis and anaphora. A discourse-pragmatic account', in R. A. Nilsen, N. Aba Appiah Amfo and K. Borthen (eds), *Interpreting Utterances. Pragmatics and Its Interfaces: Essays in Honour of Thorstein Fretheim*, 147–66, Oslo: Novus Press.

Diessel, H. (1999), *Demonstratives: Forms, Function, and Grammaticalization*, Amsterdam: John Benjamins.
Diessel, H. (2006), 'Demonstratives, joint attention, and the emergence of grammar', *Cognitive Linguistics*, 17 (4): 463–89.
Diessel, H. (2012), 'Deixis and demonstratives', in C. Maienborn, K. von Heusinger and P. Portner (eds), *An International Handbook of Natural Language Meaning*, 1–25, Berlin: Mouton de Gruyter.
Diessel, H. (2014), 'Demonstratives, frames of reference, and semantic universals of space', *Language and Linguistics Compass*, 8 (3): 116–32.
Fillmore, C. J. [1971] (1975), *The Santa Cruz Lectures on Deixis*, Bloomington: Indiana University Linguistic Club.
Fillmore, C. J. (1997), *Lectures on Deixis*. Stanford: CSLI Publications.
Forchini, P. (2012), *Movie Language Revisited: Evidence from Multi-dimensional Analysis and Corpora*, Bern: Lang.
Freddi, M. (2011), 'A phraseological approach to film dialogue: Film stylistics revisited', *Yearbook of Phraseology*, 2: 137–63.
Freddi, M. and Pavesi, M. (2009), 'The Pavia corpus of film dialogue: Methodology and research rationale', in M. Freddi and M. Pavesi (eds), *Analysing Audiovisual Dialogue: Linguistic and Translation Insights*, 95–100, Bologna: CLUEB.
Green, M. C., Brock, Timothy C. and Kaufman, G. F. (2004), 'Understanding media enjoyment: The role of transportation into narrative worlds', *Communication Theory*, 14 (4): 311–27.
Gregory, M. (1967), 'Aspects of varieties differentiation', *Journal of Linguistics*, 3 (2): 177–98.
Halliday, M. A. K. and Hasan, R. (1976), *Cohesion in English*, London: Longman.
Halliday, M. A. K. and Hasan, R. (1985), *Language, Context and Text: Aspects of Language in a Social-semiotic Perspective*, Oxford: Oxford University Press.
Hausendorf, H. (2003), 'Deixis and speech situation revisited: The mechanism of perceived perception', in F. Lenz (ed.), *Deictic Conceptualisation of Space, Time and Person*, 249–69, Amsterdam: John Benjamins.
Kirsner, R. S. (1979), 'Deixis in discourse: An exploratory quantitative study of the modern Dutch demonstrative adjectives', in T. Givón (ed.), *Syntax and Semantics. Vol. 12: Discourse and Syntax*, 355–75, New York and San Francisco: Academic Press.
Lakoff, R. (1974), 'Remarks on *This* and *That*', in M. W. La Galy, R. A. Fox and A. Bruck (eds), *CLS. Papers from the Tenth Regional Meeting of the Chicago Linguistics Society*, 345–56, Chicago: Chicago Linguistic Society.
Levinson, S. C. (1983), *Pragmatics*, Cambridge: Cambridge University Press.
Levinson, S. C. (2004), 'Deixis and pragmatics', in L. R. Horn and G. Ward (eds), *The Handbook of Pragmatics*, 97–121, Oxford: Blackwell.
Louw, W. E. (1993), 'Irony in the text or insincerity in the writer? The diagnostic potential of semantic Prosodies', in M. Baker, G. Francis and E. Tognini-Bonelli (eds), *Text and Technology: In Honour of John Sinclair*, 157–76, Amsterdam: John Benjamins.
Lyons, J. (1977), *Semantics, Vol. 2*. Cambridge: Cambridge University Press.
Margutti, P., Traverso, V. and Pugliese, R. (2016), 'I'm sorry "about that": Apologies, indexicals and (Unnamed) offenses', *Discourse Processes*, 53 (1–2): 63–82.
Messerli, T. C. (2017), 'Participation structure in fictional discourse: Authors, scriptwriters, audiences and characters', in M. C. Locher and A. H. Jucker (eds), *Pragmatics of Fiction*, 25–54, Berlin and Boston: Walter De Gruyter.

Partington, A. (2015), 'Evaluative prosody', in K. Aijmer and C. Rühlemann (eds), *Corpus Pragmatics: A Handbook*, 279–303, Cambridge: Cambridge University Press.

Pavesi, M. (2013), '*This* and *That* in the Language of Film Dubbing: A corpus-based analysis', *Meta*, 58 (1): 107–37.

Pavesi, M. (2014), 'The Pavia corpus of film dialogue: A means to several ends', in M. Pavesi, M. Formentelli and E. Ghia (eds), *The Languages of Dubbing: Mainstream Audiovisual Translation in Italy*, 29–55, Bern: Peter Lang.

Piwek, P., Beun, R.-J. and Cremers, A. (2008), '"Proximal" and "distal" in language and cognition: Evidence from deictic demonstratives in Dutch', *Journal of Pragmatics*, 40: 694–718.

Quaglio, P. (2009), *Television Dialogue: The Sitcom Friends vs. Natural Conversation*. Amsterdam: John Benjamins.

Quaglio, P. and Biber, D. (2006), 'The grammar of conversation', in B. Aarts and A. McMahon (eds), *The Handbook of English Linguistics*, 692–723, Malden, Oxford and Carlton: Blackwell Publishing.

Strauss, S. (1993), 'Why "this" and "that" are not complete without "it"', in K. Beals, G. Cooke, D. Kathman, K. E. McCullouoh, S. Kita and D. Testen (eds), *CLS, Papers from the 29th Regional Meeting of the Chicago Linguistic Society vol. 1: The Main Session*, 403–17, Chicago: Chicago Linguistic Society.

Strauss, S. (2002), '*This, That,* and *It* in spoken American english: A demonstrative system of gradient focus', *Language Sciences*, 24 (2): 131–52.

Wissmath, B., Weibel, D. and Groner, R. (2009), 'Dubbing or subtitling? Effects on spatial presence, transportation, flow, and enjoyment', *Journal of Media Psychology*, 21 (3): 114–25.

Xiao, R. and McEnery, T. (2006), 'Collocation, semantic prosody, and near synonymy: A cross-linguistic perspective', *Applied Linguistics*, 27 (1): 103–29.

2

On the usefulness of the Sydney Corpus of Television Dialogue as a reference point for corpus stylistic analyses of TV series

Monika Bednarek

1 Introduction

This chapter focuses on linguistic analysis of American television series. Major developments in recent decades such as the rise of HBO-inspired quality television and of distributors such as Netflix, iTunes, Hulu and Amazon have resulted in unprecedented changes in the US television industry. Narrative TV series are now an increasingly sophisticated and globally popular art form, which are devoured by audiences the world over. They are available on demand any time and on any device, 'binge watching' has become common, and viewers can immediately interact with TV series via the new media and forge transnational fan communities. Language is fundamental to the workings of such narratives; yet relatively little research on TV series has focused on questions of language. This gap in knowledge represents an important challenge for a range of linguistic subdisciplines such as stylistics, media linguistics and pragmatics.

While nonlinguistic research in the cross-disciplinary field of Television Studies has been undertaken since the 1970s, linguistic approaches to TV series have only started to emerge in the last decade. Within linguistics, the study of television dialogue[1] is now becoming a trend, whether in stylistics (e.g. Toolan 2011), pragmatics (e.g. Dynel 2015), corpus linguistics (e.g. Quaglio 2009; Bednarek 2010, 2018a) or sociolinguistics (e.g. Richardson 2010; Stuart-Smith 2011; Queen 2015a). Indicators of such an emerging trend include a panel on 'telecinematic discourse' (Piazza, Bednarek and Rossi 2011: 1) at the *Fourteenth International Pragmatics Conference* (Bublitz, Hoffmann and Kirner-Ludwig 2015), an international workshop on the analysis of fictional dialogue in film and television series (Mazzon and Klarer 2015), a keynote at the *Sixth International Language in the Media* conference on linguistic variation in fictional television and film (Queen 2015b) and a panel on 'Languaging the Other in TV series' at the *Sixth Critical Approaches to Discourse Analysis across Disciplines* conference (Cambria and Venuti 2016). A recent book even uses TV dialogue to teach people about language (Beers Fägersten 2016).

This emerging interest in linguistics starkly contrasts with the situation when I first started working on US TV series a decade ago (Bednarek 2007), with only a few linguistic studies and no broader engagement at conferences. A considerable amount of research has now emerged, and reviews are provided in Bednarek (2015a) and – with a focus on corpus linguistics – in Bednarek (2015b). Most of these linguistic studies focus on specific television narratives rather than analysing a wide range of series, and much work has been done on 'classic' or 'cult' shows: *Friends* (Tagliamonte and Roberts 2005; Stokoe 2008; Quaglio 2009), *Will and Grace* (Baker 2005), *The West Wing* (Richardson 2006; Wodak 2009), *Buffy* (Mandala 2007; Reichelt and Durham 2017), *Firefly* (Mandala 2008), *Star Trek* (Rey 2001; Mandala 2011), *Gilmore Girls* (Bednarek 2011a) or *Sex and the City* (Paltridge, Collins and Liu 2011; Bubel 2011). Such studies provide useful insights into these specific cultural products, but are somewhat limited in the insights they can offer into TV dialogue as a language variety, because they are not based on representative datasets. Thus, in relation to his own work on *Friends*, Quaglio (2009: 14) explicitly states: 'the results of this study should not be (and are not meant to be) generalized to television dialogue overall,' as they are limited to a particular TV series and genre (situation comedy).

There is thus scope for linguistic research that focuses on television dialogue as a *type* of language, examining a wider range of TV series (see Bednarek 2012a, 2014, 2018a). This chapter introduces a new, carefully designed dataset (corpus) of American English TV dialogue that can be used for this purpose, but that can also act as a point of reference or baseline for stylistic studies that examine one particular televisual narrative. This new corpus is called the *Sydney Corpus of Television Dialogue* (SydTV), as it was designed and built at the University of Sydney, with funding provided by the university. SydTV contains dialogue from sixty-six different US TV series. In Sections 4 and 5, I will describe the corpus in more detail and present three case studies that illustrate its potential usefulness for stylistic research on TV dialogue. However, I will first briefly discuss *why* linguists should undertake such research in the first place.

2 Why study language in television series?

As mentioned earlier, linguistic interest in the analysis of television series has only emerged fairly recently. Conversely, this means that such mass media narratives have been neglected and deemed unworthy of study for a long time. A key reason for this, especially in sociolinguistics, lies in the supposed 'artificiality' of the language used in scripted film and television narratives. This argument has been challenged by sociolinguists such as Androutsopoulos (2012) and Queen (2015a). As the latter notes,

> Is Meryl Streep's language less real when she is in character? It may be true that a character exists only in the context of the media vehicle she appears in, but the embodiment of that character is real flesh; the sounds emerging from that character's mouth are real sounds; the grammar is (usually!) the real grammar of a human language. The patterns of variability may differ from those found in non-

media communities, but that's only a problem if we assume that they should be the same. ... [F]ictional characters exist in [the broader language ecology] just as you or I do. (Queen 2015a: 161)

The reason for neglecting TV series in stylistics is different – stylistic research has long examined 'artificial' language – in this case, language created by particular writers/authors such as Jane Austen or Charles Dickens. However, such research has predominantly focused on *literary* fictional texts, rather than fictional television dialogue which originates in a cultural product that has, traditionally, not been highly valued by stylistic and literary scholars, and which has long been excluded from the scope of literary and stylistic research.[2] In fact, as I argue in Bednarek (2015b), TV series have even been assigned a lower value than other mass media narratives (films). This is despite their significance as a cultural product. I have discussed this significance in detail elsewhere (Bednarek 2010: 7–11; 2012b: 199–202), and a brief summary will suffice here.

Television series are popular cultural products, consumed by millions of viewers worldwide. They are simultaneously part of the culture and 'play a role in shaping that culture' (Queen 2015a: 21). TV series provide a window into the world we live in and some of its preoccupations. For example, medical shows such as *House* and *Nurse Jackie* address ethical and legal issues and the work–life balance; police/detective series are often propelled by current social issues or actual cases; political dramas such as *West Wing* and *House of Cards* provide searing political commentary; programmes such as *Deadwood* and *Game of Thrones* tackle human nature and morality. The dramedy *Gilmore Girls* took feminist concerns seriously and included explicit discussions by characters on dilemmas faced by women both in the past and in the present (see Bednarek 2010). Even a sitcom such as *The Big Bang Theory* may thematize social issues such as the role and treatment of women in science, or contemporary phenomena such as online verbal violence/trolling. Wodak argues that TV series such as *The West Wing* offer us models of how politics is done (Wodak 2009: 22), and Queen (2015a) points out that the scripted media provide us with an imaginary, 'fairly contained, and edited, microcosm' of sociocultural life (Queen 2015a: 21). It is worth mentioning here that the argument for taking television series seriously in linguistic research is an argument that would be unnecessary for a media or cultural studies audience.[3] Lacey (1998: 84) states: 'From a Media Studies perspective all media artifacts are worthy of investigation, particularly if they are popular. They are worthy of study because they have much to teach us about how societies are organized and how societies create meaning.' From this point of view, 'mainstream' TV series are *as* important to analyse as TV series that are sophisticated artistic creations with 'literary' qualities such as complex plots and characters.

Further, audiences engage with the characters and narratives as well as the language of these fictional worlds, including in online and offline conversations with others. More specifically, audiences spend a lot of time watching television series in general and often follow a particular TV series over many seasons – this creates significant depth of engagement. Creeber notes that TV series 'can capture an audience's involvement in a way equalled by few contemporary media' (Creeber 2004: 4). There is both psychological engagement through processes such as parasocial interaction, (wishful) identification or affinity/liking (Cohen 1999; Giles 2002) as well as linguistic engagement through texts such as threads, blogs, review columns and fan fiction about television series (Richardson 2010: 89–92).

There are manifold examples of how television dialogue is used as a resource for social interaction at a national and transnational level (Bednarek 2017a, b). To give just two anecdotal examples here, on German radio an accountant and a chemist debated nerd clichés from the US sitcom *The Big Bang Theory*, and after a misunderstanding, a German friend's Facebook comment consisted of just one word: *D'oh* – an allusion to a well-known catchphrase from *The Simpsons*. Such and similar examples also illustrate the 'mediatisation' of contemporary societies – the role of the mass and new media in transforming social life and social practices (Androutsopoulos 2014). In Coupland's (2007: 28) words, 'the media are increasingly inside us and us in them.' Contemporary engagement with TV dialogue includes practices such as:

1. The conventionalization and play with catchphrases from TV series (Richardson 2010: 100–3);
2. The referencing of TV dialogue in face-to-face conversations among young people, where such media engagement carries cultural capital (Georgakopoulou 2014);
3. The use of TV series as points of orientation in society, for example, when a commentator suggests that a political party has become 'a *Mad Men* party in a *Modern Family* world' (Queen 2015a: 1);
4. The large-scale circulation of TV dialogue via other media (e.g. as hashtags #*doh*, #*bazinga*) or in a 'mutated' form as part of language-image memes (e.g. the *I for one welcome our* [classifier] *overlords* meme originating in a *Simpsons* episode; see Zappavigna 2012: 106);
5. The engagement with TV series (and dialogue) to form transnational fan communities, for example, wearing T-shirts with quotes or asking others about their favourite piece of dialogue (Richardson 2010; Bednarek 2017a, b).

Further, TV series generate significant public discourse and debates, for instance about swearing, accents and dialects, authenticity, quality, represented values/ideologies, and so on. Queen (2015a: 239–40) provides examples of critical audience reactions to the Southern accent performed by Kyra Sedgewick in the crime series *The Closer*:

1. 'Her "Southern" accent is so over the top and farcical I am embarrassed for her';
2. 'No educated, professional Southerner speaks like that';
3. 'No one here speaks that way';
4. 'It's a touch over-exaggerated and overly gracious.'

To conclude, 'mass media are changing the terms of our engagement with language and social semiosis in late-modernity … TV in particular has put mediated linguistic diversity in front of the viewing public far more pervasively and with much richer and more saturated indexical loading than face-to-face social reality can achieve'

(Coupland 2010: 69). Several linguists have recently argued that fictional mass media require more attention (e.g. Queen 2015a) and that 'we ... need much more analysis of the structural characteristics of media representation of language, of different genres, formats' (Stuart-Smith 2011: 235). In the midst of a 'golden' age of television, the time is right for a comprehensive investigation of televisual narratives – an investigation that would be incomplete without careful examination of linguistic practices. Corpus linguistics can be a useful approach for such an endeavour and the next section will therefore briefly introduce corpus linguistics and review existing corpora of US TV dialogue.

3 Existing corpora of US TV dialogue

Corpus linguistics involves the rapid searching and sorting of electronic text collections (corpora), calculations on large amounts of data, comparison to 'reference' corpora, and both quantitative and qualitative analysis. Such techniques have successfully been applied to the study of dramatic texts (e.g. Culpeper 2009; McIntyre 2012), including to the study of television series (e.g. Rey 2001; Baker 2005; Quaglio 2008, 2009; Bednarek 2010, 2018a). Gries (2006: 200) argues that 'corpus linguistics is among the most important developments in the linguistic sciences'. Often the information that is uncovered would be impossible to detect by hand and is not accessible to intuition (Baker 2005: 5).

As already alluded to, the first corpus studies focused on 'cult' series, namely *Star Trek* and its spin-offs (Rey 2001), *Friends* (Quaglio 2008, 2009) and *Gilmore Girls* (Bednarek 2008). Mittmann (2006) analysed data from three very different TV series: *Golden Girls*, *Dawson's Creek* and *Friends* in the context of 'translationese'. Csomay and Petrovic (2012) included one TV series (*Law and Order*) in their corpus study of technical vocabulary. The more contemporary *Corpus of American Television Series* (CATS) consists of dialogue from four TV series (~160,000 words), as described in Dose (2012). The popular 'big data' approach has seen the creation of the Corpus of American Soap Operas (SOAP, Davies 2012). This corpus is described on the website as containing 100 million words from over 22,000 transcripts from ten US soap operas. However, the corpus is restricted to one genre, and it is somewhat difficult to identify the origin and accuracy of the corpus transcripts (see Bednarek 2015b). The same can be said with respect to Webb and Rodger's (2009) study, where it is unstated where transcripts were taken from, who transcribed the TV series, and how consistent and accurate the transcripts are. Their dataset consists of two episodes each from fifteen series from the 1990s as well as four older TV series. Berber Sardinha and Veirano Pinto's (2017) USTV corpus contains a wide range of different types of television texts, including twenty-eight texts from five drama series (116, 532 words) and twenty-eight texts from eight sitcoms (107, 533 words) as well as several texts from soap operas, mini series, animation series, programmes targeted at children or teens, and many other television programmes including news and reality television. As with the SOAP corpus, the texts were downloaded from websites, and their accuracy remains slightly unclear. Subtitles are also sometimes used to create corpora – see, for example, the newly released TV corpus (Davies 2019). In my own research I used corpora that contained dialogue ranging from one (Bednarek 2010, 2012b) to seven (Bednarek 2012a), ten (Bednarek 2011a), and twenty-seven (Bednarek 2014) different TV series, often relying on fan transcripts. More recently, I built and analysed a new corpus – the Sydney Corpus of Television Dialogue (Bednarek 2018b).

4 The Sydney Corpus of Television Dialogue

The Sydney Corpus of Television Dialogue (SydTV) is a specialized corpus which has been carefully designed to be representative of recent US American TV dialogue, and contains the complete dialogue from one episode from sixty-six different TV series. 'US American' is defined as having the United States as country of origin. TV dialogue is defined as the actual dialogue uttered by actors on-screen as they are performing characters in fictional TV series (cf. note 1). Series included in the corpus were first broadcast between 2000 and 2012. This specific time frame was adopted because the first decade of the twenty-first century has been dubbed a 'golden age of television'. About half of the corpus comes from comedy genres and the other half from drama genres. Different moments of textual time within the season are included in the corpus, with a healthy mix of pilot episodes, final episodes and other episodes occurring towards the beginning, middle and end of the respective season. Since the corpus contains full episodes (rather than samples) episode-based stylistic analysis is possible. However, since each series is only represented by one episode, stylistic analysis of larger narrative units is not possible (i.e. analysing the whole season or series). Because of the issues associated with using online scripts, fan transcripts or extracted subtitles (Bednarek 2015b), dialogue was mostly transcribed from scratch or existing transcripts were checked and corrected. This work was undertaken by a research assistant who followed specific transcription conventions that were developed on the basis of existing linguistic transcription standards for spoken corpora. The transcription conventions include marked pronunciation variants such as *gonna* ('going to'), *sorta* ('sort of'), the alveolar form [n] at the end of words ending in <ing> (e.g. *somethin'*) as well as contractions (e.g. *could've*), discourse markers (e.g. *oh*), hesitation markers (e.g. *uh*), listening cues (e.g *mmm*), dis/agreement markers (e.g. *uh-uh*), exclamations and interjections (e.g. *ugh*). More detail on the corpus design and transcription conventions is available in Bednarek (2018a, b, in press).

In total, SydTV comprises about 275.000 words.[4] While many contemporary corpora consist of several millions of words, these corpora are often general corpora rather than specialized corpora like SydTV. A smaller corpus size also enables the combination of quantitative and qualitative research, limits the need for random downsampling, and further permits 'total accountability' (McEnery and Hardie 2012: 15) of the data (using the entire corpus and all relevant evidence emerging from it). The transcription of spoken data is also very time-consuming. Further, as Köster rightly argues: 'What is more important than the actual size of the corpus is how well it is designed and that it is "representative"' (Köster 2010: 68). Despite its relatively small size, SydTV seems to be highly representative of recent US TV dialogue. It is important to emphasize that it contains texts from a large number of distinct cultural products (episodes from *sixty-six different* series), which makes it more representative of TV dialogue as a language variety than a much larger corpus containing dialogue from only a few programmes, only one genre or only one TV series.

5 Using SydTV

For the remainder of this chapter I want to focus on how SydTV can be used in linguistic research on TV dialogue to guard against over-interpretation, to provide a baseline or point of reference and to test hypotheses. I will do this through presenting three brief case studies that use SydTV, including two that are particularly relevant to stylistics.

In terms of my approach in these case studies it is useful to draw on the new topology for analysis of discourse proposed by Bednarek and Caple (2017). They distinguish between four zones of analysis, depending on whether research focuses on one semiotic mode or not, and whether research focuses on patterns across texts or within texts. Thus, Figure 2.1 shows that researchers can situate their study as being intrasemiotic (monomodal) or intersemiotic (horizontal axis in Figure 2.1) and intratextual or intertextual (vertical axis in Figure 2.1). These zones are considered to be clines or regions, rather than strict separate categories. Figure 2.1 also shows that I situate my case studies mainly in Zone 2: The focus is on language (intrasemiotic) and the primary interest is in patterns across texts (intertextual), rather than patterns within texts (e.g. discourse or genre structure).

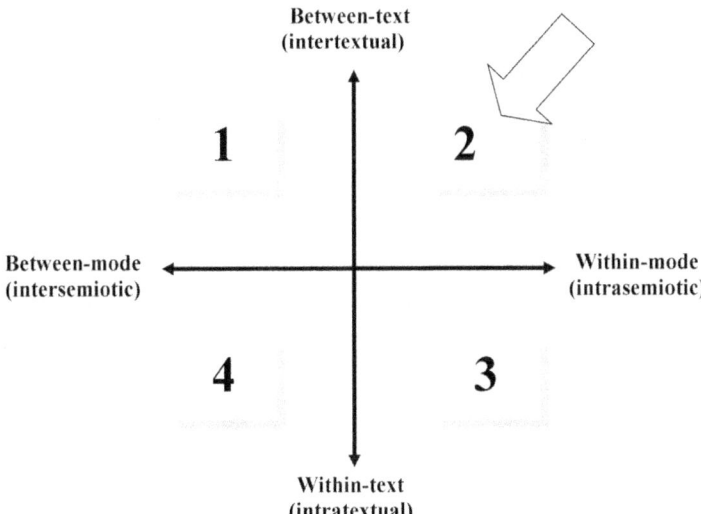

Figure 2.1 Situating the case studies.

5.1 Using SydTV as a reference corpus 1: Exploring unique linguistic features

As mentioned, SydTV can be useful for stylistic research on a particular televisual narrative, acting as a reference corpus against which the language of that narrative can be compared. I will present one case study here to show how such a comparison allows the researcher to investigate whether or not a particular linguistic feature is specific or unique to the narrative of interest or if it is simply a feature of much or most TV dialogue.

In a large-scale corpus study of the US dramedy *Gilmore Girls* (Bednarek 2010), I found that 4-grams with *talk** (*are you talking about, what are you talking* and *to talk to you*) appear to be over-represented when compared to an unscripted corpus of spoken American English (the Longman Spoken American Corpus/LSAC, as described in Mittmann 2004). More precisely, *are you talking about* is the fifth most frequent 4-gram in *Gilmore Girls*, but only the hundredth most frequent 4-gram in the LSAC, and while *what are you talking* and *to talk to you* are the seventh and seventeenth most frequent 4-gram in *Gilmore Girls* they do not rank within the top 100 most frequent 4-grams in the LSAC.[5] While I proposed that the apparent importance of talking in this series may be shared by other TV series and is related to the creation of drama (Bednarek 2010: 83–4), I also hypothesized that

> talking emerges as a central action in GiGi, where the normal expectation is that issues and problems are talked about and 'talked through', though characters may refuse to obey this expectation. This might be related to the genre of *Gilmore Girls* as a 'female' dramedy – reflecting social action that is, perhaps stereotypically, associated with women. … [W]hile *Gilmore Girls* perhaps does confirm the stereotype of 'talkative women', the portrayal of these women is sympathetic and there are strong female characters in the series. (Bednarek 2010: 83)

SydTV can be used to test whether or not talking is indeed more central in this 'female' dramedy than in other series through comparative research using SydTV. Table 2.1 provides the raw and normalized frequencies (per 100.000 words) of *are you talking about, what are you talking* and *to talk to you* in *Gilmore Girls* and SydTV.[6] Because there is overlap between the first two n-grams, frequencies are also provided for the 5-gram *what are you talking about* – which is associated with argumentative discourse or interpersonal conflict (Bednarek 2010: 83). Results for n-grams were produced using Wordsmith (Scott 2012, 2017). To provide additional insights, I used the corpus-linguistic web interface Sketch Engine (Kilgarriff et al. 2014) to identify the frequencies of all instances of the verb lemmas TALK and TELL.[7] Table 2.1 also includes results from tests for statistical significance and effect-size: log likelihood (G2), RRisk and LogRatio (produced using the calculator available at http://ucrel.lancs.ac.uk/llwizard.html, where more information on these statistics and their interpretation is also available). A G2 of 3.84 equals p <0.05; results below 3.84 indicate that findings are not statistically significant.

Table 2.1 offers up a mixed picture. On the one hand, the n-grams *are you talking about, what are you talking* and *what are you talking about* do seem to be overused in

Table 2.1 A comparison of *Gilmore Girls* and SydTV

	Gilmore Girls		SydTV (without Gilmore Girls episode)		Tests for statistical significance/effect-size		
	Raw frequency	Norm. frequency	Raw frequency	Norm. frequency	G2	RRisk	LogRatio
Are you talking about	169	15	24	9.5	5.03	1.59	0.67
What are you talking	160	14.2	19	7.5	8.25	1.90	0.92
What are you talking about	160	14.2	19	7.5	8.25	1.90	0.92
To talk to you	92	8.2	15	5.9	1.46	1.38	0.47
TALK and TELL (verb lemmas)	5090	452.9	1165	459.8	0.22	0.98	−0.02
TALK (verb lemma)	2,125	189.1	406	160.2	9.68	1.18	0.24
TELL (verb lemma)	2,965	263.8	759	299.6	9.52	0.88	−0.18

Gilmore Girls in terms of both normalized frequency and statistical significance (G2 > 3.84; p < 0.05). But as the RRisk and LogRatio values indicate, the difference between the two corpora is not huge: *are you talking about* is used about 1.6 times more often in *Gilmore Girls*, while *what are you talking (about)* is used about 1.9 times more often. Further, the combined normalized frequency of the verb lemmas TALK and TELL is almost identical, and the difference is not statistically significant. In fact, there is statistically significant *over*use of TALK in *Gilmore Girls*, which is counterbalanced by statistical significant *under*use of TELL. However, the RRisk and LogRatio values show the difference is small in both cases. Finally, while *to talk to you* appears to be overused in *Gilmore Girls* if we consider normalized frequencies, the difference is again not statistically significant (G2 < 3.84).

In sum, I would argue that my earlier interpretation – provided in the block quote above – is somewhat of an 'over-interpretation' as suggested by the consultation of a new reference corpus (SydTV). This demonstrates that SydTV is potentially useful because researchers can consult this corpus to check whether or not features are specific/unique to a particular TV series and hence avoid a potential over-interpretation of results. Once features have been identified as 'special' for a TV narrative, further analysis can focus on potential reasons – are these features overused because of idiolects of particular speakers (characterization) or do they relate to other aspects of the narrative? The comparison to SydTV can thus provide a useful starting point for more in-depth stylistic analysis.

5.2 Using SydTV as a reference corpus 2: Exploring televisual characters

Another way in which SydTV might be useful for stylistic research is in providing data from a wide range of narratives, each with their own plot and characters. In this way, a particular televisual character can, for instance, be compared not just with characters that occur within its own textual universe (e.g. comparing the character of Sheldon in *The Big Bang Theory* with other characters in this sitcom, such as Leonard or Penny) but also with *other* televisual characters.

In previous research, I used keywords/n-grams analysis to examine the language of particular TV characters: that of Lorelai (and others) in *Gilmore Girls* (Bednarek 2010, 2011b) and that of Sheldon in *The Big Bang Theory* (Bednarek 2012b). 'Keyword' analysis is a technique that uses corpus-linguistic software to identify linguistic features that are unusual in terms of frequency when a 'node' text or corpus is compared to a reference corpus (Scott and Tribble 2006: 59). The linguistic features that are unusually (in)frequent in the node corpus are identified by the software as 'key' (using the log likelihood statistic), pointing the researcher to features that characterize the language of the node corpus. These linguistic features can be individual word forms (e.g. *is, be, was*) – that is, key words – or they can be longer multi-word structures (e.g. *you know, a lot of, in the middle of*) – that is, key clusters or n-grams. Table 2.2 presents the results from my previous research on positive keywords and n-grams for the two characters when they are compared to all other characters within the respective series. In other words, these word forms and n-grams are unusually frequent in the dialogue uttered by these characters, and can be tied to aspects of their character (Bednarek 2010, 2012b).[8]

Using SydTV, it is now possible to examine if these words and n-grams are also 'key' for these two characters when their dialogue is compared against *other* televisual characters. We can do this by using SydTV as a new reference corpus against which the dialogue of these characters is compared. In this keywords analysis, the episodes that SydTV contains from *Gilmore Girls* and *The Big Bang Theory* are not included and speaker names are disregarded (e.g. *JACK: ...*).

Undertaking this analysis shows that *all* n-grams in Table 2.2 remain 'key' for Sheldon when SydTV is the reference corpus. In contrast, some of the words/n-grams are no longer 'key' for Lorelai, namely *no, cause, know, you know, kid, god, my god, oh my, oh my god*. This shows that the way Sheldon speaks is more *unique* than the way Lorelai speaks – that is, the two characters differ in the extent to which they are linguistically similar to other television characters. For instance, the results indicate that use of *you know* (possibly as discourse marker) and *god, my god, oh my god* (likely as interjection) is common among many other televisual characters, not just

Table 2.2 Character keywords/n-grams from Bednarek (2010, 2012b)

Character comparison	Selected positive keywords/n-grams (statistically speaking unusually frequent)
Lorelai vs. all other characters in *Gilmore Girls*	*mom, dad, oh, honey, no, okay/ok, inn, hon, hey, gran, hi, wow, cause, know, god, bye, and, kid, ha, coffee, yes, well, weird; my mother, the inn, my parents, you know, my god, oh no, oh my, oh my god*
Sheldon vs. all other characters in *The Big Bang Theory*	*a nobel prize; my research, number of, a series of, the fact that, lack of, the result, the possibility/possibility that, your premise, in addition, this is a, this is not a, if you will, I hardly think so, it occurs to me, going to have to, you might want to, to point, luckily for you, of course, well of course, once again, remind you, an interesting, Leonard Leonard Leonard*

unique to Lorelai. In contrast, the linguistic uniqueness of Sheldon provides further evidence for arguing that his character exhibits 'linguistically deviant behaviour' which constructs him as 'funnily abnormal' and partially 'alien' (Bednarek 2012b). While the results from this new keywords analysis are worthy of more in-depth investigation, this brief case study has demonstrated that SydTV can be useful for stylistic research into televisual characterization, as it allows a broader comparison of specific televisual characters with other characters that make up the contemporary television landscape.

5.3 *Ain't* and other variants

Finally, SydTV can be used to test hypotheses made by previous researchers on the basis of limited data, for example restricted to a particular television programme or genre. I will present one example in this section, which focuses on linguistic research on language variation, rather than stylistic research as the previous two case studies have.

In a small case study of the US daytime television drama *Days of Our Lives* (*DOOL*) it was found that most of the characters use unmarked standard American English with little phonological or grammatical variation and that 'highly stigmatized or regionally marked linguistic forms are generally absent from the DOOL data' (Queen 2012: 166). However, the non-standard, informal variant [In] (instead of the standard velar [ŋ] in participial verb morphology) occurs relatively regularly in the programme (Queen 2012: 166). Wolfram and Schilling-Estes (2006: 183) note that [In] carries social stigma, which depends on frequency of usage and status of speakers (Wolfram and Schilling-Estes 2006: 184). Finegan (2004: 26) states that in some Southern dialects [In] is predominant, and that it is only in some cases used more frequently by working-class speakers. Queen (2012) argues that [In] does not have the same negative associations with education or social background as more stigmatized forms like multiple negation or *ain't*. Queen (2015a: 39–40) mentions that 'virtually all English speakers' sometimes 'drop the *g*', and summarizes research that suggests that [In] signals social meanings such as 'masculine', 'informal' and 'friendly' as well as having an association with Western and Southern American English, whereas [Ing] signals 'articulate' and 'educated'.

SydTV can be consulted to explore if Queen's results for DOOL are true for dialogue in TV series more generally. In order to do so, we can first compare the frequencies and *range/distribution* of selected variants – that is, across how many of the sixty-six SydTV corpus files the relevant forms occur, where one file represents one episode from a different TV series. These results are presented in Table 2.3. The findings suggest that *gonna* and [In] are by far the most frequent.⁹ [In] has such a high frequency because it can occur in many different word forms. In total, there are 192 types that were transcribed as using this phonological variant (query term: **in'*). In fact, the majority of these types occur only once with [In] (n = 103); with only thirteen types occurring twenty times or more with this pronunciation: *bein'*; *comin'*; *doin'*; *fuckin'*; *gettin'*; *goin'*; *lookin'*; *nothin'*; *sayin'*; *somethin'*; *talkin'*; *thinkin'*; and *tryin'*. As indicated by the presence of *fuckin'*, several of the word forms with [In] are either taboo or swear words (e.g. *cocksuckin'*, *motherfuckin'*, *pissin'*, *shittin'*) or slang (e.g. *ballin'*, *chillin'*, *creepin'*, *eyeballin'*,

Table 2.3 Selected variants in SydTV

Variant	Raw frequency	Range	
		N° of TV series	Percentage of TV series
Gonna	1,009	65/66	98.5
[In]	992	57/66	86.4
Wanna	387	63/66	95.5
Gotta	214	58/66	87.9
'Cause	165	56/66	84.8
Ain't	92	22/66	33.3

freestylin'), but this is not a necessary condition, as other words are also pronounced in this way (e.g. *breathin'*, *complainin'*). However, *gonna* has both the highest frequency and range, reaching almost 100 per cent, while the distribution of [In] across corpus files is fairly similar to that of *gotta* and *'cause*, although it is more frequent than these forms. In contrast, *ain't* only occurs in twenty-two of the sixty-six episodes in the corpus and has by far the lowest raw frequency of all investigated forms.

We can further examine whether the non-standard or colloquial/informal variants are more common and more widely distributed than their alternatives. These alternatives are not necessarily prestigious; rather they are not stigmatized (Wolfram and Schilling-Estes 2006: 183). Figures 2.2–2.7 compare the raw frequencies of the pairs [In] and [Ing], *gonna/going to*, *wanna/want to*, *'cause/because*, the triplet *ain't/isn't/is not* and the quadruplet *gotta/got to/has to/have to*.[10]

These figures show that *gonna* is 8.9 times more frequent than *going to*, while *wanna* is 3.9 times more frequent than *want to*. In contrast, [Ing] is 3.6 times more frequent than [In], *because* is 2.5 times more frequent than *'cause*, and *isn't* is 1.8 times more frequent than *ain't*, although *ain't* and the written standard *is not* have almost the same frequency. Since *ain't* can also stand for other variants of BE (*aren't*, *'m not*) as well as variants of HAVE (*haven't*, *hasn't*) and DO (in African American Vernacular English), *ain't* is very clearly less frequent than its respective nonstigmatized alternatives. Finally, *gotta* is almost eight times more frequent than *got to*, but only about half as frequent as *has to/have to*.

Note that the difference between two compared variants is statistically significant in all cases, except when *ain't* is compared with *is not* (G2 =0.28). In terms of range/distribution, *gonna* has a higher range (r = 65) than *going to* (r = 42) and *wanna* has a higher range (r = 63) than *want to* (r = 45), while *because* has a higher range (r = 66) than *'cause* (r = 56); [Ing] has a higher range (r = 66) than [In] (r = 51); and *isn't* (r = 53) and *is not* (r = 43) have a higher range than *ain't* (r = 22). *Gotta* has a much higher range (r = 58) than *got to* (r = 20), but a slightly lower range than *has to/have to* (r = 64).

Summing up the results presented in Table 2.3 and Figures 2.2–2.7, it appears that *gonna* is the most important non-standard or colloquial/informal variant in SydTV: it is the most distributed and most frequent, and it occurs almost nine times more frequently and has a wider range than its alternative *going to*. *Wanna* is not as frequent, but has the second highest range, and occurs almost four times more frequently and has a wider range than its alternative *want to*. The variants [In], *gotta* and *'cause* are

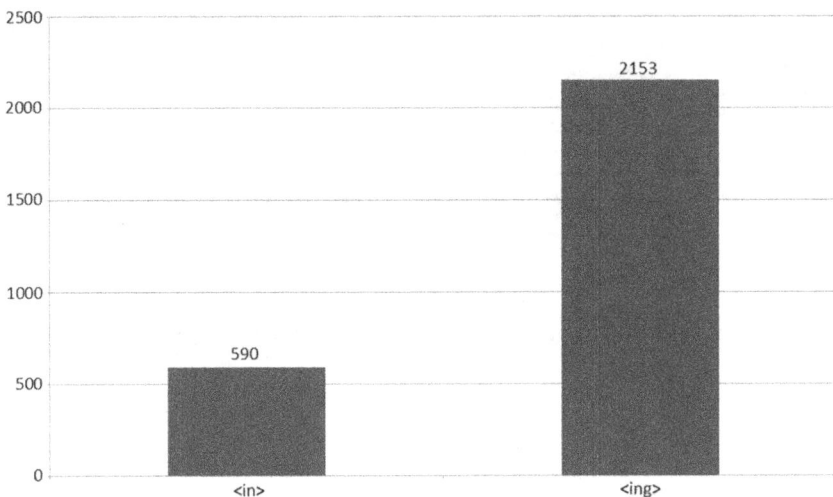

Figure 2.2 Combined raw frequencies of thirteen word types ending in [In] or [Ing] in SydTV.

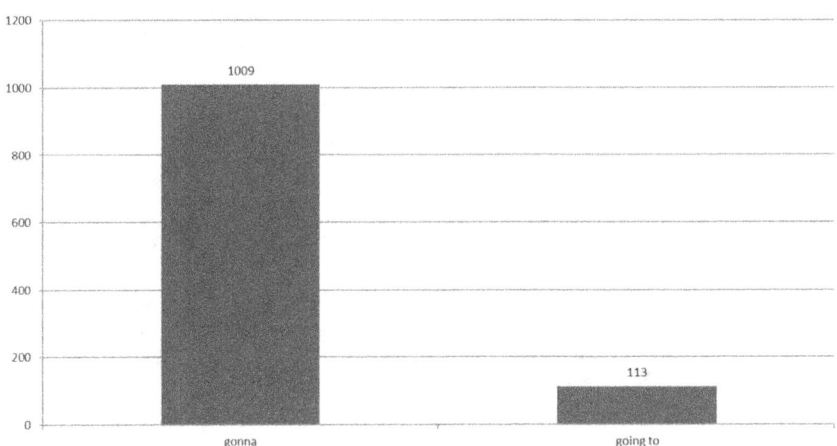

Figure 2.3 Raw frequencies of *gonna/going to* in SydTV (where to ≠ preposition).

also fairly common (especially [In]) and occur in many episodes; however, they are less frequent and less widely distributed than their alternatives.

Finally, all results indicate that *ain't* is the most stigmatized of all investigated forms: it has a lower frequency, and a much lower range than the other non-standard or colloquial/informal variants and its range and frequency are also lower than that of the spoken standard variant *isn't*. It is similar in frequency to the written standard variant *is not* (although it has a lower range), and this may reflect the fact that the dialogue imitates informal and spoken rather than formal and written American speech.

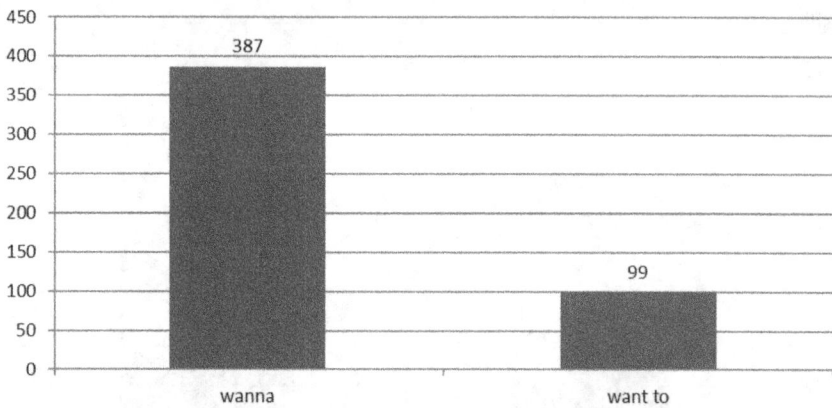

Figure 2.4 Raw frequencies of *wanna/want to* in SydTV.

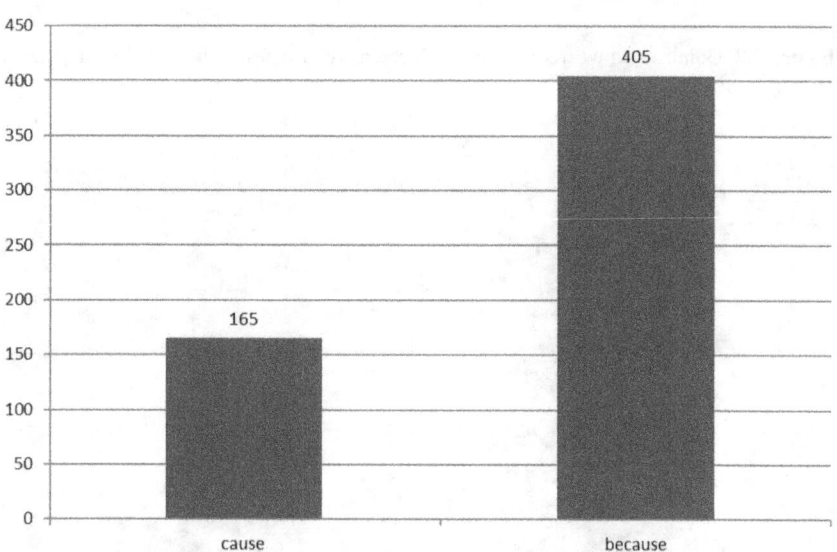

Figure 2.5 Raw frequencies of *'cause/because* in SydTV.

As a brief comparison, the distribution of frequencies in the spoken part of the Contemporary Corpus of American English/COCA (Davies 2008) in fact differ somewhat from those in SydTV: *is not* (50.164) > *isn't* (28.842) > *ain't* (3127). This part of COCA comes from transcripts of unscripted conversation on radio and television – that is, it differs from SydTV in being unscripted rather than scripted, but both corpora represent media language. Davies notes that the media context means that speakers are likely to alter their speech somewhat, including 'relatively little profanity and perhaps avoiding highly stigmatized words and phrases like "ain't got none"'.[11] In fact, *ain't* is most frequent in the fiction section of COCA (Szmrecsany and Anderwald 2018). In relation to distributional frequencies in the Corpus of American Soap Operas (SOAP,

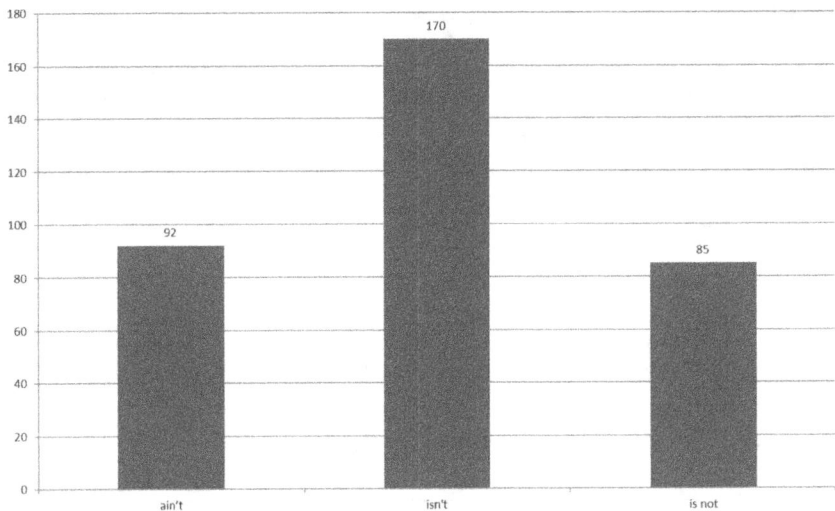

Figure 2.6 Raw frequencies of *ain't/isn't/is not* in SydTV.

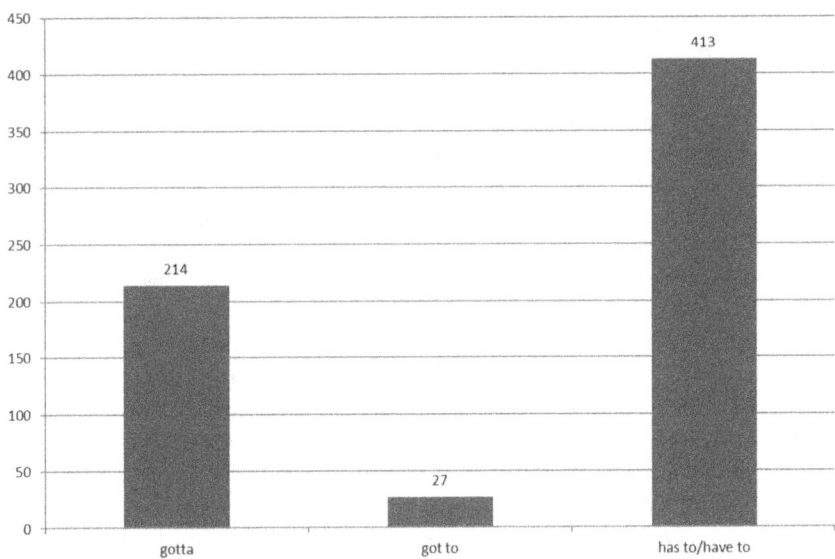

Figure 2.7 Raw frequencies of *gotta/got to/has to/have to* in SydTV (where ... *got to* is replaceable by *gotta*).

Davies 2012) – representing one TV genre – these also differ from those in SydTV: *isn't* (67.394) > *is not* (36.975) > *ain't* (3996). Thus, while *ain't* has the lowest frequency in both of these other types of American English media speech, the frequencies of *ain't* and *is not* in SydTV are almost the same, whereas *is not* occurs much more frequently than *ain't* in the spoken COCA and in SOAP. In addition, Table 2.4 and 2.5 compare

Table 2.4 A comparison of *ain't* in SydTV and COCA/S

SydTV		COCA/S		Tests for statistical significance/effect-size		
Raw frequency	Norm. frequency	Raw frequency	Norm. frequency	G2	RRisk	LogRatio
92	33.4	3127	2.9	282.06	11.70	3.55

Table 2.5 A comparison of *ain't* in SydTV and SOAP

SydTV		SOAP		Tests for statistical significance/effect-size		
Raw frequency	Norm. frequency	Raw frequency	Norm. frequency	G2	RRisk	LogRatio
92	33.4	3996	4	228.55	8.44	3.08

raw and normalized frequencies between SydTV and COCA (spoken) and SydTV and SOAP, also including results from tests for statistical significance and effect-size. According to Mark Davies (email communication), the size of COCA, and SOAP is calculated as follows: hyphens do not separate words (i.e. *force-feed* would count as one word), while ' is not allowed within words (i.e. contractions like *don't* are not counted as one word). The same token definition is used here for SydTV, that is, frequencies are normalized with respect to a corpus size of 275.074 words.

These tables indicate that *ain't* is over-represented in SydTV when compared with both COCA/S and SOAP, and that the results are statistically highly significant (critical G2 value for p < 0.0001 = 15.13). The RRisk and LogRatio show that the difference between the corpora is considerable. For instance, a LogRatio of 4 shows that the word is 16 times more common, while a LogRatio of 3 shows that the word is 8 times more common (Hardie 2014). Together, these results may indicate that COCA/S and SOAP include more formal, more standard, and less colloquial language than SydTV, or that they are less diverse as far as represented speakers are concerned.

In sum, the case study in this section has aimed to illustrate how SydTV might be used to test and further explore hypotheses based on limited data in order to gain new insights into TV dialogue as a language variety and to explore language variation and the frequency of non-standard or colloquial/informal forms across different varieties of spoken American English media discourse. From a stylistic perspective, it is also important to investigate in which episodes/TV series such variants occur most often or which characters use them (see Bednarek 2018a on a case study of *ain't*).

6 Conclusions

In this chapter, I have introduced a new resource for linguistic research on television dialogue: the Sydney Corpus of Television Dialogue (SydTV). SydTV is a small, specialized corpus that is representative of recent US TV dialogue. I presented three brief case studies to illustrate how it may be used in linguistic research, including in stylistics. Two key uses arose from this discussion:

1. SydTV can act as a reference corpus or baseline against which results from one television series can be compared, for example in relation to linguistic features or characterization. In so doing, over-interpretation of results can be avoided and a broader comparison with television narratives becomes possible.
2. SydTV can be a resource for analysing TV dialogue as a language variety, focusing on the linguistic features of this ubiquitous type of language. In this way, researchers can systematically and comprehensively identify, define and explain key features of TV dialogue and provide an in-depth understanding of the linguistic practices that millions of viewers are regularly exposed to by watching such series. Such research has the clear potential to significantly advance our current understanding of the central role language plays in contemporary television series.

While I only discussed the usefulness of SydTV for certain kinds of linguistic research in this chapter, the corpus can also be consulted in research that is situated in other linguistic subdisciplines. For instance, sociolinguistic research has seen a recent rise in interest in the analysis of mass media narratives, including film and television series (e.g. Androutsopoulos 2012; Queen 2015a). The corpus can also be used for future comparisons, for instance in relation to historically older data or data from other languages and cultures.

It is my hope that SydTV will be used by other researchers for the purposes outlined in this chapter and others – for instance testing assumptions about informality, linguistic innovation and intensifier usage made by Quaglio (2009) and Tagliamonte and Roberts (2005) on the basis of *Friends*. To enable such future research, I have made available a range of different frequency lists from SydTV that researchers can load into corpus-linguistic software such as Wordsmith and AntConc. These lists are available for download at http://www.syd-tv.com, which also provides information on how others can access and analyse the corpus itself via an online interface.

Acknowledgements

The research leading to these results has received funding from the People Programme (Marie Curie Actions) of the European Union's Seventh Framework Programme (FP7/2007-2013) under REA grant agreement n° [609305]. I am grateful to the Freiburg Institute for Advanced Studies (FRIAS), University of Freiburg, Germany, for awarding me an FCFP External Senior Fellowship. SydTV could not have been built without funding from the School of Literature, Art and Media and the Faculty of Arts and Social Sciences at the University of Sydney. I am very grateful to the university for their support. Thanks are also due to Marty Brower, Julia Elsky, Andrew Port and Mary Bucholtz for native-speaker advice on American English usage, and to Ganna Veselovska for help in formatting the reference list.

Notes

1. *TV dialogue* is here defined as the fictional speech uttered by characters in TV series on-screen (as performed by actors), where the term 'TV series' refers to scripted narrative series such as *Game of Thrones* or *Mad Men*, which viewers nowadays consume via a range of platforms (TV, mobile phone, tablet, etc.). TV dialogue includes speech by one character (voice-over, monologues, asides, etc.), between two characters (dyadic interactions) or between several characters (multi-party interactions). It does not include screen directions.
2. This has changed considerably with the rise of 'quality' television and there is now both literary and stylistic research on contemporary TV series.
3. See Pennycook (2007: 13), who makes the same point in relation to popular culture and hip hop.
4. Calculation according to Wordsmith (Scott 2017): 275.074 words (token definition: hyphens do not separate words; ' not allowed within word, speaker names excluded).
5. A comparison of ranked frequency lists (instead of keywords analysis) was undertaken as a workaround, since I had no direct access to the LSAC but had to work with published frequency lists (from Mittmann 2004).
6. The numbers in Table 2.1 include instances of *talking* and *talkin'* in SydTV. The episode from *Gilmore Girls* that is included in SydTV was removed, since the aim was to compare the dramedy with *other* TV series. The *Gilmore Girls* data was taken from Bednarek (2010) and consists of uncorrected fan transcripts. Token definition for calculating corpus size when normalizing frequencies: hyphens separate words, ' allowed as character within word: 1.123.868 (*Gilmore Girls*); 253.358 (SydTV without *Gilmore Girls* episode).
7. Sketch Engine automatically tags and lemmatizes uploaded corpora, which allows a search for a particular lemma used as a certain part-of-speech (e.g. verb vs. adjective). I uploaded a partially standardized version of SydTV where **in'* was manually changed to *ing, that is, there are no occurrences of *talkin'* or *tellin'*.
8. Table 2.2 lists only those key words/n-grams that are discussed in my previous research. I excluded *um*, *uh*, *ah*, *mm*, *hm*, *huh*, *hmm*, *ugh*, *aw* and *ooh*, because differences between the corpora might result from differing transcription procedures. I used the same software settings as in the respective published studies (Bednarek 2010, 2012b).
9. The figure for [In] in Table 2.3 includes all instances of this variant (e.g. *the feelin'* or *somethin'*), although the majority do occur in participial verb forms. The figures provided in this chapter on variants rely on the accuracy and consistency of the transcription, for which there is no 100 per cent guarantee.
10. The frequencies and range for [In] vs. [Ing] are based on the thirteen types that occur twenty times or more with [In] (*bein[g]*, *comin[g]*, *doin[g]*, *fuckin[g]*, *gettin[g]*, *goin[g]*, *lookin[g]*, *nothing[g]*, *sayin[g]*, *something[g]*, *talkin[g]*, *thinkin[g]*, *tryin[g]*), making up over half of all occurrences. This is because there are 7.014 instances of *ing in SydTV and these occurrences may not all allow the non-standard variant as alternative, since the '"rule" ... states that *–ing* in unstressed syllables may become *-in'*' (Wolfram and Schilling-Estes 2006: 173). Instances of *going to* and *got to* were manually reviewed and occurrences of *going to* where *to* is a proposition were deleted, as were all occurrences of *got to* (or verb phrases that include *got to* like *have got to*) that do not allow replacement with *gotta* (e.g. ... when I **got to** the door; ... now that I **got to** see

*you; What have you **got to** lose*), the latter with the help of native speakers of American English. Of 38 total instances of *got to*, 27 could technically be replaced with *gotta*.
11 In his comment on 'spoken transcripts', available at http://corpus.byu.edu/coca/, accessed 10 February 2016.

References

Androutsopoulos, J., ed. (2012), 'Language and society in cinematic discourse', Special Issue of *Multilingua*, 31 (2-3).
Androutsopoulos, J. (2014), 'Mediatization and sociolinguistic change: Key concepts, research traditions, open issues', in J. Androutsopoulos (ed.), *Mediatization and Sociolinguistic Change*, 3-48, Berlin: de Gruyter.
Baker, P. (2005), *Public Discourses of Gay Men*, London: Routledge.
Bednarek, M. (2007), '"What the hell is wrong with you?" A corpus perspective on evaluation and emotion in contemporary American pop culture', plenary presented at the *1st International Free Linguistics Conference*, University of Sydney, 6-7 October 2007.
Bednarek, M. (2008), '"What the hell is wrong with you?" A corpus perspective on evaluation and emotion in contemporary American pop culture', in A. Mahboob and N. Knight (eds), *Questioning Linguistics*, 95-126, Newcastle: Cambridge Scholars Press.
Bednarek, M. (2010), *The Language of Fictional Television*, London and New York: Continuum.
Bednarek, M. (2011a), 'The language of fictional television: A case study of the "dramedy" *Gilmore Girls*', *English Text Construction*, 4 (1): 54-83.
Bednarek, M. (2011b), 'The stability of the televisual character: A corpus stylistic case study', in R. Piazza, M. Bednarek and F. Rossi (eds), *Telecinematic Discourse: Approaches to the Language of Films and Television Series*, 185-204, Amsterdam and Philadelphia: John Benjamins.
Bednarek, M. (2012a), '"Get us the hell out of here": Key words and trigrams in fictional television series', *International Journal of Corpus Linguistics*, 17 (1): 35-63.
Bednarek, M. (2012b), 'Construing "nerdiness": Characterisation in *The Big Bang Theory*', *Multilingua*, 31: 199-229.
Bednarek, M. (2014), '"Who are you and why are you following us?" *Wh*-questions and communicative context in television dialogue', in J. Flowerdew (ed.), *Discourse in Context*, 49-70, London and New York: Bloomsbury.
Bednarek, M. (2015a), 'An overview of the linguistics of screenwriting and its interdisciplinary connections, with special focus on dialogue in episodic television', *Journal of Screenwriting*, 6 (2) (special issue on writing for television): 221-38.
Bednarek, M. (2015b), 'Corpus-assisted multimodal discourse analysis of television and film narratives', in P. Baker and T. McEnery (eds), *Corpora and Discourse Studies*, 63-87, Basingstoke and New York: Palgrave Macmillan.
Bednarek, M. (2017a), '(Re-)circulating popular television: Audience engagement and corporate practices', in J. Mortensen, N. Coupland and J. Thøgersen (eds), *Style, Mediation and Change: Sociolinguistic Perspectives on Talking Media*, 115-40, Oxford: Oxford University Press.
Bednarek, M. (2017b), 'Fandom', in C. Hoffmann and W. Bublitz (eds), *Pragmatics of Social Media*, 545-72, Berlin and New York: de Gruyter Mouton.

Bednarek, M. (2018a), *Language and Television Series: A Linguistic Approach to TV Dialogue*, Cambridge: Cambridge University Press.

Bednarek, M. (2018b), *Guide to the Sydney Corpus of Television Dialogue (SydTV)*. Available at: http://www.syd-tv.com/publications/.

Bednarek, M. (in press), 'The *Sydney Corpus of Television Dialogue*: Designing and building a corpus of dialogue from US TV series', *Corpora* 15 (1).

Bednarek, M. and Caple, H. (2017), *The Discourse of News Values*, New York and Oxford: Oxford University Press.

Beers Fägersten, K., ed. (2016), *Watching TV with a Linguist*, New York: Syracuse University Press.

Berber Sardinha, T. and Veirano Pinto, M. (2017), 'American television and offscreen registers: A corpus-based comparison', *Corpora*, 12 (1): 85–114.

Bubel, C. (2011), 'Relationship impression formation: How viewers know people on the screen are friends', in R. Piazza, M. Bednarek and F. Rossi (eds), *Telecinematic Discourse: Approaches to the Language of Films and Television Series*, 225–48, Amsterdam and Philadelphia: John Benjamins.

Bublitz, W., Hoffmann, C. and Kirner-Ludwig, M. (2015), 'How to do things with films – The pragmatics of telecinematic discourse', thematic panel at the *Fourteenth International Pragmatics Conference (IprA)*, University of Antwerp, Belgium, 26–31 July 2015.

Cambria, M. and Venuti, M. (2016), 'Languaging the other in TV series', thematic panel at the *Fifth Critical Approaches to Discourse Analysis across Disciplines Conference (CADAAD)*, Università di Catania, Sicily, 5–7 September 2016.

Cohen, J. (1999), 'Favourite characters of teenage viewers of Israeli serials', *Journal of Broadcasting and Electronic Media*, 43 (3): 327–45.

Coupland, N. (2007), *Style: Language Variation and Identity*, Cambridge: Cambridge University Press.

Coupland, N. (2010), 'Language, ideology, media and social change', in K. Junod and D. Maillat (eds), *Performing the Self*, 127–51, Tübingen: Gunter Narr.

Creeber, G. (2004), *Serial Television: Big Drama on the Small Screen*, London: BFI Publishing.

Csomay, E. and Petrovic, M. (2012), '"Yes, your Honor!": A corpus-based study of technical vocabulary in discipline-related movies and TV shows', *System*, 40 (2): 305–15.

Culpeper, J. (2009), 'Keyness: Words, parts-of-speech and semantic categories in the character-talk of Shakespeare's *Romeo and Juliet*', *International Journal of Corpus Linguistics*, 14 (1): 29–59.

Davies, M. (2008), *The Corpus of Contemporary American English: 520 Million Words, 1990-Present* [online]. Available at: http://corpus.byu.edu/coca/ (accessed 27 February 2016).

Davies, M. (2012), *The Corpus of American Soap Operas* [online]. Available at: http://corpus2.byu.edu/soap/ (accessed 27 February 2016).

Davies, M. (2019), *The TV Corpus: 325 Million Words, 1950–2018* [online]. Available at: https://corpus.byu.edu/tv/ (accessed 7 March 2019).

Dose, S. (2012), *Flipping the Script: A Corpus of American Television Series (CATS) for Corpus-based Language Learning and Teaching* [online]. Available at: http://www.helsinki.fi/varieng/series/volumes/13/dose/ (accessed 27 February 2016).

Dynel, M. (2015), 'Impoliteness in the service of verisimilitude in film interaction', in M. Dynel and J. Chovanec (eds), *Participation in Public and Social Media Interactions*, 157–82, Amsterdam and Philadelphia: John Benjamins.

Finegan, E. (2004), 'American English and its distinctiveness', in E. Finegan and J. R. Rickford (eds), *Language in the USA: Themes for the Twenty-First Century*, 18–38, Cambridge: Cambridge University Press.

Georgakopoulou, A. (2014), '"Girlpower or girl (in) trouble?" Identities and discourses in the (new) media engagements of adolescents' school-based interaction', in J. Androutsopoulos (ed.), *Mediatization and Sociolinguistic Change*, 217–44, Berlin: de Gruyter.

Giles, D. (2002), 'Parasocial interaction: A review of the literature and a model for future research', *Media Psychology*, 4 (3): 279–304.

Gries, S. Th. (2006), 'Some proposals towards a more rigorous corpus linguistics', *ZAA*, 54 (2): 191–202.

Hardie, A. (2014), *Log Ratio – An Informal Introduction* [online]. Available at: http://cass.lancs.ac.uk/?p=1133 (accessed 11 April 2016).

Kilgarriff, A., Baisa, V., Bušta, J., Jakubíček, M., Kovář, V., Michelfeit, J., Rychlý, P. and Suchomel, V. (2014), 'The sketch engine: Ten years on', *Lexicography*, 1 (1): 7–36.

Köster, A. (2010), 'Building small specialised corpora', in M. McCarthy and A. O'Keeffe (eds), *The Routledge Handbook of Corpus Linguistics*, 66–78, London: Routledge.

Lacey, N. (1998), *Image and Representation: Key Concepts in Media Studies*, Houndmills and New York: Palgrave.

Mandala, S. (2007), 'Solidarity and the Scoobies: An analysis of the -y suffix in the television series *Buffy the Vampire Slayer*', *Language and Literature*, 16 (1): 53–73.

Mandala, S. (2008), 'Representing the future: Chinese and codeswitching in *Firefly*', in R. V. Wilcox and T. R. Cochran (eds), *Investigating Firefly and Serenity: Science Fiction on the Frontier*, 31–40, London and New York: I.B. Tauris.

Mandala, S. (2011), '*Star Trek: Voyager*'s Seven of Nine: A case study of language and character in a televisual text', in R. Piazza, M. Bednarek and F. Rossi (eds), *Telecinematic Discourse: Approaches to the Language of Films and Television Series*, 205–23, Amsterdam and Philadelphia: John Benjamins.

Mazzon, G. and Klarer, M. (2015), *The Analysis of Fictional Dialogue in Film and Television Series: Between Narratology and Pragmatics*, International workshop, University of Innsbruck, Austria, 26–27 November 2015.

McEnery, T. and Hardie, A. (2012), *Corpus Linguistics: Method, Theory and Practice*, Cambridge: Cambridge University Press.

McIntyre, D. (2012), 'Prototypical characteristics of blockbuster movie dialogue: A corpus stylistic analysis', *Texas Studies in Literature and Language*, 54 (3): 402–25.

Mittmann, B. (2004), *Mehrwort-Cluster in der englischen Alltagskonversation. Unterschiede zwischen britischem und amerikanischem gesprochenen Englisch als Indikatoren für den präfabrizierten Charakter der Sprache.* (= Language in Performance 30). Tübingen: Gunter Narr. [*Multi-Word Clusters in English Conversation – Differences between British and American Spoken English as Indicators for the Prefabricatedness of Language.*]

Mittmann, B. (2006), 'With a little help from *Friends* (and others): Lexico-pragmatic characteristics of original and dubbed film dialogue', in C. Houswitschka, G. Knappe and A. Müller (eds), *Anglistentag 2005, Bamberg – Proceedings*, 573–85, Trier: WVT.

Paltridge, B., Collins, P. and Liu, J. (2011), 'Genre, performance and *Sex and the City*', in R. Piazza, M. Bednarek and F. Rossi (eds), *Telecinematic Discourse: Approaches to the Language of Films and Television Series*, 249–62, Amsterdam and Philadelphia: John Benjamins.

Pennycook, A. (2007), *Global Englishes and Transcultural Flows*, London and New York: Routledge.

Piazza, R., Bednarek, M. and Rossi, F., eds (2011), *Telecinematic Discourse: Approaches to the Language of Films and Television Series*, Amsterdam and Philadelphia: John Benjamins.

Quaglio, P. (2008), 'Television dialogue and natural conversation: Linguistic similarities and functional differences', in A. Ädel and R. Reppen (eds), *Corpora and Discourse: The Challenges of Different Settings*, 189–210, Amsterdam and Philadelphia: John Benjamins.

Quaglio, P. (2009), *Television Dialogue: The Sitcom* Friends vs. *Natural Conversation*, Amsterdam and Philadelphia: John Benjamins.

Queen, R. (2012), 'The days of our lives: Language, gender and affluence on a daytime television drama', *Gender and Language*, 6 (1): 153–80.

Queen, R. (2015a), *Vox Popular: The Surprising Life of Language in the Media*, New York: Wiley-Blackwell.

Queen, R. (2015b), 'Indexical authenticity and linguistic variation as evidenced in fictional television and film', plenary presented at the *Sixth International Language in the Media Conference*, University of Hamburg, 7–9 September 2015.

Reichelt, S. and Durham, M. (2017). 'Adjective intensification as a means of characterization: Portraying in-group membership and Britishness in *Buffy the Vampire Slayer*', *Journal of English Linguistics*, 45 (1): 60–87.

Rey, J. M. (2001), 'Changing gender roles in popular culture: Dialogue in *Star Trek* episodes from 1966 to 1993', in D. Biber and S. Conrad (eds), *Variation in English: Multi-dimensional Studies*, 138–56, London: Longman.

Richardson, K. (2006), 'The dark arts of good people: How popular culture negotiates "Spin" in NBC's *The West Wing*', *Journal of Sociolinguistics*, 10 (1): 52–69.

Richardson, K. (2010), *Television Dramatic Dialogue: A Sociolinguistic Study*, Oxford: Oxford University Press.

Scott, M. (2012), *WordSmith Tools Version 6*, Stroud: Lexical Analysis Software.

Scott, M. (2017), *WordSmith Tools Version 7*, Stroud: Lexical Analysis Software.

Scott, M. and Tribble, C. (2006), *Textual Patterns: Key Words and Corpus Analysis in Language Education*, Amsterdam and Philadelphia: John Benjamins.

Stokoe, E. (2008), 'Dispreferred actions and other interactional breaches as devices for occasioning audience laughter in television "sitcoms"', *Social Semiotics*, 18 (3): 289–307.

Stuart-Smith, J. (2011), 'The view from the couch: Changing perspectives on the role of the television in changing language ideologies and use', in T. Kristiansen and N. Coupland (eds), *Standard Languages and Language Standards in a Changing Europe*, 223–39, Oslo: Novus.

Szmrecsanyi, B. and Anderwald, L. (2018), 'Corpus-based approaches to dialect study', in C. Boberg, J. Nerbonne and D. Watt (eds), *The Handbook of Dialectology*, 300–13, Hoboken, NJ: Wiley-Blackwell.

Tagliamonte, S. and Roberts, C. (2005), 'So weird; so cool; so innovative: The use of intensifiers in the television series *Friends*', *American Speech*, 80 (3): 280–300.

Toolan, M. (2011), '"I don't know what they're saying half the time, but I'm hooked on the series": incomprehensible dialogue and integrated multimodal characterisation in *The Wire*', in R. Piazza, M. Bednarek and F. Rossi (eds), *Telecinematic Discourse: Approaches to the Language of Films and Television Series*, 161–83, Amsterdam and Philadelphia: John Benjamins.

Webb, S. and Rodgers, M. P. H. (2009), 'Vocabulary demands of television programs', *Language Learning*, 59 (2): 335–66.

Wodak, R. (2009), *The Discourse of Politics in Action*, Basingstoke and New York: Palgrave Macmillan.

Wolfram, W. and Schilling-Estes, N. (2006), *American English*, 2nd edn, Malden et al.: Blackwell Publishing.

Zappavigna, M. (2012), *Discourse of Twitter and Social Media: How We Use Language to Create Affiliation on the Web*, 1st edn, London: Continuum (now Bloomsbury).

3

'Drucilla, we need to talk'

The formulaic nature of problem-oriented talk in soap operas

Sabine Jautz and Verena Minow

1 Introduction

It can be argued that much of what we see and hear on-screen we have seen or heard before; in other words, there is a certain formulaicity that applies to all areas of the finished telecinematic product, ranging from the music we hear, the types of characters we are presented with, and the topics that are dealt with to the lines of dialogues the writers put into their characters' mouths. This last point may come as a surprise since it appears to contradict what manuals often urge screenwriters to do when writing dialogues:

> The TV writers who rise to the top are those who know what real people sound like when they talk, but also know how to edit that reality so their characters are more intense, more clever and more expressive than real people usually are. [...] In your teleplay, all your characters, especially your hero or heroes, should say what you would if you had the time to second-guess and third-guess and fourth-guess the words that come out of your characters' mouths, and every reader expects that's exactly what you'll do. (Brody 2003: 213–14, cited in Richardson 2010: 69–70)

Despite this urge for second-guessing, we as viewers will nevertheless often find that we are confronted with so-called stock phrases or dialogue tropes, that is, lines of dialogue that are repeatedly used in different telecinematic products in exactly the same way (cf. TV Tropes [online] 'stock phrases'). These phrases are usually regarded negatively, and numerous collections of 'overused lines' are available online. At the same time, repeated lines within the same show or franchise often become trademarks or catchphrases (cf. Richardson 2010: 100ff.). For example, James Bond will introduce himself in every film in the same way, and every *Star Wars* film so far has featured the line 'I have a bad feeling about this' – fans of the respective franchises would surely be disappointed if these lines were missing from future films.[1]

In our contribution, we focus on one formulaic utterance, namely *[name], we need to talk*, in soap opera dialogue. The trigram *need to talk* has already been identified as occurring unusually frequently in the discourse of drama series (cf. Bednarek 2012). The use of vocatives has likewise been previously mentioned to be typical of telecinematic discourse (cf. Formentelli 2013). The sequence *we need to talk* is used in telecinematic discourse to introduce what we term 'problem-oriented' conversations, which are particularly common in soap operas since here we find 'the crises and dramas of "everyday life" [being] unrealistically exaggerated in number' (Huisman 2005: 183). In soap operas, '[m]ost of what we see [...] is talk' (Fine 1981: 98) and we are interested in how exactly the drama on-screen unfolds through talk. In our approach to telecinematic discourse in general and soap opera discourse in particular, we follow the call by Androutsopoulos (2012: 143) to treat this type of discourse 'not as a substitute to something else but as a legitimate area of sociolinguistic inquiry in its own right'.

The motivation to focus on a formulaic sequence in soap operas stems firstly from the fact that they are characterized by recurring storylines and can hence be called formulaic. Secondly, soap opera discourse has for the most part been disregarded in analyses of telecinematic discourse; presumably due to researchers being more inclined to focus on 'quality television', that is, television shows such as *The Sopranos* or *Game of Thrones*, which 'successfully "remediat[e]" the aesthetics of cinema on the one hand, and the narrative structure of the 19th-century realist novel on the other' (Hassler-Forest 2014: paragraph 9). We claim that the formulaicity of soap operas will be mirrored in the dialogues. We assume that problem-oriented conversations introduced by the turn *we need to talk* in soap operas are also formulaic and that there is but a limited number of possibilities of how the conversation will unfold. Due to the dramatic nature of the data, we most often find dispreferred responses such as rejections or postponements.

2 Locating soap opera discourse within telecinematic discourse

The soap operas that form the basis of our investigation, that is, the ones that are included in the *Corpus of American Soap Operas* (SOAP; Davies 2011–), are American daytime soaps. They primarily feature characters that can be classified as middle class or upper middle class, while, in contrast, the longest running British soaps, *Coronation Street* and *EastEnders* have focused on working-class characters (cf. Allen 1995).

Daytime soaps are subject to more rigid censoring in terms of content and language that can be used; in particular, the Federal Communications Commission prohibits indecent content and '"grossly offensive" language that is considered a public nuisance' in the time slot from 6 a.m. to 10 p.m. Most soap operas are long-running, with many being or having been on air for several decades. For example, *General Hospital* and *Days of Our Lives* have been broadcast since 1963 and 1965, respectively. Unlike other television series, soap operas are thus not created with a particular end in mind;[2] they rather follow the lives of a set of characters in a given community, very often extended family or several families that are somehow connected. Since soap operas do not have a prospective end, their narrative has been described as 'non-linear' (Huisman 2005: 182), and they also do not have a plot in the traditional sense, but rather storylines which are developed in the interactions between characters (Huisman 2005: 182), and frequently reoccur in different soap operas. Many viewers will likely have encountered soap characters experiencing (usually) temporary blindness or paralysis, characters realizing that one of their parents is not their biological parent, the reappearance of a character that had been believed to be dead, as well as other typical storylines revolving around adultery (with characters often being caught in the act: 'It is not what it looks like!'), miscarriages, characters ditching each other at the altar ('I can't do this!'), and experiencing facial disfigurement requiring extensive plastic surgery (which is often used to explain a replacement of actors). We can even go as far as to say that these types of recurring storylines are expected by the soap audience alongside recurring talk situations, in the same way as other televisual genres invoke certain expectations (cf. Richardson 2010: 113f.).

Geeraerts (2001) claims that there are three main features of soap operas that distinguish them from other types of television series: first, their dramatic focus is on the characters and the way they react to the unfolding events. Second, viewers need to be able to identify with the setting and the characters. Third, the world presented in a soap opera needs to be realistic and 'the dramatic events have an air of plausibility to them' (7). As Geeraerts himself acknowledges, this third point might not be true for all soap operas: in American ones in particular we often find that characters are faced with 'murder, divorce, extramarital affairs, pimps and prostitutes, and wealthy paramours' (Fine 1981: 97), which is not exactly what the average viewer may experience in their own everyday lives.

Since the focus of soaps is so much on the characters' reactions to events, we find less action, in other words, less use of visual storytelling than in other genres. In soap operas, most of what happens does so through dialogue or, as Huisman (2005: 184) puts it, 'talk between characters is the main vehicle of the soap opera narrative'. This then means that characters need to be put in a situation where a conversation that is required for the respective storyline becomes plausible. Since, as Fine (1981: 99) puts it, '[t]he lives of the inhabitants of the American soap opera are intertwined' and the characters live in a 'small closed community' they are sure to bump into each other sooner rather than later.

What, then, is the nature of the talk in soap operas? In general, telecinematic discourse can fulfil expositional functions (cf. Richardson 2010), but it can be argued that soap opera dialogue is more expository in nature than dialogue in other genres. Unlike other series, soap operas need to accommodate new and returning viewers, and the quickest way to inform them of the ongoings is by having characters explicitly mention relevant facts. This then often results in conversations in which the Gricean maxim of quantity will be violated (Grice 1975: 45), with characters being told facts that they, strictly speaking, would not need to be told – particularly not over and over again. In addition, this practice actually goes against one of the most important commandments of screenwriting: 'Feel the need to have your characters tell each other something they would already know so you can make sure the reader or viewer knows it too? Resist it!' (Brody 2003: 218, cited in Richardson 2010: 75). Soap opera writers have no choice but to disregard the usual credo of 'show, don't tell'. Of course, this is not to say that other genres do not comprise exposition through dialogue to some extent, especially in pilot episodes of television series, in which the audience needs to be introduced to the main characters and their relationships. Example (1) presents the first two scenes with dialogue of the pilot episode of the legal drama *Suits*.

(1) 1   Louis: Gerald Tate's here. He wants to know what's happening to his deal.
    2   Jessica: Go get **Harvey**.
    3   Louis: Trust me, I can handle Gerald Tate.

Jessica gives him a look that says 'what did I just say?' Louis turns around to presumably do as he has been told.

Cut to the profile of a man in his late thirties; presumably the Harvey that was mentioned. During the conversation, the camera angles change several times to reveal that he is sitting at a table playing poker with four other men.

    4   Harvey: I'm sorry, you say the bet's to me?
    5   Player 1:   **Harvey**, when are you gonna **leave Pearson, work for a man**?
    6   Harvey: I'll leave **Jessica** any time you want, you just have to formally ask. And then after that why don't you ask Santa Claus to bring you a pony cause I'm not leaving Jessica. I check.
    7   Player 2:   Raise. Five thousand.
    8   Harvey: I'm all in.

His cell phone dings. He takes it out to check it. We can read the screen of his Blackberry. It is a message from 'Jessica Pearson (Work)' that reads 'I need you.' Harvey gets up to leave.

    9   Harvey: You can pay me later. I gotta go. Gentlemen.

           (*Suits*, 'Pilot')

Before the short exchange between Louis and Jessica, the viewer has already seen Louis leave a crowded conference room, where about two dozen lawyers were arguing, and enter Jessica's office. We do not know their names yet, but a very attentive viewer might be able to catch the name 'Jessica Pearson' and 'Managing Partner' printed on her glass office door. Most of the information about Jessica and Harvey is revealed through the dialogue, however. Harvey is mentioned by name in turn 2, and we then cut to a scene that starts with a shot of a male character's face in profile, and in turn 5 that character is indeed addressed as 'Harvey'. We also learn that the woman we have seen before is named Pearson in that same line and since Harvey refers to her as 'Jessica' in turn 6, we also get to know her first name. The shot of the Blackberry screen then confirms that her name is indeed Jessica Pearson. Here, we thus find a combination of exposition in the dialogue along with some visual cues. The expository dialogue is unobtrusive, and even the use of a first name as an address term is not remarkable since it functions as an attention getter in this case. In soap operas, however, the use of dialogue for expository purposes is more obvious and, it can be argued, less well executed; for example, there are 1,090 hits for the phrase *as you know* in the *Corpus of American Soap Operas* (Davies 2011–), which contains ca. 100 million words of soap opera dialogue, taken from ten American soap operas, that is 10.82 instances per million words. In contrast, the movie scripts in the fiction section of *The Corpus of Contemporary American English* (COCA; Davies 2008–) only yield 6.26 instances per million words. Example (2) shows a typical case of exposition in the soap opera *All My Children* introduced by this phrase in turn 7, which reveals that the character Liza is in a business relationship with a character named David. In turn 8 we then receive a recapitulation of an earlier conversation between Liza and Anna that includes crucial information to any viewer unfamiliar with Liza's storyline: at some point, she had been sick and forced into a 'research and development agreement' by David.

(2) 1 Liza: I don't know what it is you think that I might be able to tell you.
     2 Anna: I'm investigating David's connection to Maria Grey. Do you know anything about that?
     3 Liza: I don't know.
     4 Anna: He came here right before we took him into custody. Why?
     5 Liza: Have you asked him?
     6 Anna: I'm asking you.
     7 Liza: Well, **as you know, I'm in business with David**.
     8 Anna: Yeah. **You had told me that when you were sick, he had manipulated you into this research and development agreement.**
     9 Liza: You don't expect me to discuss the terms of our agreement, do you?
    10 Anna: Not yet.
    11 Liza: No, not ever, without advice of counsel.
    12 Anna: Absolutely. I'll remember that. What I'm really interested in is why he came here.
    13 Liza: He needed help.
    14 Anna: Your help?

(*All My Children*, 17 September 2002)

3 Previous research on formulaic language in soap opera and other telecinematic discourse

The fact that there are 'stock phrases' or 'dialogue tropes' in telecinematic discourse does not come as a surprise to linguists. This phenomenon has been studied within different branches of linguistics and related disciplines under a host of different terms (cf. Wray and Perkins 2000, Table 2), 'formulaic language' being one of them. Wray and Perkins (2000: 1) suggest the term 'formulaic sequence' and offer the following definition: 'a sequence, continuous or discontinuous [*sic*], of words or other meaning elements, which is, or appears to be, prefabricated: that is, stored and retrieved whole from memory at the time of use, rather than being subject to generation or analysis by the language grammar'. Among nonlinguists studying telecinematic discourse, the occurrence of formulaic sequences seems often to be frowned upon and their use is seen as a lack of creativity on the writer's part, as evidenced by the numerous collections of 'overused lines' available online; however, what these critics fail to consider is that there are many talk situations in everyday life in which speakers retrieve prefabricated sequences from their mental lexicon. In other words, formulaicity is a characteristic of discourse in general, and we can hence assume the same types of formulaic sequences to be used in telecinematic discourse as in spontaneous discourse. When situations that are typically characterized by the use of formulaic language are presented on-screen we can expect the respective formulae to occur. For example, it will not come as a surprise to witness greeting formulae and introductions to be exchanged when characters meet for the first time. At the same time, however, there may be a difference in frequency when compared to spontaneous discourse since 'particular communicative situations that necessitate the use of specific routine formulae may be more frequent in TV dialogue because television series are structured around frequent changes of different communicative situations' (Bednarek 2012: 44). For example, Quaglio (2009: 115) finds more greetings in *Friends* than in conversational discourse, but this is due to the fact that scenes in *Friends* more often feature characters meeting each other, and these exchanges are not frequently included in the conversation corpus used for comparison.

In addition, there may also be formulaic language that is connected to the genre of telecinematic discourse as a whole or to a specific subgenre thereof, that is, formulae that are less likely to be found in spontaneous discourse but frequently used in dialogues on-screen. Collections of 'overused' lines in film provide some insight into what these might be. For example, the line *you look like [expletive]* is one of those supposedly overused lines (cf. Miyamoto 2016), and a quick corpus search reveals that it occurs 2.16 times per million words in SOAP[3] and 2.57 times per million words in the movie scripts included in the fiction component of COCA, but not once in the spoken component of COCA. It can hence be argued that this is indeed a typical telecinematic formula. Of course, commenting on an interlocutor's appearance is nothing out of the ordinary, but the directness and frequency with which it is done by characters on-screen is remarkable. Other telecinematic formulaic sequences are simply due to the fact that characters often find themselves in situations that 'normal' people hardly ever experience or do not experience as often as they are shown on-screen. For instance, some of the other apparently overused lines on Miyamoto's list such as *Don't die on me!* or *Cover me. I'm going in.* are used in situations of drama on-screen, which are simply featured very often in films and television show and thus particularly salient to viewers. This does not mean to imply that these sequences are never used in real life, but they may appear to be typically associated with telecinematic discourse since we as viewers are often subjected to them.

The potential impact of writers on the use of formulaic language in telecinematic discourse also needs to be considered since the use of a particular expression may be due to a writer's or group of writers' personal preference. For example, when we compare the frequency per million words of *we need to talk* across the ten soap operas included in SOAP, we see drastic differences. While the phrase as such occurs in all soaps, it is almost twice as frequent in *Days of Our Lives* (32.48 tokens per million words) as it is in *All My Children* (16.56 tokens per million words). Even though there are usually several dialogue writers working on a given soap 'idiosyncratic differences in dialogue writing styles must be eliminated; the character must speak with a single voice' (Allen 1985: 56).

Other studies that investigate formulaicity in different genres of telecinematic discourse are Bednarek (2012) and Freddi (2011). Bednarek focuses on key words and trigrams in seven fictional television series representing five different genres; namely crime (*NCIS*), mystery (*Supernatural* and *Lost*), medical (*House*), comedy (*How I Met Your Mother* and *My Name Is Earl*), drama (*Desperate Housewives*). She finds that the language of these series is more emotional than spoken discourse since most of the words and trigrams that are over-represented in her corpus are to some extent associated with emotionality. Important for our study is the trigram *need to talk*, which occurs unusually frequently in her corpus. Bednarek lists four patterns in which this trigram occurs – *we need to talk* being one of them – and argues that '[s]uch usages […] are tied to the expression of emotion in that they express emphasis through the use of the modal verb *need* and also imply that there is a serious or urgent matter that need to be discussed' (2012: 50).

Freddi (2011) analyses formulaicity in the *Pavia Corpus of Film Dialogue* (PCFD), which comprises twelve British and American films alongside their dubbed Italian versions published between 1995 and 2004, and four additional British and American films. She mainly focuses on the eleven four-word clusters that occur most frequently in the PCFD. These are (in decreasing order of frequency) *what are you doing, what do you think, what do you mean, I want you to, I don't know what, I don't want to, thank you very much, nice to meet you, you want me to, what do you do* and *how do you know*. All of these clusters occur in at least six out of the sixteen analysed films, with *what are you doing* and *what do you mean* each occurring in eleven films (Freddi 2011: 144, Table 1). When comparing these with the spoken component of the *British National Corpus* (BNC) and the subset of face-to-face conversations in the BNC, Freddi finds that ten of the eleven clusters are used more frequently in the PCFD than in the conversations in the BNC; the only cluster that has the same frequency in the PCFD as in the face-to-face-conversations is *I don't know what* (cf. Freddi 2011: 146, Figure 2). In addition, Freddi provides an analysis of the eleven clusters in the spoken section of COCA and the movie subsection of the fiction section of COCA. Most of the clusters are more frequent in the movie subsection. However, *what do you think, thank you very much* and *what do you do* are more frequent in the spoken section of COCA; *I don't know what* and *I don't want to* have similar frequencies and are only slightly more frequent in the movies. In her conclusion, Freddi (2011: 158) states that 'the comparisons have identified very few clusters which are typical of the register under examination, i.e. scripted film dialogue, most of them being common to natural spoken data'. This seems to indicate that Freddi has a narrower view of what she considers typical of telecinematic discourse. We believe that it is not the uniqueness of a sequence that makes it typical but that the differences in frequency indeed hint at some formulae being characteristic of telecinematic discourse.

In addition to these studies focusing on formulaic language in telecinematic discourse there have been various studies by researchers that have worked with data from soap operas. There is one group of researchers who have studied soap opera dialogues to ascertain their usability in EFL/ESL teaching. Examples of these types of studies are Grant and Starks (2001), who analyse closings of conversations in the New Zealand soap opera *Shortland* and compare these with those typically found in textbooks, and Al-Surmi (2012), who uses multidimensional analyses to ascertain whether sitcom discourse (in this case *Friends*) or soap opera discourse (as featured in the 2008 season of *The Young and the Restless*) is closer to natural conversation.

Another group of researchers are those who use soap opera data as a convenient substitute for spontaneously produced informal language, which is often hard to come by. In fact, the SOAP corpus, which forms the basis of our analyses, is advertised on the website as 'a great resource to look at very informal language' and hence seems to be geared at researchers in this group. Schwarz, who makes use of SOAP for an analysis of the BE- and the GET-passive and reports a decrease of the BE-passive over time, hence motivates her choice of data as follows:

> This study is based on a large quantity of very recent, informal material, which, even though it is not authentic language data, can to some extent be argued to approximate informal spoken usage, and which ought to be particularly receptive to informal grammatical structures and to eschew overly-formal language. (2015: 153)

She is thus not so much interested in the data as such, but rather in the fact that it appears to be informal. The same can be said for Palma Fahey (2005), whose motivation for choosing soap opera data lies in the scarcity of naturally occurring data containing apologies. Elwood's choice of data for her study on variation in thanking expressions is likewise mainly motivated by the fact that 'soap operas provide a wealth of scenes involving many speech acts' (2011: 108). All three authors thus have worked with soap opera data because it is easily available and contains sufficient tokens of the linguistic features they are interested in. While they do show an awareness of the fact that conversations in soaps are scripted, they nevertheless see them as realistic enough to be, as Palma Fahey puts it, 'perceived as representative of real dialogues'. Despite their approach to the soap data being different from ours, the findings of these authors are still enlightening as they do provide us with an idea of what features can be considered typical of soap opera discourse.

Palma Fahey (2005) concentrates on apologies in the Irish soap *Fair City* and the Chilean soap *Amores de Mercado*. Here, we report only the results of the Irish English soap data. Regarding formulaic language, the most interesting result is that thirty-seven apologies occur within two hours of *Fair City*. Palma Fahey only provides the total number of words for both soaps combined (47,000), but if we assume that the Irish data make up roughly half of this, the number of apologies per million words would be 1,575. SOAP is not tagged for pragmatic information, but a search for *sorry* alone yields 146,193 tokens, which is a frequency of 1,451 per million words and hence slightly less compared to the Irish soap. Most of the apologies in *Fair City* (25/37) are remedial apologies: that is, apologies occurring after an offence. All of these feature an expression of regret, that is, either *I'm sorry* or *sorry*. In addition, 44 per cent of the apologies are enhanced by an explanation, while another 24 per cent contain an acknowledgement of responsibility. Other apology strategies occur less frequently; there are only two instances each of self-reproach and offering redress and only one promise of forbearance. Minimizing responsibility occurs four times; according to Palma Fahey this strategy 'brings down the high cost of face that the act of apologising has for the speaker'. However, this strategy also has the danger of making the apology seem less sincere, which can then be used by the scriptwriters to create further conflict. Another interesting finding reported by Palma Fahey is the fact that 24 per cent of the apologies in the Irish soap are accompanied by vocatives. Frequent use of vocatives is a typical feature of telecinematic discourse, as reported by Formentelli (2013) based on an analysis of address terms in the PCFD.

Elwood (2011) compares expressions of gratitude from two soaps, Irish *Fair City* and British *EastEnders*, and hence works within a variational pragmatics framework. She reports a difference in the forms of expressions of gratitude used in the two soaps; unadorned thanks accounted for 50 per cent of the expressions of gratitude in *Fair City* but only for 22 per cent in *EastEnders*. There was also more variation in the types of expressions used in *EastEnders*. Concerning the type of benefaction, Elwood finds similarities since in both soaps 'gratitude was most often expressed for help or participation, at roughly the same rates of frequency' (130). It is interesting that in both soaps there were quite a few cases of ironic expressions of gratitude: 18 per cent in *Fair City* and 16 per cent in *EastEnders*. Elwood explains this by saying that it is due to the nature of the data: 'It can be imagined that frequency [sic] of scenes involving disgruntled or even outraged characters might contribute to the prevalence of ironic expressions of gratitude in both programs' (131).

Finally, there is a third group of researchers who, like us, regard soap opera dialogues as a genre worthy of scholarly attention. One of the earliest studies by Fine (1981) analyses dyadic conversations in five randomly chosen episodes of four American soap operas broadcast during the 1977 season. She focuses on four aspects, namely the sex of the participants, the relationship of the participants, the topics discussed and the conversational styles. Most of the conversations are between male and female characters (151 out of 232), followed by conversations between two females (1981: 49), and conversations between two males. Concerning the relationships between the characters, Fine finds that it 'supports the image of the soap opera community as an insular society which greatly emphasizes interpersonal relationships – family, friends, and romantic relationships accounted for 68.9% of all dyadic interaction' (1981: 100). What is interesting in this regard is the fact that at that time 'a completely heterosexual pattern of romantic involvement' was portrayed in the analysed soaps (1981: 101). Not surprising is the fact that the topics discussed seem to be largely determined by the relationship between the characters; that is, spouses discuss marriage, friends discuss their friendship, and professionals discuss matters of their professional/business relationship. Most of the conversations portrayed feature a casual conversational style, which is again not surprising when considering the types of scenes that are most frequently shown. Fine concludes that the soap opera world is 'a world in which men and women live together in intimacy and harmony' and when conflict occurs '[it] exists only in terms of individual relationships; the soap opera community, as a whole, remains harmonious' (1981: 105).

Lambertz and Hebrok (2011) use the claim that soap operas are geared towards female viewers as their starting point for an analysis of features of gendered language use in two soap operas, namely Australian *Home and Away* and German *Gute Zeiten, Schlechte Zeiten*. The analysed features are sentence-prefacing disclaimers and sentence-ending tags, which were originally suggested as being typical of women's language by

Robin Lakoff (1973). In both soaps, these features are indeed used by female characters. However, in contrast to Lakoff's original assumption that these devices serve the function of hedging, the authors report that in the analysed soap episodes the opposite is the case, with *I think* very often functioning as an emphasizing device in *Home and Away*.

The scarcity of studies in the third group is not surprising since the appreciation of telecinematic discourse as a variety 'in its own right' (Androutsopoulos 2012: 143) is a fairly recent development in linguistics. What is more, even though soap operas are quite popular among viewers – albeit not as popular as they used to; of the ten soap operas included in SOAP, only four are still on the air at the time of writing (cf. 'Soap opera ratings for the 2015–16 season (final)') – they are usually regarded as less valuable than other telecinematic products, which may be another reason why linguists have so far mostly shied away from analysing them.

4 Methodology

Our investigations are based on data from the SOAP corpus (Davies 2011–). This corpus enables us to examine formulaic utterances in one particular genre of telecinematic discourse, namely soap operas, in a systematic way. The corpus contains 100 million words in more than 22,000 transcripts of ten American soap operas from 2001 to 2012. The daytime (rather than prime time) soaps under investigation are often set in fictional, medium-sized Midwestern US towns, and the focus is usually on interior settings. Here, the (mostly (upper) middle class) characters discuss family matters, harmony and disharmony in their (or other people's) relationships as well as various social issues. As already mentioned, due to the soaps being broadcast during the day, content and language use will by default be monitored. Table 3.5 at the end of Section 5 reproduces information on the composition of the corpus from the SOAP website (Davies 2011–).

From a linguistic point of view, the conversations are, among other features, characterized by recurring n-grams. The trigram *need to talk* has already been mentioned as one of the 'unusually frequent' ones in the seven TV series analysed by Bednarek (2012: 40). Due to the use of the modal *need* the addressee may expect a discussion of vital problems which do trouble not only the speaker, but, as indicated by the use of *we*, also themselves. Thus, we decided to start our search by examining the string *we need to talk* in the SOAP corpus. This search resulted in 2,527 occurrences per 100 million words, while a comparative search in the 450 million words *Corpus of Contemporary American English* (Davies 2008–) resulted in only 97 occurrences per 100 million words, which underlines that *we need to talk* is typically used in TV series.

To examine the formulaicity of *we need to talk* in more detail, we took up a finding by Formentelli (2013) that vocatives are frequently used in films and investigated the search string [np1] , **we need to talk** . (using the required syntax with blanks before punctuation marks). Not just using *we need to talk*, but also the addressee's name, makes the request more personal and thereby potentially more emotional and urgent.

Narrowing down the search further also had the advantage that we ended up with a smaller number of hits, which renders a qualitative analysis easier to manage.

In order to verify whether *we need to talk* is indeed a prototypical formulaic utterance in soaps, we also cross-checked the frequency of occurrence of other modal verbs along with *we* and *talk*. It proves justified to focus on *need* as the search for [**np1**], **we need to talk.** rendered 160 occurrences, while [**np1**], **we have to talk.** resulted in 21 hits, [**np1**], **we should talk.** was found only once and [**np1**], **we must talk.** is not attested in the SOAP corpus at all. Our search string [**np1**], **we need to talk.** includes the use of a proper name (i.e. [np1] in the search string) and specific punctuation in order to yield a manageable number of hits.

As already mentioned in Section 1, we assume *[name] we need to talk* to introduce problem-oriented conversations. We use the term 'problem-oriented' talk because it is more neutral than 'conflict' or 'confrontational' talk. The conversations we are interested in do indeed often turn out to be confrontational, but they can also be fairly amicable. The choice of the first-person plural pronoun signals the speaker's presupposition that a talk is as much in the hearer's interest as it is in their own. The topic of the talk is an issue that requires a solution or at least a conversation, but the problem as such or the solution need not be conflictual; given the dramatic nature of the genre this is very often the case. In fact, we can say that confrontation may be more prominent in telecinematic discourse than 'in corresponding real-life situations' (Richardson 2010: 110). After all, the viewers want to be entertained by the talk exchanges they witness on-screen, and it is safe to assume that dramatic exchanges are more entertaining than conversations about the weather. The 'drama' in a conversation may stem from the topic itself – this is of course often the case in soap operas – but it can also arise from the way the conversation unfolds, for example when the addressee refuses to engage in a talk about the problem.

In our coding of the data, we first checked whether *[name] we need to talk* is the first turn introducing problem-oriented talk with the addressed person. This means that we checked that there is no other language material in the turn indicating that the interlocutors have already been talking to each other and about the matter in question. We did, however, accept attention getters ('look', 'hey'), hesitators ('okay', 'well') or a repetition of the name of the person addressed as 'additional language material' used along with *[name] we need to talk*. Furthermore, this means that a response follows, that is, that *we need to talk* is not the only turn in the scene or a cliffhanger. If this was the case, the hits in question were excluded. Thereafter, we examined the data qualitatively to get a general idea what speakers actually considered necessary to be talked about. In a next step, we examined the response to the request to talk quantitatively as well as qualitatively: Responses to *[name] we need to talk* comprise – with different frequencies of occurrence – the categories agreement with the request to talk, postponement of the request to talk, rejection of the request to talk, and other responses, for example, that a third person takes the floor. For the first three categories it is possible to distinguish subcategories, as will be illustrated in Section 5.

In a final step, we had a closer look as to whether there are any patterns for females or males uttering the request to talk or being addressed by the request. As most of the methodological steps derive from interim findings of the analyses, they will be explained in more detail along with the following analyses.

5 'We need to talk': Problem-oriented talk in soap opera discourse

The following analyses aim at quantitative as well as qualitative findings. As already mentioned, our search string **[np1]** , **we need to talk** . (frequency 500) resulted in 160 hits in the SOAP corpus. However, a further investigation of all hits showed that four hits had to be excluded because they could not actually be found in the transcripts, they were duplicates of other hits, or the name covered by [np1] did not refer to the addressee. Thus, the focal data comprises 156 hits, with the sequence occurring 1.5 times per million words in the corpus. It is about three times more frequent in soap opera dialogues than in film dialogues as an analysis of the movie script subsection of COCA yields a frequency of 0.45 instances per million words.

The turn comprising *[name] we need to talk* was our first object of analysis. To guarantee a focus on formulaicity, we decided to only investigate those cases in which *[name] we need to talk* serves to introduce problem-oriented talk (i.e. it is the first turn in a conversation of the speaker and the person addressed) and is followed by a response, as explained in Section 4. This meant that a further 41 of the 156 cases had to be excluded. In these 41 cases, the search string is preceded and/or followed by further language material within the same turn which indicates that the search string is not used to introduce problem-oriented talk (27 instances; see above for accepted additional language material), the search string is the only turn in the scene in which it occurs (3 instances), or the search string serves as a cliffhanger in the scene, that is, it is not followed by a response and a continuation of the plot in the respective scene (11 instances) (cf. Table 3.1).

The remaining 115 hits are distributed in the corpus as presented in Table 3.2 (cf. Table 3.5 for the overall composition of the SOAP corpus). We can see that our search string can indeed be found in all soap operas under investigation, but with varying frequencies of occurrence.

In a second step we examined the problems one 'needs to talk' about in soap operas. These may be matters such as characters' whereabouts and what they were doing at a

Table 3.1 Overview of (Excluded) Hits

	[np1] , we need to talk .	n = 160
Hits to be excluded	not found in transcripts, duplicates or [np1] ≠ addressee	4
	additional language material pointing at ongoing conversation	27
	only turns in scenes	3
	cliffhangers	11
Total		**115**

Table 3.2 Number of Hits for [np1], we need to talk. across Soaps

Soaps	Raw Frequency	pmw
All My Children	10	0.8
As the World Turns	16	1.3
Bold and Beautiful	7	1.1
Days of Our Lives	21	1.7
General Hospital	10	0.7
Guiding Light	11	1.3
One Life to Live	11	0.9
Passions	14	2.0
Port Charles	1	0.6
Young and Restless	14	1.1
Total	**115**	

given time or issues such as gambling or drug abuse. In addition, the problems talked about often arise from the relationships between the characters involved (cf. Fine's 1981 analysis of topics in dyadic conversations). The problem can be the relationship between the interlocutors as such, as in Example (3), or the relationship the addressee is having with another character. In the latter case, the character initiating the conversation might have an intervention in mind; for example, they want the relationship to end, as illustrated in Example (4).

(3) 1 Edmund: Maria, we need to talk.
    2 Maria: I got to check on Bobby.
    3 Edmund: Please. Anita's with him. It's important. It's about us.
    (*All My Children*, 1 December 2005)

(4) 1 Brooke: I see you. Rick, we need to talk.
    2 Rick: Look, Mom, I know how you feel about Taylor and me. You disapprove. I get it.
    3 Brooke: I-I know you want to believe that this is some grand love affair.
    4 Rick: Can't we just agree to disagree, please? I don't want to fight with you anymore.
    5 Brooke: I don't want to fight with you either, honey, but this is just–
    6 Rick: Mom, there's nothing that you can say that's gonna change the way I feel about her.
    7 Brooke: *(sighs)* I want you to trust me as your mother. Whatever is going on between you and Taylor – it has to stop. It's wrong for so many reasons. I want it to end.
    (*Bold and Beautiful*, 25 March 2008)

At times, we find characters referring to information that they have about a third character that they urgently need to share with the addressee since this knowledge might change their relationship with that third character, as in Example (5):

(5) 1 Tad: Erica, we need to talk.
    2 Erica: No, we do not, not now. Please, I really do need a little space, a little time alone. I have to pull myself together before I go back downstairs.
    3 Tad: If you're going back downstairs, then what I have to say can't wait.
    4 Erica: Yeah, it will have to wait. Please, Tad, one drama at a time.
    5 Tad: No. I'm sorry. **I have to tell you something, something about Josh.**

(*All My Children*, 9 September 2006)

The problem can also be an envisaged 'scheme', in other words, an attempt by the speaker to convince the addressee to work together to the detriment of a third character:

(6) 1 Alan: There is a very important board meeting coming up, and it will be our chance to get back what Alexandra stole from us.

(*Guiding Light*, 11 February 2003)

In our data, we rarely find that the complete talk is presented in one scene. This fits in with Fine's (1981) finding that in soap operas time is often slowed down and a conversation can take place over several episodes.

Next, we combined qualitative and quantitative aspects of analysis and categorized the responses to the request to talk depending on whether they express an agreement with the request, a postponement of the decision, a rejection of the request to talk, or whether they display some other reaction. We assume that problem-oriented talk situations in soaps introduced by a character announcing 'we need to talk' follow a particular set pattern that is largely based on whether the other character's response is a preferred or dispreferred second turn.

Rejections constitute the majority of cases (46 instances) – that is, what follows *[name], we need to talk* is mostly a dispreferred second turn. There are 34 agreements to talk, which can be considered the preferred second turn. In 25 cases a decision is postponed and can hence not be unambiguously classified as preferred or dispreferred second turn. Finally, there are 10 cases in which a third person takes the floor, which means that we do not get to know the immediate reaction of the person addressed. A closer look at the hits shows that these broad categories can be further subcategorized. A summary of all categories can be found in Table 3.3.

We start our presentation of the different (sub)categories with the preferred second turns, that is, agreements with the request to talk.

(7) 1 Cassie: Look, Josh, we need to talk.
    2 Josh: Yes, we do.

(*Guiding Light*, 21 July 2008)

Here, we distinguish direct agreements including words like 'yes', 'okay', 'alright' or 'sure' as in (7) from anticipations of the topic as illustrated in (8), and more indirect ways of indicating a willingness to talk as shown in (9).

Table 3.3 Frequencies of Occurrence of Different Response Categories

	Response	n
Agreements	Direct agreements including 'yes', 'okay', and so on	11
	Addressee anticipates topic	10
	Indirect agreements indicating willingness to talk	7
	Challenging agreements	6
	Subtotal agreements	**34**
Postponements	Addressee requires clarification, for example, 'About what?'	11
	Direct postponement	9
	Indirect postponement	5
	Subtotal postponements	**25**
Rejections	Indirect rejections indicating inability to talk	14
	Indirect rejections including explanations like 'I have nothing to say to you'	10
	Direct rejections including 'no'	13
	Addressee ignores request	9
	Subtotal rejections	**46**
Other	Third person interferes/takes the floor	10
	Subtotal other responses	**10**
	Total	**115**

(8) 1 Nicole: Kate. Kate, we need to talk.
     2 Kate: Nicole, I know you weren't invited to the wedding.
       (*Days of Our Lives*, 8 September 2005)

In (8), Nicole requests Kate to talk and Kate apparently already knows what troubles Nicole. Kate's taking up the (potential) topic is an agreement to talk – but it still has to be verified by Nicole whether what Kate mentions is indeed the matter she wants to discuss. By first addressing what she believes to be the topic, Kate takes over the power herself, which makes this reaction different from the agreements shown in (7).

(9) 1 Rick: Alan, we need to talk.
     2 Alan: Rick, I hope this won't take long.
       (*Guiding Light*, 11 December 2006)

By expressing his wish for a short conversation in (9), Alan indirectly indicates that he is willing to talk to Rick – at least for a short time.

A fourth subcategory is formed by what we call challenging agreements.

(10) 1 Jack: Brad, we need to talk.
      2 Brad: Yeah, you're right, Jack, we do. The clock's ticking. I want an answer. #
       (*Young and Restless*, 6 April 2005)

In this Example (10), which is taken from the end of a scene (indicated by the hashtag #), Brad agrees with Jack's request to talk. ('Yeah, you're right, Jack, we do.') He seems to be sure which matter should be discussed, but does not name it (as in the anticipation shown in Example (8)), but takes it for granted. Just as Kate in Example (8), he takes up the topic, but does so in a much more direct and aggressive way ('I want an answer'), even indirectly threatening Jack ('The clock's ticking').

Summarizing the subcategories of agreements, we can state that direct agreements amount to 11 cases in the data at hand, addressees anticipate topics in 10 examples, there are 7 cases in which speakers indicate their willingness to talk indirectly, and 6 agreements are used to at the same time challenge the original requester.

When examining the data in detail, we came across quite a few examples in which the addressees – directly or indirectly – postpone a decision on whether they are willing to talk or not. Postponements are the next category we want to introduce. When speakers postpone a request to talk, they reject it for the time being, but not in general. The most frequent way of not directly deciding on a 'yes' or 'no' is to first require information what the conversation will be about, as illustrated in Example (11). Some speakers formulate a postponement directly (as in (12)), while others do so only indirectly, as shown in (13).

(11) 1 Carly: Holden, we need to talk.
 2 Holden: About what?
 3 Carly: About your trip with Lily.

(*As the World Turns*, 24 June 2008)

In Example (11), Holden does not reject Carly's request to talk, but does not agree to talk either – he first seeks clarification on what the conversation will be about. 'About what?' is used in 7 out of the 11 instances of this subcategory and can hence be considered formulaic. Whether the persons asking for clarification really do not know what the request to talk relates to, or whether they only want to play for time, is a different matter.

In (12) the request to talk is rejected for the time being, but the addressee directly offers to talk later and asks for Chloe's agreement ('okay?').

(12) 1 Chloe: Shawn, we need to talk.
 2 Shawn: Another time, okay?

(*Days of Our Lives*, 7 May 2002)

In contrast to (12), (13) illustrates a rejection by means of a more indirect postponement.

(13) 1 Barbara: Paul, we need to talk.
 2 Paul: This is not a good time.
 3 Barbara: Well, then make time. This is important.

(*As the World Turns*, 23 December 2009)

Paul indirectly declines Barbara's request to talk by stating that the time is not convenient. By saying that '*this* is not a good time' (emphasis added), he indirectly concedes that there will be a time which is more adequate and hence that he would be willing to talk then. This is not what he says, but this seems to be how Barbara takes his statement – she urges him to 'make time' quickly, as 'this is important'.

Indirect postponements can be found in 5 cases of our sample, direct ones form a group of 9 examples, and requests for clarification make up the largest subcategory with 11 examples.

Rejections in the narrow sense, our next category, can be subdivided into indirect and direct ones, too. The group of indirect rejections can be subdivided even further, namely, those indicating an inability to talk as illustrated in (14) and those comprising explanations such as in (15).

(14) 1 Margo: Chris, we need to talk.
      2 Chris: Yeah, I'm kind of busy.
      3 Margo: It's not a request. You and I will talk.

(*As the World Turns*, 21 January 2008)

In (14) Chris seems to agree that there is the need to talk with Margo ('Yeah'), but immediately names a factual reason which postpones a conversation about the matter in question. The indirectness of the postponement is apparent not only by the lack of a clear rejection but also by the hedge 'kind of'. Example (14) differs from Example (13) in that Chris's reply 'I'm kind of busy' indirectly rejects the actual request to talk, while the indirect refusal in (13) implies that Paul would be willing to talk to Barbara some other time. In (15) the addressee claims that she has nothing to say to the requester.

(15) 1 Miguel: Kay, we need to talk.
      2 Kay: Ugh, I have nothing to say to you.
      3 Miguel: Kay – Kay, please, you have to believe me. This is all a setup. They want you to think I tried to kill Fox to get me out of the way and to make you hate me. Oh, my God. You do hate me. #

(*Passions*, 15 February 2007)

Kay does not directly say 'no' to Miguel's request, but, as can be told by Kay's reaction, 'I have nothing to say to you' seems to be a quite powerful rejection.

There are some variations of 'I have nothing to say to you', which indicate that there are not only formulaic utterances like 'we need to talk' but also typical reactions in soap dialogues. Together with 'we need to talk', 'we have nothing to say to each other', 'we have nothing to talk about', 'I don't think we have anything to discuss' or 'I said everything I needed to' and 'we already talked' may be considered typical soap dialogues.

The most direct rejections are cases like (16) in which the addressee blatantly says 'no'.

(16) 1 Shayne: Marina, we need to talk.
      2 Maria: No.

(*Guiding Light*, 25 May 2009)

Example (17) illustrates yet another reaction by Phoebe simply ignoring Thomas's request to talk.

(17) 1 Thomas: Phoebe, we need to talk.
     2 Phoebe: Look at all this yummy food.

(*Bold and Beautiful*, 7 September 2005)

Phoebe changes the topic and thereby rejects Thomas's request to talk. However, she does not directly say so, but chooses an indirect way. A change of topic makes it more difficult for Thomas to address his matter again.

There are 9 such instances of ignoring the request to talk. Indirect rejections indicating an inability (or unwillingness) to talk form the biggest subcategory with 14 examples, another 10 examples include explanations like 'I have nothing to say to you'. Direct rejections comprising a 'no' form the second most frequent subcategory with 13 examples.

Finally, in 10 cases it is not the addressee who responds, but a third person interfering (i.e. taking the floor) as in (18). These examples form the category 'other'.

(18) 1 Oliver: Stacy, we need to talk.
     2 Kim: Who let you in?

(*One Life to Live*, 20 January 2010)

Oliver wants to have a word with Stacy, but before Stacy can reply, Kim, who is also present, takes the floor with a question. The shift of focus results in a shift of attention as far as the request to talk is concerned.

These examples form a dispreferred turn from the requester's point of view, but cannot be considered along with the other examples of dispreferred and also preferred second turns, as it is not the addressee who responds. Table 3.3 serves to summarize all frequencies of occurrence for the different subcategories introduced earlier.

In a final step, we wanted to find out whether requests to talk were predominantly uttered by female or male speakers and whether they primarily addressed people of the same or a different gender.[4] As Table 3.4 shows, the majority of speakers (60 of 115) as well as of addressees (68 of 115) is male – thus, requesting to talk seems to be a male issue in soaps. However, the most frequent constellation beyond these overall figures relates to female speakers asking male addressees to talk (39 of 115 cases). Female speakers only comparatively rarely address other females with a request to talk (16 examples), while males addressing females (31 instances) and males addressing other males (29 cases) are in-between.

Table 3.4 Gender of Speakers and Addressees

	Female speaker	Male speaker	
Female addressee	16	31	47
Male addressee	39	29	68
	55	60	

Table 3.5 Composition of the SOAP Corpus (Davies 2011–): Number of Words per Soap and Year

	2001	2002	2003	2004	2005	2006	2007	2008	2009	2010	2011	2012	Total
All My Children	472,591	1,239,762	1,206,171	1,313,737	1,320,767	1,245,559	1,225,932	1,212,690	1,185,539	1,216,456	857,417	0	12,496,621
As the World Turns	561,240	1,379,292	1,173,859	1,320,835	1,355,002	1,344,772	1,399,823	1,396,450	1,430,948	1,024,656	0	0	12,386,877
Bold and Beautiful	333,387	515,259	460,877	565,745	557,192	531,797	603,021	611,355	616,257	616,829	574,282	282,169	6,268,170
Days of Our Lives	650,116	818,525	1,067,711	1,128,858	1,278,681	1,132,098	1,241,158	1,232,301	1,186,416	1,133,875	1,212,991	600,322	12,683,052
General Hospital	354,938	1,154,240	1,143,568	1,289,225	1,290,110	1,309,304	1,379,536	1,358,357	1,365,759	1,366,452	1,364,904	704,913	14,081,306
Guiding Light	363,550	1,014,192	1,080,881	577,751	1,206,002	1,173,946	1,183,059	1,174,526	836,642	0	0	0	8,610,549
One Life to Live	294,301	1,184,530	990,652	1,262,391	1,225,763	1,213,406	1,270,986	1,257,607	1,250,391	1,269,333	1,252,450	40,040	12,511,850
Passions	604,917	846,361	973,752	1,198,128	1,278,377	1,227,179	855,657	0	0	0	0	0	6,984,371
Port Charles	642,692	686,872	486,458	0	0	0	0	0	0	0	0	0	1,816,022
Young and Restless	516,605	891,080	1,079,039	1,274,864	1,259,420	1,257,846	1,290,164	1,233,884	1,243,667	1,200,038	1,143,142	555,333	12,945,082
Total	4,794,337	9,730,113	9,662,968	9,931,534	10,771,314	10,435,907	10,449,336	9,477,170	9,115,619	7,827,639	6,405,186	2,182,777	100,783,900

6 Conclusions

We have shown that *we need to talk* can indeed be considered a stock phrase when it is used as a first turn to introduce problem-oriented talk, that is, a discussion about some issue for which some kind of solution is needed.

Following Formentelli (2013), we included the use of a vocative, namely, a proper name in our search, as vocatives are frequently used in soaps (or discourse addressed at an overhearing audience in general).[5] They do serve the function not only to attain the primary addressee's attention but also to (re)introduce an addressee to the overhearing audience and thereby make it easy especially for new or temporary recipients to follow the plot (cf. Goffman 1979; Burger 2001).

It could be shown that the use of *need* is typical of soap opera discourse. This may be due to the fact that the use of *need* conveys more urgency than could be indicated by the use of other modal verbs – which occur considerably less frequently or not at all. The urgency and relevance of the matter to be discussed becomes also apparent by the use of the first-person plural pronoun *we* including the addressee.

Our analysis has shown that *[name], we need to talk* occurs in all soaps comprised in the SOAP corpus, and it occurs much more often there than in COCA. This may be due to the fact that a person's wish to talk and the unknown reaction of the addressee promises suspense and may result in a change of the current situation. This, in turn, makes it interesting to watch a soap: It features situations (including changes) which may not happen as often in the audience's everyday routines (cf. the discussion above on overused lines, and Quaglio 2009: 115 on the more frequent use of greetings in *Friends* compared to conversational discourse).

[Name], we need to talk can thus be considered typical of soap language, even though we have to concede that there are differences: as shown in Table 3.2, *we need to talk* does not occur equally frequently in all soaps. While it is rather frequent in the romantic soap *Passions* (2 instances per million words) and the family life soap *Days of Our Lives* (1.7 instances per million words), it does not occur particularly often in the medical dramas *General Hospital* (0.7 instances per million words) and *Port Charles* (0.6 instances per million words). This could be due to writers' preferences but also to the subgenres of the soaps under investigation.

We assume that *[name], we need to talk* is used to introduce conversations about a problem concerning the speaker as well as the addressee, and that such conversations unfold in specific ways depending on whether the addressee's response is a preferred or dispreferred second turn.

Requests to talk bring about a limited set of responses. Leaving third persons taking the floor aside, addressees either agree to talk or reject the request. Postponements of different kinds range somewhere in-between: In the current conversation, they equal a rejection, but only for the moment of speaking and not (or not necessarily) in general. The question of how the requester reacts on such a nonagreement or whether there will be a discussion in the future adds to the dramatic nature of soaps.

As far as these general response categories are concerned, writers are not to blame for the limited set of responses (cf. Section 4) – agreeing, rejecting or postponing a decision are the only possibilities at hand. The subcategories (cf. Table 3.3), however, show that there is nonetheless some room for variation and hence the writers' creativity. This variation is limited with reference to the mental lexicon (cf. Section 3). When confronted with a request which may or may not be in accordance with one's own needs and which calls for a reaction, speakers (in real life as well as in soap operas) tend to resort to stock responses. Rather than spending processing capacities on a creative formulation, the former may be saved for thinking consequences through (cf. Wray 2002: 15ff.). Furthermore, a formulaically phrased request may likely trigger a formulaic response on the addressee's part (cf. Wray 2002: 99f.).

As far as the TV audience is concerned, a formulaic response covering a limited set of possibilities clarifies what is to be expected regarding the storyline. Firstly, this holds for the conversation at hand (a more or less amicable discussion or a confrontational argument about the legitimacy of the request is to be expected, cf. Section 4), and secondly, for the future plot: Soap viewers' experience has it that problem-oriented talk will often introduce unexpected changes in the protagonists' lives (cf. Taylor 2006 on the predictability of telecinematic language). And the emotionality related with such changes is what makes soaps entertaining since it is 'the presence of "dramatic" or "emotional" moments in television series that seem[s] to keep audiences interested' (Bednarek 2012: 43, cf. Al-Surmi 2012: 684 on more involved language being used in soap operas).

Taking the dramatic nature of soaps into account (cf. also Richardson 2010: 110; Section 2), it is not surprising that rejections form the largest subgroup in our analysis of responses (46 of 115 cases), and that there is also a large number of postponements, which are rejections for the time being (25 examples). Independent of and possibly in addition to the matter referred to, a rejection (be it temporary or ultimate) adds a dramatic moment to a conversation. A request is considered a face-threatening act (cf. Brown & Levinson 1987). It may be costly to the addressee to act as required by the requester rather than self-determined, and it may be costly to the speaker to require something rather than being able to care for the requested action themselves. If the requested action is contrary to the addressee's interests, he or she may insist on their not doing as requested (at least not at the moment the requester asks) and reject the need to talk, which is, in turn, a face-threatening act towards the requester. This creates even more tension: Viewers will be interested to watch whether the requester will abide by the request, or what they will do next to get the addressee to talk about the issue at hand. This emphasizes that the dramatic focus in soaps is on reactions (cf. Geeraerts 2001: 6; Section 2). Even a postponement is only a temporary solution, as the characters will surely see each other again (cf. Fine 1981: 99; Section 2).

As we have seen in the analysis, most of the conversations comprising a request to talk are mixed-gender conversations (70 out of 115 cases), followed by conversations between two males (29) and those between two females (16). Referring back to Fine's (1981) study (cf. section 3) and assuming that the soaps mostly take heterosexual relationships to be the norm (cf. Fine 1981: 101), the mixed-gender constellation with requests to talk about some problem emphasize that interpersonal relations are of great importance in soaps. If there were no talking about problems, soaps would not be entertaining. Gender does not seem to be a highly influential factor – in soaps, characters need to talk, be they men or women.

Notes

1. Thank you to Matthias Zucker for originally pointing out the *Star Wars* example to us.
2. This does not mean that television series are necessarily conceived with the showrunners already knowing how the series will end and how many seasons will be needed to tell the story.
3. The expletives occurring in the SOAP data are of course fairly mild: there are 195 instances of *you look like hell* and twenty-three instances of *you look like crap*. The movie scripts contain fifteen instances of *you look like shit*, four instances of *you look like hell*, three instances of *you look like crap* and one instance of *you look like dogshit*.
4. As far as we are aware, all the characters in the analyzed soaps are presented as either female or male.
5. Weatherall (1996) reports that 796 first names were used to refer to or address characters in five hours of *Coronation Street*.

References

Al-Surmi, M. (2012), 'Authenticity and TV shows: A multidimensional analysis perspective', *TESOL Quarterly*, 46 (4): 671–94.

Allen, R. C. (1985), *Speaking of Soap Operas*, Chapel Hill and London: The University of North Carolina Press.

Allen, R. C. (1995), 'Introduction', in R. C. Allen (ed.), *To Be Continued: Soap Operas around the World*, 1–26, London: Routledge.

Androutsopoulos, J. (2012), 'Introduction: Language and society in cinematic discourse', *Multilingua*, 31: 139–54.

Bednarek, M. (2012), '"Get us the hell out of here": Keywords and trigrams in fictional television series', *International Journal of Corpus Linguistics*, 17 (1): 35–63.

Brody, L. (2003), *Television Writing from the Inside Out: Your Channel to Success*, New York: Applause Cinema and Theatre Books.

Brown, P. and Levinson, S. C. (1987), *Politeness: Some Universals in Language Use*, Cambridge: Cambridge University Press.

Burger, H. (2001), 'Gespräche in den Massenmedien', in K. Brinker, G. Antos, W. Heinemann and S. F. Sager (eds), *Text- und Gesprächslinguistik. Ein internationales Handbuch zeitgenössischer Forschung*, 2nd vol., 1492–505, Berlin and New York: de Gruyter.

Davies, M. (2008–), *The Corpus of Contemporary American English: 520 Million Words, 1990-Present* [online]. Available at: http://corpus.byu.edu/coca/ (accessed 15 January 2017).

Davies, M. (2011–), *Corpus of American Soap Operas: 100 Million Words* [online]. Available at: http://corpus.byu.edu/soap/ (accessed 15 January 2017).

Elwood, K. (2011), 'Soap opera thankfulness – a comparison of expressions of gratitude in *Fair City* and *EastEnders*', *Waseda University Departmental Bulletin Paper*, 38 (3): 107–33 [online]. Available at: http://www.waseda.jp/w-com/quotient/publications/pdf/bun38_01.pdf (accessed 14 January 2017).

Federal Communications Commission (2016), *Consumer Guide: Obscene, Indecent and Profane Broadcasts* [online]. Available at: https://transition.fcc.gov/cgb/consumerfacts/obscene.pdf (accessed 14 January 2017).

Fine, M. G. (1981), 'Soap opera conversations: The talk that binds', *Journal of Communication*, 31 (3): 97–107.
Formentelli, M. (2013), 'Vocatives galore in audiovisual dialogue: Evidence from a corpus of American and British films', Paper presented at the *International Conference 'Address(ing) (Pro)Nouns: Sociolinguistics and Grammar of Terms of Address'*, Freie Universität Berlin, 30 May–1 June 2013.
Freddi, M. (2011), 'A phraseological approach to film dialogue: Film stylistics revisited', *Yearbook of Phraseology*, 2: 137–63.
Geeraerts, D. (2001), 'Everyday language in the media: The case of Belgian Dutch soap series', in M. Kammerer, K.-P. Konerding, A. Lehr, A. Storrer, C. Thimm and W. Wolski (eds), *Sprache im Alltag*, 281–91, Berlin and New York: de Gruyter. Available at: http://wwwling.arts.kuleuven.be/qlvl/PDFPublications/01Everydaylanguage.pdf (accessed 15 January 2017).
Goffman, E. (1979), 'Footing', *Semiotica*, 25 (1/2): 1–29.
Grant, L. and Starks, D. (2001), 'Screening appropriate teaching materials: Closings from textbooks and television soap operas', *International Review of Applied Linguistics in Language Teaching*, 39 (1): 39–50.
Grice, H. P. (1975), 'Logic and conversation', in P. Cole and J. L. Morgan (eds), *Syntax and Semantics*, vol. 3, Speech Acts, 41–58, New York: Academic Press.
Hassler-Forest, D. (2014), '*Game of Thrones*: Quality television and the cultural logic of gentrification', *TV/Series*, 6 [online]. Available at: http://journals.openedition.org/tvseries/323 (accessed 15 January 2019).
Huisman, R. (2005), 'Soap operas and sitcoms', in H. Fulton (ed.), *Narrative and Media*, 172–87, Cambridge and New York: Cambridge University Press.
Lakoff, R. (1973), 'Language and woman's place', *Language in Society*, 2: 45–80.
Lambertz, K. and Hebrok, M. (2011), 'Women's language in soap operas: Comparing features of female speech in Australia and Germany', *Griffith Working Papers in Pragmatics and Intercultural Communication*, 4 (1/2): 39–54.
Miyamoto, K. (2016), *35 Most Overused Lines of Dialogue in Screenplays* [online]. Available at: https://screencraft.org/2016/03/18/35-most-overused-lines-of-dialogue-in-screenplays/ (accessed 28 December 2016).
Palma Fahey, M. (2005), 'Speech acts as intercultural danger zones: A cross-cultural comparison of the speech act of apologising in Irish and Chilean soap operas', *Intercultural Communication* 8 [online]. Available at: https://www.immi.se/intercultural/nr8/palma.htm (accessed 13 January 2017).
'Pilot.' *Suits*, season 1, episode 1, written by Aaron Korsh, directed by Kevin Bray, USA, 23 June 2011.
Quaglio, P. (2009), *Television Dialogue: The Sitcom Friends vs. Natural Conversation*, Amsterdam and Philadelphia: John Benjamins.
Richardson, K. (2010), *Television Dramatic Dialogue: A Sociolinguistic Study*, New York: Oxford University Press.
Schwarz, S. (2015), 'Passive voice in American soap opera dialogue', *Studia Neophilologica*, 87 (2): 152–70.
'Soap opera ratings for the 2015–16 season (final).' *TV Series Finale* [online]. Available at: http://tvseriesfinale.com/tv-show/soap-opera-ratings-2015-16-season/ (accessed 15 January 2017).
'Stock phrases.' *TV Tropes* [online]. Available at: http://tvtropes.org/pmwiki/pmwiki.php/Main/StockPhrases (accessed 29 December 2016).

Taylor, C. (2006), '"I knew he'd say that!" A consideration of the predictability of language use in film', in M. Carroll, H. Gerzymisch-Arbogast and S. Nauert (eds), *Audiovisual Translation Scenarios*. Proceedings of the Marie Curie Euroconferences MuTra: Audiovisual Translation Scenarios, Copenhagen, 1–5 May 2006 [online]. Available at: http://www.euroconferences.info/proceedings/2006_Proceedings/2006_Taylor_Christopher.pdf (accessed 14 January 2017).

Weatherall, A. (1996), 'Language about women and men: An example from popular culture', *Journal of Language and Social Psychology*, 15 (1): 59–75.

Wray, A. (2002), *Formulaic Language and the Lexicon*, Cambridge: Cambridge University Press.

Wray, A. and Perkins, M. R. (2000), 'The functions of formulaic language: An integrated model', *Language & Communication*, 20: 1–28.

4

Repetition in sitcom humour

Thomas C. Messerli

1 Introduction

In his discussion of the aims and challenges that are to be expected for a stylistics of film, Toolan (2014: 459) suggests as a key area of interest 'that of shot composition and combination, the kinds of cut found in a film and the rhythm of their sequencing'. The individual shots of a film, which are themselves the result of multimodal composition, are arranged into particular narrative and aesthetic sequences. The means by which this composition and combination takes place are likened by Toolan to punctuation in written narrative, which is to say that we can regard these sequences from an onomasiological perspective as a specific expression of a certain idea. Accordingly, particular effects of telecinematic discourse (TCD) can be linked to the way in which that rhythm is constructed, which means that establishing a grammar of TCD by analysing the particular film or television series as an audiovisual text or as audiovisual language in use will provide meaningful insights into the aesthetics of telecinematic texts, the manner in which they construct meaning and the ways in which they communicate with their viewership.

Within the body of texts that are produced based on this grammar of film shots, this chapter focuses on the particular subset of the television sitcom. Sitcoms are approached with the premise that they strive to elicit humour in viewers and that they are thus also a subset of humorous texts.

The specific way in which films and television series create humorous effects has received little attention in stylistic research to date, but there are at least some relevant extant studies on the linguistics of telecinematic humour, on the one hand, and on the stylistics of humorous narratives, on the other. Within linguistics, Brock (2004) is, to my knowledge, the only book-length study of humour in fictional television. Other articles on humour in TCD have had a narrow focus on particular aspects of humour, be it its delivery in terms of prosody (Urios-Aparisi and Wagner 2011) or the complex communicative structures in which it operates (Brock 2015; Dynel 2011a; Messerli 2016). While none of these studies can present a fully fledged stylistics of telecinematic humour in and of themselves, they each contribute to the description of TCD more generally, and humour therein more specifically. Works that are more stylistic in their focus, but do not specifically focus on telecinematic texts, include Chlopicki's (1987) analysis of humorous short stories, Attardo's (2001) overview of different types of humorous texts, Ermida's (2008) study of shorter and longer humorous narratives and Marszalek's (2013) cognitive stylistic work on humorous texts. The main interest of these studies is to go beyond the analysis of a single humorous instance and to describe the larger structure and the pragmatics of humorous narratives.

In the same vein, I address humour in the audiovisual text of the sitcom as a network of individual humorous instances. However, my focus in this article is not primarily on the larger structures, but on the microscopic construction of humorous instances in the context of the larger narrative. Humour, for this purpose, is understood as a largely cognitive result of incongruity and resolution (see Suls 1972 and Section 2.1 in this chapter), and the individual humorous instance can be analysed in terms of the textual bases that are intended to result in incongruity, resolution and thus a humorous effect in television viewers.

Within the construction of the individual humorous instance as well as the textual cohesion between instances, repetition has an interesting role. On the one hand, repetition is well established as a text-cohesive device (e.g. Halliday and Hasan 1976); on the other hand, at least some forms of repetition may work against the element of surprise that is often named as a prerequisite for humour (e.g. Suls 1972: 85; Morreall 1983: 84). My qualitative and quantitative analyses of sitcom humour describe the status of repetition within sitcom humour, and at the same time use repetition as a particular lens, through which telecinematic humorous texts can be described.

The main question is then how repetition is used in TCD with the intention of achieving a humorous effect on the viewership. As will be discussed in Section 2.2, a broad understanding of repetition will be applied, which includes the recurrence not just of lexical items but also of structural parallelism as well as of such aspects of multimodality as elements of the mise en scène and character gestures. Accordingly, the question needs to be expanded to different types of repetition and the way in which they are combined to construct humorous instances. The answers to these questions are provided here based on a case study on one episode of the US American sitcom *Better with You* (ABC, 2010–2011), which serves as a randomly chosen representative of the genre of *Sitcom with a laugh track* (see description in Section 3.1). This genre was chosen because viewings of the data have shown it to be particularly rich both in terms of humorous instances and in terms of repetition. It thus promises to be as an ideal playground for an exploratory study of repetition in telecinematic humour.

Section 2 will lay the theoretical groundwork for the analysis by defining what is meant by *humour* and *repetition* as well as by discussing the roles that repetition may be expected to play in telecinematic humour. Section 3 will then describe the data and individual methodological steps that were taken in order to arrive at the findings presented in Section 4. Finally, the results will be put in context and next research steps will be suggested.

2 The role of repetition in sitcom humour

2.1 Telecinematic discourse and humour

While the pragmatics of TCD is not the main focus of this study, it is nonetheless important to briefly describe the communicative setting in which TCD takes place. The audiovisual text is positioned between a collective sender that produces it and a television audience that receives it. Accordingly, researchers have pointed to the different communicative levels or layers that need to be taken into account when describing interaction in this setting: the level between collective sender and audience, and the level between fictional characters (Dynel 2011b; Piazza, Bednarek and Rossi 2011; Messerli 2017). As has been shown elsewhere (Brock 2015; Messerli 2016), this distinction is crucial, as it leads to different audience vantage points and results in different types of humour: The audience is positioned either on the level of the characters or on that of an observer and thus laughs with or about the target of the humorous instance, respectively. Moreover, the layering of communication is in itself a resource for humour construction, for instance when intertextuality is exploited or when the inclusion of the conventionally inaccessible communicative level between sender and audience is used for comic effect.

Another way of describing this participation structure is to say that the telecinematic text is performed by a set of characters framed in a particular way, and that this performance mediates between the collective sender and its audience. This in turn entails that the dialogue spoken by the fictional characters and the multimodal actions around them are designed for a particular television audience. For instance, we can assume that producers and viewers of the television sitcom share the expectation that a humorous response is one of the intended effects of sitcom viewing.

Before I discuss repetition as a pattern in telecinematic texts, I will define and situate my understanding of humour. Humour research is traditionally separated into three main approaches: *superiority*, *relief* and *incongruity* (for comprehensive overviews of the history of humour theory see Keith-Spiegel 1972; Morreall 1983; Attardo 1994). For the purposes of this study, I will follow the incongruity tradition, which is suitable to explain the mechanisms of constructing humour and the most accepted framework within linguistic humour studies (see, for example, Veale 2004; Dynel 2013). Within this research tradition, Suls's (1972) *Incongruity-Resolution* model is still an adequate explanatory tool for the analysis of those text-immanent stimuli that trigger the cognitive processes of humour.

Humour, in this understanding, is the result of a clash between semantic frames, that is the knowledge structures that are in this case activated by the narrative (see Attardo 1994; Fillmore 2006). In the linear narrative, a first frame – narrative schema in Suls's (1972) terminology – is juxtaposed with a surprising new stimulus that does not fit the same frame.[1] While the cognitive processes involved in humour reception are not a focus of this study, they highlight what elements of the text need to be taken into account when addressing its potential for humorous effect. For Suls (1972), successful humour will trigger certain expectations in the recipient, in the case of this study the television audience, and every new bit of information will be tacitly assessed with regard to its congruence with those expectations. A non-humorous continuation of the story is the one that fits the activated frame and the viewer expectations; confusion is the result if a new stimulus is both ill-fitting and inexplicable; humour, finally, is the outcome, if a new surprising stimulus appears to be incongruous with expectations, but can then be made plausible by finding some form of cognitive or experiential rule that is able to resolve the incongruity (Suls 1972: 82).

One aspect to which Suls (1972) pays little heed is that of the context in which humour occurs. Apart from the requirement that a given incongruity must be resolvable, it also has to occur in a space in which a humorous reaction, such as laughter, is permissible. Bateson's (1953, 1955/1972) notion of *play* is one way of approaching this type of interactional framing, which communicates to the participating parties that they do not have to take the performed actions and utterances at face value, but have licence to be amused by them. In the case of TCD, this *play frame* or *joking frame* (Norrick 1996) is achieved via a range of different devices, which include the metacommunicative cues available to the television audience even before they start watching (Brock 2004: 161–4). For instance, the sitcom (i.e. situation comedy) genre as a viewing contract between producers and recipients establishes that one of its key purposes is to amuse its viewership and that therefore laughter is admissible or even expected.

When it comes to the construction of incongruities, the complex participation structure of TCD means that viewer expectations can be tied to the represented frame as well as that of its representation: This means, in the case of the traditional multicamera sitcom *Better with You*, that viewers can be expected to be familiar with dialogues between couples and in families at home and in restaurants, and with the way sitcom characters usually interact in these and other situations. Quite clearly, multilevel expectations are thus at play at any given moment, which opens up a range of possibilities when it comes to the specific way in which occurring events can be incongruous with the active frame and the ensuing viewer expectations.

The surprising stimuli that create the incongruities are not only situated on different levels of participation. Many incongruity-models of humour have a semantic background, and the prototypical incongruity indeed rests upon the juxtaposition of two similar but incompatible ideas. This notwithstanding, surprise can emerge on other levels as well, for instance, when it runs against expectations regarding the interactional organization of talk (see Stokoe 2008). Moreover, humour in TCD is also a multimodal phenomenon, with expectation-evoking and surprising stimuli being encoded in spoken dialogue as well as in character gestures and facial expressions or even in the telecinematic realization of any given scene. Finally, the resolvability of the constructed incongruities hinges on the audiovisual text offering ways for the viewers to explain to themselves why the incongruous element was present. This could be instantiated, for instance, by introducing a plot element earlier in the narrative and then reusing it in a new context as the incongruous element that will produce a humorous instance.

2.2 Characteristics and descriptors of repetition

There is to date no comprehensive and systematic discussion of the role of repetition in humour, but Norrick's (1993, 1994, 1996) studies have provided valuable observations on the subject. With those studies as a starting point, this section addresses the ways in which the two concepts affect each other, and it presents those theoretical properties of repetition and the repeated items that have informed my own categorization (see Section 3). Norrick (1993: 387) speaks of a 'dual nature of repetition', in the sense that it both indexes automaticity and 'sets the stage for abrupt variation' (Norrick 1993). The latter effect also means that repetition in jokes can serve to establish a 'background script', which refers to what Suls (1972) calls the narrative schema on which the subsequent incongruity rests.

This duality of repetition in general is mirrored in two opposed effects that repetition has on humour specifically. On the one hand, repetition in this case acts as a facilitator of humour. This is manifest in the examples Norrick (1996) gives for those aspects of humour where repetition is instrumental: (1) hyperbolic accumulation, (2) the signalling that something is intended as humorous, (3) wordplay, (4) making metalingual comments for the purposes of humour and (5) establishing a humorous form of corrective sequence. In all these cases, the humorous potential of repetition is linked to its role as a facilitator of production (following Johnstone 1987) and – together with variation – as a mechanism that can trigger a frameshift and thus establish a humorous incongruity. Coates (2007) adds to this the contribution of repetition to the establishing and maintaining of non-serious talk. She finds repetition to be 'a striking feature of talk in a play frame' (Coates 2007: 42). Repetition can render ongoing talk more and more playful, and particular words and phrases can become charged with humorous meaning and be repeated for humorous effect.

On the other hand, Morreall (1983), and Forabosco (2008) name repetition as a factor potentially conflicting with incongruity. Repetition increases familiarity, and at the same time reduces incongruity through repeated exposure (Forabosco 2008: 56). This conflict between repetition and incongruity is also already addressed by Suls (1972) who adds, however, that repeated incongruities may nevertheless retain their humorous potential. Repetition, he explains, may facilitate a positive response precisely due to familiarity and because it can reactivate the positive response associated with the first exposure (Suls 1972: 94).

In terms of its contribution to humour, repetition is thus multifunctional, and it may either facilitate or hinder humorous effect. A similar diverseness exists in the ways repetition is manifest in the audiovisual text, that is, in the range of stimuli that may be repeated and in the parameters that define each instance of repetition itself. In this vein, Aitchison (1994) discusses the different variables that have been considered in linguistic studies of repetition. In particular, she identifies as 'straightforward variables' those objective criteria that directly characterize the repeated units rather than the motivations and purposes that may have triggered their presence. They are (1) medium (spoken or written), (2) participants (self-repetition or other-repetition), (3) scale of fixity (exact or partial), (4) temporal scale (immediate or delayed) and (5) size of unit (e.g. phoneme, morpheme, word, etc.) (Aitchison 1994: 18–19).

In the case of sitcoms as an example of TCD, the medium is primarily spoken, although it is worth mentioning that the multimodal artefact may also include writing, for example, in the form of subtitles or writing that is part of the diegetic world. Moreover, speaking in the case of sitcoms is the result of an elaborate process. The spoken performance by actors in front of the camera rests on scripted dialogues that are themselves 'written to be spoken as if not written' (Gregory 1967: 191). The duality of communicative levels in sitcoms also means that repetition may both be a representation of repetitive patterns that occur in non-scripted face-to-face interaction and a property of the communication between collective sender and the television audience, that is, a planned and intentional feature of the narrative audiovisual text through which this communication occurs.

These aspects also have an effect on the second variable of participants, which most analysts of spoken conversation include as a criterion in their classification of repetition.[2] It is worth noting that in the case of TCD, the distinction of the two communicative levels is again crucial, because whereas characters can repeat themselves or other characters on the fictional level, the unidirectionality of the communication between collective sender and viewers means that any repetition is by definition a form of self-repetition on this level.

The third aspect of fixity is a gradual category in several respects. First of all, the notion of exact repetition (e.g. Tannen 1989) – also referred to as full repetition (e.g. Kim 2002), verbatim (e.g. Norrick 1996) or total recurrence (Hoffmann 2012) – can be defined as occurring 'when the original form and meaning is not changed at all' (Lichtkoppler 2007: 43). Strictly speaking, however, Johnstone (1987: 211) rightly states that 'repetition is never exact; it always involves some sort of similarity and some sort of difference, whether the difference be linguistic, as in alliteration or syntactic parallelism, or contextual, as when the same thing is said in different situations'. This includes the fact that within the chronological and linear processes of listening and reading, repeated items are inherently different because they are less novel than the item they repeat.

Leaving such ontological concerns aside, it is possible to more confidently label repetition as exact on some levels than on others. For instance, exact lexical repetition can be distinguished from partial lexical repetition based on how exactly repeated words match previously occurring ones. For aspects such as gestures, facial expressions or intonation contours on the other hand, the identification of exactness becomes even more subjective. For instance, there is no hard boundary between different hand gestures or smiles. As a result, I have distinguished between partial and exact repetition only when it comes to lexical repetition.

The notion of temporal scale can be addressed with the question asked by Johnstone (1994: 3): 'How far apart can the model and the copy get before we don't call it a repetition?' As Johnstone points out herself, there needs to be some form of restriction to more local recurrences in order not to make the concept of repetition meaningless (1994: 5). In this study, I have limited the scope for repetition to the individual sitcom episode; that is, repetition is observed as a local pattern, whereas intertextuality is excluded.

The fifth criterion of the size of unit is best addressed on different levels of language. Whereas repetition of individual words or syntactic groups can be distinguished on the lexical level, phonetic repetition can also address the repetition of specific phones, which may lead to alliterations and rhymes, for instance. In other cases, the individual gesture, the individual facial expression or the individual camera movement serve as the relevant repeatable unit.

Informed by these descriptors, but primarily driven by the analyses of the data themselves, the following types of repetition were distinguished in the empirical sections of this chapter:

1. Lexical: single word or multiple words; exact or partial
2. Structural parallelism
3. Prosodic repetition
4. Repetition of facial expressions
5. Telecinematic repetition

For each type of repetition and for repetition in general, their functions in humour will be examined based on a close-reading of examples.

2.3 Corpus and methodology

The goal of this study is to describe the role different types of simple repetition play in constructing humorous instances in TCD and thus in achieving a humorous effect on the viewership. As indicated in Section 2.2, the scope for this endeavour is the individual episode, and specifically a case study of the first episode of *Better with You*. This series was randomly selected as an example of a US sitcom with a laugh track produced in the 2010s. Since it rests on the detailed analysis of a single episode, this case study is not representative of sitcoms in general. However, my exploratory analyses can offer qualitative insights into the interaction between repetition and humour as well as a typology of repetitive patterns in the sitcom episode at hand, whose validity as a general pattern in humour should be tested on larger datasets in subsequent research.

Better with You (ABC 2010–2011) is an American sitcom which ran on ABC for twenty-two episodes. Its main characters are three couples, two sisters with their partners and the sisters' parents, and its main settings are the living rooms of each of the three couples. The first episode centres on the engagement of the younger sister Mia to Casey, who is introduced first to the older sister Maddie and her long-term boyfriend Ben, and later to the parents who, to Maddie's surprise, are thrilled about the hasty engagement. For the most part, the sitcom is filmed as a traditional multicamera sitcom, which means that the scenes are performed in a limited number of small studio sets in front of a live audience, which is typically called the *taping* of the episode. Some scenes are filmed earlier and screened to the audience during the taping (Simpson 2010). In the case of the studio scenes, usually several takes are recorded, which on the one hand offers variation in post-production, when the episode is edited for broadcast, and on the other hand is necessary when audience reactions do not conform to the expectations of the producers. In such cases, the respective scene has to be filmed anew or even rewritten (Simpson 2010).

Better with You is a sitcom that includes pre-recorded studio audience laughter, which offers a methodological advantage: As I have argued elsewhere (Messerli 2016), studio audience laughter can be regarded as a metacommunicative cue to the television audience that what immediately preceded it is intended to be funny. This is so irrespective of whether audience laughter is understood as the result of unmodified recording of a studio audience actually present during the filming of the broadcast sitcom audience or as a (partially) fabricated extra-diegetic cue that is planted by the collective sender. In the former case, the humorousness of the instance is ratified by another audience, in the latter the humorous intentions are signalled by the collective sender.

Having selected the data, humorous instances were identified using ELAN: a tool for the transcription and annotation of multimodal data, and on the basis of interactional turns which can either be followed by audience laughter or not, and thus be intended to be read as humorous or serious. This methodological step led to the identification of 149 humorous turns (henceforth HTs) in episode 1 of *Better with You*. The non-humorous turns were not examined any further, but the HTs were subsequently analysed for repetition and categorized according to different levels on which repetition may occur and as they were presented in Section 2.2. The individual repetition types will be discussed and illustrated in detail in Section 4; however, a first broad distinction was made between repetition across turns, that is, the HT at hand contained a unit repeated from a previous turn, and repetition within the particular HT. All HTs were coded for presence or absence of each category, and the coding of the categories was exhaustive but not mutually exclusive. The codebook was formulated in such a fashion that it foregrounds repeated items, that is, to code for presence only those cases in which repetition was considered salient. More generally, the coding was done from the position of a *metarecipient* (Dynel 2011b), which is to say that the stance of the analyst is similar to that of a particularly attentive and informed member of the target audience of the artefact. The orientation on the perspective of television viewers meant for instance that prosodic repetition was identified based on subjective coder impression rather than more objective measures.

In order to establish the validity of the categories, intercoder reliability was tested based on a comparable sample of the size of 60 HTs, which amounts to 46.3 per cent of the population. Due to the small size of the data considered for this case study, simple percentage agreement was used as a measure for reliability. The comparison of the two raters showed the coding of character gesture repetition to be below 75 per cent (66.7 per cent for intraturn and 70 per cent for interturn character gesture repetition), whereas all other categories were between 80 and 100 per cent and can thus be considered valid categories for the purposes of this study. Accordingly, simple descriptive statistics was done for the validated categories, which allows tentative statements as to the typicality of repetitive patterns in this sitcom episode. The categories where agreement could not be achieved were excluded from any quantification.

In Section 4, I will present the results of this categorization and illustrate the occurrences of repetition based on selected examples. One option for the second methodological step of tying this taxonomy of repetition to specific functions in telecinematic humour would have been another categorization of functions and the automatic establishment of a set of rules that would predict what type of function each instance of repetition may serve in humour. However, the close examination of the data revealed that the complex multimodal and multilevel construction of humour in sitcoms, even if it may seem generic and perhaps even unoriginal at first glance, is in fact subject to great variation, which extends to the way it makes use of repetition. Thus, while a summative overview of the range of functions will be provided for each type of repetition, this summary cannot rest on simple quantification of another set of functions as categories, and is instead provided qualitatively, based on the discussion of typical patterns and examples. This close-reading of examples will also allow me to present how repetition at different levels work together to construct humorous instances and thus to establish the stylistic means by which sitcoms create humorous effects for their audiences.

2.4 Repetition in the first episode of *Better with You*

2.4.1 Overview of repetition

Informed by the theoretical discussion of repetition in Section 2.2, the HTs in the data were analysed with regard to the role repetition plays in their construction. The results of the categorization as it is presented in this section do not yet explain how exactly the respective repetitive patterns contribute to the humorous effect of the turns. However, the outcome is a typology of repetition that demonstrates the ways this sitcom episode and perhaps TCD more generally encode specific story segments as audiovisual text. Furthermore, this typology provides the basis and context for the qualitative analysis of selected examples that link the patterns on the text surface to their humorous functions, which is discussed in the second part of each of the subsequent sections. This will be done in the form of a summary of functions observed in the data for each type of repetition, as well as by discussing selected examples.

The first distinction of the typology concerns distance, with repetition occurring both across turns (interturn repetition) and within turns (intraturn repetition). In this case and in the categorization more generally, individual categories are not mutually exclusive. Thus, the same HT may repeat a unit from another turn as well as from within itself, and it may contain different types of intraturn and/or interturn repetition.

To start with an overview, 112 (75.2 per cent) of the 149 HTs in the first episode of *Better with You* contained some form of repetition. As Table 4.1 illustrates, this is mostly due to interturn repetition, which was employed in roughly two-thirds of the analysed turns, whereas less than a fourth of all HTs employed intraturn repetition.

2.4.2 Interturn lexical repetition

The most prototypical form of repetition is repeating one or several lexical items, which occurs frequently in the data. For both interturn and intraturn repetition, the exact repetition of a single word is the most frequent pattern, but across turns, multiple words, that is, syntactic groups, are also repeated either verbatim or with some variation in word order or word morphology (partial). Since most HTs are only one or two seconds long, one explanation for the relative scarcity of that type of repetition interturn could be utterance length.

Interturn lexical repetition follows different patterns in HTs, but it often serves the creation of incongruities by means of recontextualization. For instance, words

Table 4.1 Types of Repetition in Episode 1 of *Better with You*

Type of repetition	Interturn		Intraturn	
Lexical: single word, exact	20	13.4%	9	6.0%
Lexical: single word, partial	3	2.0%	1	0.7%
Lexical: multiple words, exact	13	8.7%	3	2.0%
Lexical: multiple words, partial	14	9.4%	3	2.0%
Structural parallelism	8	5.4%	16	10.7%
Prosodic repetition	21	14.1%	25	16.8%
Repetition of facial expression	22	14.8%	11	7.4%
Telecinematic repetition	40	26.8%	0	0.0%
Any type of interturn or intraturn repetition respectively (i.e. at least one instance of any of the above types of repetition)	99	66.4%	35	23.5%

conventionally activate the particular semantic frames to which their core meaning serves as an access point, but the same words can also be explicitly associated with other semantic frames. Once established, the link between lexical item and semantic frame can be used to reactivate a frame by repeating the lexical item. A simple example occurs at the beginning of the episode, where the word *tunnel* is described as a place where couples 'fool around'. Thus, when a cab driver later asks one of the protagonists, Casey, about the route he should take, the one-word response 'tunnel' serves as a concise way of saying 'I want to fool around with my fiancée'. While there is no contrast between the core meaning of *tunnel* and the context of the taxi ride in which it is mentioned, that is, there is one consistent semantic frame, lexical repetition now also reactivates the earlier association and creates a contrast between the taxi ride and Casey's romantic intentions. It is noteworthy that, while in such cases incongruity depends on repetition, the repetitive incongruous element is nonetheless unexpected. Repetition in this case catches the television audience by surprise, because it repeats the word in an unexpected context.

Example 1, which presents three connected HTs, provides an illustration of a similar pattern of exact single-word repetition:

Example 1[3]

Ben gives advice to Casey.

HT 82   Ben: And don't make any jokes about plastic surgery. Five years ago, Mr. Putney's ears stuck out like this. now they're fine. I don't know what happened. Never asked. (whispering) Don't wanna know.

   Ben: So stick to the safe topics like wine, theatre, (.) and the Yankees.

[…]

At a restaurant, Casey is introduced to Joel Putney, his future father-in-law. Ben and the other family members are also present.

HT 92   Casey: Joel. .hh I like your ears.
HT 93   Ben: Hey, you know what you're gonna hear with those ears this year? Cheers for the Yankees!

The topic of Mr. Putney's ears is introduced in a scene somewhere in the middle of the episode, in which Ben prepares Casey for the first meeting with his future mother- and father-in-law (HT 82). Later, in a scene at a restaurant, Casey is indeed introduced to the father, and instead of heeding Ben's advice immediately blurts out a compliment about Mr. Putney's ears (HT 92). In the subsequent humorous turn (HT 93), Ben repeats the same word and thus takes up the topic of *ears*, while recontextualizing it in such a fashion that it links back to the Yankees, which he earlier described to Casey as a safe topic. Example 1 thus presents two different examples of exact interturn single-word repetition, and it illustrates cohesion through repetition – between turns more generally and HTs more particularly. The frame for the humorous instance in HT 92 is evoked by the context, that is, the mise en scène that represents a restaurant interior and character actions that are typical for a first meeting, such as the shaking of hands and the utterance 'great to meet you, Vicky', which immediately precedes HT 92. The compliment on Joel Putney's ears is incongruous because by means of simple lexical repetition it refers back to the earlier scene and thus activates the audience's knowledge that ears here constitute a taboo subject. Whereas the function of exact lexical repetition in HT 92 is similar to the aforementioned *tunnel* example, repetition of the word *ears* in HT 93 serves to motivate the humorous instance, that is, it repeats and emphasizes an element of the earlier interaction and thus cohesively ties in the subsequent incongruity with the larger narrative. This function can be linked to partial lexical multiple-word repetition in particular.

A different function of lexical repetition is illustrated in Example 2, which shows several instances of exact and partial repetition. The repeated item in this case is a syntactic group that was earlier established as a theme and is repeated several times throughout the episode.

Example 2
Maddie, standing next to her partner Ben, explains their living situation to the reception head waitress.

| HT 14 | Maddie: | Mhmmh neither of us want to be married, but we love each other. We're <u>very</u> happy. (.) It's a <u>valid</u> life choice. |

[…]
The family is discussing Mia's engagement and the fact that Maddie is not married at the restaurant.

| | Maddie: | Hey, our not being married is a va[lid-] |
| HT 111 | Vicky: | [valid] life choice. Okay, she <u>said</u> it. Everybody has to drink. |

[…]
Maddie asks her sister Mia for relationship advice in a taxi.

| HT 137 | Maddie: | Should Ben and I have gotten married a long time ago? (.) Is my life choice <u>not</u> valid? |

One of the recurring themes in the episode is the contrast between the long-term relationship of the unmarried older sister, Maddie, and the hasty engagement of the younger sister, Mia, to Casey. The announced wedding of the younger sister foregrounds that the older sister is still single and leads to a defensive stance. This stance is encoded in the phrase 'valid life choice', which is first uttered in HT 14. When Maddie is about to repeat the phrase at the restaurant, her mother interrupts her and repeats the phrase for her (exact interturn multiple-word repetition). The scene also reveals that within the fictional world

Maddie must have been using the same expression repeatedly before, and that her saying it is part of an ongoing drinking game among the others. Towards the end of the episode, in HT 137, Maddie repeats the same phrase again, when she asks, 'Is my life choice not valid?', thus transforming what has repeatedly been asserted into a negative question.

The exact repetition of the stock phrase 'valid life choice' is interesting because it explicitly includes the communicative level of the characters. Example 1 was firmly situated on the communicative level between the collective sender and the television audience, and there is no indication that anyone on the character level would be aware of the repetition and recontextualization that is taking place. Contrary to this, HT 111 illustrates that 'valid life choice' has become a mantra for the character Maddie, and that repetition is not only noticeable to the viewers but also part of the experiential knowledge of other characters. One way to interpret this is to say that, through repetition, this particular phrase becomes charged with humorous potential, which can then be exploited. At the same time, the act of repeating is itself emphasized; that is, it is established that Maddie's utterances are predictable also for the other characters. The incongruity in this case thus also rests on pragmatic principles of relevance, with repetition leading to a formulaicity that undermines the very validity of the life choice that is encoded in this phrase.

Repetition on the level of characters is also a way of representing some of the functions of repetition that have been observed in conversation (e.g. by Tannen 1989; Norrick 1987). These are affirmation through repetition and other-correction through partial lexical repetition as well as mockery through imitation. In what Goffman (1986/1974) calls *say-foring*, characters not only repeat multiple lexical items from another speaker, but do so by imitating or ventriloquizing their voice. While these repetitive practices are anchored on the character level, they are nonetheless constructed by the collective sender and serve mostly cohesive functions as they were described earlier, which is to say that they keep or render active a previously activated semantic frame in order to exploit it for (another) humorous instance.

The last function of lexical repetition that needs to be mentioned here is that of a call-back, that is, the speaking character referring back to an earlier humorous instance. This is illustrated in Example 3.

Example 3
Maddie talks to Ben about the advice she has given Casey.
HT 34   Maddie: Some quick thinking on my part. Told him it's always been Mia's dream to get engaged at the summer Olympics.
[…]
Casey kneels in front of Mia and reenacts his proposal with Maddie and Ben standing at the other side of the room as an audience.
HT 46   Casey: Mia, baby. I know it's not your dream proposal. It's not the summer Olympics.
                          ---turns around to look towards Maddie and nods conspiratorially----
[…]

Mia talks to Maddie in the kitchen.

HT 50   Mia: Not to <u>you</u>! I know you helped, and I cannot tell you how much I appreciate it. .hh although some of your ideas were a little whacky. Why did you say I thought the Olympics were romantic?

                                                    *   Casey

HT 34 creates an incongruity between Mia and Casey's engagement and the summer Olympics. This incongruity is simply repeated in HT 46 and explicitly referred back to in HT 50, which leads to two further humorous instances. Each of the three scenes and the repetition that occurs in them is framed as serious on the character level, which is to say that humour takes place solely on the sender-viewer level. While the repetition of HT 34 is not verbatim in the subsequent HTs, the example nonetheless shows all three HTs to be versions of the same humorous instance, which is achieved through lexical repetition both of the topic of the engagement, and of the incongruous element, the Olympics. In these cases it is then not just the premises that are repeated and exploited for humour several times, but the entire incongruity, which essentially means that the same joke is told three times.

On the level of characters, it can be added that this referring back to the previous mention of the same incongruity is encoded as an action that is consciously performed by the speaking character. In HT 46, this is achieved with a character gesture, in HT 50 it is encoded in Mia's utterance, when she asks Maddie an explicit question about her advice regarding the Olympics. Finally, it is noteworthy that on the character level, all three HTs are repetitions, since even HT 34 is framed as reported speech, with Maddie reporting to Ben what she has told Casey earlier. This first occurrence of humour in the story is however not part of the plot, that is, the television viewers do not actually get to see the scene all three HTs refer back to.

2.4.3 *Interturn structural parallelism*

Interturn structural parallelism, that is, a repetition of morphological and/or syntactical structure, is much rarer in the data and occurs in three different ways in the episode under investigation. In the first case, it co-occurs with lexical repetition and prosodic repetition, which together constitute the mockery of another character as it was described in the previous section.

Secondly, there are cases of structural repetition that serve functions in the represented interaction, and at the same time are cohesive insofar as they motivate the premise of the humorous instance, as Example 4 illustrates.

Example 4
At the restaurant, Mia is announcing her engagement to her parents, Vicky and Joel.

             Mia: Well, this isn't exactly the mood that I wanted to set, but, um, (.) .hh I'm getting married.
HT 101   Vicky: To who?
HT 102   Joel: Whom!

HT 103	Casey:	to ↑me:::::!
		---standing up---
HT 104	Casey:	to, I:::?
		---raises eyebrows---
		* Casey

As can be seen in this sequence of HTs, the topic of grammar, introduced earlier in the episode (HT 73–75), is exploited for humour. The role of structural parallelism in this case is to motivate the individual humorous instances by tying them in interactionally. The structure of the question in HT 101, 'to who?' is matched in HTs 103 and 104 in 'to me' and 'to I' respectively.

The third function of structural parallelism concerns the structuring of the represented speech production. In these cases, characters list several actions using the same syntactical structure and thus add to the cohesion of the scene. For instance, Ben tells Casey what he should avoid when meeting his future parents-in-law and does so by repeating a construction of the pattern *'don't' + [verb]*.

2.4.4 Interturn prosodic repetition

Another function that can be linked to representation of speech production is linked to interturn prosodic repetition. In a few HTs, the rhythm and stress patterns of the previous turn are repeated, and the respective HTs are thus characterized as instances of the same action or as separate steps in a clearly structured sequence of events.

Much more frequent, however, is prosodic repetition that is linked to characterization. As McIntyre (2014: 149) states, characterization refers to the way in which 'the personal qualities of the character in question as well as other aspects such as their social and physical characteristics' are established for the benefit of the readers, or in this case the viewers. The patterns of characterization have been studied extensively for plays by Culpeper (2001), and Bednarek (2012) offers a specific view of how characters in the sitcom *The Big Bang Theory* are constructed as nerds, which is done by associating them with selective attributes that fit nerd stereotypes. In a broad sense, the function prosodic repetition serves in characterization can again be captured by cohesion. The same character repeating the same prosodic patterns establishes consistency in linguistic behaviour and forms the impression in the viewers that this is the typical way in which the character talks, thus making it part of character identity and rendering it an affordance for the collective sender for the construction of humour. Repetition in this sense can be found for all main characters in *Better with You*, but is particularly striking for Casey, with the raised intonation in Example 4, HT 103 being a typical prosodic pattern that recurs and fits in with the character's explicit self-description as an oddball in this same episode.

2.4.5 Interturn repetition of facial expression

Characterization is also a key function for the interturn repetition of facial expressions, which often co-occur with prosodic repetition and mutually reinforce the typicality of represented character behaviour. Repeated facial expressions in the data appear to be exaggerated when compared to facial expressions that occur in spontaneous face-to-face interaction and are often incongruous simply because they do not fit the range of expressions that are typically associated with the respective frame. Related to this identification of characters is the more plot-driven function of character emotions, which are established and emphasized with repeated facial expressions that are motivated by the fictional events of the episode, but are exaggerated or ill-fitting in the context of the active frame.

2.4.6 Interturn telecinematic repetition

The final type of interturn repetition that could reliably be identified was telecinematic repetition. Camera work in a traditional multicamera sitcom like *Better with You* can be described as relatively unoriginal, which is to say that there is little in terms of angles or camera movements that would be striking enough that its recurrence would be registered as a form of repetition. However, the mise en scène, that is, the staged surroundings of the fictional characters and the way they are framed by them, is noticeable in many camera shots in the data. Even more so than was the case with repetition of facial expressions, the mise en scène tends to remain static over the period of an HT, which is why it is not surprising that no repetition of this kind occurs in the data intraturn.

Across turns, however, telecinematic repetition is frequent. One of the ways in which it occurs is to do with the juxtaposition of the three couples that are at the heart of the first episode and this sitcom more generally. For instance, the early HTs – HT 1, HT 4 and HT 5 – all show the windscreen of a typical yellow New York taxi, with the driver visible on the right side of the picture and one of the three couples sitting side by side on the rear seats. The noticeable similarity in situation established by this example of telecinematic repetition is contrasted in this case with three parallel but very different conversations that are juxtaposed in a crosscutting sequence and thus telecinematically constructed as occurring at the same time. While the most obvious use of the mise en scène is as a cue for television audiences to allow them to recognize where a particular scene takes place, it is also used to establish visual parallelism between different shots. The functions of telecinematic repetition can thus be summarized as either simply establishing narrative continuity and thus cohesion between individual HTs, which also serves to keep active a particular frame that can be exploited for humour, or as highlighting a similarity on one level that is contrasted with difference on another – thus reinforcing the incongruousness of a particular ill-fitting element.

2.4.7 Interturn character gesture repetition and semantic repetition

Before turning to the discussion of intraturn repetition, two additional types of interturn repetition need to be discussed here. First of these is character gesture repetition, which occurs frequently but turned out to be an unreliable category in this case study. The reason for this is likely the subjectivity of what gestures are similar enough to be considered recurrences of previous gestures. The definition of this category in the codebook was adapted multiple times in different cycles of coding, which improved interrater agreement to 66.7 per cent and 70 per cent, respectively. While a study on repetition in sitcoms does not warrant a more detailed subcategorization of character gestures, this seems an interesting avenue for research in its own right, and it seems likely that particular head movements, hand gestures, arm movements, and so on could be distinguished more reliably if analysed separately. For the purposes of this study, however, I will omit character gesture repetition as a separate category, while assuming that it contributes to aspects of characterization and character emotion as they have been discussed before.

The second type of repetition that I have neglected so far in the data analysis is semantic repetition. Initial views of the data showed that semantic repetition, that is, the repetition of ideas or repetition referring to the same referent, did indeed occur frequently. The categorization during pretests revealed, however, that in this broad sense, semantic repetition was present in all HT. Accordingly, it is more useful for this study to discuss semantic repetition as a general feature of sitcoms and sitcom humour rather than as an aspect that can be present or absent in individual HTs, while a more in-depth qualitative analysis of individual instances of semantic repetition needs to be done in a separate study.

2.4.8 *Intraturn lexical repetition*

Intraturn repetition is limited to the space of the individual turn and can therefore not directly contribute to text cohesion. This also means that it can be discussed on the basis of the individual HT, in which all repeated occurrences are situated by definition. A first important use of intraturn repetition in the data is for reasons of emphasis, and in particular emphatic reinforcement of a frame or of the incongruous element, that is, one of the two key elements involved in the construction of humour. Typically, this effect is achieved by employing lexical repetition, as is the case in Examples 5 and 6:

Example 5
At the restaurant, Ben has just shaken hands with Casey who he is meeting for the first time.

HT 19   Ben: Oh-hoh tough- tough? I'm not tough. uhuhuhm I mean, I work out a little.

Example 6
Casey offers to reenact his proposal to Mia for Maddie and Ben.

HT 44   Maddie: Oh no. no, no. it's really okay.

Ben is characterized in the series as a white-collar character who likes crossword puzzles rather than physical activity. In HT 19 (Example 5), he responds to Casey – who addressed him as 'tough guy' – by echoing the term 'tough' and repeating it twice more. Humour in this example hinges on the juxtaposition of salient aspects of Ben's personality, which are also encoded in his physical appearance, with the notion of toughness. In this case, lexical repetition has the purpose of unmistakeably communicating the concept of toughness in order to emphasize the contrast between strength and weakness on which this HT rests.

Example 5 also serves as another illustration of the importance of the distinction of communicative levels. On the level between collective sender and television audience, humour is the goal, and repetition serves an emphatic function. On the character level, on the other hand, the individual instances of lexical repetition are plausible because they have an identifiable function within the represented dialogue. Whereas Ben's first iteration of 'tough', repeated from Casey's 'tough guy', acknowledges the attribute, the second instance uttered with question intonation doubts it, and the third instance rejects the complement: 'I'm not tough.'

Similarly, Example 6 shows Maddie's reaction in HT 44 to Casey's offer of reenacting the proposal, with the repetition of the word 'no' amounting to an overly clear refusal. Here, too, the main function is emphasis – in this case the overly emphatic refusal of the offer – which is motivated by the experiential, privileged knowledge shared by the television viewers and Maddie. Contrary to Casey, the viewers and Maddie know that the performance of that proposal was informed by insincere advice. This piece of advice in turn was given in an attempt to prevent the couple from an overly hasty commitment to marriage. As is the case in Example 6, emphasis is often the function of intraturn lexical repetition. In other cases, this emphasis serves the reinforcement of the active frame and premise for humour, much like was observed for lexical repetition across turns.

One function of repetition observed in the literature in connection to humour is that of punning and more generally of wordplay. Interestingly, this use of repetition is largely absent from the first episode of *Better with You*. In fact, there is only one such instance in the data, and it is marked by subsequent turns as unsuccessful humour.

Example 7
Ben gives advice to Casey.

HT 77	Ben:	Uh:, let's see. call them 'Mr. and Mrs. Putney', .h even though they'll say, 'call us whatever.' oh, an- an- and don't try and make a joke and actually call them 'whatever'.
HT 78	Casey:	Why would I do that?
HT 79	Casey:	That's stupid.

In Example 7, the character Ben reports how he exploited the ambiguity in the utterance 'call us whatever' for a joke (HT 77). This form of wordplay subsequently receives a negative evaluation by Casey (HTs 78 and 79), and several humorous instances are constructed based on the assumption that Ben's attempt at a humorous reply can be interpreted as an unsuccessful joke.

2.4.9 Intraturn structural parallelism and prosodic repetition

When it comes to repetitive patterns within individual turns, structural parallelism and prosodic repetition are frequent and often occur together. Eleven of the sixteen occurrences of intraturn structural parallelism are accompanied by prosodic repetition, and three of the remaining five instances are accompanied by lexical repetition.

A first function of this kind of repetition is similar to what has been discussed for interturn repetition: Repetition establishes a list and the items of the list are identified as part of the same group through similarity in syntactic form. This list then serves as the premise for humour. Either the pattern is established with two similar instances using structural or prosodic repetition and then broken with variation that creates the incongruity; or the pattern is established and broken at the same time, in the sense that while it is structurally identical, this repetition is contrasted with opposition on the level of meaning.

Example 8
In a taxi, Ben and Maddie talk about Mia's new boyfriend Casey whom they are about to meet for the first time.

	Maddie:	I know, baby, I know. But I have a good feeling. My sister says he's totally different from other guys she's dated.
HT 6	Ben:	↑Yeah, but she said the same thing about <u>Nate</u>. and <u>Mike</u>. (.) and <u>Em</u>ma.

As Toolan (2016: 25) states, repetition can be regarded as 'the source of patterning'. Even within short HTs, presenting two similar and one different unit is a way of stressing the incongruity between the established pattern and the different last item. Example 8 shows this function based on prosodic repetition. In HT 6, Ben talks about Mia's former partners, and prosodically establishes a pattern by alternating non-stressed syllables in prepositions and conjunctions with the stressed one-syllable names Nate and Mike. The third item of the list is separated with a pause and is different in terms of phonology. This prosodic repetition emphasizes the similarity of the first two items of the list, which are two typical male names, and their difference to the final name, which is typically female. Thus, the expectations already in place because of societal norms as well as due to the shared experience of the viewers with the character Mia, namely that Ben will now provide a list of male names, are reinforced by the first two names, whose similarity is established as a pattern with the help of prosodic repetition. The final item runs counter to expectations and is thus incongruous and the trigger for the intended humorous effect on the television audience.

Example 9
Maddie tells Ben how she thinks she dissuaded Casey from proposing too soon.

HT 34	Maddie:	Some quick thinking on my part. told him it's always been Mia's dream to get engaged at the summer Olympics.
	Maddie:	So he'll have to wait till the next ones in 2012. Stuff like that.
HT 35	Ben:	So <u>quick</u> thinking. (.) not <u>good</u> thinking.

In HT 35 in Example 9, Ben repeats the noun phrase *[adjective]+'thinking'*, which emphasizes the fact that he is contrasting two different types of thinking. The similarity in structure thus serves to highlight the contrast in meaning, which in turn reinforces the incongruity on which humour is based here.

Prosodic repetitiveness often also leads to a noticeable rhythmicality in the respective character utterance. In Example 10, the mother's reaction to learning about her youngest daughter's surprise engagement is positive, which is emphasized by the rhythm established through prosodic repetition. As was mentioned for structural parallelism, prosodic repetition is also often accompanied by repetition on another level. Thus, in Example 10, Vicky not only stresses every other syllable but nods her head in the same rhythm and further reinforces the established pattern.

Example 10
Vicky reacts to the news of Mia's and Casey's wedding.
HT 107   Vicky: There's going to be a   wedding.
                    $-nods-$ $-nods-$ $-nods-$
                                             $ Vicky

On the character level, this form of rhythmic stress emphasizes the represented character emotion, which in this case runs counter to the (inferred) expectations of the other characters and to viewer expectations. Viewers at this point must base their expectations on the projections of the daughters about their mother and thus are likely to expect a negative reaction to the news of the engagement. In other examples, excitement is similarly encoded in rapid repetition of stress patterns.

2.4.10 *Intraturn repetition of facial expressions*

Intraturn repetition of facial expressions is substantially less frequent in the data than its interturn counterpart. When I have stated in Section 2.4.9 that intraturn prosodic repetition and structural parallelism often occur together, this tendency of cooccurrence with other types of repetition is even clearer in the case of intraturn repetition of facial expressions, and there are no cases in this episode where it would occur on its own. In fact, based on this case study the function of a repeated facial expression must be rendered as reinforcing the repetitiveness of the utterances it accompanies. For the most part repetition of this type co-occurs with either intraturn prosodic repetition or intraturn structural parallelism or both (ten out of eleven instances). In the only other case, it reinforces repetition on the lexical level.

3 Discussion

The presentation and discussion of occurrences of different types of repetition in the humorous turns (HTs) of the first episode of *Better with You* has demonstrated first of all that repetition is very frequent in this episode of an US American sitcom. This holds true even when purely semantic repetition is disregarded and only formal repetition is included; that is, when linguistic, paralinguistic and nonlinguistic signifiers on the surface of the multimodal text are repeated. It can further be hypothesized based on the data analysed here that sitcoms with a laugh track in general, of which *Better with You* is an example, will also make frequent use of repetition to construct HTs. However, this hypothesis will have to be verified on a larger dataset. Moreover, the analysis has shown how different types of repetition contribute to the construction of humour, which was understood as the result of incongruity and resolution (Suls 1972).

The method of analysis has distinguished between two general loci of repetition, which can be linked to the distance between repeated occurrences: Whereas interturn repetition refers to repetition across greater distances in the text – at least from one conversational turn to the next, but potentially from any earlier moment in the same episode – intraturn repetition refers to locally repeated occurrences within the same, often very short, turn. This distinction in the categorization also mirrored a difference in functions for TCD humour that will be discussed further in Sections 3.1 and 3.2.

3.1 Functions of interturn repetition in sitcom humour

In the case of interturn repetition in HTs, humour cohesion has been shown to be one key function of lexical repetition, and of exact single-word repetition in particular. This matches the understanding that lexical repetition in general is a key contributor to text cohesion (Halliday and Hasan 1976; Toolan 2016). In the case of the HTs analysed here, cohesive lexical repetition often serves to reactivate a frame that was introduced earlier in the episode and can be used later as the premise for further humorous instances. As a consequence, individual HTs and the audiovisual text in general appear to be connected, which also means that the fictional story appears to be coherent rather than a series of only loosely linked jokes. This property of sitcoms is already an important factor when it comes to characterizing them as a genre of humorous text, since other popular comedy and humour genres are different in this regard. Stand-up comedians, for instance, do of course connect their punch lines, but generally their overall routines are far less cohesive than the comparatively closed narratives of sitcom episodes; and jokes, the traditional objects of humour research, while cohesive, are typically far less complex in their structure simply because of their brevity. It seems to be characteristic for telecinematic humour, on the other hand, that it is constructed by creating humorous instances that work individually, but at the same time are cohesively linked to one or several previous humorous instances. Thus, one important effect of interturn repetition is that it is instrumental in establishing cohesion as well as coherence of the humorous text and the humour therein.

Apart from the cohesive effects, which also motivate the individual humorous instances diegetically, there is also a link to economical joke telling. Establishing viewer expectations takes time, and given the fact that in this case 149 HTs occur within twenty-two minutes, finding shortcuts to activating the desired frame are key for the collective sender. In this sense, reactivation of a frame and variation of the incongruous element is one successful strategy to create new incongruities and thus new instances of humour in an economical fashion.

When it comes to repetition as part of the incongruous element rather than the active frame, the example of the stock phrase 'valid life choice' demonstrates how a phrase can become charged with humorous potential. However, the close examination of each case of this type of lexical repetition shows on the one hand that the same incongruous element can recur in different situations and following different expectations: Incongruous elements remain surprising despite their repetition, because the moment in which they occur is unexpected for the television viewers. On the other hand, humour in these cases does not depend just on the phrase as such but also on the very fact that it is being repeated and becomes formulaic, which in the case presented here was rooted on the character level. For characters and viewers alike, repetition itself is in this case incongruous with their expectations because it does not fit conversational norms.

Other, less frequent functions of interturn repetition in sitcom humour include imitating and mocking other characters, as well as call-backs to humorous instances made before – that is, cases of repetition where both the frame and the incongruous element are repeated. These latter cases pose a challenge to the incongruity-based understanding of humour because they essentially amount to the retelling of the same joke, and should therefore no longer surprise audiences and thus result in an unsuccessful attempt at humour. The methodology used here does not allow an answer as to whether these repeated incongruities do indeed fail to amuse the viewers. However, the audience laughter does mark them as intended to be humorous, and we must assume therefore that the collective sender trusts for them to be just as successful at producing a humorous effect on the audience as any other of the humorous instances. One possible explanation for some cases is metahumour, which is to say that in these cases humour does not depend on the apparent incongruity of the utterance of the character, for example between romance and the summer Olympics (see Example 3), but on the way in which that repetition is framed. For instance, in HT 46 in Example 3, it seems that the presented discrepancy in knowledge between the two characters is crucial for the humorous incongruity. The data analysed here has only provided few examples of this kind, and this interaction of repetition and humour needs to be examined in more detail elsewhere.

While these functions were mostly observed for lexical repetition and to a lesser extent for structural parallelism, interturn prosodic repetition is often motivated by characterization. Repeated prosody establishes typical intonation patterns for the major characters. These prosodic aspects are sometimes reinforced by repeated facial expressions; they become part of the typical behaviour of the character and are then used repeatedly as an incongruous reaction to different situations. In terms of the mechanism by which incongruities are constructed, prosodic repetition thus operates similarly to the stock phrases mentioned earlier, which is to say that the repetitive intonation patterns maintain their humour potential because they are juxtaposed with different frames.

Finally, telecinematic repetition is used to establish a similarity between individual scenes and HTs, which is typically done by repeating aspects of the mise en scène. Repetition of this type often suggests a similarity between the situation in which characters find themselves, which is used in contrast with differences that are encoded on a different level. In other words, the similarity in the scene established by interturn telecinematic repetition highlights the incongruity in character behaviour and utterances.

3.2 Functions of intraturn repetition in sitcom humour

The functions of intraturn repetition in sitcom humour are different because they are confined to the individual HT and thus not directly connected to overall humour cohesion in an episode. One function of intraturn repetition concerns emphasis of the active frame, which essentially ensures that audience expectations are aligned with the design of the humorous instance and trigger the incongruity-resolution processing that may lead to successful humour uptake. As such, this function of intraturn lexical repetition can be understood as a humour-specific realization of the capacity of repetition to facilitate comprehension (see Norrick 1987; Tannen 1989). In other cases, intraturn repetition also represents some of the functions that are usually associated with repetition in conversation, for instance when lexical repetition functions as a confirmation, or when the syntactical structure of an answer matches that of the question, which serves both interactional and interpersonal functions as they were described by Tannen (1989).

Key to the construction of humour is the way in which intraturn structural parallelism establishes a pattern through repetition. In some cases, this pattern leads to expectations of continuation, which the subsequent stimulus does not meet, thus creating an incongruity. In other cases, these processes happen simultaneously, but on different levels; for example while the repetitive syntactical structure establishes similarity, there is at the same time incongruity on the semantic level. This is similar to how telecinematic repetition is used across turns.

While character identities are established over time, and thus with the help of interturn rather than intraturn repetition, structural and prosodic intraturn repetition often occur together to encode and highlight a particular character emotion, which is exaggerated or does not fit the frame in which it occurs. This highlighting of affective character reactions is often supported by repetition of facial expressions. Generally, facial expressions are repeated within HTs only when repetition also occurs on another level. The main function of this form of multimodal repetition within turns thus seems to be to reinforce the repetitiveness in character behaviour as well as the functions of the other type(s) of repetition it accompanies.

4 Conclusion

This study has provided evidence from the first episode of *Better with You* for the range of different types of repetition that are employed in the construction of incongruities and thus of humour. It has linked these cases of repetition to different functions, which was done based on the discussion of selected examples and by linking these observations to the functions of repetition in texts and conversation as they have been observed in previous research. These findings and their discussion show on the one hand that repetition in sitcoms can be theorized based on a combination of existing textual and conversational research, which means that sitcoms and TCD more generally need to be understood as multilevel and multimodal texts that need to be conceptualized both as a form of represented face-to-face interaction and as a mediated form of communication between a collective sender and an audience. On the other hand, humour in TCD also needs to be regarded separately and with a focus on its typical features that distinguish it from other humorous texts as they are more commonly studied in humour research.

Apart from the individual HTs that were analysed here, some further observations can be made for repetition in this episode of a sitcom more generally. For starters, semantic repetition, which was only discussed marginally here, appears to be omnipresent in sitcom humour. The functions of lexical repetition that were analysed here can thus be regarded as a small subset of a more general pattern of motivating individual humorous incongruities by tying the active frame to others that were previously activated or by reiterating the same semantic incongruity in a new context. Moreover, one key aspect of repetition in general is the overall rhythm it creates. Looking at the entire episode from a distance, its structure resembles that of a HT that employs structural and prosodic repetition: audience laughter, occurring every 6.5 seconds on average, serves as punctuation to the series, with a few longer gaps between laughs (upward of 20 seconds) serving as caesurae, whereas at other points short HTs with gaps between laughter of sometimes less than a second form rhythmic clusters. Such larger patterns based on the repetition of humorous instances themselves as well as the complex construction of entire sitcom scenes out of interturn and intraturn repetition of different types need to be examined based on a larger corpus of sitcom data. A larger study of this sort will also provide further evidence that can corroborate the findings of this case study on *Better with You* and offer more assertive answers to the question how sitcoms and TCD in general construct humorous instances with the help of multimodal and multilevel repetition.

In terms of these larger structures, one final function of repetition in sitcom humour that needs to be mentioned in closing here is that of maintaining the play frame. The frequent occurrences of HTs serve as a constant flow of communication from the collective sender to the television viewers that they, like the recorded studio audience they hear, are meant to laugh at the interactions that are staged for them onscreen. The sitcom episode as an audiovisual text thus also reinforces its humorousness by repeatedly communicating its own humorous intentions.

Appendix. Transcription conventions (based on Jefferson 2004; Mondada 2014)

[ ]	overlapping speech
(.)	gap between utterances
.hh	audible breathing
___	Stress
:	indicates lengthening of the previous sound
↑↓	shift to high or low pitch
. , ? !	punctuation indicates usual intonation
* ± § ^	symbols to identify participants
----	delimits action/facial expression by participant
*---->	action continues on subsequent line(s)
----*	action ends
HT 34	numbers in left-hand column list humorous turns in the data sequentially from 1–149.

Notes

1 In their seminal General Theory of Verbal Humour (GTVH), Attardo and Raskin (1991) speak of script opposition to describe the same clash between frames.
2 Apart from the term *other-repetition* (used, for example, by Tannen 1987), the repetition of another speaker's utterance (or an element thereof) is also referred to as *allo-repetition* (e.g. Tannen 1989) or *second-speaker repetition* (e.g. Norrick 1987).
3 Transcription conventions are presented in the appendix. As a general rule, only those aspects were transcribed which are directly relevant to the subsequent discussion of repetition and humour in each case.

References

Aitchison, J. (1994), '"Say, say it again Sam": The treatment of repetition in linguistics', *SPELL: Swiss Papers in English Language and Literature*, 7: 15–34.
Attardo, S. (1994), *Linguistic Theories of Humor*, Berlin: de Gruyter.
Attardo, S. (2001), *Humorous Texts: A Semantic and Pragmatic Analysis*, Berlin: Mouton de Gruyter.
Attardo, S. and Raskin, V. (1991), 'Script theory revis(it)ed: Joke similarity and joke representation model', *Humor*, 4 (3/4): 293–347.
Bateson, G. (1953), 'The position of humor in human communication', in H. von Foerster (ed.), *Cybernetics Ninth Conference*, 1–25, New York: Josiah Macy Jr. Foundation.
Bateson, G. (1972), 'A theory of play and fantasy', in *Steps to an Ecology of Mind: Collected Essays in Anthropology, Psychiatry, Evolution, and Epistemology*, 177–93, Chicago: University of Chicago Press. (Reprinted from *Psychiatric research reports*, 1955)
Bednarek, M. (2012), 'Constructing "nerdiness": Characterisation in The Big Bang Theory', *Multilingua*, 31 (2–3): 199–229. Available at: https://doi.org/10.1515/multi-2012-0010.
Brock, A. (2004), *Blackadder, Monty Python und Red Dwarf: Eine Linguistische Untersuchung Britischer Fernsehkomödien*, Tübingen: Stauffenburg.
Brock, A. (2015), 'Participation frameworks and participation in televised sitcom, candid camera and stand-up comedy', in M. Dynel and J. Chovanec (eds), *Participation in Public and Social Media Interactions*, 27–47, Amsterdam: John Benjamins. Available at: https://doi.org/10.1075/pbns.256.02bro.
Chlopicki, W. (1987), *An Application of the Script Theory of Semantics to the Analysis of Selected Polish Humorous Short Stories* (M.A. Thesis). West Lafayette, Indiana: Purdue University.
Coates, J. (2007), 'Talk in a play frame: More on laughter and intimacy', *Journal of Pragmatics*, 39 (1): 29–49. Available at: https://doi.org/10.1016/j.pragma.2006.05.003.
Culpeper, J. (2001), *Language and Characterisation: People in Plays and Other Texts*, Harlow: Longman.
Dynel, M. (2011a), '"I'll be there for you!" On participation-based sitcom humour', in M. Dynel (ed.), *The Pragmatics of Humour across Discourse Domains*, 311–33, Amsterdam: John Benjamins.
Dynel, M. (2011b), '"You talking to me?" The viewer as a ratified listener to film discourse', *Journal of Pragmatics*, 43 (6): 1628–44. Available at: https://doi.org/10.1016/j.pragma.2010.11.016.
Dynel, M. (2013), 'A view on humour theory', in M. Dynel (ed.), *Developments in Linguistic Humour Theory*, vii–xiv, Amsterdam: John Benjamins.

Ermida, I. (2008), *The Language of Comic Narratives*, Berlin: Mouton de Gruyter. Available at: http://doi.org/10.4324/9780203210000.

Fillmore, C. J. (2006), 'Frame semantics', in D. Geeraerts (ed.), *Cognitive Linguistics: Basic Readings*, 373–400, Berlin: Mouton de Gruyter.

Forabosco, G. (2008), 'Is the concept of incongruity still a useful construct for the advancement of humor research?', *Lodz Papers in Pragmatics*, 4 (1): 45–62. Available at: https://doi.org/10.2478/v10016-008-0003-5.

Goffman, E. (1986), *Frame Analysis: An Essay on the Organization of Experience*, Boston: Northeastern University Press. (Original work published 1974)

Gregory, M. (1967), 'Aspects of varieties differentiation', *Journal of Linguistics*, 3 (2): 177–98.

Halliday, M. A. K. and Hasan, R. (1976), *Cohesion in English*, London: Longman.

Hoffmann, C. (2012), *Cohesive Profiling*, Amsterdam: John Benjamins.

Jefferson, G. (2004), 'Glossary of transcript symbols with an introduction', in G. H. Lerner (ed.), *Conversation Analysis: Studies from the First Generation*, 13–31, Amsterdam: John Benjamins.

Johnstone, B. (1987), 'An introduction', *Text*, 7 (3): 205–14. Available at: https://doi.org/10.1007/978-1-4020-8021-0_1.

Johnstone, B. (1994), 'Repetition in discourse: A dialogue', in B. Johnstone (ed.), *Repetition in Discourse: Interdisciplinary Perspectives, Volume One*, 1–20, Norwood: Ablex.

Keith-Spiegel, P. (1972), 'Early conceptions of humor: Varieties and issues', in J. H. Goldstein and P. E. McGhee (eds), *The Psychology of Humor: Theoretical Perspectives and Empirical Issues*, 4–39, New York: Academic Press.

Kim, H. (2002), 'The form and function of next-turn repetition in English conversation', *Language Research*, 38 (1): 51–81. Available at: http://s-space.snu.ac.kr/bitstream/10371/86198/1/3. 2225610.pdf.

Lichtkoppler, J. (2007), '"Male. Male". – "Male?" – "The sex is male". – The role of repetition in English as a lingua franca conversations', *Vienna English Working Papers*, 16 (1): 39–65.

Marszalek, A. (2013), '"It's not funny out of context!": A cognitive stylistic approach to humorous narratives', in M. Dynel (ed.), *Developments in Linguistic Humour Theory*, 393–421, Amsterdam: John Benjamins.

McIntyre, D. (2014), 'Characterisation', in P. Stockwell and S. Whiteley (eds), *The Cambridge Handbook of Stylistics*, 149–64, Cambridge: Cambridge University Press.

Messerli, T. C. (2016), 'Extradiegetic and character laughter as markers of humorous intentions in the sitcom 2 Broke Girls', *Journal of Pragmatics*, 95: 79–92. Available at: https://doi.org/10.1016/j.pragma.2015.12.009.

Messerli, T. C. (2017), 'Participation structure in fictional discourse: Authors, scriptwriters, audiences and characters', in M. A. Locher and A. H. Jucker (eds), *Pragmatics of Fiction: Handbooks of Pragmatics, vol. 12*, 25–54, Berlin: Mouton de Gruyter.

Mondada, L. (2014), *Conventions for Multimodal Transcription* [online]. Available at: https://franz.unibas.ch/fileadmin/franz/user_upload/ redaktion/Mondada_conv_multimodality.pdf (accessed 2 July 2015).

Morreall, J. (1983), *Taking Laughter Seriously*, Albany: State University of New York Press.

Norrick, N. R. (1987), 'Functions of repetition in conversation', *Text*, 7 (3): 245–64. Available at: https://doi.org/10.1515/text.1.1987.7.3.245.

Norrick, N. R. (1993), 'Repetition in canned jokes and spontaneous conversational joking', *Humor*, 6 (4): 385–402. Available at: https://doi.org/10.1515/humr.1993.6.4.385.

Norrick, N. R. (1994), 'Repetition as a conversational joking strategy', in B. Johnstone (ed.), *Repetition in Discourse: Interdisciplinary Perspectives, Volume Two*, 15–28, Norwood: Ablex.

Norrick, N. R. (1996), 'Repetition in conversational joking', in C. Bazzanella (ed.), *Repetition in Dialogue*, 129–40, Tübingen: Niemeyer.

Piazza, R., Bednarek, M. and Rossi, F. (2011), 'Introduction: Analysing telecinematic discourse', in R. Piazza, M. Bednarek and F. Rossi (eds), *Telecinematic Discourse: Approaches to the Language of Films and Television Series*, 1–17, Amsterdam: John Benjamins.

Simpson, M. (2010), *My Experience at a Taping for Better with You* [online]. Available at: https://hollywoodthewriteway.com/2010/09/my-experience-at-taping-for-better-with.html (accessed 20 December 2016).

Stokoe, E. (2008), 'Dispreferred actions and other interactional breaches as devices for occasioning audience laughter in television "sitcoms"', *Social Semiotics*, 18 (3): 289–307. Available at: http://doi.org/10.1080/10350330802217071.

Suls, J. M. (1972), 'A two-stage model for the appreciation of jokes and cartoons: An information-processing analysis', in J. H. Goldstein and P. E. McGhee (eds), *The Psychology of Humor: Theoretical Perspectives and Empirical Issues*, 81–100, New York: Academic Press.

Tannen, D. (1987), 'Repetition in conversation: Toward a poetics of talk', *Language*, 63 (3): 574–605.

Tannen, D. (1989), *Talking Voices: Repetition, Dialogue, and Imagery in Conversational Discourse*, Cambridge: Cambridge University Press.

Toolan, M. (2014), 'Stylistics and film', in M. Burke (ed.), *The Routledge Handbook of Stylistics*, 455–70, New York: Routledge.

Toolan, M. (2016), *Making Sense of Narrative Text*, New York: Routledge.

Urios-Aparisi, E. and Wagner, M. (2011), 'Prosody of humor in sex and the city', *Pragmatics and Cognition*, 19 (3): 507–29. Available at: https://doi.org/10.1075/pc.19.3.06uri.

Veale, T. (2004), 'Incongruity in humor: Root cause or epiphenomenon?', *Humor*, 17 (4): 419–28.

Television series

Goldberg-Meehan, S. and Burrows, J., Dir. (2011), 'Pilot', in S. Goldberg-Meehan (Creator), *Better with You*, Los Angeles: ABC.

5

Ideology in the multimodal discourse of television documentaries on Irish travellers' and gypsies' communities in the UK

Roberta Piazza

1 Introduction

This chapter investigates the portrayal of the minority community of travellers and gypsies in a sample of factual films broadcast on public and commercial television.[1] Like for many other scholars, for Blommaert (2005), who emphasizes the importance of contextualization in Critical Discourse Analysis (CDA), no text is ideology-free. This is certainly true for such complex texts as television documentaries, which through a combination of narrative and interviews, along with embedded footage and visual images, purport to offer a seemingly balanced and neutral account of some issues, when, in fact, they convey a specific view through an ideological discourse (Piazza, Bednarek and Rossi 2015). The discussion concentrates on the 'representation' in documentaries, understood as a non-transparent and non-objective 'mediating' process 'whereby an event (…) filtered through interpretive frameworks (…), acquires ideological significance' (Poole 2002: 23). The chapter highlights how the linguistic and visual choices in these films create a 'subjective representation' of the reality of these groups, which is offered to the viewers as a set of 'objective beliefs and perceptions' (Bhatia 2015: 1–2).

Following on from previous research (Piazza, Bednarek and Rossi 2015), this study categorizes documentaries as films that are a complex amalgam of three distinct text genres, namely expository, argumentative and instructive (Hatim and Mason 1990). Most documentaries are hybrids between an expository and an argumentative text; as factual films, they seemingly present and discuss an issue with the clear objective of informing viewers, but, as they do so, they develop a 'claim' of a particular kind and express a specific stance. In line with Pollak (2008: 80), the study attempts to answer the following questions by analysing mainly the verbal discourses in the three selected documentaries but with some consideration of the visual level:

1. What perspective does the documentary endorse and which does it hide or minimize?

2. What values are upheld in the topics discussed/investigated?
3. How are the social actors presented, in this case travellers and settled residents?
4. How is the credibility of the documentary established?

The three documentaries, which were broadcast on British television over a two-year period, all report on the disenfranchised and marginal communities of travellers and gypsies. They are as follows: *The Town the Travellers Took Over* was broadcast by the commercial Channel 5 in July 2013; *My Life: Children of the Road* (henceforth *Children*) appeared on public BBC One in May 2011; and *Gypsy Eviction: The Fight for Dale Farm* (henceforth *Eviction*) was shown on Channel 4 in September 2011. Given the documentaries' diverse perspectives on the topic, the study is intended as an initial reflection on the ideological aspects of representation of the chosen groups. While they all focus on the same mobile communities, the three documentaries' sub-topics, styles and functions (Corner 2002) are markedly different. *Eviction* is a piece of hard-news reportage about the then-impending forced closure of Dale Farm, the biggest travellers' site in England; *Children* is a piece of social journalism that reflects on the condition of travellers' children in the same site; finally, *The Town the Travellers Took Over* is an example of classic investigative journalism, in this instance focusing on an international scam by a travellers' gang who sold faulty generators across Europe.[2]

A brief synopsis of the documentaries will make it easier for the reader to understand the analysis. *Eviction* follows the demise of the biggest campsite in England where the travellers having bought a piece of green belt land adjoining a legal site, illegally built their homes. The dramatic story ended in the site's violent eviction, but the documentary follows the stages prior to that event when the travellers and a massive number of supporters attempted a negotiation with the authorities. *Children* explores the life of Dale Farm children, their games, beliefs, traumatic memories, aspirations and through their voices we learn about the travellers' community at large and above all how these young adults are often victims of discrimination by permanent residents. *The Town the Travellers Took Over* starts from the story of Rathkeale – a quiet town in Ireland that has become the Mecca for travellers who are trying, we are told, to purchase all the properties and slowly push out the original residents. The film explains the provenance of the travellers' wealth by tracing a gypsy gang who have set up an international scam selling faulty generators and operating throughout Europe and as far as Australia. Although TV documentaries are often produced by independent film makers and journalists, most of them are specifically commissioned by television networks (Lichtenstein 2015). While they cannot be taken as directly reflecting the views and values of a specific network, they necessarily take into account its political leanings and, in part, adapt to its style of delivery (with regard, for instance, to film segmentation in view of commercial breaks). This chapter, therefore, also reflects on how although they are not the direct product of the network that broadcasts them, the three factual films are relatively in synchrony with the television network's character. More specifically, the films broadcast by the public providers, BBC One and Channel 4, greatly differ from the documentary on Channel 5 which is 'a commercial operation [directed to] a young target audience, and, consequently, tends to adopt a more populist approach' (Gaber et al., 2016: 638). Finally, the three documentaries are one off, stand-alone films therefore their choice of angle and topic is much more crucial than it is in the case of a series in which different aspects of the gypsy communities can be shown each time (an example being Channel 5's *The Truth about Travellers* and BBC One Scotland's *The Travellers*, cf. Piazza, Bednarek and Rossi 2015).

The study focuses primarily on the role of the authorial voice of the documentary narrator that overarches and orchestrates the various voices within the film. Following that, the questions posed by the interviewer are considered in detail and reference is made to the concepts of a documentary's credibility and authoritativeness interpreted as the means through which television journalists validate the representation they offer of the travellers' communities. Finally, some attention is paid to the visuals in the documentaries' trailers.

2 Context: The community of travellers and gypsies

In the present time of diaspora and mobility, travellers and gypsies are still treated with a great deal of suspicion by settled people (Kabachnik 2009), stigmatized (Powell 2008), exoticized[3] or, more generally, excluded or 'othered' (Holloway 2005). Travellers is the generic name for the Irish nomadic community investigated in this study, but it also refers to English, Welsh and Scottish mobile people. Gypsy, often in association with the qualifier Romany, is the other synonymous term that defines such itinerant groups who have no permanent residence as they choose to change location on a fairly continuous basis. In the past, they led a life in tune with nature, selling their trade and services as they moved from place to place. As a consequence of their lifestyle, however, they have fallen behind the times often remaining illiterate, trapped in a patriarchal family structure strongly supported by a communitarian non-capitalist life style in which solidarity among the community members has a major role especially with regard to the raising of children. Nowadays, however, travellers appreciate the value of education for their families. Some also accept to be housed and are happy to live in permanent sites but others choose to remain fully or partially mobile. Ideally, a traveller family would gladly limit travelling to the summer months and be sedentary during school time in their caravan parked in a campsite.

Travellers' relation to a continuously redefined place is crucial to a proper understanding of their group identity (Piazza and Fasulo 2014). Their immediate space is the caravan in which they invest most of their financial resources. Beyond the caravan is the encampment or site; this can be authorized, rent-based and serviced by the local Councils (that provide gas, electricity, communal toilets and showers), or non-authorized when travellers occupy for short periods parks and other green areas in and around mostly urban centres. Travellers are constantly evicted from these illegal spaces so their relationship with settled society is generally through law enforcement. The problem lies in the shortage of living arrangements for these communities who, according to the 2011 Population Census, totalled 54,895 people in England.

In the UK, Travellers, Gypsies and Roma or Romanies are a threatened community, with ethnic minority status (TGR); most people do not have any substantive contacts with them and generally hold very negative opinions and attitudes towards them, because they are regarded as being antisocial and parasitic in various ways including their untidiness and engagement with theft. The media, therefore, have an important role in the representation of this community as they could potentially increase the knowledge of relatively very large TV audiences concerning these marginal groups. Yet, at least in the case of television, the travellers' community is invariably covered only if some major event or incident makes the news, as in the case of the eviction of Dale Farm, the biggest illegal site in Essex, England. Generally television encourages negative stereotyping by portraying travellers and gypsies as exotic circus creatures good for entertainment (as in the *Big Fat Gypsy Wedding*, Channel 4, famous for its rococo' clothes galore), or violent brawlers or crooks (as in *The Travellers' Secret Cash Stash*, Channel 5).

The three documentaries under scrutiny rely on specific 'categorizations' (Sarangi and Candlin 2003) of the traveller and gypsy communities. Categories serve as 'spectacles through which we routinely, albeit largely unconsciously, observe and classify events and experiences' (Sarangi and Candlin 2003: 117). In this instance, Irish travellers are categorized as groups engaged in certain kinds of activities and occupations. Another related concept is 'framing' (Goffman 1986; Tannen 1979, 1993; Bednarek 2015 among others) that facilitates the way in which film makers and journalists organize knowledge and present reality for the viewers through linguistic and visual means. Such framing activates 'structures of expectations' (Tannen 1979: 144) by offering prototypical categorizations of events and people among viewers. As frames tend to be stable (Bednarek 2015: 690), it is crucial to capture the various ways in which the case study documentaries view and understand the travelling community. Such framing and categorizing are realized in the film through a verbal and visual discourse that assigns the travellers to a particular category of people.

Being one of the expressions of the 'authoritative voices [...] of the elite groups in society' (Bhatia 2015: 15), in documentaries TV journalists construct a discourse of authoritativeness and credibility by providing evidence of the accounts they offer and speaking from documented experience (Montgomery 1999, 2001). In various ways, but mainly through interviewing experts and witnesses, as well as speaking from their direct month-long experience within the Irish travellers' community and hence showing 'expertise-based legitimacy' (Bhatia 2015: 14), the reporters in these three films present themselves as authoritative and impartial commentators.

A lexical analysis of words that are frequently used in the narrator's voice-over (henceforth VO) reveals the dominant categorizations and frames of these two groups which underpin these documentaries. Reporters' questions similarly tend to reinforce these categorizations and frames. A brief discussion of the images in the films' trailers and how they support the narrative will complete the investigation. Such triangulation, it is hoped, will provide sufficient evidence of how a particular discourse on the Irish community of travellers is constructed in the three films.

3 Theoretical background: Ideological discourse and the documentary genre

The concept of 'ideology' is closely associated with Marxist theory with a strong emphasis on its role in generating or reinforcing false consciousness and of political praxis in countering this. However, for the purposes of this analysis ideology is understood as a 'system of prejudices, stereotypes, patterns, or ideas' shared by a community (Calzada-Pérez 1998: 41). Standing in a 'complex and often quite indirect' relation with discourse (van Dijk 2006a: 124), ideology is not forcefully imposed from above by dominant groups, rather it is a dynamic phenomenon and the site of power struggles that sustain or vice versa resist dominant forces (Bhatia 2015). Identifying ideology in the discourse of the media and television in particular therefore means to analyse the language that is used, echoing the Sapir-Whorf hypothesis, to construct a particular view of the world. It also means following van Leeuwen's (2008) Foucauldian approach, to identify the semantic constructions of reality by focusing on how a particular event or 'social practice' is 'recontextualized' in discourse, which represents the roles, the settings and the actions of the people involved. Crucially, the relationship between discourse and ideology is not simple and direct and 'we may ask ourselves whether specific discourse features, such as passive sentences or nominalizations are "intentional" aspects of ideological discourse, or whether such structures are largely automatized and hence hardly consciously controlled' (van Dijk 2006b: 127).

Documentaries are factual, as opposed to fictional, films that promise a degree of truth or at least 'the experience of an attempt at truth' (Routt 1991). Discussing news and television programmes as multimodal texts, Montgomery (2007) believes that it is not unrealistic to assume that the verbal and visual content of factual television to a degree is taken by viewers as being informative and hence credible. Similarly, van Leeuwen (1991) who believes in the supremacy of the verbal plane in television documentaries observes that, especially when it accompanies the voice-over, 'the visual authenticates, particularises and exemplifies the verbal' (113).

However, other scholars focus more on the ideological component of documentaries. Routt (1991), for example, who is preoccupied with the philosophical issue of truth in documentaries, asserts that the very act of selecting the materials to include in a factual film falsifies it. As television narratives, documentaries are subject to the logic of dramatization that makes any television product appealing but also contributes to the film falsity and precludes an accurate representation (Routt 1991: 65). Bruzzi (2000) and Nichols (2001) also note that the degree of accuracy in presenting information and the internal narrative coherence of the films often offer a semblance of truth to viewers when, in fact, a particular interpretation of reality is being presented. Through a number of interviews with documentary-makers, Mueller and Crone (2015) emphasize how it is very challenging 'for a documentary to function as an objective, authentic representation of reality' (p. 293). The reflectivist and constructivist approaches to documentaries thus emphasize the role of the visual and verbal in the construction of an ideological discourse. In line with these latter studies, this chapter considers the truth of documentaries as relative and limited (Routt 1991: 65) and factual films as ideological products; it thus explores the stylistic choices through which a partisan view of the issue in hand is realized in them.

The three documentaries under scrutiny rely on specific 'categorizations' (Sarangi and Candlin 2003) of the traveller and gypsy communities. Categories serve as 'spectacles through which we routinely, albeit largely unconsciously, observe and classify events and experiences' (Sarangi and Candlin 2003: 117). In this instance, Irish travellers are categorized as groups engaged in certain kinds of activities and occupations. Another related concept is 'framing' (Goffman 1986; Tannen 1979, 1993; Bednarek 2015 among others) that facilitates the way in which film makers and journalists organize knowledge and present reality for the viewers through linguistic and visual means. Such framing activates 'structures of expectations' (Tannen 1979: 144) by offering prototypical categorizations of events and people among viewers. As frames tend to be stable (Bednarek 2015: 690), it is crucial to capture the various ways in which the case study documentaries view and understand the travelling community. Such framing and categorizing are realized in the film through a verbal and visual discourse that assigns the travellers to a particular category of people.

Being one of the expressions of the 'authoritative voices [...] of the elite groups in society' (Bhatia 2015: 15), in documentaries TV journalists construct a discourse of authoritativeness and credibility by providing evidence of the accounts they offer and speaking from documented experience (Montgomery 1999, 2001). In various ways, but mainly through interviewing experts and witnesses, as well as speaking from their direct month-long experience within the Irish travellers' community and hence showing 'expertise-based legitimacy' (Bhatia 2015: 14), the reporters in these three films present themselves as authoritative and impartial commentators.

A television documentary usually presents to viewers the result of its investigation into a particular issue or event. To do so many are the affordances used, the main and canonical one being the voice-over, whether in the form of a reporter speaking to the camera or a narrator's disembodied voice. Together with the interviews, and accompanied by the witnesses' and experts' voices, the VO narrates often in a present form and brings together all the various threads in the film. Functioning as a direct address to the viewers, such hetero-diegetic VO has attracted scholars' criticism especially when in the form of an unidentified and disembodied narrator. For many such 'voice of God' (Nichols 2001) is synonymous with a patronizing, domineering and patriarchal narrative mode (Bruzzi 2000: 42) that assumes the audience needs to be guided through the film with the viewer lacking agency vis-à-vis the images, the interviews and the events being reported. This study, on the other hand, takes a more neutral attitude to the VO and shows how this technique by itself cannot be necessarily and acritically associated with ideological representation.

The three documentaries investigated in this study exhibit different VO modalities. In *The Town the Travellers Took Over* (henceforth *TT*) (Channel 5, July 2013), the male reporter speaks to camera and in voice-over; in *Children* (BBC One, May 2011), an invisible disembodied female narrator ensures the story coherence by speaking over the images and alternating with an equally invisible male reporter who conducts the interviews; *Eviction* (Channel 4, September 2011) favours transparency therefore in it the female interviewer is also the VO narrator. The focus of this chapter is on the narrator's VO that conveys the most crucial part of the film message and undoubtedly the most direct address to the audience; the analysis however will discuss how such a modality interacts with other verbal and visual elements in the documentary, all contributing to the televisual representation of the Irish travelling community in the UK.

4 Analytical framework

The analysis of the various voices in the documentaries brings to the fore the representation of the traveller and gypsy communities, highlighting how in the media this is not a 'transparent report' but 'always a decision to interpret and represent [information] in one way rather than another' (Fairclough 1995: 54). As the voice of the narrator whether identifiable (in the case the narrator speaks to the camera, indicated in the excerpts as CAM) or disembodied (indicated simply as VO) is what presents to the viewers the main information, the analysis starts from a semantic deconstruction of this affordance in the films. A lexical analysis of words that are frequently used in the narrator's VO (with the help of WordSmith Tools 4, Scott) reveals the dominant categorizations and frames of these two groups which underpin these documentaries. Such focus on frequent words (both such function words as pronouns that immediately refer to the person orchestrating the narrative, and lexical words that suggest particular topics and themes) not only highlights the centrality of particular concepts and ideas in the VO but, by presenting the text in which specific words appears, guarantees an entry point into the discourse of the film and reveals the degree of ideological dominance that various interpretations of the VO can realize.

Following the analysis of the narrator's voice, the analysis moves to reporters' questions that similarly tend to reinforce the categorizations and frames encouraged in the documentaries. By examining the questions that are asked to witnesses and experts, the analysis moves from '"primary discourse" (the representing or reporting discourse) [to] "secondary discourse" (the discourse represented or reported' (Fairclough 1995: 54–5). Such attention to indirect and direct discourse highlights the frames as ways of seeing the world that are encouraged in the documentaries as well as the proposed categorizations of the participants involved. The combined examination of the documentaries' discourse also reveals how the journalists construct their legitimacy and institutional identity as reporters.

A brief foray into the visuals of the film trailers and a discussion of how they support the narrative completes the investigation. Such triangulation, it is hoped, will provide sufficient evidence of how a particular discourse on the Irish community of travellers is constructed in the three films.

5 Analysis: Inside the documentaries

A prima facie indication of ideology in the three documentaries is the choice of topic, therefore from this perspective Channel 5 *TT*'s sensationalist, tabloid concentration on a gang of crook travellers does nothing but reinforce a negative stereotype while *Children* and *Eviction* show understanding. However, as anticipated, the following analysis goes in much more depth.

5.1 The reporter's word in the documentaries

This section discusses the narrator's VO in the three films with particular attention being paid to the pronouns used and the lexical preferences. Each film is different with regard to these elements partly because the space that the VO occupies is not the same. In *Eviction*, the VO amounts to 43 per cent of the total word count (ca 6,600 words), in *Children* it totals 36 per cent of the total (ca 5), which are both much lower than the percentage of VO's words in *TT*, 84 per cent (of a total of ca 6,600)

5.1.1 *The VO's we*

In Channel 4 *Eviction*, the use of *we* associated with such verbs as *investigate* often refers to the particular documentary series, *Dispatches*, which is reporting on travellers. This is a well-known and widely respected series which reports on a wide range of topics mainly about British society, health, religion, politics, environment and current affairs. As such, *Dispatches* reporters have a reputation for being part of a hard-hitting and insightful documentary brand.

(1) *Eviction* VO. Tonight on Dispatches *we investigate* the battle between the travelling community, their neighbours and the law. Gypsies and travellers say there are not enough places for them to live. We *investigate* why some people don't want them next door. We *ask* how far these minority groups can keep their culture and still integrate with the wider world.

Within such a civic service-frame, the VO's *we* serves to construct an authoritative narrator who has the moralizing duty (Baym 2000) of bringing to the fore the legal anomalies that make travellers' life difficult (e.g. traveller complaints about lack of permanent sites and their desire to maintain their traditions) as well as the attitudes of mainstream society (*viz* people rejecting travellers). BBC One *Children* similarly embarks on the moral task of helping us understand the predicament of travellers' children by focusing exclusively on them (with the exception of a few questions put to one child's father). From this angle, the use of *we* indexes the team of reporters who approach the children by name in a neutral but also friendly manner: 'We meet Salina and Francesca out on the site.' / 'Because we're not allowed into the caravan, Roger brings out some family photos.' By contrast, in Channel 5 *TT*, the journalist glorifies his role as reporter. The VO's 'I' occurs forty-four times with verbs attributing visible agency to the reporter (*I learned, I exposed, I'd be conned, I wanted to know, I'd walked away without a scratch, I had a receipt, I then paid a visit, I went undercover, I tracked down, I made my approach, I saw, I was given*). Thus, the reporter portrays himself as a daring investigator of a community of crooks that forces him to use unorthodox measures ('Determined to find out why, I tried again. This time, wearing a hidden camera') (Figure 5.1). Later as he summarizes the thrust of his search, the journalist stands in a medium shot in front of the viewers against the ruins of an old church, the focus visually on him and his enterprise rather than the travellers' community. While this strategy ensures suspense and entertainment, it acts at the expense of true insight into the nomadic community and categorizes the travellers as a threatening group.

TT presenter Paul Connolly is Irish (and his documentary is shot in Ireland, while the other two discuss the Irish community of travellers in England). For this reason, he plausibly acquires immediate credibility in the viewers' eyes as an appropriate person

Figure 5.1 *TT*'s reporter and VO using a hidden camera. 'The Town the Travellers Took Over' © Channel 5 2013.

to approach travellers. In line with CH5 'infotaiment' (Thussu 2008) spirit, however, Connolly's credibility seems to depend on the construction of his professional identity as 'heroic' (Smith 2013) and daring because in conjunction with the frame of illegality and the categorization of travellers as dangerous people:

(2) *TT* VO. The deal was done, I had a receipt in my pocket and, *thankfully, I'd walked away without a scratch.*

(3) *TT* REP CAM.[4] Over the course of a six-month investigation, one which unexpectedly led *me* across Europe and home again, *I drilled down to the core* of Rathkeale's many secrets that answered questions which, *for decades now*, cast long dark shadows over the town the travellers plan to one day take over completely.

In conclusion, an attention to pronouns provides a first entry into the role of the reporters, which is inextricably linked to the representation of travellers portrayed in each film. In terms of the realization of the overarching narrative, a disembodied VO is not necessarily and immediately associated with a damning judgement of the Irish community; *Children* which adopts the invisible narrator mode shows an attempt at presenting the travellers' children in a friendly and non-judgemental way at least in terms of the VO.

5.1.2 Lexical choices: **Traveller**

This section examines how the lexical preferences in the films – revealed again with the use of a concordancer – indicate the ideological stance through the ways in which the reporters refer to travellers as actors, the degree of agency and responsibility they attribute to them and settled residents and, consequently, how they indicate the understanding and respect (or lack of these) towards them.

The very frequent word *traveller/s* is crucial. CH 5 *TT* shows throughout a negative semantic or discourse 'prosody' (Gabrielatos and Baker 2008: 11; Sinclair 1991) of this word due to the collocates of the node *traveller* pertaining mostly to a domain of illegality and criminality (*crooked, crime, amassed, monied, con, scam, rival, muscled, do as you please, faulty generators*).

(4) *TT* VO. I had, almost by chance, unearthed links to national and international crime. *Travellers* from within Rathkeale had told me of a vastly profitable criminal network that crisscrossed the globe running scams.

(5) *TT* VO. I was told to be at a Limerick hotel in two days' time, and that a monied *traveller* from Rathkeale would be waiting and willing to talk on camera, provided I protect his identity.

Expectedly, in line with such negative prosody, this documentary favours the term *illegal campsite* in contrast to Channel 4 *Eviction*'s preference for the more neutral *unauthorized* site. The frame encouraged by lexical choices in *TT* is once again that of unlawfulness while the categorization of travellers is that of a group of people sustaining themselves through activities that are banned by mainstream society.

By contrast with *TT, Children* and *Eviction* show a less negative attitude when the VO uses the lemma *traveller/s*. In both films, the term is used mainly as a noun rather than a premodifier and descriptor, which makes it easier to attach agency to the travellers and present them as actors of a number of processes:

(6) *Eviction* VO. There are neither temporary stopping places nor permanent sites for *travellers* in Bournemouth. / Then, late this afternoon, the *travellers* won a last-minute court injunction.

(7) *Children* VO. The council says it'll do whatever it can to provide alternative housing for those that have nowhere else to go, and still hopes the *travellers* will agree to leave Dale Farm.

BBC One *Children* pays tribute to travellers' history: 'Some gypsies can trace their roots right back to northern India, but Irish travellers are different. They originally come from Ireland.' *Children* also recognizes the ordeal travellers go through due to restrictive laws and scarcity of space.

(8) *Children* VO. The travellers here are trying to make Dale Farm their permanent home, but the case has been heard in many different courts, and the travellers have now lost. Travellers first began settling here in the 1960s, when permission was granted for forty families, but over the past few years more and more families have moved to Dale Farm, often having been evicted from elsewhere. They bought land on an old scrap yard, and now live there illegally.

Crucially, BBC One *Children* implicitly attributes blame to mainstream society for children's exclusion at school,[5] which forces travellers' families to resort to home teaching:

(9) *Children* VO. Some parents at Dale Farm say they teach their children at home because they're worried about them being accepted at the local comprehensive. [...]

They go to the local primary school in a nearby village. There are ninety pupils at the school. All but two are *travellers*. The school used to be full of local kids, but as more and more travellers joined, their parents moved them.

Similarly, in CH 4 *Eviction*, *traveller/s* are the actors of a number of processes and they are often commended for their resilience and tenacity: 'the travellers *haven't given up yet*' or 'they *won international support* from religious leaders'. Also, the programme blames mainstream society's contradictory laws for the travellers' dramatic situation:

(10) CH 4 *Eviction* VO. ... there's already a national shortage of several thousand caravan places. *Authorities like Leeds are caught between public outrage if they spend money on more sites, and furious reaction when they don't*. These gypsy families stay around Leeds, but there's no space on any council or private sites. Wherever they stop, within days bailiffs move them on.

In terms of how travellers as 'participants of social practices' (van Leeuwen 2008: 23) are represented, *TT* focuses on the pressures the group puts on the settled community. For example, how 'the settled community now claim to be under siege, and in this, the town the travellers took over, a cross-cultural tug-of-war has reached boiling point'. And again, '[Rathkeale]A once-thriving settled community are now very much in the minority and can lay claim to less than 20 per cent of the town'; how its activities are obscure and damaging to the social environment ('Often, properties aren't bought to be lived in [...] most of the owners live abroad. [...] properties are deserted, boarded-up.'); and how travellers are involved in straightforward illegality when the journalist reports on being sold faulty generators by a con-businessman belonging to an international network:

(11) *TT* VO. My investigation into Rathkeale, the town that travellers took over, had unexpectedly led me to Paris in France, where I tracked down and came face-to-face with a crew of traveller con men, all of whom are residents in or have strong links to the Limerick town [Rathkeale]. Posing as a customer, I went undercover to buy one of several hundred faulty generators they were hawking on the streets of Paris for what sources claimed was up to ten times the market value. I then paid a visit to an independent expert, an electrical engineer, who proved beyond a doubt that I'd been conned.

Eviction also reveals that travelling 'men are five times more likely to be jailed than the national average'. However, this documentary frames the issue of illegality among travellers not so much as a feature of the community but as the inevitable yet not always fair perception that settled society has of these mobile people: 'Perhaps the most sensitive issue to address is *a view* that gypsies and travellers prey on the vulnerable. *It tarnishes the reputation of their whole community, even though only a few are guilty*'.

Travellers' criminality, therefore, is treated not as the topic or the subject matter of the discussion but as a 'topos' or 'the common-sense reasoning typical for specific issues' (van Dijk 2000: 97–8; cf. also Sedlak 2000; Reisigl and Wodak 2001). The mention of the existence of con men among travellers seems to be offered as a concession to an expected mainstream view of the community that the film maker cannot ignore. However, it is not at the core of the documentary narrative.

Finally, it is worth noticing how the three films use various techniques to (de)personalize travellers. In CH 4 *Eviction* and BBC One *Children*, the viewers make the acquaintance of some of the travellers in a direct way through the use of personal identification and personalization (van Leeuwen 2008: 42). In the former, Mary is portrayed as the fierce fighter for justice ready to sacrifice her life to keep Dale Farm open ('*They better bring body bags and ambulances 'cos we're willing to die for our homes*'); similarly, in the BBC One *Children* documentary, we empathize with young Roger who is still suffering emotionally from the trauma of a previous violent eviction and with Tammy who dreams of a future as a hairdresser but is unable to train as one because of the racism of mainstream society that does not welcome a young traveller girl into a beauty salon. The empathy with the travellers' predicament that the documentary encourages through the use of first names is, on the contrary, totally absent in *TT*, where travellers are portrayed as an anonymous depersonalized entity.

In conclusion, the analysis of the lemma, *traveller/s* grants us entry into the discursive representation offered in the films. While *Children* and *Eviction* categorize travellers as a nomadic group in a dynamic relationship with mainstream society and often attribute blame to the permanent community, *TT* portrays travellers as a group of crooks and con men who take advantage of naive people and whose investigation can put the journalist himself at risk.

5.1.3 Community *and* law

Remaining on the plane of semantic choices, it is worth noting that, apart from *traveller/s*, the only words frequently shared by the three VOs are *community* and *law*. Again, a close look at how these terms are used is indicative of the different frames encouraged in the films and the ways in which travellers are categorized.

CH 5 *TT* has a menacing and ominous tone attributing to the travelling *community* a series of negative meanings and presenting the permanent community as being very concerned about it. In the VO's words (excerpts (12) and (13)), travellers appear as a social threat as they keep buying properties in Rathkeale with the settled residents losing control of the town and slowly becoming the minority.

(12) *TT* REP VO. For the traveller *community*, owning real estate in Rathkeale, their spiritual home, is seen as a status symbol. Often, properties aren't bought to be lived in, but are instead used as holiday homes or simply as a showpiece. As for all but two months of the year, most of the owners live abroad. During that time, properties are deserted boarded-up. Now that practice has spread to Main Street, Rathkeale, where once-booming businesses lie empty and unused.

(13) *TT* REP CAM. There is, however, no escaping the fact that the settled *community* are steadily vanishing from Rathkeale. As they're perfectly entitled to do, Rathkeale's travellers continue to buy up what land and property they can.

Worse still, while a group of travellers has associations with international crime, the VO claims that, although not involved, the entire travellers' community has been forcefully silenced, which suggests the collusion of the travellers' community at large (excerpt (14)).

(14) REP VO. It soon became clear that, in the background, there was someone pulling the strings. The wider *community* had been warned off talking to the media, ordered to stay tight-lipped. I wondered what, if anything, they were hiding and who was giving the orders.

As for *law*, the semantic associations with this term in *TT* are equally negative as many travellers are described as 'choosing to operate outside the law':

(15) REP VO. The vast majority of Rathkeale's wealthy travellers have, of course, earned their money legitimately through antiques, property and other concerns. But, according to my sources, some chose to operate *outside the law*. That *dirty money lines some of Rathkeale's streets* is a huge claim, but I soon found *floods of evidence* to support it.

Again, by contrast, Channel 4 *Eviction* offers a relatively neutral use of the two terms *community* and *law* ('Estimates of numbers for both groups of the travelling community reach 300,000 / The law is clear, half the site is illegal'). BBC One *Children* adopts a more negative categorization (Sarangi and Candlin 2003; Sacks 1992) of the travellers' children which results in their 'negative othering' (Riggins 1997). Travellers' boys are portrayed as exotic little men doing extraordinary things in a locked up and isolated *community* where illegality and disrespect for norms thrives (excerpts (16) and (17)).

(16) *Children* REP VO. It's *against the law* not to go to school unless you can show you're being taught at home. Tammy hasn't been to school for two years.

(17) *Children* REP VO. It's *against the law* for children to drive because it's dangerous. They drive here because they're on private land and it's part of the traveller way of life, but if children were to drive on a public road, they would get into serious trouble with the police.

In excerpt (16), the implicature – or 'information that is communicated to the viewer (reader/listener) implicitly' (Sperber and Wilson 1995: 273) – that can be drawn from the VO's words is that Tammy is breaking the law by missing school. Indeed, the whole narrative concerning these travellers' children is built around the notion that they are different and do not lead normal lives; it is thus not implausible to think that these children may consider driving outside their encampment on public roads at some point. The fact that later on the documentary explicitly blames mainstream society with charges of racism for preventing these children from attending school does not reduce the impact that the narrator's 'discursive group polarization (de/emphasize good/bad things of Us/Them)' (van Dijk 2006b: 374) produces in the film.

With regard to the treatment of the term *community*, the BBC One *Children* documentary is quite neutral with a much stronger emphasis on the travellers' predicament and group characteristics. ('They accept a life of family, work, friendship and marriage within the traveller *community*.') In excerpt (18), the choice of the verb *squatting* again conjures up associations with illegality; however, the following utterances offer a clear sense of the travellers' aspiration that even go against their traditions ('for the sake of their children') as well as a justification for the travellers' behaviour and a clear condemnation of mainstream society at least through the community's eyes ('they say').

(18) REP VO. But Britain has changed. There are very few places for them to go. And for the sake of their children, this *community* wants to stay put. They hate *squatting* on the land, but say they have no choice. There are no other sites; there is nowhere else for them to go.

In excerpt (19) from the same film, the female VO's involving comment '*you're* expected to get married' points the finger at the travellers' customs of marrying young.

(19) REP VO. The *community* that the travellers have built up is a rather traditional place, where extended families live together, where religion is important for everyone, and where *you're expected to get married*.

In *Eviction*, the term *community* is often associated with the blaming of mainstream society and a seeming understanding of the travellers' hardship (excerpts (20) and (21)).

(20) REP VO. Every *community* has to have some level of interaction with mainstream society. Otherwise that degree of separation becomes a real problem, when they're just cast apart, and they become fair game. At Dale Farm, almost all *their contact with mainstream society has been unwelcome*.

(21) REP VO. The gypsies and travellers we met said they couldn't be held responsible for the actions of a small minority of their *community*. They know how they're regarded by many people. *That's partly why they choose to stay separate from the mainstream world.*

In conclusion, the ways in which specific words are used in the films encourage particular frames and categorizations for the travellers. Travellers for instance can be portrayed as sleazy crooks (*TT* VO 'To those with inside knowledge, Rathkeale is referred to as the money-laundering capital of Ireland and has, I learned, been the focus of countless investigations by the Criminal Assets Bureau'/'In listening to stories of backhanded payments, bribery and fraud, the enormous scale of the wealth in and around this sleepy rural town crashed into sharper'); alternatively the focus can be laid on how the authorities often find themselves in a double bind with regard to the treatment of these communities (*Eviction* VO 'Authorities like Leeds are caught between public outrage if they spend money on more sites, and furious reaction when they don't./ The operation will cost Basildon Council £8 million pound, the police another 10 million./ Coventry Council admitted conditions could be improved.')

A lexical analysis of the VO's verbal text suggests that while *Eviction* and *Children* offer a more neutral representation, *TT* insists on a categorization of travellers as outlaws and the frame it conjures up is that of an illegal world onto which the reporter heroically sheds light.

The next section analyses the questions addressed to the experts, witnesses and the average person (Vox Pop) that often function as authentication of the VO. This will provide a wider angle of inspection on the overall language of the three texts under study.

5.2 Beyond the VO: The power of questions

Besides the narrator's embodied or disembodied VO, an essential part of documentaries is the interpellation of witnesses, experts and the voices of the average person or Vox Pop. Realized through the voice of the investigating journalist generally following the narrator, questions have the twofold aim of adding more information to what the VO presents and, crucially, ensuring the VO's credibility by providing the necessary evidence of his/her statements. In the process of eliciting information from different people as a legitimation device, the interviewers accomplish their institutional identity as reporters (Emmertsen 2007) but also tend to enforce the VO's ideological discourse not differently from what happens with questions in other television contexts/genres, for example news interviews (Clayman 1992 and 1993; Heritage and Greatbatch 1989).

Being the result of a scripted dialogue and careful editing, the questions asked by documentary reporters cannot be considered extemporaneous. Rather, they reflect the director's specific stance vis-à-vis the topic. Noticeably, a crucial change in the form of address occurs in the switch from the VO to the reporter's questions. The VO narrative directly addresses the viewers (both verbally and, at times, visually if the VO looks at the camera establishing eye-contact with the viewers). By contrast, questions are only indirectly aimed at them in virtue of the double articulation, or double plane of dialogue between speakers on-screen and viewers at home who act as 'over-hearers' (Bubel 2008: 62), which characterizes films. Questions also assume a good degree of shared knowledge and thus contribute to creating a common ground with viewers (Piazza, Bednarek and Rossi 2015: 9).

Sarangi (2003) focuses on the interpretive procedures enacted in interview talk. He specifically looks at how interviewers and interviewees accomplish the exchange by focusing on the identity of the questioner and respondent and, more important to the present discussion, he explores the inferences that can be plausibly drawn from the text. This section looks at the type of questions that reporters in documentaries ask a variety of individuals as part of the investigation into the travellers' community reported in the film. The classification according to different question types brings to the fore the attempt to convey neutrality or vice versa encourage a particular view.

This is done by questions that, as a result of their syntactic form and their pragmatic force, are open and relatively non-biased, in contraposition to others that are blame-implicative, raise particular implicatures and are ideological.

The grouping of questions under various categories shows they can best be viewed on a continuum from the most neutral to the least objective; as other features in the films, questions suggest the inevitable presence of the film maker's beliefs and convictions. In all three documentaries, the time devoted to questions occupies less than the VO's. In CH 5 *TT*, where the male questioner is same as the VO, the number of words in the questions is 21.5 per cent of the total, in CH 4 *Eviction* where the questioner and VO are the same female journalist, they are 14 per cent and, in BBC One *Children* where the male questioner is different from the female, it is almost half.

In addition to the type of questions in the three films, it also necessary to distinguish between questions chastising mainstream society and those criticizing travellers; it is through such attribution of responsibility to one group or the other that the documentary's reporter (besides the VO) realizes the journalist's moralizing duty (Baym 2000) interpreted as the call for addressing issues of a moral nature and advocating justice and fairness.

5.2.1 Open questions

(22) *Eviction* REP. What's it mean to be a gypsy?

Robert: Everything. Live on the land, work the land, take off the land what you want to take off the land, 'cos God said it.

The question put to an adult male traveller, Robert, follows the journalist's reported speech ('Robert doesn't deny his past, but says all gypsies are tarred with the same reputation because people don't understand their culture') and yields an insightful personal and poetic response by the interviewee.

Of course, it can be argued that a certain degree of bias is inherent to the previous question in that it assumes the need to explain what being a mobile individual is. However, in general open questions are very effective (Oxburgh, Myklebust and Grant 2010: 46–8) because they do not appear forceful and, in this case, they represent the travellers as individuals in tune with nature and as countryside lovers.

A similarly felicitous open question in BBC One *Children* triggers a narrative of mainstream society's rejection and exclusion of the travellers' community.

(23) *Children* REP. What do people think of you outside of here?

Boy one: I don't know. We never really meet any people outside of here.
Boy two: They don't really chat to us. They don't like us.
Boy three (Roger): They don't really like us. Because we're different.
Boy four: They're probably jealous.
Boy two: They think we're different because we stays in caravans, they stays in houses, but it's really nothing different.

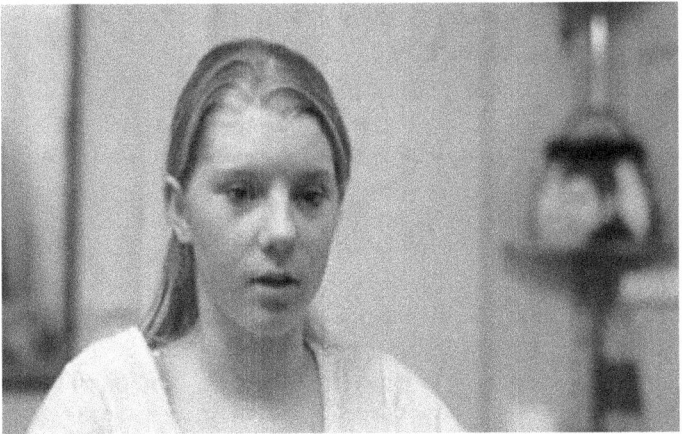

Figure 5.2 Tammy answers questions in close-up. 'My Life: Children of the Road' © BBC1 2011.

Following this question while the camera is on close-up on the boys first as a group and then on each one of them when taking turn at speaking – an endearing technique that brings them closer to the viewers – the reporter's leading query hints at mainstream community racist tendencies. (*Children* REP. What kind of things do they call you? Boy four. Gypsies and pikeys, stuff like that.)

However while the camera is on Tammy in close-up (Figure 5.2), it is this young girl's dramatic narrative that blames settled society most blatantly for its cruel and unjustified Othering of travellers only on the basis of their different accent.

(24) *Children*. Tammy. We used to walk down to the shop, down to the park. We used to walk places for fresh air. Then, when we were walking, everyone keeps looking out at you and stops you from playing. It got kind of hard when everyone is looking at you, so we stopped going everywhere.
REP: You don't look different from anybody else.
Tammy: No...
REP: How do they know?
Tammy: Because we were having a laugh. When we're talking they know. We all have different accents. We come from Ireland. We have different accents from everyone else. As you can see when I'm talking.
REP: Can you think of other examples where people have teased you?
Tammy: Yeah, we were in the cinemas last week. It was my friend's birthday. We were playing and eating pizza, they all moved away. All of the people moved away from us on the tables.
REP: So, people moved away from you in a pizza restaurant?
Tammy: Yeah, they moved away from us.
REP: Why do you think they did that?
Tammy: Because they thought we had germs or something.

5.2.2 Confirmation-aimed, probing and leading questions (including yes/no questions)

Although seemingly neutral, the questions in this broad category are those that Griffiths and Milne (2006 in Oxburgh, Myklebust and Grant 2010: 51) define as 'un-productive' in that they do not yield very informative answers because respondents provide preferred responses. Questions of this type generally assume the existence of a problem, for instance that the travellers' children are not being treated fairly as in excerpt (24) when Tammy says, 'All of the people moved away from us on the tables.'

And the reporter asks, 'So, people moved away from you in a pizza restaurant?' or that wishing to expel travellers is a legitimate desire (25). Similarly, they can be leading if due to their syntactic formulation or the presupposition on which they are based, they are meant to elicit a specific reply from the interviewee in agreement with the stance expressed by the questioner as in (26). Questions can also be expressed by statements that in the particular context, need to be confirmed or refuted as in the case of 'some of the residents will say you're asking to be a special case' which elicited the traveller's reply 'And we agree 100 per cent with them, we have a heart, we do understand where they're coming from.'

(25) *TT* REP. Do you want the travellers out of Rathkeale?

Witness: It'd be nice to see them gone.

(26) *TT* REP. If you buy properties in Rathkeale, you can do what you like. So, in Rathkeale, the same planning laws simply don't apply?

Witness: Not one bit.

5.2.3 Blame-implicative questions

Any of the questions in the three groups described earlier can express bias and implicate blame against travellers or vice versa the settled society. Such ideological stances either can be formulated as a statement that is expected to be confirmed, as in 'the travellers are trying to *take over* Rathkeale' or contain blame-implicative lexis as in 'How have Rathkeale travellers *amassed* such *enormous wealth*?' (both from CH 5 *TT*). In the latter example, the choice of the verb *amass* in the sense of 'to gather or collect (something, such as a large amount of money) especially for yourself' (Merriam-Webster) and the qualifier *enormous* suggest the individualistic and utilitarian nature of the travellers' wealth. Similarly, in the following excerpt, the implicature of *take over* is that Rathkeale is a desirable place that travellers aim to appropriate.

(27) *TT* REP. Do you think that the travellers are trying *to take over* Rathkeale?

Witness: From the outside looking in, it looks that way.

Besides the type of questions that can encourage more or less directly and clearly a particular view of travellers, the evaluation they (in)directly express can be in favour or critical of either travellers or the settled society. The reporter's leading question in (28), for instance, criticizes mainstream society for not providing the necessary space for mobile communities; similarly in (29) the accusation of thieving directed to the young travellers offers the opportunity of a critique of the settled community. However, the question in (30), following a witness' complaint about the discovery of human excreta in the woods, chastises travellers' unhealthy and antisocial habits by blaming them for not using the toilets in their caravans.

(28) *Eviction* REP. But there's no space on any of those sites?

Woman traveller: We do not have any ... *No, there 'sn't*. There may be one or two.

(29) *Children* REP. So, why do you think travellers have such a poor reputation?

Young boy: Because some travellers pulls in and people thinks 'ou're digging up the fields, doing this, but we pulls in, stays a week and goes. *You'an't get staying anywhere.* 'ou're probably there for half an hour and no, get out of my place. T'at's the way it is in life.

(30) *Eviction* REP. Do you not have little toilets in the caravans?

Traveller girl: *We 'on't use them*. No way. Imagine cooking your dinner and then some'ne's in the toilet. You wou'dn't do it, no way.

CH 4 *Eviction* has fewer questions than the other two films[6] due to its prevalently narrative style while CH 5 *TT* exhibits the highest number. More interesting is to observe the presence of blame-implicative questions. *TT* has the highest number of questions blaming travellers in the category of y/n and open questions for instance, 'How have so many of the town's traveller population come to be so incredibly wealthy?' and 'Would they intimidate customers into paying?' BBC One *Children*[7] shows an equal number of such questions blaming indirectly travellers and settled society. *Eviction* blames travellers four times and settled society twice as many times with such direct questions as 'Why have councils been so reluctant either to provide council sites or give planning permission for private sites?'

Importantly the REP's questions fulfil the crucial function of supporting the VO's views. At times they can provide an opportunity for eliciting on the part of the respondent an outspoken critique of settled society's discrimination of travellers (cf. (41)) or instead favourable comments as in (42) in which Michael's answer confirms the VO's statement and uses a poetic metaphor to describe how travellers are forced into stationary life (both from *Children*).

(31) *Children* VO. It's against the law not to go to school unless you can show you're being taught at home. Tammy hasn't been to school for two years. She dreams of becoming a hairdresser.

REP. Do you think you will become a hairdresser?

Tammy. I don't know. I don't think so. *They really don't employ people like us. 'Cos they really don't live us in hairdressers or salons that much.* If we go get our hair done, that's why we does it ourselves. That's how we learned to do it.

(32) *Children* VO. Roger's dad [Michael] agrees to talk to us as long as we don't show his face. He tells us he may not get work locally if people knew he lived in Dale Farm.

Michael: You know we didn't have anyone to tell us where to go – not like now, you know what I mean? *Then it was a fabulous life*, you know.
REP: Did you have a life on the road, were you travelling?
Michael: All my life. *Today, what they want to do is like catching a little wild bird and put it in the cage*, what they're trying to do to the travellers today.

In conclusion, as for the lexical choices in the VO's language, the three documentaries can be differentiated on the grounds of the use of questions. Particularly relevant seems to be the ascription of blame as a form of moral evaluation (Baym 2000). In light of this, once again CH 4 *Eviction* exhibits the most varied questions and ascribes responsibility for the travellers' ill fate to settled society more than the other two films do.

5.3 VO and visuals

This last section returns to the narrator's voice as that which provides the main entry into the film and briefly discusses the images that illustrate the verbal meaning of the VO's words in the first minute and a few seconds of each documentary's introduction or trailer, which showcases the film content in *Eviction, Children* and *TT.*

CH 4 *Eviction* (trailer length 1:29) opens with an image of travellers protesting in Dale Farm barricaded against police and bailiffs. As the VO explains, 'This is the entrance to Britain's biggest traveller site' in which the linguistic intensification (or gradation, Martin and White 2005) contained in the premodifier *biggest* emphasizes the size of the problem and the consequent protest. Long and medium shots from high and low on the scaffolding at the entrance (Figure 5.3) showing protesters ready for the fight stress the travellers' power and tenacity in saving their place and convey the film director's positive social evaluation (Martin and White 2005).

Following this, a series of quick archival references to previous evictions underline the historicity of travellers' problems. Footage is then shown of the British prime minister at the time, David Cameron in Parliament speaking against travellers' alleged legal abuses. These archival sequences are interspersed with pictures of traditional horse-driven carriages, a concession to a stereotyped old-fashioned vision of travellers. However, in the subsequent long shot a woman blames the authorities for treating travellers 'like animals' and another recounts how the bailiffs 'shifted' them (in the sense of 'moved') in the morning without respect for their families. Following these travellers' traumatic personal narratives, the subsequent scene seems to redress the balance. As the VO recites, 'we investigate why some people don't want them next door', in a close-up shot a man mentions the debris travellers leave behind, while the camera is on a piece of what appears to be toilet paper in the woods.

Ideology in the Multimodal Discourse of Television Documentaries 133

Figure 5.3 Protesters at Dale Farm. 'Gypsy Eviction: The Fight for Dale Farm' © Channel 4 2011.

Figure 5.4 Feisty Mary. 'Gypsy Eviction: The Fight for Dale Farm' © Channel 4 2011.

Significantly, the trailer ends with a visual and verbal reminder of the travellers' unfortunate destiny: the camera is on a close-up on Candy Sheridan, a supporter and a traveller herself, who refers to her community as 'vilified, hated, misunderstood'; this is followed by one more shot on the barricaded site and a close-up of Mary, the main woman traveller in the documentary (Figure 5.4). Both shots introducing some of the characters in the film appear truthful and credible in that the two interviewees do not establish a 'vector' or imaginary line (Kress and van Leeuwen 1996) with the camera, as they are involved in their conversation with the reporter.

In short, in the documentary's trailer, the combination of images and VO's words seems to propose an empathetic or at least balanced view of the travellers, portrayed as an endangered and persecuted minority. The camera panning on the travellers' site emphasizes its size (and is, therefore, a reminder of the large number of families living there); as it accompanies the VO's words that insist on the travellers' tenacity in resisting the authorities and blame political parties for the situation ('Travellers were encouraged to buy their own land after the Conservatives abolished the duty of councils to provide sites in the mid '90s'), the long shot may invoke the viewers' solidarity with the community of travellers.

BBC One *Children* (trailer length 1:10) opens with a medium shot of a group of joyful boys walking and jumping towards the camera, while the VO recites 'these children are outsiders'. The direct deictic reference to 'these children' links the actors to the desolate context in which they operate (Chapman 2011: 40) and the deictic works as a direct appeal to the viewers. The emphasis on 'these' may signal that these children who are like any others are actually outsiders or alternatively, that they are outsiders while still behaving like normal children. The surrounding context is grim, with visible scaffolding, puddles on the unpaved road, barbed wire and bent fences possibly suggesting the travelling community's poor conditions and its resistance to the site's enforced enclosure. Next is a close-up of a small boy jokingly showing his fists to the camera. The implication is that the youth live in a unhealthy and threatened camp but in spite of this they are still normal children playing in front of the camera.

A panoramic shot of Dale Farm accompanies narrator Rani Price explaining in VO that over 1,000 travellers live on the site, the biggest in Europe; as in the previous documentary, this visual and verbal intensification (Martin and White 2005) suggests the size and severity of the issue. A long shot of young girls with prams follows; the likely implicature is that they are looking after small children or even babies without any adults' supervision although they are children themselves (as the final medium shot on some young girls playing 'Eeny, meeny, miny, moe' confirms) (Figure 5.5).

Figure 5.5 Young girls and prams in Dale Farm. 'Gypsy Eviction: The Fight for Dale Farm' © Channel 4 2011.

In short, compared to *Eviction*, this second documentary's trailer visually encourages a categorization of the children's 'normal abnormality' and sets a negative interpretive frame centred on the difference between the greater sense of responsibility of settled society versus the burden that travellers lay on children as guardians of the younger ones. However, as was discussed, in the course of the documentary at the level of discourse (both through the VO's words and the reporter's questions), although this view is not refuted, the reasons behind the travellers' diversity and exclusion are duly explored.

Finally, CH 5 *TT* (trailer length 1:2) opens with gloomy and ominous music on images of a wrought iron gate towering over the viewers from a bottom shot, followed by a yellow flower field, the roof of a house with a bird in the eave, chimney smoke, the front of a blue car, a close-up on a one-eyed dog, all aiming to suggest the quiet ordinariness of the town of Rathkeale that the travellers have been violently disrupting. At the same time, the VO narrates: 'Rathkeale, County Limerick, may seem like any other sleepy rural village though it's anything but.' A close-up of an image of Christ on a wall as the VO says that travellers have made Rathkeale 'their spiritual home, their Mecca' is a visual realization of a metaphor (Mecca as desired place) re-contextualized in a Catholic frame. An extreme close-up on an interviewed gangster-looking man with Ray Ban sunglasses visually sets the illegal frame of the film. The image of a broken window (Figure 5.6) symbolizing lack of upkeep but also violence accompanies the VO's mention of the fact that residents of Rathkeale – as the sign in English and Irish 'Rathkeale/Ráth Caola' appears – feel under siege.

The images that contrast poor travellers' caravans and wealthy mansions are followed by close-up shots of interviewees; as one of them, a Rathkeale resident, says, 'we're going nowhere'. The visual frame encouraged by these visuals is that of a town besieged by unwanted travellers who are dramatically altering the place's original cultural heritage. The trailer concludes with a medium shot of the journalist in a derelict roofless church behind an open gate talking about his investigation on travellers' wealth in Rathkeale. As a strategy that can be frequently observed in news reports, this 'blending of visual images and verbal text in a metaphoric relationship

Figure 5.6 Grim ordinariness in Rathkeale. 'The Town the Travellers Took Over' © Channel 5.

is intended to influence the viewers' comprehension' (Wiggin and Miller 2003: 269; Piazza and Haarman 2016). In this case, the open gate functions as a visual metaphor for the reporter opening the viewers' eyes to the mystery of the Irish town.

From the above quick foray into the range of images at the opening of the documentaries, once again *Eviction* seems to show empathy with the travellers' fate while *Children* portrays the community occupying a grim and unhealthy space. The opening images of *TT* are relatively cryptic and unappealing; however, what they seem to suggest is the atmosphere of both ordinariness and abandonment mixed with tension in the town of Rathkeale. In terms of the visually encouraged frames, while *Eviction* proposes a 'mental representation' (Bednarek 2015: 689) of the travelling community as threatened also due to mishaps of mainstream society, *Children* immediately encourages a categorization of travellers' children as different and invites an indirect criticism of their adultless community.

6 Conclusion

Treating factual films as documents that reflect their time and as representations of particular contexts of production can contribute to a better understanding of past and present developments and societal forms of expression (Pollak 2008: 77). This chapter has identified salient points that both on the visual and verbal plane, both in the words of the narrator and in those of the interviewer, can be plausibly seen as encouraging particular interpretive frames and representations of the Irish travelling community in contemporary Britain.

Although with particular reference to TV news, historically impartiality has been regarded as a token of professionalism and inspired broadcasts' guidelines. However, as 'neutrality is impossible and truth does not lie in the middle', Boudana (2016) invokes 'accuracy' in representation as this is 'better served by fairness than by a delusive position of impartiality' (p. 600). The analysis proposed in this chapter confirms the central thesis of this research: documentaries are not impartial nor are they particularly accurate in their depiction of the travellers' community and the truth they offer is only one-sided and 'murky' (Bruzzi 2000: 3).

Behind a seemingly neutral VO or interviewer's intervention, these films frame a topic in a particular way and encourage a given categorization of the social actors involved. This said, marked differences have been identified between the three films. Focusing entirely on travellers' corruption and illegality, CH5 *TT* sacrifices any serious consideration of travellers' communities to a journalistic style aimed at engaging and entertaining viewers through the ability of the reporter as investigator and the extraordinariness of his account. He then becomes a hero who at the risk of his own life, exposes the malaise within the travelling community thus indirectly justifying the racism to which travellers are subjected by permanent residents in Rathkeale and beyond. In spite of the fact that the reporter is himself Irish, a factor that endows him with immediate credibility, this film most directly feeds into stereotypical views of Irish travellers as outlaws and crooks. Although it deals with the very delicate issue of minors and shows understanding of the complexity of their existence and sheer incredulity at the reasons behind their discrimination, *Children* occasionally gives in to biased views and stereotypes about travellers. Once again partiality is a trend of this documentary although, it may be argued, as a consequence of its attempt to represent travellers with a degree of accuracy. *Eviction* is the most balanced of the three films, showing a degree of empathy with travellers and above all often taking to task settled society for its incoherent and contradictory laws.

Moreover, while CH 4 *Eviction* and BBC One *Children* can be seen as having a social function as 'instruments for the propagation of democratic civics' (Mueller and Crone 2015: 295) by reporting on a disenfranchised and anti-capitalist minority, for *TT* travellers are simply a pretext to report on a sensationalist journalistic inquiry. While documentaries are independent products and cannot be unproblematically associated with the mission statement of a particular broadcaster, they certainly take into consideration the programme/series of which they are part and the style of the network. In the present case, while objectivity reflects the ethos of public television, in the case of commercial providers ideology is realized through a multimodal discourse that sacrifices impartiality and accuracy to sensationalism and entertainment.

Notes

1   This chapter has been published by the author under the same title in *Critical Approaches to Discourse Analysis across Disciplines*, 9 (1) (2017): 63–90, and is here reprinted with the permission of the journal.
2   The choice of topic is not fortuitous. In my work with Irish travellers in the south of England (Piazza and Fasulo 2015), I noticed how the interviewees repeatedly pointed out that the limited knowledge that settled society has about them specifically comes from television programmes as the excerpt below from one of my interviews attests. (indicates overlapping talk and @ stands for laughter)

   Interviewer: Do you think they know anything about you, about your community? Do you think they know anything about traveller's lives? [And about who they are?
   Traveller: [Y: no, they didn't, they didn't … but since big fat gypsy weddings
   Interviewer: yes
   Traveller: I think they do now, they understand more 'cos of that programme
   Interviewer: yeah @
   Traveller: I think they learnt a lot from that, even more so than ever
   Interviewer: in a good way or a bad way do you think they learnt by that programme?
   Traveller: both in a good and bad, 'cos everyone's got different opinions haven't they? Everyone's got different opinions about different things so some people would understand it in a good way, some people wouldn't like it.

3   As in such films as *Chocolat* 2000 with Juliette Binoche and Johnny Depp as the seductive gypsy. Very different is the case of the autobiography by Mikey Walsh, a painful self-critical representation of Romany gypsy communities offered by an outcast insider.
4   In the excerpts REP CAM stands for 'Reporter speaking to camera'.

5. Gypsy, Traveller and Roma pupils are very vulnerable in schools where they are victims of severe bullying (DfE 2014 in Equality and Human Right Commission report 2016).
6. The questions in the three films are summarized below:

	Confirmation, leading and y/n	Open	Blaming travellers	Blaming mainstream society
Eviction	19	16	4	8
Children	46	37	4	4
TT	33	35	13	0

7. Incidentally probably because they are addressed to children, *Children*'s questions are rather simplistic (e.g. REP: How many dogs live on this site, do you reckon?/ REP: Roger, I've seen lots of boys around here driving. Roger: Yeah. REP: Can you drive? Roger: Yeah. REP: How old are you now? Roger: 12) with occasionally more insightful ones aimed at highlighting discrimination (e.g. REP: You learned to do hair dressing because you couldn't get into the hairdresser's?).

References

Baym, G. (2000), 'Constructing moral authority: We in the discourse of television news', *Western Journal of Communication*, 64 (1): 92–111.

Bednarek, M. (2015), 'Voices and values in the news: News media talk, news values and attribution', *Discourse, Context and Media*, 11: 27–37.

Bhatia, A. (2015), *Discursive Illusions in Public Discourse*, London: Routledge.

Blommaert, J. (2005), *Discourse: A Critical Introduction*, Cambridge: Cambridge University Press.

Boudana, S. (2016), 'Impartiality is not fair: Toward an alternative approach to the evaluation of content bias in news stories', *Journalism*, 17 (5): 600–18.

Bruzzi, S. (2000), *A New Documentary: A Critical Introduction*, London and New York: Routledge.

Bubel, C. (2008), 'Film audiences as overhearers', *Journal of Pragmatics*, 40 (1): 55–71.

Calzada-Pérez, M. (1998), 'Studying prejudices: An ideological approach to Alan Bennett's Bed among the Lentils', *Text-Interdisciplinary Journal for the Study of Discourse*, 18 (1): 39–66.

Chapman, S. (2011), *Pragmatics*, Houndmills: Palgrave McMillan.

Clayman, S. (1992), 'Footing in the achievement of neutrality: The case of news interview discourse', in P. Drew and J. Heritage (eds), *Talk at Work: Interaction in Institutional Settings*, 163–98, Cambridge: Cambridge University Press.

Clayman, S. (1993), 'Reformulating the question: A device for answering/not answering questions in news interviews and press conferences', *Text-Interdisciplinary Journal for the Study of Discourse*, 13 (2): 159–88.

Corner, J. (2002), 'Performing the real: Documentary diversions', *Television & New Media*, 3 (3): 255–69.

Emmertsen, S. (2007), 'Interviewers' challenging questions in British broadcast debate interviews', *Journal of Pragmatics*, 39 (3): 570–91.

Equality and Human Rights Commission (March 2016), *England's most Disadvantaged Groups: Gypsies, Travellers and Roma*. An Is England Fairer review spotlight.

Fairclough, N. (1995), *Critical Discourse Analysis*, Harlow: Pearson.

Gaber, I., Piazza, R., Haarman, H. and Caborn, A., eds (2016), 'Values and choices in television discourse: A view from both sides of the screen' (Book review), *Journal of British Cinema and Television*, 13 (4): 637-9.

Gabrielatos, C. and Baker, P. (2008), 'Fleeing, sneaking, flooding: A corpus analysis of discursive constructions of refugees and asylum seekers in the UK press, 1996-2005', *Journal of English Linguistics*, 36 (1): 5-38.

Goffman, E. (1986), *Frame Analysis*, Boston: Northeastern.

Griffiths, A. and Milne, B. (2006), 'Will it all end in tiers? Police interviews with suspects in Britain', in T. Williamson (ed.), *Investigative Interviewing*, 167-89, Cullompton: Willan.

Hatim, B. and Mason, I. (1990), *Discourse and the Translator*, London: Longman, 1990.

Heritage, J. and Greatbatch, D. (1989), 'On the institutional character of institutional talk: The case of news interviews', in *Discourse in Professional and Everyday Culture: Linko Ping*, 47-98, Sweden: Department of Communication Studies, University of Linko Ping.

Holloway, S. (2005), 'Articulating otherness? White rural residents talk about Gypsy-Travellers', *Transactions of the Institute of British Geographers*, 30: 351-67.

Kabachnik, P. (2009), 'To choose, fix, or ignore culture? The cultural politics of Gypsy and Traveler mobility in England', *Social and Cultural Geography*, 10 (4): 461-79.

Kress, G. and van Leeuwen, T. (1996), *Reading Images*, London and New York: Routledge.

Lichtenstein, O. (2015), 'Documentary-making: A commercial and public broadcaster perspective', in R. Piazza, L. Haarman and A. Caborn (eds), *Values and Choices in Television Discourse*, 216-22, Houndmills: Palgrave McMillan.

Martin, J. and White, P. (2005), *The Language of Evaluation: Appraisal in English*, Houndmills: Palgrave Macmillan.

Montgomery, M. (1999), 'Speaking sincerely: Public reactions to the death of Diana', *Language and Literature*, 8 (1): 5-33.

Montgomery, M. (2001), 'Defining "authentic talk"', *Discourse Studies*, 3 (4): 397-405.

Montgomery, M. (2007), *The Discourse of Broadcast News*, London: Routledge.

Mueller, F. and Crone, V. (2015), 'The reel claiming the real: An actor network approach to understanding the achievement and management of documentary authority and authenticity', *Journal of Applied Journalism & Media Studies*, 4 (2): 293-308.

Nichols, B. (2001), *Introduction to Documentary*, Bloomington and Indianapolis, IN: Indiana University Press.

Oxburgh, G. Myklebust, T. and Grant, T. (2010), 'The question of question types in police interviews: A review of the literature from a psychological and linguistic perspective', *The International Journal of Speech, Language and the Law*, 17 (1): 45-66.

Piazza, R. Bednarek, M. and Rossi, F., eds (2015), *Telecinematic Discourse*, Amsterdam and Philadelphia: Benjamin.

Piazza, R. and Fasulo, A., eds (2015), *Marked Identities*. London: Palgrave.

Piazza, R. and Haarman, L. (2016), 'A pragmatic cognitive model for the interpretation of verbal-visual communication in television news programmes', *Visual Communication*, 15 (4): 461-86.

Pollak, A. (2008), 'Analyzing TV documentaries', in R. Wodak and M. Krzyzanowski (eds), *Qualitative Discourse Analysis in the Social Sciences*, 77-95, Houndsmill: Palgrave McMillan.

Poole, E. (2002), *Reporting Islam: Media Representations of British Muslims*, London and New York: I.B.Tauris.

Powell, R. (2008), 'Understanding the stigmatization of gypsies: Power and the dialectics of (dis)identification', *Housing, Theory and Society*, 25 (2): 87–109.

Reisigl, M. and Wodak, R. (2001), *Discourse and Discrimination: Rhetorics of Racism and Anti-Semitism*, London: Routledge.

Riggins, S. (1997), 'The rhetoric of othering', in S. Riggins (ed.), *The Language and Politics of Exclusion: Others in Discourse*, 1–30, Thousands Oakks: Sage.

Routt, W. (1991), 'The truth of the documentary', *Continuum: The Australian Journal of Media and Culture*, 5 (1): 65–6.

Sacks, H (1992), *Lectures on Conversation*, vol. I and II, Oxford: Blackwell.

Sarangi, S. (2003), 'Institutional, professional, and lifeworld frames in interview talk', in van den Berg, M. Wetherell and H. Houtkoop (eds), *Analyzing Race Talk: Multidisciplinary Approaches to the Interview*, 64–84, Cambridge: Cambridge University Press.

Sarangi, S. and Candlin, C. (2003), 'Categorization and explanation of risk: A discourse analytical perspective', *Health, Risk & Policy*, 5 (2): 115–24.

Scannell, P. (1996), *Radio, Television and Modern Life*, London: Sage.

Sedlak, M. (2000), 'You really do make an unrespectable foreign policy', in R. Wodak and T. Van Dijk (eds), *Racism at the Top: Parliamentary Discourses on Ethnic Issues in Six European States*, 107–68, Klagenfurt: Drava.

Sinclair, J. (1991), *Corpus, Concordance, Collocation*, Oxford: Oxford University Press.

Smith, P. (2013), 'Heroic endeavours: Flying high in New Zealand reality television', in N. Lorenzo-Dus and P. Garcés-Conejos Blitvich (eds), *Real Talk*, 140–65, Houndmills and New York: Palgrave McMillan.

Sperber, D. and Wilson, D. (1995), *Relevance: Communication and Cognition*, Oxford and Cambridge: Blackwell Publishers.

Tannen, D. (1979), 'What's in a frame? Surface evidence for underlying expectations', in R. Freedle (ed.), *New Directions in Discourse Processing*, 137–81, Norwood: Ablex.

Tannen, D., ed. (1993), *Framing in Discourse*. Oxford: Oxford University Press.

Tannen, D. and Wallat, C. (1987), 'Interactive frames and knowledge schemes in interaction: Examples from a medical examination/interview', *Social Psychology Quarterly*, 50 (2): 205–16.

Thussu, D. K. (2008), *News as Entertainment: The Rise of Global Infotainment*, London: Sage.

Van Dijk, T. (2000), 'New(s) racism: A discourse analytical approach', in S. Cottle (ed.), *Ethnic Minorities and the Media*, 33–49, Milton Keynes: Open University Press.

Van Dijk, T. (2005), 'Contextual knowledge management in discourse production', in R. Wodak and P. Chilton (eds), *A New Agenda in (Critical) Discourse Analysis*, 71–100, Amsterdam and Philadelphia, PA: John Benjamins.

Van Dijk, T. (2006a), 'Discourse and manipulation', *Discourse & Society*, 17 (3): 359–83.

Van Dijk, T. (2006b), 'Ideology and discourse analysis', *Journal of Political Ideologies*, 11 (2): 115–40.

Van Leeuwen, T. (1991), 'Conjunctive structure in documentary film and television', *Continuum: Journal of Media & Cultural Studies*, 5 (1): 76–114.

Van Leeuwen, T. (2008), *Discourse and Practice*, Oxford: Oxford University Press.

Walsh, M. (2010), *Gypsy Boy*, London: Hodden & Stoughton.

Wiggin, A. and Miller, C. (2003), '"Uncle Sam Wants You!" Exploring verbal-visual juxtapositions in television advertising', in L. Scott and R. Batra (eds), *Persuasive Imagery: A Consumer Perspective*, 267–95, Mahwah and London: Lawrence Erlbaum.

6

Voice-over and presenter narration in TV documentaries

Jan Chovanec

1 Introduction

Not unlike other types of telecinematic discourse, the genre of the TV documentary constitutes a narrative that has a relatively clear and coherent internal structure. After all, TV documentaries are creative non-fiction narratives that revolve around 'telling a story' about a particular topic or issue (Bernard 2011). This can take various forms, for example, a discovery quest pursued by the main protagonist who, in a final narrative resolution, discovers the operation of natural/technical phenomena or completes a specific mission. On a lower level, the overall macronarrative of the whole programme is mirrored in the structure of some of the individual scenes, acts and sequences that constitute more or less self-enclosed sub-narratives with their own narrative elements (Labov and Waletsky 1967; Labov 1972).

While the overall narrative in documentaries emerges out of the complex interplay between the visual track and the sound track, my primary interest here is in the latter. The soundtrack consists of two elements: the verbal track and the music track, typically spliced together and overlapping. Within the verbal track, we find multiple voices (Bakhtin 1981; cf. also the notion of 'accessed voices' introduced by Hartley 1982) that co-construct the narrative in complex ways. While some attention has been paid to the nature of narrativity in telecinematic discourse by communication and media scholars, both concerning films (Bordwell 1985; Chatman 1990) and such non-factual genres as the travelogue (Gieve and Norton 2007), relatively little research has been done on narrative voices in non-fictional broadcast productions from the perspective of stylistic pragmatics. One of the few notable exceptions is Lorenzo-Dus (2009), who deals with narrative commentary and celebrity narrators in documentaries.

The aim of this chapter is, thus, to investigate more systematically the interplay between the diegetic and non-diegetic narrator voices (see Section 2) and to identify several techniques by means of which switches between the two voices are realized, resulting in the dominant role of one or the other voice in a given narrative segment (Section 4). The theoretical background to the analysis is grounded in the pragmatic analysis of 'telecinematic discourse' (Piazza, Bednarek and Rossi 2011) and the discourse-analytical tradition of broadcast talk (Tolson 2006; Thornborrow 2015).

Methodologically, these approaches draw on a close textual analysis of microlinguistic phenomena involved in the conversational interaction between participants, in the tradition of conversation analysis applied to spoken media texts (Clayman and Heritage 2002; Hutchby 2006). The combined interdisciplinary perspective yields findings that are relevant for linguistics as well as media and communication studies. As regards the analysis of narrative, there has been a long research tradition into this topic both in film studies (Bordwell 1985; Kozloff 1988; Chatman 1990) and in structurally and functionally oriented literary stylistics (Genette 1980; Simpson 1993; Semino and Culpeper 2002; Leech and Short 2007). Recently, this area has enjoyed much renewed interest in pragmatics, particularly in connection with the emerging communicative practices found in modern social and public media (Hoffmann 2010; Page and Thomas 2011; Page 2012; Dynel and Chovanec 2015). In spite of these developments, the more traditional and well-established genre of the TV documentary still remains a relatively under-researched topic, perhaps with the exception of some studies in the field of audiovisual translation (Franco 2001; Matamala 2009).

2 Narrator voices in telecinematic discourse

One of the main characteristic narrative features of the TV documentary genre is the use of a dual communicative frame. This means that there are two narrators who construct the narrative on two levels – diegetic (i.e. present within the scene itself) and non-diegetic/extra-diegetic (i.e. added during post-production to supplement the narrative in the scene; O'Sullivan 2011). These levels are communicatively separate from each other, coming into existence through editing during the post-production stage, yet they are juxtaposed and intertwined in a very coherent way. Together, they form the dynamically changing and varied narrative situation of modern documentary programmes.

The diegetic level is made up of the participants in the scenes shown within the visual track. In TV documentaries, it comprises the presenter and other individuals who interact with the presenter and/or appear on the camera. The most prominent from among these diegetic voices is the presenter narrator, around whom the entire programme is structured. The second, non-diegetic level consists of the voice-over that is superimposed on the diegetic level. Voice-over narration, then, refers to the use of non-diegetic voice during the narration of the story in film or television productions. While it can be uttered by a character, this type of narration tends to be more commonly used by an off-screen narrator in non-fictional telecinematic works, where it provides the necessary background, having a strong informative nature (LaRocca 2016), particularly in traditional expository documentaries (Lorenzo-Dus 2009: 30). One of the distinctions between the presenter narrator and the voice-over is that the presenter is not only heard but also seen in the programme (Bonner 2011: 6). In this sense, voice-over narrators in the documentary are off-screen; hence, they are literally 'invisible narrators' (Kozloff 1988).

The same kind of hierarchical narrative organization is found in many fictional cinematic genres (Kozloff 1988). This occurs whenever an external narrator or a character provides 'heterodiegetic' narration (Genette 1980).[1] The voice-over functions as the non-diegetic narrator since it 'belongs only to the exegesis and does not narrate about himself as a character in the diegesis, instead narrating exclusively about other people' (Schmid 2010: 68). This results in the typical impersonal, detached style and third-person accounts of events and actions in the diegetic frame, for example, when the voice-over refers to what the on-screen characters have done, are doing, or are about to do, on the camera.[2] The cinematic narrator (Chatman 1990) is not only extra-diegetic but can also be omniscient – Lorenzo-Duz (2009: 33) even calls it 'the authoritative voice of God'. In that sense, it is the privileged voice: its superimposed, extra-diegetic position of a hierarchically higher communicative frame allows it to pass comments also on the 'inter-character diegetic dialogue' (Kozloff 2000: 97). This kind of involvement of the non-diegetic voice in the diegetic world appears to be the rule in TV documentaries; as observed by Chatman, for instance, voice-over can interpret 'when the visual track presents a shallow picture of events' (1990: 136).

One might be tempted to view the contrast between cinematic art and non-fictional screen genres along the axes of scriptedness versus authenticity. That, however, would be a simplification. Non-fictional genres of telecinematic discourse – which include the TV documentary – typically follow a script as well, even though they seem to be showing 'real' individuals in the 'real' world. Criticizing the intuitive binary view of documentary films as presenting 'footage that seems to be making an assertion about the kind of representation it is (e.g., as true or as corresponding with the world it purports to show)', LaRocca (2016: 4) argues that 'documentary film is just another form of poetic imitation, in its variety of instances and complexity of fabrication, it is just as much caught up with the limitations – and effects – of mimetic art, including fiction film'.

Indeed, the characters, the individuals and the voices that viewers experience in cinematic fiction on the one hand and in non-fictional programmes such as documentaries on the other are likewise somewhat similar. The non-authenticity of the discourse produced by actors playing various characters in film (cf. Quaglio 2009; Richardson 2010; Bednarek 2010) is actually akin to the conscious on-camera performance of individuals appearing in non-fictional programmes since their behaviour is subject to a high degree of stylization as well (Lorenzo-Dus and Garcés-Conejos Blitvich 2013; Thornborrow 2015). Indeed, there is little 'real authenticity' about documentaries: while the participants do not play any character roles, they are certainly not 'being themselves': they have social roles to perform in the design of the programme. Thus, what they do is put on their public personas and project their public identities, being engaged in frontstage performance (Goffman 1981) that follows preplanned and partly or fully scripted scenes.[3]

3 Characterization of the data

The data analysed in this chapter comes from the documentary series *How Britain Worked*, produced and aired by the British TV station Channel 4 in 2012. In six instalments, the series traces some of the major British engineering inventions from the time of the Industrial Revolution. The programme is designed around the central role of the presenter, a young British lorry mechanic and motorcycle racer Guy Martin, who gets involved in various reconstruction projects around the whole country, such as a steam engine, a water mill, a seaside pier, and so on. In this sense, each programme constitutes a self-enclosed narrative (Cobley 2013) with a distinct storyline and a gradual development culminating in the final closure – the successful accomplishment of the reconstruction.

As regards its genre classification, the programme is essentially classifiable among expository documentaries that 'claim to offer a truthful view of the socio-historical world that they show' (Lorenzo-Dus 2009: 30). However, in spite of a strong educational component, it also contains some features of reality TV, and hence classifies as an instance of a hybrid documentary. The genre of reality TV is, in general, characterized by the participation of 'ordinary people' (Bonner 2003; Tolson 2006: 130; Garcés-Conejos Blitvich and Lorenzo-Dus 2013: 17) and the observational role of the TV audiences who follow the pursuits of such individuals (Coles 2000: 34). The presenter in this documentary programme is actually an individual who enjoys a celebrity status in the UK thanks to his successful racing career. Within the programme, however, the presenter – while also holding a significant amount of modern technical expertise – engages in tasks for which he lacks the appropriate professional experience requiring the historical knowledge of technical procedures and production processes. As a result, he needs to rely on step-by-step guidance from other experts, which makes him susceptible to occasional failure (Chovanec 2016b). It is this experiential dimension of the programme that makes it possible to classify the programme as having a reality-TV element to it: the presenter is observed in the performance of tasks and is subject to evaluation (by the experts, the voice-over, and ultimately the viewers) of his eventual success. Despite the frequent appearance of laughter in this programme (Chovanec 2018), the production goal appears not to be entertainment, as is the case with many reality TV and entertainment programmes (such as the motor show *Top Gear/Grand Tour*, cf. Bonner 2010; or various 'docusoaps' of the *Big-Brother*-style, cf. Coles 2000), but rather the positive celebration and appreciation of the achievements of past British generations and ordinary workers.

The present chapter analyses a sequence of scenes from the fourth part of the series, where Guy Martin assists in the reconstruction of the last specimen of an eighteenth-century Newcombe engine in a British coal mine. The analysis is intended to identify some of the ways of how the voices of the voice-over narrator and the presenter narrator interact and how they jointly construct the story. While the strategies that are identified below are quite typical of the whole programme and can be found in many other modern TV documentaries, the focus on a connected sequence of scenes in the analysis below is meant to emphasize how the individual strategies are combined in order to assure variety. Arguably, this diversity of narrative techniques and the frequent switches between the narrative voices contribute to the appeal of TV documentary programmes.

4 Analysing narrative voices in the documentary

The qualitative analysis, based on a close textual reading of the data, focuses on the interplay between the two voices that are involved in the narration of the main story line of the documentary programme: the voice-over narrator and the presenter narrator. In *How Britain Worked*, the non-diegetic voice-over is produced by the Manchester-born English voice artist and actor Bernard Hill, whose authoritative voice, punctuated with frequent dramatic pauses (a typical feature of voice-over in documentaries; cf. Lorenzo-Dus 2009: 33), provides the factual background to the visual narrative (cf. Osgood and Hinshaw 2009). His standard English pronunciation, tinged with a slight regional accent, contrasts sharply with the diegetic voice of the show's main protagonist and presenter Guy Martin, who provides the second main narrative voice in the documentary. The latter's strong Lincolnshire accent is occasionally almost unintelligible when he spontaneously launches into fast, emotional outbursts. Arguably, the contrast between the accents, as well as the marked difference in the tempo of the narrators' speech, contributes to the dynamism existing between the two narrative voices and, by extension, of the entire programme. By marking the celebrity presenter as non-elite, Guy Martin's accent enhances his 'ordinariness' and combines with the non-eliteness of his social status as a blue-collar professional. The regional accent spoken by the presenter, as well as the numerous other individuals he interacts with throughout the programme, serves to orient the viewers to the diegetic world (cf. Kozloff 2000: 35) and anchor the given scene in the particular regional and social environment that serves as the setting of the programme.

As regards the interplay between these two narrative voices, the analysis in this section identifies several strategies of how the narrative is built through their interaction, depending on how much control each voice has in the story telling. It is based on a close watching and transcription of the six-hour programme and the identification of the most important kinds of relationship between the voices as regards the dominant role of one or the other in the construction of the narrative. The analysis of the data has revealed a limited set of strategies that keep occurring throughout the programme. In this way, we can identify segments of the documentary where

(a) the voice-over is the dominant narrator, with the presenter narrator having only very incidental involvement (Section 4.1);
(b) the voice-over frames conversational interaction between the presenter and another individual while still retaining its dominance as regards the expository mode of the discourse (Section 4.2);
(c) the voice-over yields to a more extended dialogical interaction between the characters on the diegetic level and, thus, gives up its dominance (Section 4.3); and
(d) the voice-over and the presenter jointly narrate the story in turns, complementing each other more or less equally (Section 4.4).

4.1 The dominance of the voice-over narrator

From the production point of view, the voice-over narration is part of a soundtrack that is added in post-production when the individual shots are edited into a coherent visual narrative. During this process, the non-diegetic soundtrack (and music) becomes superimposed onto the diegetic narration within a hierarchically superordinate frame.

While in some documentaries, the voice-over constitutes the only narrative voice telling the story and accompanying the visual track, it is much more common for the off-camera voice-over to be interlaced with utterances that originate within the communicative frame constituted by the scene that is shown on the camera. The latter can include utterances produced by the presenter narrator as well as a number of other individuals. Modern documentaries are thus characterized by a constant switch between the superimposed narrator voice within the higher-level frame and other voices on the lower-level frame.

One of the typical techniques for realizing this switch between narrators in TV documentaries is given in Extract 1. With this technique, the narrative is told exclusively through the voice-over, with the accessed voice of the presenter narrator not developing the story in any significant way. In the example, the presenter narrator has only a very minimal involvement. His voice appears to be added in order to make the scene come to life by enabling the audience to momentarily hear what is going on among the participants currently shown on the screen. In this sense, the diegetic voice animates the visual track and prevents the perception of a potential disassociation between the verbal and the visual tracks:

Extract 1. Telling the story through voice-over (*How Britain Worked* 4, 4.14–4.49, Extraction of coal from a mine)[4]

1	VO	Over the coming months (.) Guy will help the
2		experts re<u>store</u> the ma<u>chine</u>. They'll need to
3		replace the rotting exterior <u>frame</u>,
4		recondition the <u>boiler</u>, rebuild the crumbling
5		<u>shaft</u> <u>wall</u> (.) and refurbish nearly all of
6		the engine's FIFty working parts.
7	GM	A::::h...save it for the gentle persuasion...
8	VO	Along the way, Guy will find out just how
9		<u>tough</u> eighteenth-century <u>mining</u> <u>was</u>.
10	GM	Not fair that-
11	Man	You're working t'coal now man
12	VO	And discover how the men and women of the
13		first mining towns (.) forged a new [way of
14		life.
15		[Heh
16		he::::h...(.) it's cracky <u>that</u>! Hey?

In this segment, the documentary provides an initial overview of what is to come later in the programme. Hence, it essentially functions as a teaser which showcases the highlights of the programme in order to secure the interest of the audience. To this end, it pulls 'key excerpts from the scenes to come' (Fox 2010: 211), doing so both verbally and visually. The technique is reminiscent of film trailers, where excerpts inform the viewers of what to expect.

As regards the verbal component, the voice-over narrator is entirely dominant, producing a coherent series of 'flash-forwards' – utterances that describe the processes to be shown later in the documentary. They are among some of the typical features of narrative discourse (Simpson and Montgomery 1995: 141). However, the voice-over narrative is not entirely continuous because it is interrupted on three occasions by the presenter narrator. On these occasions, the voice track gives access to the presenter's voice originating within the scene that is currently being shown on the screen. In the first of these, Guy Martin is hammering on a metal bolt. His emotional and evaluative comment underscores the male participants' ironic understanding of the activity as having a gendered nature ('Ah... save it for the gentle persuasion' in line 7).[5] In the second one of these interruptions (by the non-diegetic voice-over narrative), the presenter complains about the physical demands of coal mining (line 10), which generates an explanatory reaction from a miner who follows him inside the coal mine in which he is presently working (line 11). The third instance occurs at the end of the scene, when the presenter's laughter (line 15) overlaps with the voice-over's final words in this segment. Note, though, that at this point Guy Martin is still off-screen and it is not obvious to the viewer what motivates his laughter (line 16). The visual track switches to the presenter only once the voice-over terminates, revealing that Martin is actually taking a bath in an old-style bathtub. This creates an interesting and potentially mildly humorous discrepancy between the proposition conveyed by the voice-over and the visual track. The soundtrack thus moves in and out of the otherwise fully coherent voice-over narrative by including the verbal comments from the presenter. Those comments neither develop the narrative – that is, they do not provide any additional description or exposition – nor are they structurally necessary to complement the voice-over narrator. The presenter's comments and reactions serve to break up the monologic flow of the voice-over narration into shorter segments, specifying, exemplifying and dynamizing the more general voice-over description, and thus making it more tangible for the viewer.

However, the comments from the presenter are related to the voice-over in that they are timed to illustrate what the voice-over is currently talking about. Thus, the first interruption of the voice-over provides a commentary on the physical demands of the reconstruction work, the second illustrates Guy's experiential processes primed by the voice-over narrator's remark ('Guy will find out just how tough eighteenth-century mining was' in lines 8–9) and the third links the narrator's reference to Guy's discovery of the 'new way of life' of people living at that historical era (cf. Swender 2009). Funnily enough, with the last example, the visual track opens with a two-second historical shot of a miner washing in a tub and ends with the brief (blurred) shot of naked Martin enjoying a hot bath and commenting on his experience, thereby potentially undermining the seriousness of the matter by pointing out Guy's physical enjoyment of his quasi-historical experience of bathing (see Figure 6.1).

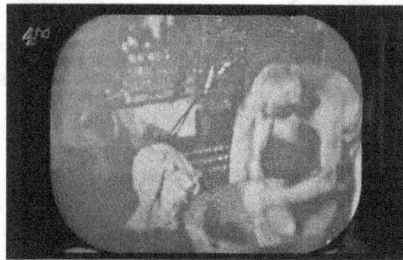 

Figure 6.1 Humorous displacement between non-diegetic voice-over ('a new way of life') and the visual track. 'How Britain Worked' © Channel 4 2012.

Two more observations need to be made. First, the visual track in this segment is more complex than the sound track: the former consists of a series of brief scenes and shots that change in a quick succession. On the other hand, the voice-over frames the entire segment and is assisted by the music track, which provides an additional level of unity of this part of the programme. The assemblage of visual material is explained by the voice-over that specifies the general nature of the work ('Guy will help the experts restore the machine') as well as the specific tasks identified in the verbal track. However, there is some discrepancy here as well – for instance the more general description given by the voice-over in lines 4–5 ('rebuild the crumbling shaft wall') is complemented with a very brief shot of the presenter throwing clay into a brick mould, that is, an activity that is much more specific than the actual description synchronically verbalized by the voice-over in the sound track. The visual shot is actually a flash-forward to an activity that is shown later on in the programme; it is an intricate aspect of the visual cohesion of the TV programme.

The second observation concerns the temporal disconnection between utterances in the verbal track and the actual shots and scenes shown. The use of the future tense by the voice-over (instead of, say, the present perfect or the past tense) to describe events that have already happened betray the ultimate orientation of these utterances to the audience, signposting the audience's imminent exposure to the activities within the documentary programme. The motivation for this linguistic feature is, of course, to be sought in the overall function of this segment as the preview or teaser for what is to come within the rest of the programme rather than, say, in an individual scene that might follow.

4.2 Interplay of voices

Another strategy for realizing the interplay between the voices of the narrator and the presenter goes beyond their mere juxtaposition. The voices are already poised in a mutual relationship. This can take several forms. Extract 2 illustrates two of them: the framing use of the voice-over narration to introduce an embedded conversational interaction, and the mutual dialogical interaction of the voices indicating their close interdependence:

Extract 2. The framing use of voice-over (*How Britain Worked* 4, 4.54–5.42, Identification of rotten beams)

1	VO	The first job facing the team (.) is a big one
2		(1.5) The entire oak frame above the mine
3		shaft has decayed and needs to be replaced.
4	GM	So it's >actually proper< rotten.
5	Man	Rotten.
6	GM	Oh now [all righ'
7	Man	[wi'a lo'o' 'and cream it'll come jus'
8		Clean
9	GM	We'll see to that. Right 'ere.
10	Man	Right 'ere.
11	GM	((GM groping the bottom of a beam)) Proper
12		rotten. (3.0) ((scene cut; coordinating a
13		crane)) Right there? 'appy enough?
14	Man	Yeah yeah. ((GM hand-sawing a beam))
15	VO	Guy is helping to take the old frame apart.
16	GM	Are ya' all right?
17	VO	A crane will complete the job (.) pulling out
18		the dismantled sections. Once cleared (.) it
19		will be re<u>placed</u> with <u>new</u> (.) <u>English</u> <u>oak</u>.
20	GM	>You wan' me to cu' em up all right?<
21	VO	When the engine was first built, it
22		represented cutting-edge technology.
23	GM	<Ro:::le>, we'll be lifting it >from the top<.

In this segment, the voice-over narration provides a background framework, within which the talk between the presenter and a worker are embedded. The utterances produced by the voice-over narrator are not, unlike the example discussed in the previous section, independently coherent, though they make sense with respect to the visual track. In lines 1–3, the voice-over sets up the context for the scene. The voice-over talk contains a recognizable text pattern of the 'problem-solution' kind (Hoey 1983), which is also reminiscent of some of the sequenced structural elements of narrative storytelling identified by Labov and Waletzky (1967). In this narrative episode, the voice-over first sets the scene and provides an orientation ('the first job facing the team'), and then it introduces some problematic part of the event ('the entire oak frame ... has decayed'). This step, constituting Hoey's 'problem' move, is followed by a statement that implies the 'solution' that the subsequent action will achieve ('needs to be replaced').[6] The statements could also be interpreted as a sequenced pattern of 'complication' and 'resolution' within Labov and Waletzky's narrative model. This act of storytelling is framed within the narrator's positive evaluation ('the first job ... is a big one'), which serves to prime the audience's appreciation of the eventual successful achievement of the reconstruction by Guy Martin's team.

The switch from the narrator to the presenter at this point is coupled with the presenter repeating, through his verbal comments and physical acts, the structural moves of the local narrative that has been outlined through the narrator voice. Thus, the presenter repeats the move of complication by describing the beam he is inspecting as 'proper rotten' (line 4). The adjective 'rotten' forms a co-referential cohesive chain with the synonymous expression 'decayed' introduced shortly before by the voice-over. The expression is subsequently repeated verbatim by an expert who inspects the beam with Guy Martin. By echoing Martin's word, the man confirms the problem and affirms its seriousness ('Rotten', line 5). The mutual joint negotiation of the problematic issue involves the specification of the location ('Right 'ere', line 9), the further enhancement of the seriousness of the problem ('Proper rotten', lines 11–12) as well as the suggestion of a general solution that is imminent ('We'll see to that', line 9). While all these acts are jointly achieved by the presenter and the expert, representing their own personal discovery procedure, the localization of the rotten part of the beam merely affirms and interactionally develops what the voice-over narrator had already established shortly before.

At this point, the voice-over interferes: it provides a running commentary on what the viewers can see in the next scene. The relevant utterance ('Guy is helping to take the old frame apart', line 15) articulates the presenter's active participation in the resolution of the problem, assigning meaning to the visual track in which the men coordinate their activities. The diegetic level resurfaces in Guy Martin's utterance which is addressed non-specifically to one of the workers ('Are you all right?', line 16), cut off by the voice-over narrator providing technical details about the solution ('A crane will complete the job...', line 17). The diegetic level is accessed once more, with voice given to Guy Martin, who makes another transactional utterance whereby the physical activity of the workmen is being coordinated and his reliance on the expertise of others is highlighted ('You wan' me to cu' em up all right?', line 20). The presenter's utterances at this point have a merely emblematic function since they do not contribute to the construction of the narrative. They serve a similar purpose as the brief utterances constituting the minimal involvement of the voice of the presenter narrator in the programme documented in Section 4.1.

Throughout the extract, the voice-over narrator is in the expository mode, that is, presenting information from an authoritative viewpoint of the omniscient narrator. Unlike Example 1, however, in this particular case it more distinctly structures the entire segment, providing a framework for the presenter narrator to either verbally repeat or physically perform what the voice-over has described or is describing. In this way, the voice-over provides guidance to the viewers, both framing the interaction between the participants on the diegetic level and interpreting the on-screen action.

4.3 The expository mode of diegetic voices

It is hardly surprising to see the voice-over operate in the expository mode, that is, presenting factual information. This is, after all, the most usual (default) function of the non-diegetic narrator. This function, however, is occasionally also assumed by the presenter narrator or other informed individuals whose voices are accessed for the purpose of imparting information. In this case, the dominant voices responsible for the development of the narrative are located on the diegetic level of the individual scenes making up the documentary programme: a situation which is exemplified in Extract 3. Here, the presenter narrator initially shifts into the expository mode (lines 1–11) and then tries, with varying degrees of success, to ease out information from one of the workers, Keith Jones (KJ; lines 17, 22, 24, 27, 31–32, 37, 39, 41). In this case, it is the diegetic voices that move the narrative forward, with only a marginal assistance of the voice-over narrator:

Extract 3. Fictionalizing the narrative and engaging the expert (*How Britain Worked* 4, 5.43–6.53, Presenter-expert discussion)

1	GM	1712 and folk would've been looking at that
2		and saying (.) <'what is it?' (.) 'what's it
3		doing?'> Folk would've >never seen anything
4		like this before< ever. It'd've been like, a
5		bit of, wouldn't it, like witchcraft or
6		something … what's happening here, wouldn't it,
7		that's what it would be, like a bit of
8		witchcraft or something, 'U::O::::H', you
9		know, like that, is that what folk do?
10		'UU::::H' (.) we still do that in Lincolnshire
11		(.) <aeroplanes>.
12	VO	Keith Jones is supervising the new timberwork
13		on the beam engine. He knows he's got a ha:rd
14		act to follow.
15	KJ	1712 no cranes as we're seeing today no hard
16		hats no bother like that no=
17	GM	No bother like that [all right heh heh
18	KJ	[=They just got on and did
19		it what we're doing today with two or three
20		people they'd have had twenty thirty people
21		doing it-
22	GM	You reckon?
23	KJ	Oh yeah.
24	GM	Yeah?
25	KJ	Blocks'n'tackles, an' horses an' ropes an' you
26		know=
27	GM	Blocks'n'tackle
28	KJ	=blocks'n'tackle and the best computer in the
29		world your brains get on do it. You know, it's
30		just <u>staggering</u> what they achieved
31	GM	You're im, you're impressed you're genuinely
32		[impressed
33	KJ	[Oh yea, genuinely impressed. How they got
34		some of those lumps of wood up there I mean
35		that main beam on that engine probably weighs
36		best part of three tons.
37	GM	Is that one solid piece of oak?

38	KJ	One solid [piece of oak
39	GM	[all right three ton you reckon?
40	KJ	Easily. Probably more than that.
41	GM	You reckon?
42	KJ	Yes.

The transition from the non-diegetic narration at the end of Extract 2 (i.e. immediately preceding the beginning of this extract) to the diegetic voice of the presenter talking to the camera at the beginning of Extract 3 is also formally marked and enhanced by the termination of the music track, which correlates with the termination of the framing function of the earlier voice-over narration. Thus, for the duration of Extract 3, the soundtrack consists only of diegetic sounds, save for a brief intervention from the voice-over to introduce the expert (lines 12–14).

The scene shows the presenter talking directly to the camera and ruminating on the historical machinery. Because of the cutting and editing of the documentary programme, Guy Martin's monologic exposition comes immediately after the scene that shows the replacement of the rotten beam, and it may be less evident to the viewer what exactly he is referring to with the pronouns 'that' and 'it' ('folk would have been looking at that and saying "what is it?", "what's it doing?"' in lines 1–3). The pronouns lack any antecedents and the visual track does not, at this point, enable its anchorage to some object presented visually. The likely antecedents are to be sought in the preceding scene and, more specifically, in the voice-over narrator's last reference to an engine and, more generally, technology ('When the engine was first built, it represented cutting-edge technology', lines 21–22 in Example 2). Here, cohesion is constructed across the individual voices and scenes.

From a pragmatic point of view, the presenter narrator also introduces fictional voices of eighteenth-century people through so-called *ventriloquizing* (Tannen 2010). Guy Martin uses these voices to express the people's assumed amazement over what must have been unique and ground-breaking technology at its time. In his monologue, the presenter skilfully juxtaposes these fictionalized voices with his own voice, while establishing and developing a verbal quasi-contact with the audience (cf. the tag 'wouldn't it' and the discourse marker 'you know', lines 5 and 8–9) in an instance of synthetic personalization (Fairclough 1989; Tolson 1991). His monologue ends with an act of joking, when he likens the failure of common eighteenth-century people to comprehend the Newcomen engine to the (assumed) reactions from the people of his home county to aeroplanes ('"UU::::H" we still do that in Lincolnshire (.) aeroplanes', lines 10–11). Through this obvious exaggeration, the presenter not only presents people from his region as somewhat backward but – importantly – also aligns himself to the rural locality and 'the common folk'. In this way, he performs his 'ordinariness' for the camera and boosts the credibility of the persona he is presenting in the documentary series.

After this initial exposition and evaluation by the presenter, the verbal track switches momentarily to the non-diegetic voice-over that introduces the identity of a man who is currently working together with Martin ('Keith Jones is supervising the new timberwork on the beam engine', lines 12–13). The voice-over narrator, with his omniscient approach, specifies the expert's mental process as 'knowing' ('He knows he's got a hard act to follow', lines 13–14). In this segment, the specification serves as a transition point for switching back from the voice-over to diegetic narration. The voice-over then terminates, and the communication between the individuals portrayed in the scene becomes accessible to the viewers.

The ensuing conversation between the presenter and the expert is characterized by the presenter backgrounding his own communicative role by prompting the expert to enter into the expository mode and share his expertise. The exchange starts with the expert stating some obvious pieces of historical information ('1712 no cranes as we're seeing today no hard hats ...', lines 15–16). Rhetorically, the utterance contains a three-part series of phrases starting with 'no', with the third element actually setting up an implied contrast with the present time ('...no bother like that no'). This wins an instant emotional reaction from the presenter through echoing and backchannel acknowledgement ('no bother like that, all right', line 17). Another factual statement by the expert (lines 18–21) is similarly rewarded by the presenter's phrase 'You reckon?' (line 22), which both expresses his appreciation and encourages the expert to elaborate. At this point, however, the expert merely concurs ('Oh yeah', in line 23), which is instantly echoed by the presenter ('Yeah?', line 24) in an attempt to keep the communication going. This time, the expert makes another informative utterance, referring to the equipment used by the workers, and the first part of that utterance is once again echoed by the presenter in a backchannel acknowledgement of the content ('Blocks'n'tackle', line 27). The expert repeats the phrase verbatim and develops his contribution further. In the remaining eight turns, the conversation between the presenter and the expert continues in a similar manner: the presenter always picks up some element from the expert's previous utterance, prompting him to follow it up or develop.

Throughout the exchange, the presenter, who is responsible for the extraction of information from the expert, takes a very active approach. In his frequent backchannels and prompts, he also demonstrates the mutual conversational alignment of the two speakers, who are presently involved in cooperative communication and display communicative harmony. While the diegetic participants construct the narrative jointly, their face-to-face conversational interaction also provides the possibility for the display of such positive interpersonal values as camaraderie and bonding (cf. Bonner 2010), and also a shared appreciation of eighteenth-century workers. Segments like these affect the participation framework of the documentary programme: while expository narration through the voice-over's or the presenter's monologue positions viewers as addressees, here the viewers assume the role of overhearers observing conversational encounters among others. Arguably, this observational nature of the viewers' participation enables a different kind of engagement from when they are talked to directly by the various narrators. Aware of the performative aspect in the behaviour of the on-screen individuals, the viewers may be more prone to draw pleasure and enjoyment from observing others engaged in serious as well as playful activities (cf. Corner 2002: 263; for examples of playful exchanges in TV documentaries, see Chovanec 2018).

4.4 Co-construction of narrative by voice-over and presenter

Apart from the development of the narrative through the conversational interaction between characters on the diegetic level of the programme, there are situations when the expository mode is adopted, in a more or less equal manner, by both the voice-over narrator and the presenter narrator.

In this section, this kind of interplay between the two voices is illustrated with two examples. While Extract 4 documents an instance of a relatively independent presentation of information through the voice-over narrator and the presenter, Extract 5 shows a tighter connection between the two voices, pointing out how they intertwine and complement each other in a joint construction of the narrative.

Extract 4. Complementary exposition through non-diegetic and diegetic voices (*How Britain Worked* 4, 6.55–8.55, Description of principles of engine operation)

1	VO	Behind all this hard labour lay one man's
2		ingenuity. No pictures survive of Thomas
3		Newcomen (.) but we know that he came from
4		Devon (.) and was an ironmonger by trade. Many
5		of his customers ran local <u>tin</u> <u>mines</u> where
6		workers faced the daily danger of <u>drowning</u>.
7		Newcomen <u>solved</u> their problem by cracking an
8		age old puzzle. He successfully <u>harnessed</u> the
9		power of steam (2.0) To work out <u>how</u> he did
10		it, Guy's found himself a perfect copy of his
11		machine (1.0) in miniature.
12	GM	Yes, so >what we've got here< is the Newcomen
13		beam engine (1.0) The boiler down here (.)
14		she's obviously boiling the water [...]
15		((description of process omitted: 7.45-8.18))
16		It's BRILliant. <ABSOlutely> brilliant. (3.5)
17		Yes, >all we've got'ere is just< a (.)
18		miniature version (1.0) on nearly exact scale
19		of a (1.0) >you know< ((pointing a finger))
20		the engine we've got 'ere.
21	VO	The original's three-ton oak beam and FIFty
22		moving parts are <u>still</u> lying <u>idle</u>. But if the
23		team succeed, they'll have resurrected the
24		first mechanical wonder of the <u>industrial</u> <u>age</u>.
25	GM	This one 'ere's gonna take a bit of work to
26		(.) get her ship shape again. >It'll run like
27		this< an'it might take a bit of work yet but
28		we'll >get it running like this<.

This segment starts with the voice-over giving an encyclopedia-style overview on the inventor of the Newcomen engine. The narrative structure of this introduction follows, once again, the three-part story structure of a micronarrative by presenting the set-up ('Many of his customers ran local tin mines', lines 4–5), outlining the problem ('workers faced the daily danger of drowning', line 6), and hinting at a resolution ('Newcomen solved their problem by cracking an age old puzzle', lines 7–8). The micronarrative serves as a lead-in for the description of the technical process by the presenter in the next turn.

The visual track running next to the voice-over within this segment initially continues with the previous scene, where Guy Martin and Keith Jones hammer on bolts. This is replaced by several moving aerial shots of the English coast and countryside to illustrate the inventor's region of origin. Once the voice-over mentions the resolution ('Newcomen solved…', line 7), the visual track switches to a scene of the presenter operating a model of the machinery. For several seconds, there is a lack of alignment between the words and the image: the viewers are able to see Guy Martin and the model before the voice-over actually describes that reality in words ('Guy's found himself a perfect copy of his machine in miniature', lines 10–11). This moment is potentially interesting: during the few seconds of the non-alignment between the verbal and the visual tracks, the presenter is actually metaphorically represented on the screen as the original inventor. By linking the verbal with the visual track, the voice-over indicates that a turn transition point has been reached.

At this point, there is a switch in the narrative voice. The presenter identifies the object in front of him (the formulation indicates that he acts on a prompt from the production team, cf. 'Yes, so what we've got here …', line 12) and starts an elaborate technical explanation, lasting almost a whole minute (left out of the previous extract). During this time he describes the design and the operation of the engine in a long monologue addressed to the camera. With this description, the presenter fully adopts the expository mode. Together with the way he is aligned to the viewers, talking directly to the camera and claiming common ground through the inclusive pronoun *we* (cf. 'you know the engine we've got 'ere' in lines 19–20), the scene is ideally structured to meet the primary goal of the documentary, which is 'producing understanding in the audience' (Dromm 2016: 421).

Such extensive expository monologue produced by the presenter on camera is a very recognizable element of TV documentaries. It is probably the most direct method of conveying informational content to the viewers. In this documentary series, it is found once or twice in each of the programmes. Clearly, it cannot serve as the only technique for conveying information since its overuse could have some adverse effect on the audience. The high level of sophistication, combined with the monologic delivery of this kind of exposition, runs the risk of alienating the audience, for example, through a feeling of being excessively mentored by the presenter. Also, should this technique be used too often, an imbalance might arise in the programme between the traditional communicative roles of the voice-over and the presenter that assign the ultimate knowledgeability to the former. The voice-over narrator in TV documentaries operates, by default, as the omniscient narrator, while the presenter – as a direct participant in the documentary – is there to experience the real events. That affects the role of the viewers as well: they change from being the recipients of informational content that is narrated to them to witnessing events and being observers of lived-through experience.

As regards the mutual relationship between the two voices, we can see that the voice-over narrator hands over the floor to the presenter narrator, and upon the termination of the presenter's expository monologue, the voice-over continues with the exposition. It proceeds to develop the narrative by refocusing on the reconstruction project. However, as the next example shows, the relationship between the non-diegetic and diegetic voices can be even more dynamic.

Extract 5 illustrates how several techniques can be used within a relatively short stretch of the documentary and how the relationship between the narrative voices constantly develops. While in the first two pairs of turns we find the techniques identified in the earlier part of this chapter, the second half of the transcript captures how the narrators alternate, taking turns in a relatively short succession and complementing each in a more coherent way. Instead of merely switching from one narrator to another, the technical editors have skilfully sequenced the narrative voices so that the whole narrative can be built through the joint telling by both of the voices.

Extract 5. Multiple forms of voice-over and presenter interaction (*How Britain Worked* 4, 9.20–11.12; Dangers of mining)

1	VO	The engine's new oak head frame has been
2		delivered. Guy's helping the restoration team
3		to put it in place. The last few <u>bolts</u> need
4		to be se<u>cured</u>.
5	GM	Oh, it's looking a treat.
6	VO	Newcomen's engine protected miners from
7		drowning. But the new deep mines presented
8		other dangers. And while Guy waits for the
9		team to move on to the next stages of the
10		project, he finds out <u>more</u> <u>about</u> them.
11	GM	From 1750 (.) to 1950, there was a 150
12		thousand people killed down in mine >I mean
13		that's not a hundred and fifty<, that's a
14		hundred and fifty THOUsand (.) <that's a lot
15		o'folk> that. And I'm just looking here hey
16		((showing a photograph to camera)) ehm you
17		can see really you can see why (.) I mean
18		.hhh we've got the roof supports here, just
19		with a (.) wedge (.) out in the, >↑you know,
20		it's no wonder so many folk was killed<, hey
21		(1.0) that's not gonna >pass for
22		health'n'safety now< is it, hey (1.0) we got
23		that there >↑look here< (.) what's 'appened
24		↑THERE? >what's there? Your fella's in there
25		with 'is pickaxe< smashing at the face (1.0)
26		these boys aren't messing about (.) that's
27		↑proper ↑work that's (.) ↓proper work.

28	VO	One of the biggest challenges facing miners
29		was <u>seeing</u> what they were <u>doing</u>.
30	GM	They had these (.) you know they 'ad these.
31		Stuck on the side of their 'elmets with clay.
32		Clay-mounted lights (.) I mean (1.0) you're
33		not gonna see a lot with that are you really,
34		I mean a blind man might be pleased to see
35		wouldn't he by 'eck, hey.
36	VO	Carrying a naked flame could be <u>deadly</u> (.)
37		because of underground <u>gases</u> that <u>miners</u>
38		called FIREDAMP. The main culprit was
39		methane. Guy's about to find out just how
40		<u>dangerous</u> it could be. (4.0)
41	GM	You know with the right concentration it's
42		lethal. >It'd 'ave 'ad to be< <u>explo</u>sions down
43		there >you know you've got< a naked light
44		>stuck on the side of your helmet< you're
45		gonna set these explosions off are you? so
46		yeah dangerous business ((cut to a new scene,
47		GM talking camera crew)) I'll be all right
48		'olding the thing I'll be just standing there
49		honestly I'll be all right.

As suggested earlier, there are three different techniques through which the narrative voices are mutually related in Extract 5. The first two (which have been identified and discussed in detail in connection with Extracts 1 and 4) are represented by (a) the incidental remark by the diegetic presenter that interrupts the continuity of the voice-over narration (while not being addressed to any specific recipient, cf. line 5), and (b) the extensive expository monologue delivered by the presenter to camera when talking about a historical photograph showing miners at work (lines 11–27). While the first adds the purely experiential dimension to the informational content provided by the voice-over, the second uses many linguistic features of synthetic personalization ('you can see', 'we've got the roof supports here', 'you know', 'look here', etc.) in order to establish a relation with the viewers and communicate the content in terms of juxtaposing historical facts with the present-day situation that the viewers are likely to be familiar with. This is done both explicitly ('that's not gonna pass for health'n'safety now, is it', lines 21–22) and through implicit inference ('these boys aren't messing about. That's proper work,' lines 25–27).

The third technique, which is the focal point of my analysis at this point, comes into play in the second half of the extract. It constitutes a peculiar instance of 'multiple tellership' (Page 2012: 117) that is established through editorial cutting during the post-production stage. This is characterized not only by the juxtaposition of the voices but also through their sequencing in such a way that they complement each other telling the story.

The segment opens with the statement uttered by the voice-over ('One of the biggest challenges facing miners was seeing what they were doing,' lines 28–29). This introduces another micronarrative by establishing the textual move of a 'problem' (cued by the expression *challenges*). The next element within the structure of the micronarrative, however, is taken up by the presenter, who presents the solution. He does so initially in a rather vague way by using the pronoun *these*, which has an exophoric reference to a miner's lamp that Guy Martin is currently holding in his hand ('They had these (.) you know they 'ad these,' line 30). The presenter then gives a description ('Stuck on the side of their 'elmets with clay,' line 31) before naming the lamp in a very general way ('Clay-mounted lights, I mean', line 32). He never uses the technical name of the device, thereby indicating his lay status of a non-expert.[7]

The presenter's seemingly spontaneous talk (which includes an instance of joking about 'a blind man', cf. line 34) is cut short by the voice-over that refers to the naked light that is shown in the scene ('Carrying a naked flame could be deadly', line 36). Apart from linking the presenter's action in the visual track to the voice-over commentary in the verbal track, this piece of information serves as yet another 'problem' move. Unlike the previous turns, however, it is not resolved immediately – it finds its narrative resolution only several turns later when an expert explains to the presenter some technical innovations that eventually solved the problem. Instead, the voice-over narrator first specifies the nature of the danger ('The main culprit was methane,' lines 38–39) and then sets the ground for another switch between the voices. His utterance at this point ('Guy's about to find out just how dangerous it could be,' lines 39–40) has a discourse-organizing function: it structures the narrative of the programme by indicating the next scene – an experiment carried out by the presenter.

In the next turn, the presenter continues with the factual exposition about the dangers of methane in mines, while preparing for the experiment. Effecting a shift of footing in the final part of his turn, he addresses a series of utterances to the production team, and ultimately the audience, to dispel their possible worries. The multiple assurances show that he is in control of the situation ('I'll be all right 'olding the thing I'll be just standing honestly I'll be all right,' lines 47–49). They further boost the experiential dimension of the presenter's involvement in the documentary.

All in all, the extract shows how the two narrators jointly move the narrative forward, almost in a tango-style manner. Through editing, their narrative voices are woven together, with coherence established through multiple cohesive links not only between the narrators' utterances but also between the verbal and the visual tracks. Arguably, this dynamic presentation and the successions of switches between the voices contribute towards making the presentation of content particularly attractive to the audience.

5 Conclusions

As shown in the analysis, the mutual relationship between the diegetic and non-diegetic narrative voices in TV documentaries is both complex in terms of the structural organization of the entire programme and very dynamic as regards the situation in specific programme segments and scenes. All of that has a number of implications for our understanding of how the narrative is constructed and how the production of the entire programme is designed with respect to captivating the audience. By way of summing up, let me relate the key findings to the following three main points: the interplay between the voices, the roles of the narrators, and the broader structural organization of the documentary, including the relationship between the soundtrack and the visual track. While these findings are based on the analysis of the material at hand, they apply in a general way to the construction of narrative in the genre of the TV documentary.

First, the narrative storytelling in the documentaries is developed through the combination of the voice-over narrator and the presenter narrator in ways that show a changing dynamic between the voices, sometimes even within a single scene. Through editing in post-production, various mutual positions between the voices can be established. While the voice-over tends to be the authoritative, dominant way of conveying information, the presenter – depending on the nature of the programme – occasionally shifts into the full expository mode as well, delivering technical information in a monologue on the camera, thus directly establishing a communicative frame with the viewers. The framing role of the non-diegetic voice-over becomes strongest when the presenter's contributions are merely complementary and illustrative of what is happening on the diegetic level, providing the viewers with a momentary 'glimpse' right into the action. More sophisticated kinds of relationship occur when the voice-over has an evaluative function, for example, commenting on and glossing over the verbal interaction in the diegetic level (including conversational dialogic interaction between the presenter and other individuals), and a discourse organizational function, for example, by means of verbal flash-forwards and flashbacks.

As regards their communicative roles, a certain lack of balance is observable between the two voices. In general, the non-diegetic voice-over narrator in TV documentaries provides a level of 'certainty': this is the authoritative voice of an omniscient narrator that provides a frame for the entire programme, guiding the viewers from the beginning till the end. Importantly, the knowledge status of the voice-over does not change during the programme. That stability, however, opens up the possibility for the presenter narrator voice to assume the opposite role. The presenter's knowledge and communicative role may shift dramatically scene from scene. These dynamic changes sometimes correlate with shifts of footing: when the presenter talks on camera, he may opt to adopt the expository mode marked with a high level of knowledge and characterized by technical information being conveyed to the audience. Thanks to the imparting of information, the presenter is constructed as a knowledgeable individual, who explicitly orients towards the TV audience rather than the other participants or the activity that he is involved in in the scene.

By contrast, when the presenter engages in conversations with other participants in the diegetic frame, his knowledge status typically changes. So does the nature of his narration – he becomes responsible for teasing the technical expertise out of the experts and thus has to position himself as a less knowledgeable individual. At the same time, the fact that the presenter is physically present in the diegetic scene means that his narrative can assume a significant experiential nature, manifested in his evaluative comments on various phenomena. As a result, while the non-diegetic voice-over uses the third-person narrative form when referring to the embedded frame, the diegetic presenter tends to alternate between moving the narrative forward (either in monologue or in dialogue), and consciously self-reflecting on his own experience (evidenced by first-person utterances). The disinterested knowledge of the voice-over narrator thus contrasts with the personalized and experienced knowledge of the presenter.

The last point that needs to be highlighted concerns the broader structural relations that link the issue of narrative voices to the technical design of the programme. Thus, within the macrostructure of the narrative of the entire programme, for instance, both the voice-over and the presenter produce relatively self-enclosed micronarratives, consisting of some of the fundamental constructional elements of narratives such as the set-up, the complication and the resolution. A complex relationship between the voices may develop between the voice-over and the presenter, for example, with the former establishing the set-up and postulating the complication, and the latter detailing the resolution. The micronarrative is thus constructed jointly across the communicative levels by both the non-diegetic voice-over and the diegetic presenter. This appears to be a particularly effective technique of storytelling in TV documentaries since it allows for the shifts between the narrative voices to move almost seamlessly from one to the other.

Related to that is yet another dimension of the broader structural level, namely the (non-)alignment of the sound and the visual tracks. While non-diegetic sounds (such as music) serve a connecting function within a single scene or across several scenes, the verbal track is very often misaligned with respect to the visual track. The discrepancy can be either between the voice-over narrator and the visual scene (e.g. with the voice-over anticipating what is yet to come or describing the action with a slight delay) or between the presenter narrator and the visual track (e.g. with the presenter's voice providing cohesion across an assemblage of edited shots or with historical video footage on the screen). Arguably, it is in this direction that we may look for some promising future pragma-stylistic research in the area of TV documentaries.

Notes

1 Lorenzo-Dus (2009: 21) refers to the latter type as 'heterodiegetic narration'. The detachment, typical of such 'voice of God' narrators, contrasts with homodiegetic narrators, who 'become personally involved in their acts of telling'. Since this distinction might be somewhat problematic in the case of some documentaries (cf. also Lorenzo-Dus 2009: 30), I prefer to use the expression 'diegetic' and 'non-diegetic'. This usage follows the practice in the literature on broadcast talk and TV documentaries and stresses the structural/production aspect of the genre, that is, whatever is added to

the soundtrack after the recording to the scene is identified as 'non-diegetic' (i.e. the voice-over, additional sounds, music, etc.).
2   There are, of course, documentary formats where the voice-over narrator and the presenter narrator are the same person (as with the documentary programmes produced and narrated by David Attenborough) or where the voice-over uses the first-person plural pronoun *we*. Those cases, however, are beyond the scope of my interest here.
3   The real, authentic backstage selves are revealed only on rare occasions, such as in microphone gaffes in live broadcasts (Chovanec 2016a), or in some special programme designs such as the candid camera or 'fly-on-the-wall' documentaries that aim to frame unsuspecting participants (Brock 2015).
4   VO = the voice-over narrator Bernard Hill; GM – the presenter Guy Martin.
5   This appears to tie in with the trend of male participants in various TV shows to perform their gendered identity in more or less explicit ways. They do this for the purpose of masculine bonding and camaraderie, which are based on the image of the tough, working-class male (cf. Smith 2008; Bonner 2010).
6   As observed by Coles (2000: 33), the problem/resolution format is a 'common structuring device used both in documentary and drama'. Lorenzo-Dus confirms this finding, arguing that the structure is crucial in the design of the programme's storytelling. It is one of the ways of overcoming 'dullness' (2009: 22).
7   The technical term for the lamp is then used only later on in the presenter's discussion with an expert – a lamp maker.

References

Bakhtin, M. M. (1981), *The Dialogic Imagination: Four Essays*, Austin and London: University of Texas Press.
Bednarek, M. (2010), *The Language of Fictional Television: Drama and Identity*, London and New York: Continuum.
Bernard, S. C. (2011), *Documentary Storytelling: Creative Nonfiction on Screen*, 3rd edn, Amsterdam: Focal Press.
Bonner, F. (2003), *Ordinary Television: Analyzing Popular TV*, London: Sage.
Bonner, F. (2010), 'Top Gear: Why does the world's most popular programme not deserve scrutiny', *Critical Studies in Television*, 5 (1): 32–45. http://journals.sagepub.com/doi/pdf/10.7227/CST.5.1.5.
Bonner, F. (2011), *Personality Presenters: Television's Intermediaries with Viewers*, London: Routledge.
Bordwell, D. (1985), *Narration in the Fiction Film*, London: Methuen.
Brock, A. (2015), 'Participation frameworks and participation in televised sitcoms, candid camera and stand-up comedy', in M. Dynel and J. Chovanec (eds), *Participation in Public and Social Media Interactions*, 27–47, Amsterdam and Philadelphia: John Benjamins.
Chatman, S. (1990), *Coming to Terms: The Rhetoric of Narrative in Fiction and Film*, Ithaca and London: Cornell University Press.
Chovanec, J. (2016a), 'Eavesdropping on media talk: Microphone gaffes and unintended humour in sports broadcasts', *Journal of Pragmatics*, 95: 93–106. doi: 10.1016/j.pragma.2016.01.011.

Chovanec, J. (2016b), '"It's quite simple, really": Shifting forms of expertise in TV documentaries', *Discourse, Context and Media*, 13 (A): 11–19. doi:10.1016/j.dcm.2016.03.004.

Chovanec, J. (2018), 'Laughter and non-humorous situations in TV documentaries', in V. Tsakona and J. Chovanec (eds), *The Dynamics of Interactional Humor: Creating and Negotiating Humor in Everyday Encounters*, 155–79, Amsterdam and Philadelphia: John Benjamins.

Clayman, S. and Heritage, J. (2002), *The News Interview: Journalists and Public Figures on the Air*, Cambridge: Cambridge University Press.

Cobley, P. (2013), *Narrative*, London: Routledge.

Coles, G. (2000), 'Docusoap: Actuality and the serial format', in B. Carson and M. Llewellyn-Jones (eds), *Frames and Fictions on Television. The Politics of Identity within Drama*, 27–39, Exeter and Portland: Intellect.

Corner, J. (2002), 'Performing the real: Documentary diversions', *Television and New Media*, 3 (3): 255–269.

Dromm, K. (2016), 'Understanding (and) the legacy of the trace: Reflections after Carroll, Currie, and Plantinga', in D. LaRocca (ed.), *The Philosophy of Documentary Film*, 413–30, Lanhan and London: Lexington Books.

Dynel, M. and Chovanec, J., eds (2015), *Participation in Public and Social Media Interactions*, Amsterdam and Philadelphia: John Benjamins.

Fairclough, N. (1989), *Language and Power*, London: Routledge.

Fox, B. (2010), *Documentary Media: History, Theory, Practice*, Harlow: Pearson Education Inc.

Franco, E. P. C. (2001), 'Voiced-over television documentaries: Terminological and conceptual issues for their research', *Target: International Journal of Translation Studies*, 13 (2): 289–304.

Garcés-Conejos Blitvich, P. and Lorenzo-Dus, N. (2013), 'Reality television: A discourse-analytical perspective', in N. Lorenzo-Dus and P. Garcés-Conejos Blitvich (eds), *Real Talk: Reality Television and Discourse Analysis in Action*, 9–23, Basingstoke: Palgrave Macmillan.

Genette, G. (1980), *Narrative Discourse*, Oxford: Basil Blackwell.

Gieve, S. and Norton, J. (2007), 'Dealing with linguistic difference in encounters with others on British television', in S. Johnson and A. Ensslin (eds), *Language in the Media*, 188–210, London and New York: Continuum.

Goffman, E. (1981), *Forms of Talk*, Philadelphia: University of Pennsylvania Press.

Hartley, J. (1982), *Understanding News*, London and New York: Routledge.

Hoey, M. (1983), *On the Surface of Discourse*, London: Allen and Unwin.

Hoffmann, C., ed. (2010), *Narrative Revisited: Telling a Story in the Age of New Media*, Amsterdam and Philadelphia: John Benjamins.

Hutchby, I. (2006), *Media Talk: Conversation Analysis and the Study of Broadcasting*, Maidenhead: Open University Press.

Kozloff, S. (1988), *Invisible Storytellers: Voice-over Narration in American Fiction Film*, Berkeley: University of California Press.

Kozloff, S. (2000), *Overhearing Film Dialogue*, Berkeley: University of California Press.

Labov, W. (1972), 'The transformation of experience in narrative syntax', in W. Labov (ed.), *Language in the Inner City: Studies in the Black English Vernacular*, 354–96, Philadelphia: University of Pennsylvania Press.

Labov, W. and Waletzky, J. (1967), 'Narrative analysis', in J. Helm (ed.), *Essays on the Verbal and Visual Arts*, 12–44, Seattle: University of Washington Press.
LaRocca, D. (2016), 'Introduction: Representative qualities and questions of documentary film', in D. LaRocca (ed.), *The Philosophy of Documentary Film*, Lanham and London: Lexington Books.
Leech, G. N. and M. Short (2007), *Style in Fiction: A Linguistic Introduction to English Fictional Prose*, 2nd edn, Harlow and London: Pearson Education.
Lorenzo-Dus, N. (2009), *Television Discourse: Analysing Language in the Media*, Basingstoke: Palgrave Macmillan.
Lorenzo-Dus, N. and Garcés-Conejos Blitvich, P., eds (2013), *Real Talk: Reality Television and Discourse Analysis in Action*, Basingstoke: Palgrave Macmillan.
Matamala, A. (2009), 'Main challenges in the translation of documentaries', in J. Díaz Cintas (ed.), *New Trends in Audiovisual Translation*, 109–32, Bristol: Multilingual Matters.
Osgood, R. J. and Hinshaw, M. J. (2009), *Visual Storytelling: Videography and Post-production in the Digital Age*, Boston: Wadsworth Cengage Learning.
O'Sullivan, C. (2011), *Translating Popular Film*, Basingstoke: Palgrave Macmillan.
Page, R. (2012), *Stories and Social Media: Identities and Interaction*, New York and London: Routledge.
Page, R. and Thomas, B., eds (2011), *New Narratives: Stories and Storytelling in the Digital Age*, Lincoln: University of Nebraska Press.
Piazza, R., Bednarek, M. and Rossi, F., eds (2011), *Telecinematic Discourse: Approaches to the Language of Films*, Amsterdam and Philadelphia: John Benjamins.
Quaglio, P. (2009), *Television Dialogue: The Sitcom Friends vs. Natural Conversation*, Amsterdam and Philadelphia: John Benjamins.
Richardson, K. (2010), *Television Dramatic Dialogue: A Sociolinguistic Study*, New York: Oxford University Press.
Schmid, W. (2010), *Narratology: An Introduction*, Berlin and New York: Walter de Gruyter.
Semino, E. and Culpeper, J., eds (2002), *Cognitive Stylistics: Language and Cognition in Text Analysis*, Amsterdam and Philadelphia: John Benjamins.
Simpson, P. (1993), *Language, Ideology and Point of View*, London: Routledge.
Simpson, P. and Montgomery, M. (1995), 'Language, literature and film', in P. Verdonk and J. J. Weber (eds), *Twentieth Century Fiction: From Text to Context*, 138–64, London: Routledge.
Smith, A. (2008), '*Top Gear* as a Bastion of Heterosexual Masculinity', in K. Ross and S. Price (eds), *Popular Media and Communication: Essays on Publics, Practices and Processes*, 83–102, Newcastle upon Tyne: Cambridge Scholars Publishing.
Swender, R. (2009), 'Claiming the found: Archive footage and documentary practice', *The Velvet Light Trap*, 64: 3–10.
Tannen, D. (2010), 'Abduction and identity in family interaction: Ventriloquizing as indirectness', *Journal of Pragmatics*, 42 (2): 307–16.
Thornborrow, J. (2015), *The Discourse of Public Participation Media: From Talk Show to Twitter*, London and New York: Routledge.
Tolson, A. (1991), 'Televised chat and the synthetic personality', in P. Scannell (ed.), *Broadcast Talk*, 178–90, London: Sage.
Tolson, A. (2006), *Media Talk: Spoken Discourse on TV and Radio*, Edinburgh: Edinburgh University Press.

Transcription conventions

(Following Hutchby 2006)

[	turns that start simultaneously
=	latched utterances
.hhh	an audible intake of breath
↑↓	rise or fall in pitch
<u>under</u>line	speaker emphasis
CAPITALS	speech markedly louder
< >	slow talk
> <	fast talk
sou::::nd	stretching of a sound or a word
((note))	description of non-verbal activity
(1.5)	length of pause in seconds
(.)	brief pause (less than 0.5 seconds)
heh	laughter token

7

A mixed-method analysis of autism spectrum disorder representation in fictional television

Susan Reichelt

1 Introduction

Autism spectrum disorders (ASD) have been explored in several ways in telecinematic contexts (see Belcher and Maich 2014), creating recognizable patterns and stereotypes of those diagnosed, including the savant, the compulsive, the socially awkward or the overly literal (Draaisma 2009).

This chapter introduces a twofold method of investigating the portrayal of a character diagnosed with Asperger's syndrome in a recent fictional television series. The study does not dwell on questions of authenticity or 'realness' of the portrayal of ASD, but rather focuses on how pragmatic competence of characters identified with and around an ASD diagnosis is indexed within the telecinematic context. A quantitative character analysis of the use of pragmatic markers (*you know*, *I mean* and *kind of*) across different characters is set alongside a qualitative scene analysis that investigates interaction between characters and mise en scène. This approach is based on Androutsopoulos's multileveled framework, which investigates sociolinguistic difference as character styling (2012: 301–2) and enables an incorporation of different aspects of sociolinguistic analysis in order to fully explore meaning-making processes of audiovisual performances (2012: 323).

The first part of the chapter addresses previous accounts of ASD representations in audiovisual media, providing a backdrop of why predominant focus has been given to pragmatic competence, and what the present paper adds to the discussion. The second part of the chapter consists of two analyses of pragmatic competence, using the television series *Parenthood* as a case study. Lastly, the discussion emphasizes the gained insights a mixed-method approach might yield, particularly when considering audiovisual media. Precisely because character styling occurs multi-modally, an analysis of multiple aspects of sociolinguistic difference offers differentiated interpretations of indexed representations.

2 Representation of ASD in audiovisual media

This chapter deals with a particular type of autism spectrum disorder commonly known as Asperger's syndrome (after Asperger 1944), defined as high-functioning on the autism spectrum. In recent years, popular culture, from movies and television to novels and picture books, has increasingly featured characters with ASD, and they seem to follow certain stereotypical trends in their depictions. Draaisma (2009: 1476–7) argues that stereotypes of ASD are so prolific that, while older examples of ASD characterizations would usually come with an expert introducing the disorder ('the topical white-coat scene'), newer depictions would drop these altogether. Audiences know what to expect when a character is introduced as diagnosed with Asperger's, and audiences even leap to an unconfirmed diagnosis when particular character cues appear. According to Belcher and Maich (2014), who conducted a cross-media analysis into the representation of ASD in popular media, fictional television characters with ASD diagnoses (or indications thereof) are usually 'portrayed as intellectually stimulating geniuses' (2014: 97). In fact, four of the five characters associated with ASD that are discussed here are exceptionally skilled scientists (Reid in *Criminal Minds*, Brennan in *Bones*, Sheldon in *The Big Bang Theory* and Mary McDonnell in *Grey's Anatomy*).

The representation of Asperger's in audiovisual media seldom extends past these stereotypes, something that has been criticized as it creates unrealistic perceptions of the disorder that may even be harmful to those not fitting into these moulds (cf. Belcher and Maich 2014: 98).

Stereotypes are not always directly linked to autism spectrum diagnoses, although popular culture relies on audiences drawing their conclusions about certain characters. One such character often connected to Asperger's but never officially confirmed by the series creators is *The Big Bang Theory's* Sheldon Cooper. McGrath (2014) claims that even though Sheldon is never directly said to be diagnosed, his characterization as being 'outside the norm due to communication difficulties' (2014: 140) is catering towards an ASD interpretation. Her analysis consistently shows Sheldon to be ill-equipped when it comes to pragmatic competence and how to appropriately communicate in different social situations (cf. 2014: 158ff). She says that one key characteristic of Sheldon that is explored throughout the series is 'that he cannot read others' emotions' and is generally unable to read 'social situations and emotions' (2014: 160). Bednarek, in a study analysing characterization of 'nerdiness', finds similar patterns and remarks that Sheldon's 'inability to understand sarcasm and irony, and his difficulty with non-literal phrases and expressions' (2012: 215), that is, again, aspects of pragmatic competence, are generally associated with Asperger's.

The characterization of ASD and Asperger's is thus established through seemingly typical pragmatic behaviour (see also Section 4). Many of these indexes are based on what the characters talk about (or, what they never talk about) and how they explicitly comment on their own and others' behaviour (cf. Bednarek 2012, on keywords in Sheldon's dialogue). What is unclear, however, is whether and how implicit pragmatic cues (cf. Culpeper 2001) are strategically used in combination with explicit cues or meta-commentary. This paper focuses on pragmatic markers that are not stereotypically associated or indexed with mental disorders, but rather belong to the expected, and thus unmarked repertoire of spoken dialogue. In that, their strategic use for characters with ASD would imply additional layers in the sociolinguistic characterization of fictional speakers. For this, I am focusing on one particular character with ASD from the television series *Parenthood*.

3 *Parenthood*

Parenthood is an American dramedy that was broadcast on network television (NBC) from 2010 to 2015. The seasons are of varying length and amount to a total of 103 episodes. Included in the present study are seasons one to four, which equal 68 episodes and a total of 2,856 minutes of screen time (assuming a typical runtime of 42 minutes per episode).

Parenthood is an ensemble series, meaning that instead of a main character, the series has several core characters with a variety of storylines across season arches. The story revolves around the Braverman family: grandparents Zeek and Camille, as well as their four grown-up children with their respective families. Adam, married to Kristina, is the oldest of the four. He and Kristina have two children: teenager Haddie and Max. In the first season, Adam goes into business with his younger brother Crosby. Their sister Julia is a successful lawyer who struggles with her shared commitment to her job, her marriage and her young daughter Sidney. Finally, Sarah, single mother to Amber and Drew, is introduced as lost and unfocused in her career. The series begins with Sarah's decision to move back into her parents' house, creating a multigenerational focus point around which most of the drama is created.

The first season starts with Max's diagnosis and, following from that, ASD is a reoccurring theme throughout the series' six seasons. The audience is thus part of the first moments in which Adam and Kristina wonder if something about Max is different, the actual diagnosis and how they tell their families, the adjustments in school and friendships, his own handling of the diagnosis and following identification with it, as well as how his ASD relates to other familial circumstances. One such situation serves as a case study for the qualitative scene analysis in the present study. In a study focusing on the first season of the series, Holton (2013) illustrates that Max's portrayal is largely defined by isolation and othering. He argues that much of the portrayal of ASD is channelled through explicit outside evaluation, that is, other characters voicing concern about Max, and remarked-upon deviance from what is established as 'normal'. Whether this is confirmed in the use of implicit cues will be addressed in the character analysis.

The corpus of the first four seasons of the series was collected from transcripts of the original aired episodes. Transcripts were written by fans of the series and uploaded online. This method of obtaining linguistic data has previously been used (cf. Bednarek 2010; Quaglio 2009) and found to be reliable. While relying on other people's transcription skills is no doubt risky and tied to considerable time spent checking

Table 7.1 Word Count for Characters in *Parenthood* by Number of Episodes

Character	Word count	Episodes (seasons 1–4)
Julia	17726	68
Crosby	40039	68
Amber	21094	68
Zeek	19603	68
Haddie	12483	56
Sarah	44579	68
Camille	8933	68
Max	11208	68
Adam	58206	68
Kristina	38037	68

content, the efforts of transcribing the whole content exceeds that time by far. Valuable insights into using transcripts are discussed by Adams (2013). Episode transcripts were downloaded and checked for accuracy against the audiovisual originals. Accuracy here not only applies to the exact transcription of what was said on-screen but also includes consistency in transcription conventions and general spelling. Once a representative number of episodes were checked (between four and six per season depending on the length of the season), the transcripts were manipulated into usable corpus files.

The analysis does not include every single character from the series, as only characters with representative speaking portions are comparable with each other across the series. Further, a considerable amount of spoken words also indicates more established speech patterns. Characters included in the analysis, as well as their word and episode counts are included in Table 7.1.

Speech portions for each character included in the analysis were manually extracted from the main data (through filtering within the csv files) and put into season specific txt files. These were read into corpus tools for the extraction of variables for manual coding (using AntConc, Anthony 2016). For the quantitative analysis, the overall amount of spoken words for each character was taken into consideration and all variant frequencies were normalized to represent a 'per 1,000 words' value. This enables a more direct comparison between the characters.

4 Pragmatic competence as an index for ASD

4.1 Pragmatic competence

Pragmatic competence is the ability to use language in socially appropriate ways and an impairment in this area, defined as failing 'to observe the social expectations prevalent in their [the characters'] culture about what one can appropriately say to others without jeopardising good social relations' (Semino 2014: 151), is a central ASD symptom (cf. Landa 2000; Volden et al. 2009; Lam and Yeung 2012). With pragmatic competence considered as the most stigmatized and stereotyped trait people with ASD diagnoses are said to inhibit (Landa 2000: 125), it seems self-evident that it is also the trait most productive in character styling.

Landa et al. (1992, 2000) present nineteen typical pragmatic behaviours that co-occur with ASD diagnoses. These roughly map onto general tendencies for inappropriateness and awkwardness, impoliteness, rudeness, overly formal and direct language, topic preoccupation, and so on. All of these can, in one way or another, be indexed through a wide range of linguistic strategies and so it seems sensible for an analysis to focus on a limited set of these possible cues. Semino (2014), for instance, investigates ASD-associated characters in three novels and focuses on three particular aspects of pragmatic failure: relevance, impoliteness and interpretation of figurative language. She locates her interpretation within the framework of mind style, that is a character's mental state as reflected in linguistic representation (Fowler 1977), and finds that in all three novels, the depiction of ASD is accompanied by pragmatic failure. Semino w rites further that '"deviation" from default or conventional expectations [...] may be sufficient to attribute a (mental) trait to a character' (2014: 155). This perceived link between linguistic deviance and character type, that is the indexicality between pragmatic failings and ASD, is at the base of this investigation which expands Semino's work twofold through asking (1) how salient this indexicality is with features not immediately associated with pragmatic failure, and (2) how linguistic deviance is complemented on-screen representations.

In order to address these questions, I follow Androutsopoulos's framework of analysing sociolinguistic difference in audiovisual media (2012). He proposes a three-tiered analysis of audiovisual characterization, starting from a macro-level repertoire analysis (i.e. which languages or dialects are spoken by each character) to character analysis (i.e. which linguistic variables are chosen by characters), and finally a scene analysis (i.e. how scenes display salient indexes). Similarly to Bednarek (2012), I am focusing on only two of the three levels in the present study by combining a quantitative analysis of pragmatic marker variation with a scene analysis of pragmatic competence and cinematography.

4.2 Pragmatic markers as possible indexes for pragmatic competence

Pragmatic markers (elsewhere also discourse markers (Schiffrin 1987; Schourop 1999), discourse particles (Schourop 1985) or pragmatic expressions (Erman 1987)) are part of a group of discourse features that is still relatively ill-defined in (socio)pragmatic research (cf. Andersen 2001: 22, 39; Tagliamonte 2012: 269–70). Aijmer (2015) alluded to this, saying that 'they [pragmatic markers] have a large number of functions, there is no consensus about the linguistic model needed to describe them, and the relationship between form and function is complex' (2015: 195). Many studies have assigned a plethora of functions to the individual features and the contexts in which they appear. This multifunctional nature of pragmatic markers and interpretation bias can cause difficulties in determining general meanings: 'precise categorisation and percentages are thus difficult to ascertain, and a certain fuzziness is inevitable' (Beeching 2016: 34). Schiffrin (1987: 318) points out that the features function on a discourse managing level with what she refers to as 'core meanings' and Fox Tree and Schrock (2002) proposed as 'basic meanings'. Holmes and Stubbe (1995) claim that a distinction can be made between self-oriented and other-oriented markers, depending on the personal pronoun that is part of the marker. With regards to the markers chosen for the present study, a self-oriented marker is *I mean*, whereas *you know* can be described as other-oriented. This is comparable to the basic meanings suggested by Fox Tree and Schrock (2002), who said that *I mean* serves the speaker in forewarning adjustments to the utterance (2002: 744) and *you know* is used to invite 'addressee inferences' (2002: 744).

An example from the *Parenthood* corpus is given below:

> Adam: And I hope you don't take it the wrong way but, *you know*, just cause it's the music business, *you know*, it doesn't mean that, *you know*, we expect you – or that you have to dress a-a certain way.

In this utterance, Adam tries to talk to his assistant about the way she dresses, which makes him clearly uncomfortable. He is trying to mitigate ('don't take it the wrong way'), pre-emptively giving her an excuse ('just cause it's the music business'), hesitating ('a-a'), and being vague ('a certain way') in order to save her face. In using pragmatic marker *you know* in three instances here, Adam acknowledges the fact that he might overstep their professional relationship, hedging his approach. All tokens of the pragmatic marker could be omitted from this utterance without the propositional message being changed, though it would arguably make his statement more forward and possibly face-threatening.

Pragmatic marker *you know* can be found clause-initially, mid-clause and clause-final. There were four main functions of *you know* found in the *Parenthood* corpus: the propositional use (1) where the knowledge of the interactant is mentioned and the phrase oftentimes co-occurs with an object (here 'what'), the emphatic use (2) where the propositional meaning is highlighted, the pragmatic marker use (3) where the phrase does not add to the propositional meaning of the utterance and the utterance is made non-committal, and finally the pragmatic marker use (4) where the marker implies certainty. Here, the interactional function is not hedging or non-committal but rather condescending, what Beeching called impositional (2016: 106).

(1) Amber: No, *you know* what? You're right.
(2) Sarah: How can he be mad at me that I don't want him to stay by himself in the house after he, you know – *you know*.
(3) Adam: Um, *you know*, I'll need some help here at the house
(4) Crosby: Look, this isn't a job that a monkey can do, *you know*. I have to be present.

The distinction between the last two functions of pragmatic marker *you know* is discernible mostly through the context of the conversation and intonation (with intonation rising for the hedging pragmatic marker and falling for the impositional use). Similarly to *you know*, *I mean* can have propositional meaning in conversation. While propositional *you know* can occur without an object however (as a minimal response for instance), propositional *I mean* almost always co-occurs with an object, either preceding the phrase (5), or following (6). Pragmatic marker *I mean* (7) is not syntactically restricted, although it seldom appears in clause clause-final position in the *Parenthood* corpus.

(5) Julia: No, *I mean* they could charge us with breaking and entering.
(6) Zeek: You are gonna be fantastic. *I mean* great.
(7) Amber: And, look, there's not even sunlight in here. *I mean*, this is, like, a nightmare, right, guys?

Schiffrin (1987), in her seminal work on discourse markers, defines these features as 'sequentially dependent elements which bracket units of talk' (1987: 31), not themselves carrying propositional content within the sentence, they contribute to the interactional or pragmatic context of the conversation. In that, these markers can act as turn-taking orientation, politeness and face-saving acts, vagueness markers, hesitation devices and/or repair signs. This places the appropriate use of pragmatic markers squarely within the realm of pragmatic competence. Pragmatic markers are, in their multifunctional nature, broadly used for the organization of communication and, as Landa (2000: 138) claims, 'within a discourse event, individuals with HFA [high-functioning autism] and AS [Asperger's syndrome] have difficulty using linguistic strategies'. With reference to pragmatic competence in using these markers, it could be expected that where pragmatic markers are used for functions contributing to the communicative event (not the propositional function), people with ASD might show fewer instances of usage overall.

Similar expectations apply to the third marker: *kind of*. Lakoff first established linguistic features such as *kind of* as part of a linguistic category he called hedges: 'words whose meaning implicitly involves fuzziness – words whose job it is to make things fuzzier or less fuzzy' (1973: 471). These hedges are classed as adverbs that pre- or postmodify a word (or the whole phrase) as 'fuzzier', vague and imprecise.

Syntactically, these hedges can appear in pre-modification of nouns (8), verbs (9), adjectives (9), as post-modifiers (11) and as minimal responses (11) (cf. Aijmer 1984: 120–1).

(8) Amber: Cause that was *kind of* a trick question.
(9) Adam: So it *kind of* leaps off the page, you know?
(10) Kristina: This is getting *kind of* silly.
(11) Zeek: Yeah, they're comfortable, *kind of*, I mean …
(12) Kristina: What happens here stays here. Okay?
    Max: So it's like in Vegas?
    Kristina: *Kind of*. And if dad asks, grandma picked you up.

In terms of inclusion in the analysis, I differentiated between tokens that showed purely pragmatic functions, and those that carried propositional meaning, which were in turn discarded.

In the Example (13) for instance, *kind of* describes a specific type of kid (the kind that eats Bouillabaisse), rather than a vague or non-committal reference to a kid. Here, the feature is not used as a hedging device, but rather a device of specification or typification.

(13) Julia: What *kind of* kid eats Boullabaisse?

This distinction between hedge and typification is exclusive to tokens occurring in noun phrases. With regards to tokens that modify noun phrases, Fetzer summarizes the scaled fuzziness component of the feature in terms of their immediate syntactic context: 'The anchoring of the object at hand to the scale is not arbitrary but depends on the semantics of the hedge' (2010: 51).

All tokens for *I mean, you know* (as well as *y'know*) and *kind of* (as well as *kinda*) were extracted from the corpus and coded manually for their function within the context of the interaction. Where concrete functions were unclear from the token context (fifty characters before and after the token), the transcript was used to determine the function. This was the case in some instances of *you know*, where it was used as a minimal response and only the full transcript was able to show exactly how it was used.

Following Landa's list of ASD cues, these markers, in their respective pragmatic functions, are unlikely to be used at high frequencies by a character who is styled following ASD stereotypes. Further, none of these features are particularly sociolinguistically marked, as opposed to, for instance, discourse marker *like*, which is stereotypically used for young female speakers. That means that other character traits, while important to consider, are unlikely to interfere to a significant degree.

5 ASD representation in Parenthood

5.1 Character analysis: Pragmatic markers

The following analysis focuses on three pragmatic devices that can be linked to pragmatic competence in that their occurrence is unexpected with, for instance, overly direct or formal speakers (see Section 4.1 for other cues of ASD). This character analysis focuses on the sociolinguistic difference between characters' uses of pragmatic markers across the first four seasons of the series' runtime.

Figure 7.1 shows the distribution of *you know*, by character and per 1,000 words, with Max's use highlighted in black.

For *you know*, the pragmatic marker that is described as inference-seeking and dependent on shared knowledge between conversation participants is unsurprisingly

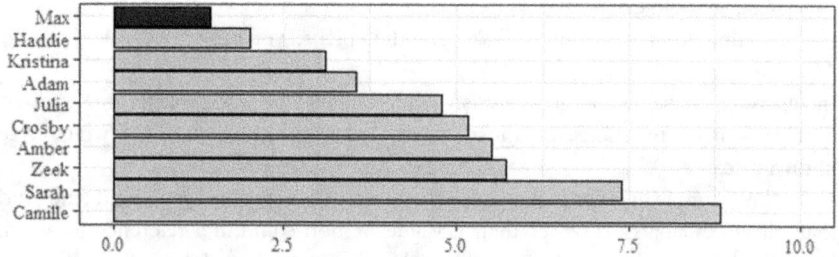

Figure 7.1 Pragmatic marker *you know*, per 1,000 words.

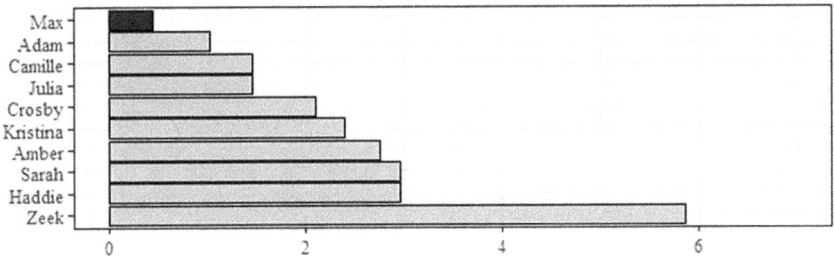

Figure 7.2 Pragmatic marker *I mean*, per 1,000 words.

low for Max. Following established stereotypes of ASD and Asperger's, it is not expected that he would organize or manage the communicative event. Importantly however, Max is not styled as completely unable to use these features, and in his use, he is actually closest aligned with the rest of his immediate family (Haddie, Kristina and Adam). In terms of representation of ASD then, it is worth noting that there is not a lack of competence, but rather a diminished competence associated with Max. This is in so far relevant as that this may impact the general evaluation of ASD representation from the audience.

For *I mean* (Figure 7.2), the distribution for Max is similar to that of *you know*, while most other characters from the series shift in their use compared to *you know*. As a feature aimed at self-repair and hedging, the expectations would be that characters who are styled as uncertain and self-doubting would lead in their use of this pragmatic marker. This is visible from the distributions on both ends of the scale. Zeek, who self-repairs because he is often found in situations where he needs to clarify himself, and Haddie and Sarah, who both struggle with their respective sets of insecurities throughout the series, are using *I mean* as a pragmatic marker most frequently. On the other hand, Max, again, shows a very low use of the pragmatic marker. The interpretation of an ASD-associated character being othered thus holds true for these types of cues as well.

With both variables quite varied in functions, a next step would be to further analyse the concrete instances in which Max *did* use the markers and what the exact functions were in the various contexts. While outside of the scope of the present study, this first quantitative analysis already provided a brief overview of how these markers could be used as indexical markers by the writers/actors in establishing styling of ASD in telecinematic discourse.

Moving on to hedges, the patterns are more of the same. Figure 7.3 shows that Max is using *kind of* least frequently of all the characters.

Interestingly, both Adam and Camille, who were also similar to Max for *I mean*, are again joining him on this end of the frequency scale. As an interpretation of the quantitative representation of possible ASD traits in characters' language, it is important to point out that there are no binaries between ASD and non-ASD linguistic patterns. Rather, we see Max at the end of a scale that is overall varied across characters. That means that, linguistically speaking, an ASD diagnosis for a character does not imply a completely unique and isolated set of features. I will return to this point in the discussion.

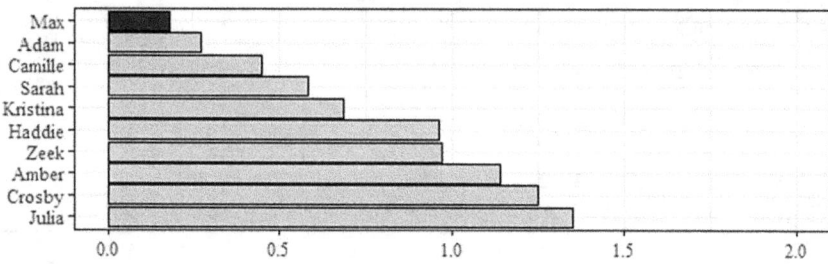

Figure 7.3 Hedge *kind of*, per 1,000 words.

The quantitative account gives a brief overview of how pragmatic competence can be investigated with reference to a character introduced as being diagnosed with ASD. While rather surface-level at this point, it provides indications on possible interactions of variables that might be worth investigating further. Additionally, it might be useful to see what other features provide similar patterns. As a character analysis, this has shown that Max is defined by a lessened use of pragmatic features that function in terms of certainty, directness and communication management.

5.2 Scene analysis

The scene chosen for the scene analysis is taken from the final episode of season two of the series (*Hard Times Come Again No More*, first aired on 19 April 2011). Androutsopoulos argues that salient features contributing to characterization will be exposed in emotionally heightened scenes (2012: 307), scenes that include 'antagonistic, conflictual interactions' (Georgakopoulou 2000: 125). Thus, a dramatic scene where Max's inability to conform to the as normal established behaviour likely yields additional evidence of how ASD might be styled.

After a tumultuous season for Sarah and her daughter Amber, the latter is part of a critical accident. The episode opens with Sarah, Drew, Camille and Zeek sitting in the waiting room waiting for news on Amber's well-being. One after another, other family members join them. The scene opens at fifty seconds into the episode and lasts roughly until minute four, at which point the surgeon steps out into the waiting room. With all characters that are included in the corpus portion of the study present here as well, there is an opportunity to see whether quantitative patterns found are congruent with the more qualitative analysis – not just for Max. The scene is very emotional for most of the ensemble and juxtaposes Max's competence in judging moments and communicative means against that of others.

Table 7.2 gives an overview of the scene with time stamps for the dialogue, brief descriptions and what is happening on-screen, as well as selected tracings of screen shots to accompany the analysis. A subsequent discussion of non-verbal features such as gaze and body posture will highlight multimodal aspects of characterizations and how these tie in with previously observed dialogue patterns.

The scene starts very quietly and non-verbal, with a slow vocal track as the accompanying music. Up until minute 1:40, none of the characters say anything.

A special focus of the camera is on the faces of each characters, with several close-ups. When Adam, Kristina, Haddie and Max enter the waiting room, the audience is situated within the waiting area alongside Sarah and sees the four newcomers approaching from afar. A close-up then shows Adam and Kristina hugging Sarah, with Haddie looking on in the close background (see image at 0:50). What is notable here is that there was no focus on Max. While visible as they approach, he is out of the picture frame for the close-up hug and only as the camera slowly pans away (see image at 1:24), he is again in the frame off to the side (*).

When the scene opens again, the camera shifts quickly between family members, focusing again on faces and gaze. With the audience taking part in the scene at eye level and almost shaky picture frames (as if sat in one of the waiting room chairs), an atmosphere of intimacy is drawn on. When Max starts talking, the audience's eye (the camera) is still preoccupied with Crosby and only focuses on the new situation with a slight delay.

As Max talks, his gaze is directed at a steady point someplace just in front of Adam and does not change until Max gets up from his chair. When Adam tries to appease his son with other food, Max is getting increasingly loud and dismissive of anything other than his plan. His dealing with change of schedules is an often-repeated theme throughout the series, and it becomes clear that the other characters in the room are not surprised at the start of this discussion. The audience's position is still on eye level with most of the other characters and the camera does not follow Max as he gets up, causing him to be almost cut off from the frame (see image at 2:58/9). While the audience seemingly remains a part of the intimate family gathering, Max is stepping out (by getting up and out of the ideal frame) and is alienating himself from the others. Several brief close-up frames of family members show their discomfort in only quickly glancing up at Max and immediately looking away again. Adam, the only one engaging with his son, is still trying to calm Max down. In saying 'this is one of those times we talked about', he indicates to the audience that situations such as these have been discussed with Max, highlighting that this is something Max has been struggling with in the past.

Max is getting increasingly upset and starts pacing between the rows of chairs of the waiting room. He recounts the, for him, logical reason why waiting here is nonsensical. His gaze is randomly focused on different areas of the room, but still not in contact with any of the other characters. In saying that even in the case of Amber's death, them waiting would not make a difference, the audience can see first reactions in Zeek, who shakes his head (3:20).

Max, getting to the highpoint of this outburst, is standing in the middle of the room with a rather static posture. His arms pressed to his sides, he leans slightly forward as he starts shouting (see image at 3:26). His body thus seems very controlled despite the fact that he is screaming. Still not looking at anyone directly and with rigid body movements, Max shows that even though he is emotionally driven (in that he is angry), he is not actually giving in to what might be expected from an emotional outburst.

As Zeek gets up and steps in, the scene quickly escalates. With Zeek shouting at Max ('Then get a frickin' Danish, okay!'), both Max and Adam start talking over each other, making the rest of the scene almost unintelligible for the audience. This

Table 7.2 The Hospital Scene

Time	Screen	Scene description
0:50		Scene opens to hospital waiting room. Amber's immediate family (mother Sarah, brother Drew, and grandparents Zeek and Camille) are already in the waiting room. They look exhausted. Doors to the left open to reveal Julia, Joel and Sidney (their daughter), as well as Crosby joining. They all hug and huddle together.
1:24		Adam, Kristina, Haddie and Max join the family gathering. Max sits down (*) while the others go on to hug Sarah and other family members.
1:40		Drew is trying to reach his father on the phone. Haddie's boyfriend Alex joins the family. Julia and Kristina talk about how Haddie seems more grown-up. Crosby's ex-fiancée Jasmine joins, causing him and Joel to exchange meaningful glances.
2:50		Max starts complaining to his father about being hungry and wanting to leave. M I want to eat.
2:52		A Alright, let's see what they have here.
2:53		M No, dad, you said that we could go to get pancakes, and now I've been here for an hour and half [and I want to go:]

2:58		A	[Look at this.] Max we have Danishes.
2:59	Adam opens a pastry box and turns towards Max. Max gets up from his seat.	M	No: I don't want a Danish.
3:00		A	Max, take it easy. This is one of those times where you have to be patient, okay? We're here for Amber and Drew.
3:05	Max starts pacing between the chairs where the rest of the family is sitting.	M	No. You said that Amber wasn't gonna die, right? So if Amber's not gonna die, then. You know, even if she was gonna die, we're not doctors we can't do anything to help
3:15		A	Max we [talked about this …]
3:15		M	[sitting here right now isn't helping.]
3:17		A	[This is one of these things we talked about. This is what it means]
3:20	Zeek is shaking his head.	M	[I'm hungry!]
3:21		A	Okay, we have to be there for each other, and right now we're here for Amber.
3:23		M	No, dad, I don't care about Amber right now.

(*Continued*)

Table 7.2 (Continued)

Time	Screen	Scene description		
3:26		Zeek suddenly gets up and faces Max	A	Max, [please don't say that.]
3:27		Max reaches the top of his outburst, getting louder with every word.	M	[I'm hungry, and I want to eat no:w!]
3:28		Zeek shouts at Max.	Z	Hey, Max!
3:28		Max stops. Other family members look alarmed that Zeek lost his composure. Max, Zeek, and Adam all talk on top of each other.	A	[Don't cause a scene, okay?]
3:30			Z	[Then get a frickin' Danish, okay?]
3:31			M	[Shut up, grandpa!]
3:33			A	[Max!]
3:33			Z	[Don't] tell me to shut up.
3:34		Kristina gets up and walks over to Max, tries to calm him.	K	Max. I'm so sorry. [Let's take a break.]
3:36			M	[Dad, I want food!]
3:38		Kristina grabs Max's arm and steers him towards the exit past Zeek, who is still standing. Max is trying to push her away, yet willingly leaves the waiting room.	K	I'm gonna give him a break, okay? [Don't.] Please don't hit me. Stop it. Max, stop. Out
3:42			M	[Ah!]
			K	Stop.
3:50		Scene shifts as doctor walks in.		

is unique for television series where dialogue is usually carefully arranged not to overlap. The end of the scene is also the only time Kristina, Max's mother, reacts. As soon as Zeek starts shouting, the audience can see her getting up while apologizing to Sarah. What we see here in particular are the very different reactions and approaches of family members to Max. Throughout the scene the camera focuses on each of the character's faces and up until the end of it, when the doctor steps in, reactions are those of exhaustion rather than upset. It seems here that the family, all aware of Max's diognosis, are neither surprised by his outburst nor particularly shocked by what he says. A theme throughout the series is that even though the situations involving Max and his diagnosis are oftentimes depicted as negative, the family around him is more or less neutral and resigning that this behaviour is routine. More subtly then, when Kristina apologizes, it seems that there is a heightened awareness surrounding Max and social inappropriateness that at times needs to be negotiated.

Comparing the dialogue between Adam and Max in this scene, it is striking to see how they both exhibit styles at completely different ends of a directness scale. While Max, as previously mentioned, bluntly states his thoughts, indifferent who is listening in, Adam is extremely cautious in replying (14).

(14) Adam: Max, take it easy. This is one of those times where you have to be patient, okay? We're here for Amber and Drew.
Max: No. You said that Amber wasn't gonna die, right? So if Amber's not gonna die, then. You know, even if she was gonna die, we're not doctors we can't do anything to help
Adam: Max we [talked about this …]
Max: [sitting here right now isn't helping.]
Adam: [This is one of these things we talked about. This is what it means]
Max: [I'm hungry!]
Adam: Okay, we have to be there for each other, and right now we're here for Amber.
Max: No, dad, I don't care about Amber right now.

Adam, by using vague reference markers and being non-descript in saying how they are helping, or what the concrete reasons are for why being in a waiting room is necessary at this point in time, is not addressing his son's apparent lack of reasoning for being in this situation. The reasons for that are linked to exactly the things Max struggles with: politeness and mitigation. Within the emotional situation, Adam is unable to clearly state the severity of the situation because Sarah, who is worried about her daughter possibly dying, is an overhearer of the discussion. We can see here how Max's rather marked characterization as socially awkward and struggling with emotions is highlighted by putting him in a situation that demands high competence in social appropriation.

6 Discussion

This chapter highlights how different modes in telecinematic discourse work together in creating a character with ASD. Notable here is that it is not the character in isolation that is defined, but rather a character and how they behave compared to their surroundings, as well as with regards to audience's expectations.

ASD, an increasingly used plot point in all kinds of popular media, is rather stereotypically conceptualized in fictional contexts. With a range of seemingly typical characteristics, ranging from communicative problems, lack of self-awareness, missing of social cues, no eye-contact and avoidance of emotionality, both mentally and physically, most television series employ what the audience knows. Further, as previous research has shown, fictional contexts also overuse the idea of ASD being equal to savant-like statuses.

While fictional representations are arguably limited in showing full range of possibilities and, in fact, realities, the ways in which characterization is achieved is manifold. A mixed-method approach, such as what was attempted here, gives a little insight into a diverse range of characterization processes that can and need to be considered in telecinematic discourse.

A quantitative analysis, such as the character analysis here, will always achieve an overview of what is happening systematically within a series (or even just an episode) and enables researchers to compare characters against each other, as well as analyse a character's development over time. However, it is unable to catch detailed contexts and might gloss over peculiarities that are important for any characterization. A qualitative analysis, as the scene analysis has shown, provides a very detailed opportunity to include not only dialogue but individual turns, non-verbal communication and extra-diegetic factors such as music or framing. It captures a multitude of characterizing facets, but fails to provide knowledge of whether this is consistently applicable to the medium as a whole.

Joining these two approaches is thus rewarding in that it gives a more complete idea of how characters are created: language patterns over time, their comparability to the ensemble and their situation-specific behaviour.

What we find with Max's representation in *Parenthood* is that he is styled as deviant from the rest of the cast: implicitly and explicitly. In scenes that highlight his Asperger's, the various pragmatic competency cues are likewise highlighted. These include the content of conversation (Max bluntly stating facts that are socially inappropriate), the way he talks (demanding focus, no turn-taking strategies), mise en scène (he is almost always to the side or completely missing from the frame, the camera does not follow his movement), posture and gaze. The character analysis has shown that, throughout the episodes, his use of pragmatic devices consistently deviates from the other characters'. Importantly here though is the finding that his language use does not single him out as being different, that is, there is no perceived binary between ASD and non-ASD. His ASD diagnosis thus consistently impacts his linguistic repertoire (in that he uses fewer pragmatic devices for instance), but it does not significantly isolate him from his family members. Scenes where the diagnosis is at the forefront of characterization will exacerbate his diminished pragmatic competence and it is these moments where ASD will be represented the most stereotypically.

7 Conclusion

With an ever increasing variety of character types in audiovisual media, the need to investigate how representation is achieved, particularly when it concerns possibly stigmatized character types, is apparent. This chapter analysed how a complex character trait, such as Asperger's, is styled on different levels in order to achieve an encompassing characterization. Representations of particular character traits, such as mental disorders, are still highly dependent in stereotypes. This study has shown that these stereotyped moments can be accompanied by strategic patterns of unmarked linguistic features (such as pragmatic markers and hedges), which shows that characters can be styled with linguistic nuances that do not reduce characterization to a single trait.

The present study only managed to capture a small range of patterns here and it will be interesting to see how new corpora as well as new approaches may be able to capture the multimodal nature of telecinematic discourse in more detail.

References

Adams, M. (2013), 'Vignette 13b - working with scripted data: Variations among scripts, texts, and performances', in C. Mallinson, B. Childs and G. Van Herk (eds), *Data Collection in Sociolinguistics – Methods and Applications*, 232–5, New York: Routledge.

Aijmer, K. (1984), '*Sort of* and *kind of* in English conversation', *Studia Linguistica*, 38 (2): 118–28.

Aijmer, K. (2015), 'Pragmatic markers', in K. Aijmer and C. Rühlemann (eds), *Corpus Pragmatics*, 195–218, Cambridge: Cambridge University Press.

Andersen, G. (2001), *Pragmatic Markers and Sociolinguistic Variation: A Relevance-theoretic Approach to the Language of Adolescents*, Amsterdam: John Benjamins.

Androutsopoulos, J. (2012), 'Repertoires, characters and scenes: Sociolinguistic difference in Turkish German comedy', *Multilingua*, 31 (2/3): 301–26.

Anthony, L. (2016), *AntConc [Computer Software]*, Tokyo: Waseda University. Available at: http://www.laurenceanthony.net/software (accessed February 2017).

Asperger, H. (1944), 'Die „Autistischen psychopathen" im Kindesalter', *Archiv für Psychiatrie und Nervenkrankheiten*, 117 (1): 76–136.

Bednarek, M. (2010), *The Language of Fictional Television: Drama and Identity*, London: Continuum.

Bednarek, M. (2012), 'Constructing 'nerdiness": Characterisation in The Big Bang Theory', *Multilingua*, 31 (2): 199–229.

Beeching, K. (2016), *Pragmatic Markers in British English: Meaning in Social Interaction*, Cambridge: Cambridge University Press.

Belcher, C. and Maich, K. (2014), 'Autism spectrum disorder in popular media: Storied reflections of societal views', *Brock Education*, 23 (2): 97–115.

Culpeper, J. (2001), *Language and Characterisation: People in Plays and Other Texts*, Harlow: Longman.

Draaisma, D. (2009), 'Stereotypes of autism', *Philosophical Transactions of the Royal Society B: Biological Sciences*, 364 (1522): 1475–80.

Erman, B. (1987), *Pragmatic Expressions in English: A Study of You Know, You See and I Mean in Face-to-Face Conversation*, Doctoral dissertation, Almqvist and Wiksell International.

Fetzer, A. (2010), 'Hedges in context: Form and function of *sort of* and *kind of*', in G. Kaltenböck, W. Mihatsch and S. Schneider (eds), *New Approaches to Hedging*, 49–72, Bingley: Emerald Group Publishing Limited.

Fowler, R. (1977), *Linguistics and the Novel*, London: Methuen.
Fox Tree, J. E. and Schrock, J. C. (2002), 'Basic meanings of *you know* and *I mean*', *Journal of Pragmatics*, 34: 727–47.
Georgakopoulou, A. (2000), 'On the sociolinguistics of popular films: Funny characters, funny voices', *Journal of modern Greek studies*, 18 (1): 119–33.
Holton, A. E. (2013), 'What's wrong with Max? Parenthood and the portrayal of autism spectrum disorders', *Journal of Communication Inquiry*, 37 (1): 45–63.
Lakoff, G. (1973), 'Hedges: A study of meaning criteria and the logic of fuzzy concepts', *Journal of Philosophical Logic*, 2: 458–508.
Lam, Y. G. and Yeung, S. (2012), 'Towards a convergent account of pragmatic language deficits in children with high-functioning autism: Depicting the phenotype using the pragmatic rating scale', *Research in Autism Spectrum Disorders*, 6: 792–7.
Landa, R. (2000), 'Social language use in asperger syndrome and high-functioning autism', in A. Klin, Volkmar, F. and Sparrow, S. (eds), *Asperger Syndrome*, New York: The Guildford Press.
Landa, R., Piven, J., Wzorek, M., Gayle, J., Chase, G. and Folstein, S. (1992), 'Social language use in parents of autistic individuals', *Psychological Medicine*, 22 (1): 245–54.
McGrath, K. (2014), 'Communication deficiencies provide incongruities for humor: The Asperger's-like case of The Big Bang Theory's Sheldon Cooper', *The Popular Culture Studies Journal*, 2 (1): 140–71.
Quaglio, P. (2009), *Television Dialogue: The Sitcom Friends vs. Natural Conversation*, vol. 36, Philadelphia: John Benjamins Publishing.
Schiffrin, D. (1987), *Discourse Markers*, Cambridge: Cambridge University Press.
Schourup, L. (1985), *Common Discourse Particles in English Conversation*, New York and London: Garland Publishing.
Schourup, L. (1999), 'Discourse markers', *Lingua*, 107: 227–65.
Semino, E. (2014), 'Pragmatic failure, mind style and characterisation in fiction about autism', *Language and Literature*, 23 (2): 141–58.
Stubbe, M. and Holmes, J. (1995), 'You know, eh and other "exasperating expressions": An analysis of social and stylistic variation in the use of pragmatic devices in a sample of New Zealand English', *Language & Communication*, 15 (1): 63–88.
Tagliamonte, S. (2012), *Variationist Sociolinguistics: Change, Observation, Interpretation*, Chichester: Blackwell Publishing.
Volden, J., Coolican, J., Garon, N., White, J. and Bryson, S. (2009), 'Brief report: Pragmatic language in autism spectrum disorder: Relationships to measures of ability and disability', *Journal of Autism and Developmental Disorders*, 39: 388–93.

8

The visual discourse of shots and cuts

Applying the cooperative principle to horror film cinematography

Christoph Schubert

1 Introduction

The process of creating and watching a feature film resembles the act of storytelling, since in both cases a narrator uses a semiotic system unfolding in time to relate a sequence of events to an audience. In contrast to purely verbal texts, however, multimodal film discourse also incorporates visual signs as well as non-verbal acoustic signs such as music and sound effects (cf. Kress 2010: 148; Wildfeuer 2014: 9–10). Therefore, by analogy with the syntax or 'grammar' of film (Arijon 1991: 15), it is possible to speak of the 'pragmatics' of cinematic discourse, which Richard Janney has defined as 'the audiovisual discourse of film narration itself' (2012: 86). More specifically, he argues that cinematic discourse involves 'an implicit communicative pact between the participants (a cooperative assumption)' (2012: 88), which relies on the producers' and recipients' common ground, mutual understanding and complementary intentions. While the audience of mainstream feature films has certain expectations and specific background knowledge, the scriptwriters and directors will usually try to model an implied addressee with the aim of producing a commercially successful film that appeals to a large target group.

On the basis of these premises, it is feasible to apply Herbert Paul Grice's well-known cooperative principle (1975, 1989) to the discourse of cinematography, which accounts for the central part of the visual language in films. This is further corroborated by Grice's assessment that conversation is 'a special case or variety of purposive, indeed rational, behaviour', so that the maxims show 'analogues in the sphere of transactions that are not talk exchanges' (1975: 47). Thus, in order to adapt the cooperative principle to films, Grice's 'conversational' maxims, which prototypically refer to dialogical verbal interaction, are here reconceptualized in the sense of *communicative* maxims, covering the conceptually monological mode of feature films as well. Along these lines, the central aim of this study is to demonstrate that cinematography as 'visual storytelling' (Brown 2012: 67) may either ostentatiously obey or deliberately fail to observe the communicative maxims. This results in cinematic implicatures, which closely involve viewers, because implicated ideas rely on common ground and default principles of rationality. Film makers may thus use such implicatures as tools to evoke important narrative meanings and cinematographic effects, relating to plot development, characterization and the creation of suspense.

This chapter focuses on-camera work, in particular on film shots, which are based on the static or dynamic representation of visual space from different angles and distances (cf. Dick 2002: 54–77). Simultaneously, special attention will be paid to cuts, defined as visual transitions between adjacent shots. In this way, shots add up to cohesive sequences, which are created in the process of 'continuity editing' (Bednarek 2010: 20). While shots are the basis for 'visual composition' in cinematography, the combination of shots is a matter of 'visual punctuation' (Arijon 1991: 18). In addition, different types of lighting, such as low or high key, will be taken into consideration, since they may closely cooperate with the design of shots and cuts, ultimately constituting the 'grammatical tools of the film language' (Arijon 1991: 15). As Michael Toolan similarly argues in an article on the stylistics of film, 'one area of great interest is that of shot composition and combination' (2014: 459), since these techniques to some extent form the equivalent of sentences and punctuation marks in a written literary text. Hence, as far as the theoretical framework is concerned, this article is located in the continuously growing area of pragmatic stylistics, which has recently been fostered by a number of volumes (e.g. Hidalgo-Downing 2000; Black 2006; Chapman and Clark 2014; Schubert and Volkmann 2016).

The dataset underlying this study contains a selection of eight well-known films from the horror genre, since here cinematography manipulates the affective reception of the audience in original ways. For the sake of suspense or shock effects, cinematographic techniques such as close-ups or shaky camera motion are often taken to their extreme, so that functions of visual cinematic discourse are particularly striking. Owing to this peculiarity of horror film cinematography, an important role will be played by the concept of discursive 'deviance' in the crime and horror genre, as defined by Christiana Gregoriou (2007: 1) and Roberta Piazza (2011a: 87). By ways of a detailed qualitative analysis, this chapter extracts and contextualizes key scenes from the films, so as to investigate each of the communicative maxims with regard to visual implicatures triggered by cinematography. It will become clear that visual implicatures are a subtle yet effective way of conveying narrative meaning that successfully complements more explicit techniques of multimodal storytelling.

2 The communicative situation in cinematic discourse

Although the discourse-analytical and media-pragmatic research on film discourse has considerably gained momentum in the new millennium, relevant studies used to concentrate mainly on the speech of fictional characters. This communicative plane in film is aptly called the 'inter-character level' (Dynel 2011: 312), as opposed to the producer–recipient level, which comprises the wider participation framework of scriptwriters and viewers (cf. Piazza, Bednarek and Rossi 2011: 9). Apart from a few monographs on spoken conversation in television series (cf. Bubel 2006; Quaglio 2009; Bednarek 2010), there are studies on the forms and functions of dialogue in different film genres (Kozloff 2000), on the use of dialects in film (Hodson 2014) and on the relationship between verbal dialogue and visual film language (Piazza 2011b). In principle, film dialogues can be examined in the same way as verbal interaction in drama and character speech in narrative fiction.

More recently, as a complementary development, several studies have focused on the multimodal discourse of film, taking into account both the visual and the auditory modes (cf. Bateman and Schmidt 2012; Janney 2010, 2012; Wildfeuer 2014). Janina Wildfeuer, for instance, in her multilayered approach examines 'how filmic devices are intersemiotically combined to narrative structures' (2014: 1) to establish a multimodal textuality of film. In doing so, she propounds the five categories of 'shot', 'shot description', 'audio track', 'spoken language' and 'music' (cf. 2014: 24–6). By means of a parallel analysis and juxtaposition of these parameters, the pragma-stylistic effects of film discourse at the producer–recipient level can be revealed in detail. In this chapter, the focus is on shots and their description, while the three remaining features are considered only if they are indispensable for understanding the discursive context.

As regards the production and reception of film discourse, there is a 'collective sender', as represented by the 'film crew (directors, scriptwriters, editors, actors, etc.)' (Dynel 2011: 313). Hence, it is the task of this creative group to conduct a number of elaborate production steps in storyboarding, scripting, shooting and editing a film. The actual reception process of cinematic discourse can be paraphrased as 'screen-to-face conversation' (Bubel 2008: 64), carried out by a mass audience in cinemas or in front of private television sets. Although the viewers are not directly addressed by the characters in films and therefore seem to have the role of mere 'overhearers' (Bubel 2008: 62), audiences are still 'ratified' participants in Goffman's understanding (1981: 146) since cinematic discourse ultimately addresses the external spectators.

Owing to the commercial foundation of the mainstream film industry, the positive reception of films by the target audience is an indispensable prerequisite for the existence and continuation of cinematic discourse at large. In order to achieve a box-office success, film producers typically place emphasis on a careful 'overhearer design' with regard to the 'implied spectators' (Bubel 2008: 64). Along these lines, directors make assumptions about the audience's world knowledge as well as cognitive and emotional expectations to create common ground. The addressees' previous knowledge may comprise other productions by the same director or actors, metadiscursive texts such as film reviews, or intertextual pretexts, including prequels or sequels in a series of films, all of which are likely to have an impact on the duration and intensity of the respective reception process. Thus, although the discourse of films is ostensibly monological and non-interactive, the producers conceptualize a target audience with specific conjectures and interests. The producer–recipient level of cinematic discourse is at the centre of the present analysis, whereas the inter-character level will play only a minor role, whenever its inclusion is necessary for a complete comprehension of cinematographic devices.

3 The horror genre and the dataset

In order to achieve and enhance the default perlocution of suspense, shock or even revulsion, horror film cinematography tends to employ discursive techniques that may deviate from the regular aesthetic cooperation of film narrative. In general, the linguistic idea of 'deviation' or 'deviance', which are here used synonymously (cf. Gregoriou 2007: 1), is emphasized already in Geoffrey Leech's (1969) classic account of poetic language. Leech points out that divergence from a norm cannot be assessed in absolute terms but only with regard to varying 'degrees of abnormality' (cf. 1969: 31) on a scale between linguistic convention and creativity. Referring to Russian formalism à la Roman Jakobson, Lesley Jeffries and Dan McIntyre further elaborate that deviation 'may occur at any of the levels of linguistic structure' (2010: 31) and that it is a case of foregrounding in the wider area of linguistic defamiliarization in literary discourse. Along these lines, the notion of deviance is applied to crime fiction by Christiana Gregoriou, who argues that 'by employing deviant language to portray the criminal mind, novelists allow access to criminals' reasoning and conceptualization of reality' (2007: 152). She underscores her findings mainly with respect to the linguistic levels of semantics and lexicology, giving examples of personifications, deviant connotations and literalized idioms and metaphors.

In a more fine-grained definition, 'external' deviation means that a complete text or genre is distinct from other texts or genres, whereas 'internal' deviation refers to the fact that within a given text a specific character may linguistically stand out from the remaining text (cf. Jeffries and McIntyre 2010: 32). Accordingly, both internal and external deviations are possible in horror cinema, for one character may deviate from other characters in a film, or horror films may generally display deviating cinematographic techniques. With regard to internal deviation, Roberta Piazza argues that horror films contain 'indicators of visual deviance that make the representation of the unconventional characters more complete' (2011a: 87). Her principal conclusion is that perpetrators typically act in uncooperative ways, as indicated by both verbal and visual means. In the present study, however, the focus is on *external* deviation, since it elaborates on specific visuals of the horror genre at large, which differs from other fictional film genres such as romantic comedies as well as non-fictional genres such as television news or documentaries.

For a definition of the horror genre, it is necessary to point out that it shows occasional overlaps with other genres such as science fiction (cf. Hutchings 2013: 2). While the Western genre, for instance, is defined by a specific historical and geographical setting (Hutchings 2013: 6), horror is mainly marked by its frightening perlocutionary effect on the audience, as made explicit in the genre's very name (cf. Kawin 2012: 4; Sipos 2010: 5). This strong emotional reaction is expected and in fact perceived as enjoyable by a vast majority of the audience because of a variety of reasons, including possible cathartic effects and psychological stress relief (cf. Sipos 2010: 247–58).

Correspondingly, as far as cinematic genre analysis is concerned, the central question is, how do features of form and content achieve this kind of viewer response? Formally, cinematographic techniques in the horror genre often include low-key lighting, extreme close-ups, subjective camera and surprising camera angles, such as the low-angle shot of the shower head in the famous shower scene in Hitchcock's *Psycho* (cf. Dick 2002: 172; Pramaggiore and Wallis 2011: 384). Moreover, the cinema of horror and suspense often contains impediments to seeing, which form a precondition for surprising revelations and correspond to the technique of 'fallible focalization' (Schubert 2005: 224) in the literature of crime and detection. Such obstructions to visual perception can be achieved, for instance, by shots from great distances or restricted angles, by insufficient lighting, by a selective focus on the screen or by accelerated camera movements that result in blurred vision.

As regards the contents of horror films, the plot is typically marked by an 'unnatural threat' to vulnerable characters, who usually have no option of escape and are confronted with phenomena 'outside the realm of normalcy, reality, or history' (Sipos 2010: 6; cf. also Pramaggiore and Wallis 2011: 383). The three main types of such threats are (a) 'the supernatural', as exemplified by demons, vampires or witches; (b) 'the monsters of nature and science', such as space aliens, King Kong, carnivorous dinosaurs or Frankenstein's creature; and (c) 'the human psyche's dark side (horror psycho)', as personified by characters such as Norman Bates in *Psycho*, Michael Myers in *Halloween* or Hannibal Lecter in *The Silence of the Lambs* (Sipos 2010: 10). To some extent, the horror genre shows an 'apparent formulaic repetitiveness' (Hutchings 2013: vii), but this genre is still hard to delineate, since 'like one of its own shape-shifting monsters, it is always changing, always in process' (Hutchings 2013: 9). For this kind of horror film textuality, Philip Brophy has coined the term 'horrality', which he defines as 'the construction, deployment and manipulation of horror – in all its various guises – as a textual mode' (1986: 5).

The dataset analysed in this study consists of eight contemporary feature films released between the years 1979 and 2008, thus covering a period of three decades at the turn of the millennium (cf. Table 8.1). Recent canonical examples of the genre have been randomly selected, comprising a wide range of content-related subgenres from supernatural and psychological mystery as well as creature and science fiction horror to vampire movies. The chosen films have not only received critical acclaim but also achieved great popularity in combination with tremendous commercial success. A central reason for these accomplishments certainly is the fact that they manage to

Table 8.1 Survey of Horror Films in the Dataset

	Title	Director	Year	Running time	Horror subgenre
(1)	*Alien*	Ridley Scott	1979	01:51:53	Creature, science fiction
(2)	*The Shining*	Stanley Kubrick	1980	01:54:43	Supernatural, psychology
(3)	*Bram Stoker's Dracula*	Francis Ford Coppola	1992	02:02:13	Vampire
(4)	*Jurassic Park*	Steven Spielberg	1993	02:01:22	Creature, science fiction
(5)	*The Sixth Sense*	M. Night Shyamalan	1999	01:42:54	Supernatural
(6)	*Signs*	M. Night Shyamalan	2002	01:42:10	Supernatural, science fiction
(7)	*Paranormal Activity*	Oren Peli	2007	01:22:05	Supernatural
(8)	*Cloverfield*	Matt Reeves	2008	01:21:12	Creature

trigger an emotional maximum of suspense and horror through original and efficient camera work. Hence, as to formal techniques, the eight films cover both the stable-image cinematographic style connected with sophisticated continuity editing (e.g. *The Shining* or *Bram Stoker's Dracula*) and more recent handheld camera productions and found footage aesthetics (e.g. *Paranormal Activity* or *Cloverfield*). The running time of the individual films ranges between 01:21:12 and 02:02:13, adding up to a total of 13 hours, 58 minutes and 32 seconds of cinematic discourse.

The maxims of quantity, quality, relation and manner were applied to the cinematography in the films, so as to determine prototypical and representative examples of their characteristic (non-)observance. Accordingly, most of the samples were extracted from highly suspenseful sequences that mark potential turning points in the characters' lives, while other examples were chosen because they include visual perspectives that reveal dramaturgically significant insights. In general, most attention is paid to shots rather than cuts, for the former constitute the basic building blocks of cinematography, while the latter mainly serve as linking devices. Furthermore, the focus is on the visual communication in relation to events and actions on the screen, while verbal dialogues are taken into account only if they are needed to clarify the situational background in the plot.

4 The cooperative principle applied to cinematography

Herbert Paul Grice's (1975, 1989) influential cooperative principle (CP) comprises the four general maxims of quantity, quality, relation and manner. If a maxim is disregarded in an obvious way, this process of flouting may result in a 'conversational implicature' (Grice 1975: 49). From a terminological perspective, Bethan L. Davies points out that Grice's technical notion of 'cooperation' is different from the everyday meaning of the term, which would be 'high levels of effort on the part of the speaker, perfect utterances, and avoidance of misunderstandings' (2007: 2311). In the framework of Grice's other philosophical writings, it becomes clear that he is mainly interested in rationality, which is an 'accountable system' and a 'logic' (Davies 2007: 2328) behind the literal meaning, so that his concept of cooperation is adaptable to cinematographic communication.

Grice's theory has triggered numerous (neo-Gricean) approaches and a variety of applications in diverse domains, as enumerated by Lindblom (2001: 1607–8), Bultinck (2005: 25) and Huang (2012: 31–6). Among the neo-Gricean models, two prominent examples are Laurence Horn's work on the Q- and R-Principles (1984) and Stephen Levinson's monograph on the generalized conversational implicature, which he defines as a 'default inference' (2000: 11). More recently, David Lumsden argues that Grice's idea of cooperation does not necessarily imply that interlocutors are cooperative in general, yet the CP can still be maintained by defining it in a narrower sense as 'linguistic or formal' cooperation (2008: 1907), which is also evident in the formal communication of cinematographic patterns. From a meta-perspective, Kenneth Lindblom distinguishes between three types of CP studies, examining discourse as utterance, as social interaction or as social context (cf. 2001: 1603). Along these lines, the present investigation of cinematography belongs to the first category, since film is an extended multimodal utterance which is not immediately interactive and does not directly respond to social context. As for other applications of Grice's principle to diverse discourse situations, there is research, for instance, on language teaching (White 2001), gender studies (Rundquist 1992) or humour and irony (Pan 2012; Schubert 2009).

Numerous studies in the area of pragmatic stylistics apply the conversational maxims to fictional dialogue at the inter-character level (cf. Cunico 1998: 105–15; Leech 2008: 120–35; Jeffries and McIntyre 2010: 100–10; Lambrou 2014: 142–50; Chapman 2014: 46–53). As Sonia Cunico argues, fictional characters are analogies of real-life people, so that their social and discursive practices in the imaginary textual world can be interpreted in similar ways (cf. 1998: 105). With regard to pragmatic principles, Geoffrey Leech further emphasizes that the utterances of literary characters may deviate from norms of 'cooperative or polite behaviour for a given conversational situation' (2008: 120) so that fictional figures can be discursively characterized as pragmatically abnormal at the inter-character level.

In contrast to studies exclusively dedicated to inter-character dialogue, Siobhan Chapman also touches upon the issue of how the narrator may trigger a quantity implicature that needs to be interpreted by the reader (cf. 2014: 53) so that she also includes the topic of audience response. Accordingly, the following paragraphs will give a survey of arguments for the adaptation of the CP to cinematographic communication also at the producer–recipient level, supporting the claim that the 'Gricean approach can be applied both to interaction between writers and readers and to interaction between characters' (Chapman and Clark 2014: 5). The central arguments can be subsumed under four headings, as will be outlined subsequently:

[1] Salience of producer–recipient implicature in carefully edited film discourse
[2] Pragmatic similarity between cinematic discourse and other forms of mass communication
[3] Real-life analogy between everyday storytelling and cinematic narratives
[4] Implied contract between viewers and filmmakers regarding the filmic illusion

[1] Geoffrey Leech and Mick Short mention the concept of the 'author-reader implicature' (1981: 303), which is said to be especially salient in authorial digressions from the linear fictional narrative. Since novels as written texts undergo a careful process of writing, revising and editing, 'it is arguable that adherence to the cooperative principle must be assumed even more strongly than for everyday talk exchanges' (Leech and Short 1981: 302). As the same is true of multimodal film discourse, any non-observation of maxims is particularly noteworthy also in the case of cinematography.
[2] Applying pragmatic perspectives to film, Richard Janney points out that cinematic discourse is

> assumed to follow pragmatic principles analogous to, if not in all instances identical to, those underlying other forms of public communication: it would be seen to be goal-oriented, involve intentional agents, employ a shared medium, require a certain amount of common knowledge and assumed sincerity, and so forth. (2012: 88)

Thus, from the vantage point of media pragmatics, the multimodal discourse of film ultimately represents a specific text type in the area of popular mass communication, so that the principle of cooperation plays an indispensable role.

[3] In her textbook on pragmatic stylistics, Elizabeth Black (2006) likewise argues for the application of the CP to both communicative levels of fictional discourse. She claims a 'real-life analogy' also in the utterances of the authorial narrator, for 'we tell each other stories, often for a range of interpersonal reasons' (2006: 32). For instance, just like a boring everyday story, a lengthy or tedious cinematographic sequence can also disregard the quantity maxim, since it may be less informative than anticipated and may thus fail to meet the viewers' default expectation of pleasurable entertainment. [4] Black also raises a highly relevant issue when she refers to

> the implied contract we all enter into when we read a fictional work: we may suspend some of our disbelief, but nevertheless we are likely to process the text in much the same way as other types of discourse, though we play the credulous reader. (2006: 32)

In a similar way, horror films will reach their aim of scaring the audience only if the viewers are enabled to identify and empathize with the protagonists on the screen. Although spectators are aware of the fictitious nature of feature films, they are usually willing to submit to the illusion during the short period of watching, especially in a darkened cinema theatre.

Accordingly, by flouting communicative maxims, horror film cinematography triggers specific cinematic implicatures. The central phenomenon under investigation is the shot, best defined as 'a single uninterrupted series of frames, [which] is film's basic unit of expression: an image whose meaning unfolds through time' (Pramaggiore and

Figure 8.1 Screenshot from *The Shining* (minute 00:26:31). 'The Shining' directed by Stanley Kubrick © Warner Brothers. 1980. All rights reserved.

Wallis 2011: 133). The temporal succession of images in cinematographic discourse is further determined by the technique of the cut, conceptualized as 'the joining of two separate shots so that the first is instantaneously replaced by the second, showing something that the preceding shot did not' (Dick 2002: 82). Cuts may in turn be semantically subdivided into different visual transitions that create specific emotional and cognitive effects. In the case of 'straight cuts', images are abruptly replaced, while a 'dissolve' means a gradual transition and a 'jump cut' creates a spatial gap between shots (cf. Dick 2002: 82–6). For instance, after the protagonist of *The Shining* has been shown in a medium shot for a few seconds while looking at a maze (see Figure 8.1), this image is replaced by an aerial shot of the maze by means of a straight cut (see Figure 8.4 in Section 5).

As the editing process combines shots into sequences, this procedure will lead to film discourse cohesion, since '[f]ilm depends to a large extent for its perceptual connectivity on the presence of cohesive visual ties between frames in shots, shots in sequences, and sequences in larger narrative units' (Janney 2010: 247; see also Tseng 2013: 2–6). As a result, the basic units of film analysis in ascending order are the levels of 'frame', 'shot', 'sequence', 'episode' and the entire 'narrative' (cf. Janney 2010: 248). Correspondingly, shots and cuts are here examined with regard to their forms and functions within the superordinate unit of the respective sequence.

5 The communicative maxims in the visual discourse of horror films

The following analysis concentrates on the (non-)observance of each of the four communicative maxims, including the respective submaxims. In order to adapt the CP to the visual communication of film, the chapter provides numerous examples of cinematic implicatures. All samples are embedded and contextualized in the filmic plots, with particular reference to the interaction between fictional characters and respective mortal threats.

5.1 The maxim of quantity

In horror films, the two submaxims of quantity can be correlated to specific cinematographic techniques by means of which they are typically flouted. The first submaxim, '[m]ake your contribution as informative as is required' (Grice 1975: 45), is flouted whenever visual clues deliberately lack informativity in comparison to the default situation of sufficient light, full visual access and unimpaired views. As the following instances will demonstrate, flouts can be caused by a selection of specific shots (zooms, close-ups, point-of-view, unbalanced and reaction shots), the handheld camera technique, methods of lighting (spotlights, low-key and bottom lighting) and types of focus (rack or shallow focus).

The typical function of flouting the first submaxim of quantity is to withhold visual details to create the implicature of a hidden threat that is not fully visible at present.

This is commonly achieved by zooms or close-ups, which are much less informative than full shots. Accordingly, in a suspenseful nightly sequence of *Jurassic Park*, only the eye of a Tyrannosaurus rex is initially discernible through a car window, as a teenage girl named Lex Murphy points a battery torch at the dinosaur's eye before it attacks the car (Spielberg 1993: minute 01:02:45). This visual *pars pro toto* conveys less information than would be presently required to fully comprehend the situation, yet through the cinematic context it is implicated that a life-threatening danger in the form of a large creature is to be expected. As the viewers adopt the character's restricted point of view, they are bound to empathize with the fear and horror experienced by the girl in the car. What is more, this shot corresponds with Bernard F. Dick's observation that '[e]xtreme close-ups of the eye are, in fact, standard in horror films' (2002: 55).

A close-up can also function as a reaction shot, implicating that the reason for a character's emotional response is about to be given. This is the case, for instance, when farmer Graham Hess in *Signs* first perceives the mysterious crop circles (i.e. 'signs') in his field: the perspective widens considerably and the camera eventually zooms out in an aerial shot (Shyamalan 2002: minute 00:04:35). The initial presentation of the protagonist's puzzled and shocked facial expression is particularly suitable to arouse curiosity and to trigger a feeling of anticipation in the audience.

In another suspenseful sequence of *Signs*, the quantity maxim is flouted in a more pronounced way through drastically reduced informativity (Shyamalan 2002: minute 00:57:57). Since the extraterrestrial invader, whose visual appearance is still unknown to the audience, is trapped in the pantry of a house, protagonist Graham Hess puts his head on the floor to get an impression of the alien through the crack under the door. The viewers, however, see the protagonist's countenance from the creature's restricted point of view from inside the pantry (see Figure 8.2). In contrast to close-ups, this type of shot does not provide a meronymic image, but merely puts the spectator in the alien's position, so that the degree of informativity is even lower. As a consequence, the mere camera perspective implicates that an unknown danger is presently hiding behind the door.

In general, deficient visual informativity and corresponding flouts of quantity are common in horror films whenever the actual perpetrator or creature is not overtly shown but merely implicated. A classic example is Steven Spielberg's *Jaws* from 1975,

Figure 8.2 Screenshot from *Signs* (minute 00:57:57). 'Signs' directed by M. Night Shyamalan © Touchstone Pictures. 2002. All rights reserved.

in which the great white shark does not appear during the first two-thirds of the film, while its presence is being only suggested by revealing effects such as ocean waves, its dorsal fin or the theme music (cf. Edge 2008: 6–7).

The use of a handheld camera may also be employed so as to reduce informativity, as in an example from *Paranormal Activity*: the character Micah puts the camera on the ground to support his girlfriend Katie, who has collapsed and is lying on the floor (Peli 2007: minute 01:16:17). From the camera's point of view, only their legs and torsos are visible, while their heads are visually cut off by the frame. By way of implicature, this shot foreshadows that their lives are in great danger, as corroborated in the remainder of the film. In terms of visual composition, such an 'unbalanced shot', which deletes significant details, steers and focuses the viewers' attention and creates 'strong emotional or aesthetic effects' (Sipos 2010: 66).

Signs contains a similar scene, in which Graham Hess's son Merrill appears in a medium shot in frontal position, standing beside his adversary Lionel Prichard, who is sitting at a table (Shyamalan 2002: minute 00:27:03). Since Merrill's head is visually cut off by the frame, the absence of his facial expression flouts the quantity maxim, but his clenched fist and his menacing body language implicate aggression towards Lionel (see Figure 8.3).

A love scene in *Bram Stoker's Dracula* likewise flouts quantity, for in a full shot Mina Harker kneels on her bed, seemingly embracing and kissing a lover that is invisible to the audience (Coppola 1992: minute 01:37:45). In this way, the shot cinematographically implicates Dracula's elusive and uncanny existence.

Apart from the shot type and distance, there are also other means of holding back visual information and thus flouting the first submaxim of quantity. In particular, low-key lighting often leaves parts of the scenery literally in the dark, while specific items may be foregrounded by spotlights. For instance, in *Signs*, while the family is in the basement of their house hiding from the aliens, Graham Hess's son Morgan uses a battery torch to highlight his face from below, creating a stark contrast with the surrounding scenery (Shyamalan 2002: minute 01:16:35). While bottom lighting in general 'gives a sinister air' (Dick 2002: 110), the cinematic implicature here is that

Figure 8.3 Screenshot from *Signs* (minute 00:27:03). 'Signs' directed by M. Night Shyamalan © Touchstone Pictures. 2002. All rights reserved.

unknown dangers may be lurking in the dark. In the same scene, a few minutes later, the torch lies on the ground and illuminates Morgan's sister Bo through a spotlight, but her head is visually cut off, which again implicates mortal dangers (Shyamalan 2002: minute 01:19:23).

Similarly, in a memorable sequence from *Alien*, Captain Dallas crawls through the narrow and unlit ventilation shafts of his spacecraft. While his body is singled out by a spotlight, the low-key lighting of the scenery reveals the spatial restrictions and the impenetrable darkness in both directions of movement (Scott 1979: minute 1:12:21). The contrast in lighting here constitutes a 'visual metaphor' (Brown 2012: 70), as it foregrounds human bravery against the background of pitch-black alien malevolence. Through the decreased visual informativity, it is cinematically implicated that the character may be assaulted at any time by the evil creature, while the restricted location offers no option of escape.

In addition to shot distance and lighting, selected features on the screen may be emphasized by being in focus, whereas other items appear as a mere blur. This technique occurs in *Signs*, when the family hides in its home and the father's head is clearly visible in the foreground, while the other three family members are out of focus in the background (Shyamalan 2002: minute 01:07:05). This instance of 'shallow focus' (Dick 2002: 69) directs the viewers' attention to the front of the cinematic space and implicates the father's central role as the protective agent in the family. A few minutes later, the film shows an example of 'rack focus' (Dick 2002: 69), since visual perspicuity here alternates between items in the front and in the back (Shyamalan 2002: minute 1:09:41). In this shot, first the baby monitor in the foreground is a blur, until, after a few seconds, the family in the background is out of focus and the baby monitor, which suddenly receives alien signals, is the clearly marked centre of attention. This wavering allocation of interest and informativity implicates a close interplay between the characters' emotions and the eerie sounds emanating from the baby monitor.

While flouts of the first quantity submaxim thus can depend on a great variety of cinematographic techniques, flouts of the second submaxim, '[d]o not make your contribution more informative than is required' (Grice 1975: 45), are caused chiefly by highly detailed long shots and the over-informative split-screen technique. In particular, a long shot may cause information overload by means of too many details in too little time. One sequence in *Bram Stoker's Dracula*, for example, contains a shot of a crowded London street at night, showing a multitude of individual persons within only a few seconds of film (Coppola 1992: minute 01:19:26–01:19:35). This instance of boosted informativity implicates the overly busy character of the city, which stands in stark contrast to Dracula's solitary castle in Transylvania and allows wrongdoers such as vampires to disappear in the crowd.

As far as enhanced informativity is concerned, the split-screen technique is highly salient as well, as another sequence from *Bram Stoker's Dracula* demonstrates (Coppola 1992: minute 01:03:52). While on the left of the screen the character Mina Harker is seen meditating, the right-hand side provides a turbulent flashback of her medieval alter ego's life. This technique implicates that the two identities of the character are cognitively intertwined in highly complex ways that cannot be represented in a sequential but only in a concurrent manner.

5.2 The maxim of quality

The application of the quality maxim to horror films poses challenges that need to be taken into account in the analysis. First, since viewers are aware of the fantastic nature of these narratives, the occurrence of supernatural creatures or events is both intended by the filmmakers and expected by the audience, so that corresponding special effects are not likely to trigger cinematic implicatures. For example, Dracula's shadow has a life of its own when Jonathan Harker visits him in his castle (Coppola 1992: minute 00:16:53), and when Harker sits in the train to Transylvania, Dracula's giant eyes appear in the sky (Coppola 1992: minute 00:08:36). Such scenes underline the villain's supernatural powers and are thus consistent with the internal logic of the horror genre, so that the maxim of quality is not affected. Second, the focus of this chapter is not on the truthfulness or plausibility of the plot itself but on the ways in which specific *cinematographic* techniques contribute to the (non-)observance of the quality maxim. On the basis of these premises, the examination of the dataset yields particular functions of the handheld camera style and the subjective camera technique, as will be pointed out in the following.

Some horror films specifically intend to convey the impression of authenticity, so that they ostentatiously simulate the observance of the two quality submaxims. This is the case especially in the so-called 'found footage' subgenre, which equals pseudo-documentaries, since it pretends to provide authentic recordings of horrific events, while the persons involved are usually declared dead. The effect of this subgenre is a heightened emotional response by viewers, as the illusion of reality is underscored by pervasive shaky camera motion, which imitates a genuine perception of events. This is the case in *Paranormal Activity*, where the documentary style is further supported by calendrical dates, the exact time of supernatural incidents and consecutive numbers allocated to the different nights throughout the narrative. Since the events are supposedly documented by the protagonists Micah and Katie themselves, the cinematographic form resembles the style of amateur home videos (Peli 2007: minute 01:13:14). Similarly, the opening credits in *Cloverfield*, stylistically reminiscent of official government documents, inform the audience that the film is found footage from a 'camera retrieved at incident site "US-447" – area formerly known as "central park"' (Reeves 2008: minute 00:01:15). The claim to realism and the blatant adherence to the maxim '[d]o not say that for which you lack adequate evidence' (Grice 1975: 46) have the function of enhancing the horror experienced by the viewers. Accordingly, *Cloverfield* is marked by the handheld camera style of personal videos, which here 'translates fear and conflict between characters into a visually upsetting experience' (Pramaggiore and Wallis 2011: 147). In the final showdown, for instance, when the creature attacks the protagonists Beth and Rob, the realistic presentation mode of the shaky camera gives the viewers a strong impression of immediacy (Reeves 2008: minute 01:06:30). Analogously, when a news broadcast in *Signs* airs a private recording of an alien, this sequence is also marked by shaky camera motion and blurred images (Shyamalan 2002: minute 00:56:29). In order to underline the observance of the quality maxim, this footage is additionally classified as 'genuine' by the news speaker (Shyamalan 2002: minute 00:55:18).

Apart from the pronounced *adherence* to quality, in several horror films this maxim is *violated* so that cinematic discourse is 'liable to mislead' the audience (Grice 1975: 49), even if only for a section of the film. While an objective shot 'represents what the camera sees', a subjective shot '(sometimes referred to as a *subjective camera*) represents what the character sees' (Dick 2002: 58), which means that in the latter case the viewers are put in the position of a character. In *The Sixth Sense*, for instance, almost the entire plot is conveyed from the unreliable point of view of the protagonist, the child psychologist Dr Malcolm Crowe. When Crowe at the end of the film discovers a bloody spot on the back of his shirt (Shyamalan 1999: minute 01:35:46), he realizes that he has actually been dead all along, since he was shot by a former patient in the beginning of the film. The audience is therefore tricked until this final revelation, although the film provides a few hints on Crowe's situation, which, however, can hardly be decoded before the disclosure at the end. Hence, this type of unreliability caused by a violation of the quality maxim prepares the ground for a concluding plot twist that is surprising for both the fictional character and the film audience.

The subjective camera also looms large in *The Shining*, when the young boy Danny Torrance rides his tricycle through the vast corridors of the abandoned Overlook Hotel and eventually stops to see two dead girls who invite him to play (Kubrick 1980: minute 00:35:38). This point-of-view shot violates the quality maxim, for it shows the audience horrific visions that are only accessible to this particular character. In this case, the subjective perception does not chiefly surprise the viewers but discloses past murders in the hotel and foreshadows later events in the film.

5.3 The maxim of relation

The communicative maxim of relation is significant whenever a visual transition between shots appears to lack relevance and thus the covert relation between the shots triggers an implicature. Hence, this maxim mainly corresponds to the degree of 'visual cohesion' (Arijon 1991: 475), which is caused by different types of cuts that connect shots. Just as the maxim of relation deals with the issue of 'how to allow for the fact that subjects of conversation are legitimately changed' (Grice 1975: 46), film discourse cohesion covers 'repertoires of shot composing and editing techniques' (Janney 2010: 247), resulting in filmic continuity. In cinematographic terminology, continuity can be divided into the four types of 'content', 'movement', 'position' and 'time' (Brown 2012: 78). For the present goal of examining implicatures that are caused by flouts of the maxim of relation, the two categories of *movement* and *position* will be subsumed under the superordinate term of *spatial* continuity.

As regards continuity of content, *Jurassic Park* contains a straight cut from a mosquito enclosed in amber to a dinosaur bone (Spielberg 1993: minute 00:05:15). In the beginning of the film, this juxtaposition creates a logical link between the two images and serves as a foreshadowing of later plot developments, when dinosaurs are actually created from DNA found in mosquitoes. Along similar lines, in two of the eight films of the dataset, straight cuts establish relevance between physically brutal deeds and fictional characters eating meat. In *Jurassic Park*, after a cow has been killed by a raptor, theme park owner John Hammond asks the question 'who's hungry', which is followed by a shot of a lunch plate (Spielberg 1993: minute 00:32:56), while in *Bram Stoker's Dracula*, Professor van Helsing cuts off a slice of a medium rare roast after Lucy Westenra's head has been severed from her body (Coppola 1992: minute 01:24:15). By the construction of relevance through juxtaposition, the cinematography implicates that the human consumption of meat is comparable to acts of physical violence. In addition, such original cuts add irony and dark humour to the mostly terrifying and sombre plotlines.

Concerning the continuity of time, the relevance of a cut may be rather difficult to reconstruct if the action alternates between different temporal levels. In *Cloverfield*, for instance, the plot occasionally switches between April and May 2009. At the end of the film, after New York City has been destroyed on 22 May, the found footage tape contains a straight cut back to a trip of the protagonists to Coney Island on 27 April (Reeves 2008: minute 01:10:14). The relevance of this non-chronological sequence becomes obvious by watching the shot in more detail, since that reveals a very small unidentified object falling from the sky in the background (Reeves 2008: minute 01:10:21). Hence, this cut implicates that this mysterious entity hitting the Atlantic Ocean may have brought the destructive creature to New York.

In a similar way, *Signs* comprises a few flashbacks to the deadly accident of Graham Hess's wife (Shyamalan 2002: minutes 00:44:22, 01:22:30, and 01:30:22), which likewise implicate a cause–effect relationship between events from the past and the present, since the woman's final words 'tell Merrill to swing away' (minute 01:31:32) give the protagonist hints on how to defeat the alien intruder in the final showdown. Moreover, in one of the concluding sequences of *Signs*, a very slow horizontal camera pan in a room flouts the maxim of relation, because the season changes from late summer in one window to snowy winter in the next (Shyamalan 2002: minute 01:35:40 to 01:36:21). This seemingly unrelated succession of frames implicates a leap in time that has not only changed the weather but has also affected the characters, since farmer Graham Hess has resumed his previous profession of a priest.

As far as spatial continuity between shots is concerned, *Bram Stoker's Dracula* flouts the maxim of relation in a sequence that shows Jonathan Harker shaving in the bathroom of the count's uncanny castle. In a point-of-view shot from Dracula's perspective, the vampire's hand approaches Harker's shoulder from behind, while the bathroom mirror does not show the count's reflection. When Harker suddenly turns around, the shot following the straight cut displays Dracula standing by the door several steps away from Harker (Coppola 1992: minutes 00:25:27 and 00:25:33). The implicature triggered by this deviant spatial continuity is that the count has superhuman abilities and poses a serious physical threat to Harker's life. Moreover, this cinematic cut corresponds to the plot also in a metaphorical way, as Harker actually cuts himself while shaving.

Finally, a special type of transition between shots is called *crossfading* or *dissolve*, defined as a 'gradual replacement of one shot by another' (Dick 2002: 85), so that, in contrast to straight cuts, one shot slowly merges into the next one frame by frame. This cinematographic technique frequently manifests itself in a 'metaphorical dissolve' (Dick 2002: 86), involving a semantic transfer across shots. For instance, in *Bram Stoker's Dracula*, the teeth marks on Lucy Westenra's neck merge into the shining eyes of a wolf (Coppola

1992: minute 00:49:05). Hence, by flouting the maxim of relation, this dissolve implicates a logical relationship between the initial violent act of biting and the animal metamorphosis, thereby serving the purpose of foreshadowing. If two images have a similar shape, as in this case, the transition is additionally labelled as a 'form dissolve' (Dick 2002: 87). Another characteristic instance occurs in *Bram Stoker's Dracula*: an extreme close-up of one of Mina Harker's eyes gradually turns into a glass of absinthe, which is subsequently shown in a high-angle shot (Coppola 1992: minute 01:01:10). By way of implicature, it is thus suggested that Mina Harker is increasingly intoxicated by Dracula's pernicious influence.

5.4 The maxim of manner

Finally, the maxim of manner may be disregarded in its various submaxims, for horror cinematography often achieves its frightening effects by blatantly avoiding the corresponding 'supermaxim – "Be perspicuous"' (Grice 1975: 46). In order to surprise and keep viewers in suspense, visual details are deliberately withheld or concealed through the strategic use of shots and cuts. Accordingly, the metaphor of 'obscurity' in the first submaxim '[a]void obscurity of expression' (Grice 1975: 46) can be taken literally, owing to frequent low-key lighting and nightly scenes. This may additionally be supported by fast movements, as in a scene in *Cloverfield*, where the protagonists run through the streets of New York during night time while being filmed by the person following them (Reeves 2008: minute 1:01:40). The shaky handheld camera in combination with darkness and blinding police floodlight not only enhances realism (see Section 5.2) but also implicates emotional agitation and disorientation of the character serving as the cameraman, so that audiences are invited to identify and empathize with the diegetic figures.

Obscurity of visual expression can also be the result of screen objects that are out of focus and therefore drastically blurred. A case in point is the amateur footage of the alien in *Signs*, which not only underscores authenticity (see Section 5.2) but also implicates the opaque and mysterious character of the extraterrestrials, thereby arousing the viewers' curiosity (Shyamalan 2002: minute 00:56:29). Hence, through such intentional obscurity, the cinematography implicates that a scene contains 'hidden or unseen threats' (Sipos 2010: 58), which causes fear and suspense. Another instance of an indistinct menace occurs near the end of *Signs*, when the alien that is holding Graham Hess's son in its hands is at first only perceived as a reflection in the black TV screen in the family's living room (Shyamalan 2002: minute 01:29:13). Thus, along with the characters, the audience will be horrified and eager to get a full view of the intruder, which is eventually provided by changes in the cinematographic perspective.

The second submaxim, '[a]void ambiguity' (cf. Grice 1975: 46), is disobeyed whenever visual images are equivocal and require interpretation or disclosure. In one sequence of *The Sixth Sense*, the nine-year-old boy Cole Sear slowly approaches a woman from behind, assuming that she is his mother (Shyamalan 1999: minute 00:53:15). However, when she turns around after a few seconds, a close-up of her face reveals that she is a complete stranger whose wrists have been slit (minute 00:53:19). Through this horrible surprise, both the viewers and Cole will be shocked and scared, while it is implicated that the boy lives in a dangerous and hostile world in which many things are not what they seem to be. An alternative form of ambiguity appears in *The Shining* when family father Jack has a close look at a model maze in the hotel lobby (Kubrick 1980: minute 00:26:31, see Figure 8.1 in Section 4). The following shot shows a bird's eye view of the maze (minute 00:26:40, see Figure 8.4), but gradually, by slowly zooming in, it becomes clear that this perspective shows the real maze outside the hotel, which is presently explored by his wife and son. Although the zoom eventually resolves the equivocal perception, the ambiguity implicates that Jack has acquired almost supernatural omniscience during his stay at the Overlook Hotel.

In contrast to the second quantity maxim, which refers to visual information overload (see Section 5.1), the submaxim '[b]e brief (avoid unnecessary prolixity)' (Grice 1975: 46) is disregarded whenever shots are redundant or artificially prolonged by means of pauses, repetitions or extremely slow camera movement. In the horror genre, lengthy shots or sequences may be employed to gradually build up suspense, which may culminate in a jump scare. In *Paranormal Activity*, for instance, the young couple installs a static video camera in one corner of their bedroom ceiling to record anything unusual that happens during the night. In several sequences, the viewers see them sleeping peacefully for some time until something mysterious takes place; for example, their blanket is moved or Katie is violently pulled out of bed by an invisible force (Peli 2007: minute 01:13:51). In accordance with the logic of repetition and escalation in this film, the monotonous shots of the stationary camera increasingly implicate the imminence of scary incidents.

Finally, the submaxim '[b]e orderly' (Grice 1975: 46) is flouted whenever the chronological order of events is undermined, as previously pointed out in the examples

Figure 8.4 Screenshot from *The Shining* (minute 00:26:40). 'The Shining' directed by Stanley Kubrick © Warner Brothers. 1980. All rights reserved.

from *Cloverfield* or *Signs* (see Section 5.3). The typical implicature is that different sections of the plotline are intertwined and mutually affect each other, independently of the linear progression of time.

Alternatively, shots can flout the maxim of orderliness also in spatial terms, which is the case in one of the final sequences of *Cloverfield*. After the monstrous creature has devastated Central Park and Rob's friend Hud has been killed, the video camera falls to the ground. The camera then unsuccessfully tries to autofocus and produces a shot in which Hud's head is upside down in a close-up (Reeves 2008: minute 01:06:38). The obvious implicature is that natural order is inverted and that the diegetic characters are utterly disoriented by the horrific events, so that the film audience will likewise experience consternation and bewilderment. Similarly, in the final sequence of *Paranormal Activity*, the demonic presence unexpectedly throws Micah's body against the camera, so that it suddenly tilts to the right and conveys a skewed image of the room (Peli 2007: minute 01:20:55). This disorderly shot implicates that the couple's intention to impose rational order on the unnatural events in their home has failed miserably.

6 Conclusions

As I have demonstrated in this chapter, Grice's CP can be adapted and applied to horror film cinematography, since this type of visual discourse involves a communicative understanding between film producers and recipients. While the viewers have specific genre-related expectations, scriptwriters and directors intend to appeal to their target group through the process of audience design. The examples have shown that the cinematographic deviance of the horror genre is a gradual phenomenon that does not manifest itself in totally unique techniques but rather in a pronounced or boosted realization of specific features such as extreme close-ups, shaky camera movement or subjective point-of-view shots. Thus, although the verbal dialogues are indispensable for the situation-dependent reconstruction of the plotlines, cinematic implicatures are ultimately triggered by the idiosyncratic visual language of the camera work. Within the horror genre itself, varying degrees of deviance can be found, ranging from rather conventional mainstream blockbusters such as *Jurassic Park* to experimental low-budget productions such as *Paranormal Activity*. As regards the different functions of shots and cuts, the former are pertinent to all four communicative maxims, for they form the basic building blocks of visual composition. Since cuts represent the filmic counterpart of punctuation, they are particularly salient in the application of the maxim of relation, which covers the interconnectedness of discursive segments.

As far as the first submaxim of quantity is concerned, withholding visual information is a central cinematographic technique of the horror genre. Through visual meronymy, extreme close-ups commonly flout this submaxim, since, in contrast to full shots, only a fraction of the complete picture is provided. Hence, this practice typically implicates an imminent threat or danger, so that it arouses the audience's curiosity and results in suspense. A similar effect is achieved by restricted point-of-view shots through small openings, by the use of a handheld camera showing only snippets of reality, or by a reaction shot of a startled character. Visual informativity may also be reduced by low-key lighting or blinding spotlights against a dark background. In addition, shallow focus may provide a detailed impression of the foreground, while the background is blurred and out of focus. In such cases, implicatures direct the spectators' attention to selected visual aspects on the screen. As to the second submaxim, the split-screen technique or too many details in a relatively brief sequence may lead to inflated informativity, which causes implicatures that potentially characterize individuals or display bustling activity.

The quality maxim is an exception among the four maxims, for it is usually not flouted but rather reinforced by the personal video camera style in found footage films. This technique results in a documentary look that serves the functions of realism, immediacy and illusion, aiming at an enhanced affective reaction of spectators through identification with the character holding the camera. Alternatively, the quality maxim is occasionally violated through the use of the subjective camera technique, which presents unreliable perspectives by specific characters. Such idiosyncratic perceptions may either result in a surprise of the audience, whenever the respective character is deluded, or they fulfil the function of foreshadowing, in case the character in question has visionary qualities.

The maxim of relation is flouted by visual transitions between shots, which may superficially appear non-cohesive with regard to content, time or space. This is typically caused by an obvious lack of filmic continuity in cuts, so that specific relations are implicated and need to be inferred by viewers. In terms of content, the innovative juxtaposition of apparently incongruous shots can culminate in original logical relations or dark humour. Blatant flouts of chronological order, as in the case of narrative time leaps, often implicate a cause–effect relationship. Whenever spatial continuity is flouted, this frequently leads to the implicature of supernatural abilities or events. While the default transition between shots is the straight cut, a noteworthy exception is the dissolve, which usually implicates semantic transfer or similarity across adjacent shots.

With regard to flouts of the manner maxim, the deviant images of horror cinematography are often obscure, owing to insufficient lighting or blurred vision. Likewise, misperceptions, visual ambiguity and protracted shots with a minimum of action are frequently used to initiate surprise or shock effects. Just like tilted camera angles, these techniques implicate disorientation, confusion and bewilderment of characters caused by psychological or physical threats.

All in all, since the present study is based on a relatively small dataset of eight films, it could only give a first insight into the (non-)cooperative character of horror film cinematography. Furthermore, as the chapter exclusively deals with visual communication, it would be desirable for future pragma-stylistic research to examine other aspects of multimodality in the horror genre as well. First, verbal dialogues may collaborate with cinematography in flouting or violating selected maxims, depending on the respective character speaking. Second, in horror films the audio track plays a major role, since acoustic signs intersemiotically contribute to implicatures that enhance surprise or shock, as in the case of uncanny sound effects or unexpected bangs that accompany jump scares. Third, the soundtrack also comprises the film score, which not only supports the rhythm of shots and cuts but also strengthens the affective impact on viewers, as in the case of suspenseful music developing into a gradual crescendo. Despite these limitations concerning multimodality, the present investigation of the visual plane has sought to demonstrate that the (non-)observance of maxims in horror films is a genre-related strategy that strongly supports the perlocution of pleasurable thrills in the audience.

Cinematic dataset (DVDs)

Coppola, F. F., dir. (1999/1992), *Bram Stoker's Dracula*, Culver City: Columbia Pictures.
Kubrick, S., dir. (2001/1980), *The Shining*, Burbank: Warner Brothers.
Peli, O., dir. (2010/2007), *Paranormal Activity*, Hollywood: Paramount Pictures.
Reeves, M., dir. (2009/2008), *Cloverfield*, Hollywood: Paramount Pictures.
Scott, R., dir. (2007/1979), *Alien*, London: Twentieth Century Fox.
Shyamalan, M. N., dir. (2003/2002), *Signs*, Burbank: Touchstone Pictures.
Shyamalan, M. N., dir. (2004/1999), *The Sixth Sense*, Burbank: Warner Brothers.
Spielberg, S., dir. (2001/1993), *Jurassic Park*, Universal City: Universal Studios.

References

Arijon, D. (1991), *Grammar of the Film Language*, Los Angeles: Silman-James.
Bateman, J. and Schmidt, K.-H. (2012), *Multimodal Film Analysis: How Films Mean*, New York: Routledge.
Bednarek, M. (2010), *The Language of Fictional Television: Drama and Identity*, London: Continuum.
Black, E. (2006), *Pragmatic Stylistics*, Edinburgh: Edinburgh University Press.
Brophy, P. (1986), 'Horrality: The textuality of contemporary horror films', *Screen*, 27 (1): 2–13.
Brown, B. (2012), *Cinematography: Theory and Practice – Imagemaking for Cinematographers and Directors*, 2nd edn, Amsterdam: Elsevier.
Bubel, C. M. (2006), *The Linguistic Construction of Character Relations in TV Drama: Doing Friendship in Sex and the City*, Saarbrücken: Universität des Saarlandes. Available at: http://scidok.sulb.uni-saarland.de/volltexte/2006/598/pdf/Diss_Bubel_publ.pdf (accessed 28 November 2016).
Bubel, C. M. (2008), 'Film audiences as overhearers', *Journal of Pragmatics*, 40 (1): 55–71.
Bultinck, B. (2005), *Numerous Meanings: The Meanings of English Cardinals and the Legacy of Paul Grice*, Amsterdam: Elsevier.
Chapman, S. (2014), '"Oh, do let's talk about something else-": What is not said and what is implicated in Elizabeth Bowen's *The Last September*', in S. Chapman and B. Clark (eds), *Pragmatic Literary Stylistics*, 36–54, Houndmills: Palgrave Macmillan.
Chapman, S. and Clark, B. (2014), 'Introduction: Pragmatic literary stylistics', in S. Chapman and B. Clark (eds), *Pragmatic Literary Stylistics*, 1–15, Houndmills: Palgrave Macmillan.
Cunico, S. (1998), 'Who's afraid of maxims? The co-operative principle from H. P. Grice to G. Leech with an application to contemporary British and American dramatic

discourse', in C. T. Rorsello, L. Haarman and L. Gavioli (eds), *British/American Variation in Language, Theory and Methodology*, 105–16, Bologna: CLUEB.

Davies, B. L. (2007), 'Grice's cooperative principle: Meaning and rationality', *Journal of Pragmatics*, 39 (12): 2308–31.

Dick, B. F. (2002), *Anatomy of Film*, 4th edn, New York: St. Martin's Press.

Dynel, M. (2011), '"I'll be there for you!" On participation-based sitcom humour', in M. Dynel (ed.), *The Pragmatics of Humour across Discourse Domains*, 311–33, Amsterdam: John Benjamins.

Edge, L. B. (2008), *Steven Spielberg: Director of Blockbuster Films*, New York: Enslow Publishers.

Goffman, E. (1981), *Forms of Talk*, Oxford: Blackwell.

Gregoriou, C. (2007), *Deviance in Contemporary Crime Fiction*, Houndmills: Palgrave.

Grice, H. P. (1975), 'Logic and Conversation', in P. Cole and J. L. Morgan (eds), *Syntax and Semantics*. Vol. 3: *Speech Acts*, 41–58, New York: Academic Press.

Grice, H. P. (1989), *Studies in the Way of Words*, Cambridge, MA: Harvard University Press.

Hidalgo-Downing, L. (2000), *Negation, Text Worlds, and Discourse: The Pragmatics of Fiction*, Stamford: Ablex Pub. Corp.

Hodson, J. (2014), *Dialect in Film and Literature*, London: Palgrave.

Horn, L. R. (1984), 'Toward a new taxonomy for pragmatic inference: q-based and r-based implicature', in D. Schiffrin (ed.), *Meaning, Form, and Use in Context: Linguistic Applications*, 11–42, Washington DC: Georgetown University Press.

Huang, Y. (2012), 'Relevance and neo-Gricean pragmatic principles', in H.-J. Schmid (ed.), *Cognitive Pragmatics*, 25–46, Berlin: de Gruyter Mouton.

Hutchings, P. (2013), *The Horror Film*, London: Routledge.

Janney, R. W. (2010), 'Film discourse cohesion', in C. Hoffmann (ed.), *Narrative Revisited: Telling a Story in the Age of New Media*, 245–65, Amsterdam: John Benjamins.

Janney, R. W. (2012), 'Pragmatics and cinematic discourse', *Lodz Papers in Pragmatics*, 8 (1): 85–113.

Jeffries, L. and McIntyre, D. (2010), *Stylistics*, Cambridge: Cambridge University Press.

Kawin, B. F. (2012), *Horror and the Horror Film*, London: Anthem Press.

Kozloff, S. (2000), *Overhearing Film Dialogue*, Berkeley: University of California Press.

Kress, G. (2010), *Multimodality: A Social Semiotic Approach to Contemporary Communication*, London: Routledge.

Lambrou, M. (2014), 'Stylistics, conversation analysis and the cooperative principle', in M. Burke (ed.), *The Routledge Handbook of Stylistics*, 136–54, London: Routledge.

Leech, G. (1969), *A Linguistic Guide to English Poetry*, London: Longman.

Leech, G. (2008), *Language in Literature: Style and Foregrounding*, Harlow: Pearson Longman.

Leech, G. and Short, M. (1981), *Style in Fiction: A Linguistic Introduction to English Fictional Prose*, London: Longman.

Levinson, S. C. (2000), *Presumptive Meanings: The Theory of Generalized Conversational Implicature*, Cambridge, MA: The MIT Press.

Lindblom, K. (2001), 'Cooperating with Grice: A cross-disciplinary metaperspective on uses of Grice's cooperative principle', *Journal of Pragmatics*, 33 (10): 1601–23.

Lumsden, D. (2008), 'Kinds of conversational cooperation', *Journal of Pragmatics*, 40 (11): 1896–1908.

Pan, W. (2012), 'Linguistic basis of humor in uses of Grice's cooperative principle', *International Journal of Applied Linguistics and English Literature*, 1 (6): 20–5.

Piazza, R. (2011a), 'Pragmatic deviance in realist horror films: A look at films by Argento and Fincher', in R. Piazza, M. Bednarek and F. Rossi (eds), *Telecinematic Discourse: Approaches to the Language of Films and Television Series*, 85–104, Amsterdam: John Benjamins.

Piazza, R. (2011b), *The Discourse of Italian Cinema and Beyond: Let Cinema Speak*, London: Continuum.

Piazza, R., Bednarek, M. and Rossi, F. (2011), 'Introduction: Analysing telecinematic discourse', in R. Piazza, M. Bednarek and F. Rossi (eds), *Telecinematic Discourse: Approaches to the Language of Films and Television Series*, 1–17, Amsterdam: John Benjamins.

Pramaggiore, M. and Wallis, T. (2011), *Film: A Critical Introduction*, 3rd edn, London: Laurence King Publishing.

Quaglio, P. (2009), *Television Dialogue: The Sitcom Friends vs. Natural Conversation*, Amsterdam: John Benjamins.

Rundquist, S. (1992), 'Indirectness: A gender study of flouting Grice's maxims', *Journal of Pragmatics*, 18: 431–49.

Schubert, C. (2005), '*Fallible Focalization*: Zur Linguistik der Sichtbehinderung im fiktionalen Text', *Germanisch-Romanische Monatsschrift*, 55 (2): 205–26.

Schubert, C. (2009), 'Punchlines in context: cooperation and relevance as key issues in humour studies', in L. Eckstein and C. Reinfandt (eds), *Anglistentag 2008 Tübingen: Proceedings*, 471–80, Trier: Wissenschaftlicher Verlag Trier.

Schubert, C. and Volkmann, L., eds. (2016), *Pragmatic Perspectives on Postcolonial Discourse: Linguistics and Literature*, Newcastle: Cambridge Scholars Publishing.

Sipos, T. M. (2010), *Horror Film Aesthetics: Creating the Visual Language of Fear*, Jefferson: McFarland and Company.

Toolan, M. (2014), 'Stylistics and film', in M. Burke (ed.), *The Routledge Handbook of Stylistics*, 455–70, Oxford: Routledge.

Tseng, C.-I. (2013), *Cohesion in Film: Tracking Film Elements*, Houndmills: Palgrave Macmillan.

White, R. (2001), 'Adapting Grice's maxims in the teaching of writing', *ELT Journal*, 55 (1): 62–9.

Wildfeuer, J. (2014), *Film Discourse Interpretation: Towards a New Paradigm for Multimodal Film Analysis*, London: Routledge.

Effectful advertising?

Film trailers and their relevance for prospective audiences

Heike Krebs

1 Introduction

In April 2000, *The Guardian* reported the record number of 1.7 million downloads of the new trailer for the upcoming *The Lord of the Rings* trilogy (*The Guardian* 2000). This number alone, combined with the actual box-office receipts (Mikos et al. 2007: 245), might support the notion that film trailers are among the most effective ways of advertising (Hediger 1999: 112). What all of them have in common is their multimodal composition, which includes audiovisual as well as textual elements. However, while the number of multimodal analyses of films is steadily growing, closer examinations of trailer-related filmic discourse are still rare and often constrain themselves to a film historical perspective or one of movie marketing (see, for example, Kernan 2004; Hediger 2001).

Using Richard Janney's claim that 'film making and film viewing can be understood as interrelated aspects of a complex form of public audiovisual discourse' (2012: 87), this chapter focuses on trailers as multimodal texts situated within this type of discourse. Since trailers are made to persuade, the question arises how their creators manage to convince viewers to go out and watch the related feature film. In many ways, pragmatic stylistics seems to provide the suitable theoretical groundwork necessary to tackle this question. So, we may ask how trailers develop their advertising function and to what extent the multimodal fabric of trailers tends to maximize it?

To this end, this chapter introduces a new framework based on relevance theory (RT) (Sperber and Wilson 1986, 1995), specifically designed to capture and analyse film trailers as multimodal advertising texts. Various examples used by Dan Sperber and Deirdre Wilson show that their approach does not exclusively focus on verbal language. For instance, they show that body movement or gaze can be used for specific communicative purposes, such as indicating an approaching person or possibly bad weather conditions (1995: 48f, 51); they even discuss the context dependent relevance of the smell of gas or auditory phenomena (1995: 151). Given that in film trailers verbal language is consciously combined with non-verbal modes like moving images or sound, this makes an important prerequisite for the application of their theory. Another main advantage of their model is its capability to account realistically for the speed of human comprehension (Forceville 2014: 55; Padilla Cruz 2016: 10) and provide empirical proof for central claims (Wilson 2016: 6). The former seems especially relevant regarding the complexity of multimodal texts like film trailers. Furthermore, a number of studies have already applied RT to various multimodal examples, especially within advertising (e.g. Díaz Pérez 2000; Taillard 2000).[1]

Film trailers as multimodal advertising, however, have not been discussed from a relevance theoretic perspective so far. Therefore, this chapter aims at a combination of both perspectives. In this respect, Charles Forceville's question 'What does each modality contribute to the optimization of relevance?' (2014: 67) will be taken as a starting point in order to explore the notion of relevance in the specific genre of film trailers. To this end, a multimodal analysis of a film trailer of *The Lord of the Rings*[2] (henceforth *LotR*) will show how its multimodal construction can cause specific relevance for different target audiences based on the use of different semiotic modes.

In a first step, the specific characteristics of film trailers as telecinematic advertising will be explained. On the theoretical basis of Sperber and Wilson's seminal publication of 1995, the general prerequisites of optimally relevant trailers will be used to develop a relevance theoretic framework for a trailer recipient design and to examine how a trailer's typical combination of descriptive and interpretative uses of modes contributes to its persuasive potential. Finally, an exploratory case study of a *LotR* trailer will focus on the semiotic modes of written and spoken language, (moving) image and music, as well as the combination of them, in order to expose the merits of this relevance theoretic framework for multimodal analysis.

2 Film trailers as telecinematic advertising

In order to provide a thorough analysis of film trailers in Chapter 4, some considerations as to their structural and functional classification are necessary. Both are prominent in Carmen Maier's central definition about the multimodal structure and persuasive function typical of trailers: 'Film trailers are multimodal texts in which several semiotic modes are combined, and parts of texts created for other purposes are transferred, rearranged and supplemented in order to attain a promotional purpose' (2009: 160). Apart from Maier's papers (see also Maier 2011), there are only three monographs focusing on film trailers, all of which take a film historical stance, albeit from different perspectives.[3] Recently, trailers have also been subject to multimodal argumentation studies.[4] This chapter, based on a closer look at the multimodal structure of trailers and the main semiotic resources relevant to the following analysis will categorize film trailers as telecinematic advertising. This includes some basic considerations about their multimodal structure, their production background and classification as (tele)cinematic discourse, as well as their 'promotional purpose' (Maier 2009: 160) of advertising a film.

Starting with a closer description of film trailers, a first aspect for their classification as cinematic discourse can be found in Janney's definition, that understands the 'technical cinematic apparatus [as] multimodal and multicoded' (2012: 91). However, taking a linguistic point of view, instead of talking of semiotic resources or (semiotic) modes like Maier (2009: 160), Janney prefers using the terms 'smaller expressive subsystems, each with its own heuristic practices, forms, and discursive functions' (Maier 2009) to describe the contents of this apparatus. As such subsystems, he lists language, staging, gesture, cinematography, editing and post-production. For my examination of film trailers, I will be dividing language into a spoken and written mode (*speech* and *writing*) and subsume staging, gesture and cinematography under the semiotic mode of *(moving) images*. Finally, considerations about *sound* and *music* will conclude my selection of the five most important semiotic modes in a film trailer, all of which can be classified according to their sensory channel as visual or auditory. The case of *editing* as a filmic mode shows the difficulty of this sensory subdivision, because its classification as exclusively visual might not go far enough, as by linking subsequent shots, editing is rather time-based. Therefore, it will serve as a sixth, filmic mode, which as such has a direct effect on other modes, for example when editing creates a rhythmic change of shots, which might be supported by music.

Taking Gunther Kress's definition of modes as 'socially shaped and culturally given resource[s] for making meaning' (2014: 60) as a basis provides the opportunity to emphasize the social aspect of meaning-making, which also brings along a rather dynamic understanding of meaning, that goes along with Sperber and Wilson's view of communication as inferential (see chapter 3.1). Kress goes on to list '[i]*mage, writing, layout, music, gesture, speech, moving image, soundtrack* [as] examples of modes used in representation and communication' (2014, emphasis in the original), pointing out their functional purpose. Depending on the different affordances or meaning-making potentials of the different modes, they can be used – individually or in a combined way – for certain aims, like the promotion of a film.

As trailers will be considered cinematic discourse based on their use of 'audiovisual discourse of film narration' (Janney 2012: 86), they are, secondly, also subject to different types of layering. In a very simplified way, the production of trailers can be seen as a two-step process, starting with the material of the film to be advertised, which is then 'transferred, rearranged and supplemented' (Maier 2009: 160) during the trailer production. For the description of this production level of films – which can also be applied to trailers, as I claim, Marta Dynel (2011) introduces the term *collective sender* to include several instances, which are collectively responsible for the production of filmic discourse[5], 'embracing among others: the scriptwriter, the director, camera operators, actors, picture and sound editors' (42). The collective sender of a film trailer additionally integrates the respective editors, voice-over artists and so on from a distinct trailer production company, which is usually commissioned for this task (Hediger 2001: 21). With regard to specific discourse within films – or trailers – another layering can be made out, which different authors have examined (Dynel 2011: 48). Most prominently, Herbert Clark's approach of layered discourse (1996) springs to mind, which has also been used for criticizing Sperber and Wilson's RT for lacking concrete applicability for such multilayered, fictional discourse (1987).[6] Central to this approach is the idea that discourse is to be differentiated into an '*inter-character/characters*' *(communicative) level* and the *recipient's (communicative) level*, on which meanings are communicated to the viewer' (Dynel 2011: 49, emphasis in the original). Similarly, Francisco Yus Ramos 'draw[s] a symbolic line between author/spectator communication and character/character communication' (1998: 5), which seems especially useful for advertising discourse, too (1998: 7). In order to analyse how trailers develop relevance for specific audiences, this chapter will focus on the recipients' communicative level (Dynel 2011: 49), which the collective sender uses to pursue their aim of advertising.

Finally, according to their 'promotional purpose' (Maier 2009: 160), trailers will be categorized as telecinematic advertising, expanding their cinematic classification to the realm of television and other media,[7] where trailers can be found increasingly. In this respect, Forceville lists four special characteristics of advertising that 'differ [...] from the kind of communication that dominates *Relevance*' (Forceville 1996: 99, emphasis in the original): 'non-co-presence in time', 'number of communicators involved', the 'multi-media [sic!] character of advertisements'[8] and 'ambiguity of the textual part of advertisements' (1996: 99–104).[9] Additionally, Forceville classifies advertisements as '*mass*-communication' (1996: 99). Similarly to the production level of films, advertising also involves several contributors who communicate their mutual advertisement to a mass audience that can be more or less easily defined in terms of the prospective target group of a certain product, brand or film (Forceville 1996: 100). Due to 'non-co-presence in time', advertising in general does not provide any opportunity of direct feedback in case of misunderstanding (Forceville 2014: 62, 1996: 100), contrary to typical face-to-face communication, which is the basis of Sperber and Wilson's (1995) majority of examples.[10] That means that advertisers have to be extremely conscious about the form of their messages, which is why advertising often uses ambiguous or weak forms of communication, such as images, metaphors or music (Cook 2006: 50f), as well as multimodal combinations (Forceville 1996: 102), in which the responsibility of drawing a suitable conclusion lies with the addressee (Forceville 1996: 102–4). In order to show how the specific combination of weak and strong forms of communication enables the address of specific audiences, RT can provide a helpful framework.

3 Relevance in trailer communication

After sketching out the basic features of the discourse of film trailers, the following chapter will expound the main notions of RT for the application to film trailers. Other than Paul Grice's approach (1989), RT does not rely on the premise of cooperation, which may be especially useful for the application to advertising discourse (Taillard 2000: 153). A main reason might be the condensation of Grice's cooperative maxims to just two principles of relevance (Sperber and Wilson 1995: 162). Of these, the first, cognitive principle of relevance is the general basis of their theory and states that '[h]uman cognition tends to be geared to the maximisation of relevance' (Sperber and Wilson 1995: 260). More important than this is the second, communicative principle of communication, which will serve as a basis for the subsequent analysis: 'Every act of ostensive communication communicates a presumption of its own optimal relevance' (Sperber and Wilson 1995: 260).

On the basis of the premises for an application of RT to film trailers (3.1), the following chapter will explain the core idea of their second communicative principle, that is a balance between optimal effect and effort from the perspectives of the audience (3.2). From the perspective of the collective sender, who is the communicator of the trailer, further considerations about the different uses of language or other modes of a trailer will be made (3.3).

3.1 Premises for optimally relevant trailers

At the heart of Sperber and Wilson's theory lies the classification of communication as 'ostensive' and 'inferential'. While the latter describes the process of understanding by inferencing, in contrast to encoding and decoding processes, the former contains information about the communicative situation itself. In order to apply RT to a specific domain like film trailers, it must be clear that communication in this field can be considered ostensive in the first place. For Sperber and Wilson, '*ostensive* behaviour or simply *ostension*' is 'behaviour which makes manifest an intention to make something manifest' (Sperber and Wilson 1995: 49), 'manifest' meaning 'perceptible or inferable' (Sperber and Wilson 1995: 39). Note that the authors do not only talk about ostensive *utterances* but instead deliberately use the more general term ostensive *behaviour*.[11] Employing a rather broad concept of behaviour, in their theory, they enhance its scope of application to multimodal forms of discourse. In the case of film trailers, I claim that the collective sender's distribution of an attractive trailer can be seen as ostensive behaviour, as will be shown.

The definition of 'ostension' centrally includes the notion of intention and 'provides two layers of information to be picked up: first, there is the information which has been, so to speak, pointed out; second, there is the information that the first layer of information has been intentionally pointed out' (Sperber and Wilson 1995: 50). The former, informative intention is directed at the information within a certain utterance, which can on the one hand consist of concrete narrative information about the advertised film, additional information about the cast, or an idea about its genre classification. On the other hand, considering trailers as parts of film marketing and thus of 'commercial advertising', their 'informative intention always boils down to some kind of positive claim about the product or service advertised' (Forceville 1996: 99). Applying Forceville's claim of 'modern Western man's familiarity with the genre of advertising' (1996: 106) to the more specific genre of film advertising – that is, trailers – it can hence be assumed that the audience generally notices the positive claim within the trailer, so that the informative intention of the trailer is at least recognized, if not even fulfilled, which is the case when the audience actually believes it (Forceville 1996: 99).

The second, communicative intention is recognized when the audience knows about the communicator's intention to convey certain information. In film trailers, this can be the case by recognizing the form of the trailer itself, which is typically used for intentional advertising of the respective film. This recognition – that is, the audience's assumption that the trailer is a piece of advertising for a certain film – may also be influenced by the individuals' cognitive environments, consisting in their physical environment (e.g. in the cinema) and cognitive abilities (e.g. former experience with or knowledge of trailers) (Sperber and Wilson 1995: 39).

Furthermore, Sperber and Wilson (1995: 153) include the notion of 'stimulus' as a 'phenomenon designed to achieve cognitive effects' (1995), which will be explored further in the next chapter. They elaborate that stimuli can be ostensive, too. As visual, auditory or tactile perceptions, they first serve to get the audience's attention, at the same time ensuring that the audience becomes aware of the communicator's intentions (1995), thus serving as an important element within trailers, as will be shown.

3.2 Audience – Effect and effort

The core idea of Sperber and Wilson's theory is that all communication is based on a principle of optimal relevance, which relies on a cost-benefit balance between the effort of processing, which must be optimally small, and the effect of the input, which must be optimally large for the input to be relevant (Sperber and Wilson 1995: 164, 267). This effect is defined as a 'cognitive effect that contributes positively to the fulfilment of cognitive functions or goals' (Sperber and Wilson 1995: 265). Concretely, a positive cognitive effect can be an 'epistemic improvement, i.e. an increase in knowledge' (Sperber and Wilson 1995: 266), for example, but also 'the reorganization of existing knowledge, or the elaboration of rational desires' (Sperber and Wilson 1995). Wilson (2016: 5) further specifies the need of new information to be linked to existing knowledge to be relevant for the addressee:

> what makes an input relevant to an individual is that it interacts with contextual information he has available to yield worthwhile cognitive effects (e.g. warranted conclusions, warranted strengthenings or revisions of available information). (Wilson 2016: 5)

Hence, relevance in Sperber and Wilson's sense includes three different effects within ostensive communication, which are necessary for the input to be relevant:

1. New information that can link to existing cognitive environment, that is existing knowledge,
2. Strengthenings of existing assumptions and
3. Weakenings of existing assumptions.

Forceville adds a fourth effect, consisting in 'sharing an emotion or evaluation with an addressee' (Forceville 2014: 54). Considering these effects, a trailer will be relevant if it presents new information, which can be linked to existing knowledge. In the case of the *LotR* trailer analysed in this chapter, the existing knowledge is – at least partly – based on the films' character as literary adaptation, which, similar to a trailer for a remake of a film, makes the activation of knowledge possible. In order to be relevant to viewers who might not know the original books, however, other ways of connecting existing knowledge or assumptions are necessary, which will be explored in the detailed analysis in Section 4.

The processing effort needed is more difficult to show. It includes the quantity of information to be processed and the number of mental operations, such as deductions (Sperber and Wilson 1995: 125–7). For linguistic utterances, it can be assumed, for instance, that a rather long utterance containing the same proposition as a shorter utterance will need a greater effort to process or that an utterance containing additional information without further contextual effects is thus less relevant (Sperber and Wilson 1995: 127). For film trailers, the case is more complex as they simultaneously use different modes for conveying an impression about the promoted film. However, the abundant use of film scenes can be seen as a way of keeping the effort as low as possible, given that the recognition of filmic action, as long as certain editing rules are obeyed, might be less taxing than, for example the decoding of the same information if it were presented only in written form.[12]

Considering the popularity of trailers as film advertising might lead to the conclusion that their assumed relevance – that is, the balance between maximal effect and minimal effort – is indeed recognized by their respective audience. As a closer inspection of the audience's effort is not possible in the scope of this chapter, the following case study (chapter 4) will focus on the question of effect and asks how the combination and interaction of modes contributes to a trailer's relevance.

3.3 Collective sender – Saying and showing

Assuming that trailers are a type of ostensive communication, as was done in 3.1, does not automatically mean that trailers do exclusively use overt communication. On the contrary, ostension, too, is a scalar notion. On these grounds, the following reflections directed at the communicator in the form of a collective sender will discuss different kinds of uses of language or other semiotic modes in a trailer.

In this respect, Sperber and Wilson claim that there is 'a continuum of cases of ostension ranging from "showing", where strong direct evidence for the basic layer of information is provided, to "saying that", where all the evidence is indirect' (1995: 53). They give the example of Peter 'leaning back ostensively to let Mary see William approaching' (1995). Despite this strong direct evidence of the approaching figure, the ostensive movement can still be understood as an instance of weak communication, as Mary may derive several assumptions about its meaning. That is why non-verbal communication can generally be considered 'relatively weak' (Sperber and Wilson 1995: 60). On the other hand, in saying that William is approaching, Peter must rely on his credibility if he does not only want to have his informative, but also communicative intention fulfilled. In film trailers, this opposition is resolved by a combination of 'saying' and 'showing', which involves a combination of descriptive and interpretive uses of modes.

> On the most basic level, every utterance is a more or less faithful interpretation of a thought the speaker wants to communicate. An utterance is descriptively used when the thought interpreted is itself entertained as a true description of a state of affairs; it is interpretively used when the thought interpreted is entertained as an interpretation of some further thought: say, an attributed or a relevant thought. (Sperber and Wilson 1995: 259)

For an application of this distinction between descriptive and interpretative use of utterances to film trailers, the special construction of film trailers must be considered. Roughly, the trailer can be seen as a multilevel and multimodal utterance of a 'positive claim' (Forceville 1996: 99) about the film it advertises. The film scenes included in the trailer are used as a form of interpretation of the original film scenes, for example often presented in a cut version, similar to direct quotations or summaries, which resemble the original but differ from it (Sperber and Wilson 1995: 227f).

In terms of the descriptive use of filmic material, semiotic modes 'show' the audience what they can expect from the film, for example images of characters played by certain actors. Thus, the descriptive use is mostly found on the microlevel of concrete semiotic modes, especially in the form of moving images or spoken language of the film, which iconically resemble and indexically represent the original film scenes. Such a 'description of a state of affairs in the actual world' (Sperber and Wilson 1995: 231) or in a given fictional world (Sperber and Wilson 1995: 289) is for instance also the release date of the films (1:04–1:22) or the names of the cast (1:24), given in written language. The interpretative use, on the other hand, is usually constructed by combining different semiotic modes, aiming at mirroring the film's narrative, for example, which is itself a function of multimodal construction work. Within this interpretative use, a trailer can itself develop its own narrative, for example, which need not be exactly the same as the one in the film it advertises – even though it is constructed largely from the same filmic material.

Hence, the advertising function of trailers works on at least two levels: On the one hand, the different semiotic modes and their combinations can cause different cognitive effects, enabling the address of different target audiences. On the other, based on the same multimodal construction, a specific combination of descriptive and interpretative uses of modes can give rise to an especially powerful advertising effect. The following chapters will merge these aspects with the respective potential of weak and strong forms of communication and show how this relevance theoretic framework functions by use of a case study.

4 The multimodal structure of the *LotR* trailer and its relevance for different audiences

4.1 Corpus and method

The following relevance theoretic analysis will focus on one trailer of the *LotR* trilogy. It is the first trailer for the whole trilogy, which was screened about a year before the release of the first film (Mikos et al. 2007: 70). It serves as advertising for the whole trilogy. As the first trailer of the trilogy promoted the film about one year in advance, it had to raise a general awareness for the trilogy before other trailers followed which focused on the first film of the trilogy.[13] *LotR* is a special case in that it is a literary adaptation and could thus address former readers of the literary original (Mikos et al. 2007: 56, 65). As such, it was part of an extensive marketing campaign (Mikos et al. 2007) and provides the advantage that a comprehensive reception study

(Mikos et al. 2007; see also Jöckel 2005) can underpin assumptions about potential audiences with quantitative evidence.[14] Therefore, among the different target audiences identified in the study by Mikos et al. (2007: 209),[15] this analysis will focus on one distinction, that is spectators who have or have not read the original books.

Considering Sperber and Wilson's communicative principle of relevance, the main focus will lie on the positive cognitive effects the trailer offers for readers and non-readers of the literary original as revealed by a multimodal analysis (4.2). After the identification of the five modes of speech, writing, images, sound and music, as well as their combinations, they will be classified regarding their potential of raising (different) cognitive effects for readers or non-readers of the books. A new framework will finally combine Sperber and Wilson's classification of strong and weak communication with the respective multimodal background and assign it to respective descriptive or interpretative uses of modes or multimodal combinations (4.3).

4.2 Multimodal recipient design

For the films of the *LotR* trilogy, Jöckel has shown that their success can be explained by their attractiveness for diverse social groups (2005: 209). Therefore, I assume that the trailers as part of a larger marketing strategy are also aimed at different audience groups and that this can be explained within their multimodal structure. So, while Sperber and Wilson's RT can provide insights as to how audiences develop positive cognitive effects (see chapter 3.2), a second theoretical concept, that can only be touched upon within the scope of this chapter, frames the analysis in terms of a multimodal recipient design: Building upon Alan Bell's audience design (1984, 1991), Dynel uses the notion of recipient design, originally brought up by Harvey Sacks, Emanuel Schegloff and Gail Jefferson (1974), in a telecinematic context:

> Recipient design is here understood as a set of discursive (as well as cinematographic) techniques enabling the target viewer's interpretative processes and arrival at meanings, in accordance with the collective sender's plan. The latter's choice of strategies, and effects consequent upon them, are dependent on the presupposed target audience. (Dynel 2011: 52)

Both audience design, which was developed for explaining intra-speaker variation in the context of news discourse, and recipient design can account for stylistic choices, which Sperber and Wilson see as important means for the communicator to imply her relevance (Sperber and Wilson 1995: 219; see also Padilla Cruz 2016: 11). Considering that discursive as well as cinematographic techniques on the recipients' level – that is, aimed at the film or trailer audience outside the screen – are based on multimodal structures, the use and combination of different modes will be understood as stylistic choices within a trailer. On this basis, a multimodal analysis will show in which ways the recipients of trailers profit from positive cognitive effects like the generation of new knowledge, strengthening or weakening of assumptions or being conveyed an emotion or evaluation (Forceville 2014: 54). Following reception studies about the *LotR* trilogies (Mikos et al. 2007; Jöckel 2005), the following analysis will focus on two main target groups, explaining how readers of the *LotR* novels might gain maximal cognitive effects in comparison to audience members who are not aware of the literary original.

Given the readers' existing knowledge about the novels by John Ronald Reuel Tolkien (1954), its characters, plot and maybe also about the cultural discourse around the work, such as the common assumption that it was deemed too complex for filmic adaptation, the cognitive environment they could build upon is different from so-called non-readers, who watch the trailer without background knowledge of the books. In the trailer, these different backgrounds are activated by a combination of forms of weak and strong communicational means. In general, non-verbal modes, that is, images, music and sound are seen as 'relatively weak' by Sperber and Wilson (1995: 60), which means that their interpretation can vary to a rather large degree depending on the addressee (Forceville 1996: 106–7). In the case of this trailer, the advantages of weak communication, which is commonly used in advertising (Forceville 1996: 107), become clear, as it further supports the specific address of the different audiences.

So, while images give rise to the recognition of various aspects of the known literary works for readers thereof, the same images can be considered relevant for spectators without knowledge of the books for other reasons. A rather long scene towards the end of the trailer (1:02–1:22) is a good case in point. The images alone show altogether nine male persons in a mountainous landscape walking towards the camera in different outfits. Readers might recognize them because their outfits or props suggest their character, for example the wizard Gandalf with a pointed hat and a staff, Legolas carrying a bow and the bearded Gimli an axe, others might notice that some of them have appeared earlier in the trailer (e.g. Gandalf in 0:35 and 0:45, Frodo in 0:38, 0:42, 0:54 or Aragorn in 0:32 and 0:46), which might suggest their importance, and viewers without knowledge of the books might simply know an actor – either case leads to recognition that improves the relevance for the viewers. The new knowledge about book characters' appearance can additionally lead to strengthening or weakening readers' assumptions held about the looks of certain characters – an effect that non-readers will miss, however. Instead, the assumptions they might gather from visual stimuli generally refer to the film's assumed genre or atmosphere. The central part of the trailer, for instance, consists of a sequence of sixteen different shots presented in 18 seconds (0:28–0:46). Not only do these give a very broad overview of different protagonists and rather impressive landscapes, which different kinds of audiences can integrate differently in their existing knowledge. Also, the editing of these scenes in quick succession strengthens different assumptions. On the one hand, readers, having recognized parts of the trailer as a possible filmic adaptation of the *LotR* novels, might (start to) assume that their idea of Tolkien's story being unfilmable because it stretches over decades in the original, which were hard to imagine within the length of a mainstream film, has to be revised – that is, their assumption weakened. On the other hand, non-readers can use the visual information for the formation of new assumptions about the advertised film's genre, which seems to be somewhere between action, adventure and fantasy. The fact that single scenes show fights, for example by two figures with long robes and a staff (0:42) or battle related scenes, such as a man with a sword leading an army (0:46) or a marching army of orcs (0:28) can support this impression.

Additionally, other typical examples of weak communication are provided by sounds and music. The two parts of the trailer that are accompanied by music (0:28–0:48, 1:00–1:42) each gain specific energy and momentum, for example by rhythm as sub-mode of both music and editing. Especially the assumption about the adventurous character of the film conveyed by the editing mentioned earlier (0:28–0:46) is further strengthened. A potential meaning of sounds, however openly communicated, is harder to pin down, whereas their relevance potential in the form of ostensive stimuli has been claimed explicitly by Sperber and Wilson. These 'must satisfy two conditions: first, they must attract the audience's attention; and second, they must focus it on the communicator's intentions' (1995: 153). Given that prominent phenomena like 'sudden loud noises such as shouts or doorbell chimes, striking visual stimuli such as hand waves, flashing lights or bright posters, or vigorous tactile stimulation such as prodding or grasping' (1995) are especially prone to human attention (Sperber and Wilson 1995: 40), the first condition is fulfilled. Their combination with other modes in trailers, then, can offer the function of directing the audience's attention according to the communicator's intentions (Sperber and Wilson 1995: 153).

Therefore, instances of weak communication, especially those directing the audience's attention, will often be combined with strong forms of communication like language in both written and spoken forms. In the example of the approaching figures mentioned earlier (1:02–1:22), this works by the combination with language, written in this case, which Sperber and Wilson generally describe as 'a kind of explicit communication' (1995: 55) with the 'advantage [...] that it gives rise to the strongest possible form of communication' (1995: 60). This use of writing towards the end of the trailer provides a frame for the otherwise mostly visual impressions the viewers obtain and presents the titles of the single films of the trilogy, each followed by their general release date (1:04–1:22), for example 'Christmas 2001' (1:01). While some quiet, ethereal music accompanies the scene in the background, the appearance of each film title and release date is introduced by a muffled beat of a kettledrum, leading the viewer's attention to the written information. The interaction of writing and images might also lead to new assumptions about how the presented persons fit to single films of the trilogy: 'The Fellowship of the Ring' (1:04) might in fact consist of the shown persons and a story about their experiences. The title 'The Return of the King' (1:17) presented simultaneously with two men approaching might bring up the question of reference: Is one of the two men rightfully referred to as king? The fact that the last person appearing was already presented twice before in this trailer can be seen as a higher relevance, as he will be recognized on the grounds of pre-existing knowledge more probably than the person walking in front of him.

Therefore, from a perspective of RT, the film titles and dates alone would not be very relevant, despite being a strong form of communication. By their combination with other modes and their position at the end of the trailer, however, they can refer to the new knowledge about the film they advertise – for readers and non-readers alike. Depending on how interested the viewers have become, the dates present a very relevant input, if the interaction of recent impressions of the film with the new knowledge about the release dates, has the cognitive effect of the decision to see the film.

Finally, speech is rather rare in the analysed trailer and only occurs three times. A large part at the beginning of the trailer is taken up by an off-screen narrator quoting the ring verse 'One Ring to rule them all / One Ring to find them / One Ring to bring them all / and in the darkness bind them' (Tolkien 1954: 1, 0:08–0:24). This verse creates the first explicit differentiation of the trailer audience: Those who are acquainted with Tolkien's books can recognize it as the ring verse in *LotR*, thus connecting it to their existing knowledge of the literary original, which results in a high relevance for them. Probably, hearing the ring verse in spoken form within a trailer – fans will even recognize it in the language of Mordor, uttered before the English version begins – will raise the strong assumption of a film adaptation being advertised. The interpretation of others will be more open after decoding the utterance.[16] A similar differentiation can be assumed for the other two instances of speech, which on the one hand (re-)activate knowledge about the original plot ('Even the smallest person can change the course of the future,' 0:49–0:51) and on the other strengthen assumptions about the advertised film's atmosphere and genre ('This Christmas, the most extraordinary tale ever told will come to life,' 0:35–0:44). Equally interesting is the classification of speech in terms of its descriptive or interpretative use, which can be applied to the latter sample of speech and which contributes to a new theoretical framework for the multimodal analysis of trailers.

4.3 Double usage structure of trailers

As has been shown from a relevance theoretic perspective, weak forms of communication can in fact be considered 'even preferable to the stronger forms' (Sperber and Wilson 1995: 60) and the combination of both can be used efficiently for the advertising effect of a film trailer. In the following, the general effectiveness of a trailer will be discussed on the basis of its double usage structure of saying and showing, that is descriptive and interpretative uses of certain modes or multimodal combinations.

The basis for this special communicative feature of trailers lies in the character of trailers itself, which typically use the material of the film that they advertise, as mentioned in chapter 3.3, but not only 'transfer' this material to an advertising context but also 'rearrange[...] and supplement[...]' (Maier 2009: 160) it. The latter features can be seen as foundation for the suitability of Sperber and Wilson's interpretative use of modes in trailers. At first sight, this interpretation makes sense especially with regard to the mentioned combination of modes, for instance not only by enriching a scene with the addition of background sounds or music or making it seem especially vivid by editing a sequence of short shots, but also because this specific multimodal combination can imply a certain interpretation, 'saying that' the advertised film is especially suspenseful, for example (see Table 9.1). However, the mode of speech in the analysed *LotR* trailer partly[17] works in a similar way, as it makes suggestions that do not only describe the advertised film but give an interpretation of it. In this respect, 'This Christmas, the most extraordinary tale ever told will come to life', articulated by a male voice-over, (0:35–0:44) does not only refer to the release date of the first film of the trilogy in terms of 'an actual state of affairs' (Sperber and Wilson 1995: 232), which is tantamount to a descriptive use. It also, interpretatively, uses the superlative 'most extraordinary tale ever told' and thus provides the audience with further points of departure for individual inferences. For instance, viewers can relate the use of 'tale' to own experiences of adventurous (fairy) tales, thus concluding that the prospective film might belong to a fantasy genre. However, despite the explicit character of language, this – interpretative – utterance needs further proof to be relevant, let alone credible, for the audience.

Therefore, the trailer makes use of literally 'showing' reasons why the advertised film is relevant for certain audiences and therefore worth watching. For instance, the mode of writing 'describes' an actual state of affairs (Sperber and Wilson 1995: 232) by announcing that the films will screen 'Christmas 2001' (1:01). Also, the use of scenes from the film, that is, the mode of images taken individually or audiovisual combinations that can be interpreted as scenes from the film, work this way, providing direct evidence for the attractiveness of the advertised film (e.g. the shot-reverse-shot sequence of Galadriel and Frodo (0:49–0:51) or the diverse scenes used in the short-shot sequence in the middle of the film (0:28–0:46)). Interestingly, it is also the visual mode that is used because of its indirectness in terms of recipient design: being a weak form of communication, it can be interpreted rather openly, which contributes to the potential of addressing a diverse audience.

Hence, this double usage structure also makes use of the specific affordances of different modes, however, differently from the ways used in the formation of a multimodal recipient design. Here, weak forms of communication like images are used for providing direct evidence of the film in question, that is, support the positive claim about the film directly, while rather strong forms of communication like spoken language can only substantiate the claim they make in an indirect way.

This is especially obvious for the case of a voice-over narrator, who is not part of the fictional layer but can rather be attributed to the collective sender, that is, communicator, herself. However, I claim that in general, also other instances of speech and writing are used, at least partly, in an interpretative way with regard to the advertising aim of the communicator of the trailer.[18]

The special context of advertising, that usually entails a certain lack of trust towards the advertiser (Tanaka 1996: 39–40), therefore makes appropriate adjustments necessary so that the communicator can achieve her aim of offering a relevant message to her audience, that is, potential viewers of the advertised film. Especially in non-reciprocal

Table 9.1 Double Usage Structure of Trailers

Use	(Multimodal) preference	Form of communication
Interpretative use 'Saying that'	Single mode: *speech* (off-screen narrator), *writing* (intertitle)	Strong communication
~ indirect evidence for positive claim about film	Multimodal: *editing, music* (used additionally to audiovisual scenes)	Weak communication
Descriptive use 'Showing that'	Single mode: *images* (e.g. landscapes, characters/actors), *writing* (e.g. release dates, names of cast)	Weak communication, strong communication
~ direct evidence for positive claim about film	Multimodal: audiovisual scenes	Combination of weak + strong communication

communication like advertising, the communicator, that is, collective sender of the trailer, 'has to [...] adapt her informative intentions to her credibility' (Sperber and Wilson 1995: 63) in order to create the mutual cognitive environment necessary for the communication of further details. For example, this mutual cognitive environment can entail knowledge about constituents of the collective sender – for example the director or production company of the advertised film – as well as, in terms of the 'cognitive ability' of the addressee, the possibility to recognize the trailer as film advertising due to its comparability to other trailers or its presentation in a cinema, which makes up the physical environment, which is also part of the (mutual) cognitive environment (Sperber and Wilson 1995: 39). For trailers, this means that in order to fulfil their informative intention of conveying a positive image of the advertised film, the communicator must resort to appropriate ways of presentation. This can be done by presenting certain content. The corporate logo of the production studio of the advertised film shown in the beginning of the trailer ('New Line Cinema – A Time Warner Company' (0:01)), for example, can be interpreted as a guarantee for certain quality as it evokes positive memories about previous popular films produced by the same film studio (Grainge 2008: 85). Keiko Tanaka (1996: 39–40) furthermore gives the example of a salesperson to illustrate the situation of a possibly untrustworthy communicator, who, lacking obvious trust, 'has to aim to achieve [her] intended effects by means of an artfully crafted stimulus' (Tanaka 1996: 40). In the case of trailers, the collective sender similarly aims at raising interest in the promoted film by creating a trailer that is attractive for its target audience, containing an 'artful' combination of diverse multimodal stimuli, so that it can even receive acclaim in the form of the Golden Trailer Award.[19] However, the special case of film advertising lies in the direct connection of this artful presentation to the source of the employed material, which is the advertised film. To this end, the communicator makes use of the specific kind of double usage structure of saying and showing in order to make her sales message both credible and worthwhile the viewers' attention.

5 Conclusion

Using a *LotR* film trailer as a case study, this chapter has developed a relevance theoretic framework for the multimodal foundation of a trailer recipient design and has shown how RT helps to explain the address of two exemplary target audiences. Secondly, the use of certain modes has been merged with a more abstract structure that might provide an explanation for the effectiveness of trailer advertising. This 'double usage structure' of trailers illustrated for the sample analysis that the verbal modes *speech* and *writing* can be used differently: While in the case study writing is mostly used descriptively, giving rather concrete release dates or names of the cast, for example, speech is also used in an interpretative way in that it presents the positive claim about the advertised film – to be shown and substantiated directly by the help of otherwise weak forms of communication, such as images.

For this exploratory case study, the use of a trailer for a pre-sold property – that is, an advertised product whose advantage is that it is already known among a group of potential customers (Mikos et al. 2007: 56) – was very helpful in terms of the identification and selection of a well-defined audience group. Further studies, however, need to show how a trailer recipient design can resort to other and possibly multiple target audiences, also exploring the use of modes in more detail. Moreover, further empirical studies from an interdisciplinary perspective, especially including reception studies or the rather new branch of neurocinematics, might offer closer insights into the applicability and scope of this relevance theoretic framework for film trailers.

Notes

1. For a relevance theoretic model for media discourse, see Yus Ramos (1998); Pinar Sanz (2013) has applied RT for political advertising and Piazza and Haarman (2015) have most recently developed a framework for verbal–visual relations in television news programmes.
2. *Lord of the Rings: The Fellowship of the Ring – Trailer* [online]. Available at: <https://www.youtube.com/watch?v=z_WZxJpHzEE>
3. *Coming Attractions. Reading American Movie Trailers* by Lisa Kernan (2004) aims at a rhetorical analysis of trailers from three different eras (1920–1999) and wants to explore how trailers address their (implied) audience. Keith M. Johnston's *Coming Soon. Film Trailers and the Selling of Hollywood Technology* (2009) uses the method of 'unified analysis', which combines textual analysis of trailers with a historical analysis of the trailers' contexts, for example concerning their production, distribution or reception (11f), specifically focusing on the connection to technology. Vinzenz Hediger's analysis in *Verführung zum Film. Der amerikanische Kinotrailer seit 1912* (2001) offers a historical classification of different types of trailers, which he frames with respective background information about film advertising.
4. See, for example, Wildfeuer and Pollaroli (2017), Pollaroli (2014).
5. Film discourse according to Dynel (2011: 42) defines linguistic discourse within a film, that is, usually among the filmic characters, and has to be distinguished from '*cinematic discourse*, which conflates an array of cinematographic techniques, which are studied primarily outside linguistics' (ibid., see also Janney 2012: 86). Given the scarcity of film discourse in the examined trailer, this study will consider it as only one of several parts of the broader notion of (tele)cinematic discourse, that also Christian Hoffmann and Monika Kirner-Ludwig refer to in their introduction to this volume.
6. That RT can indeed be used will hopefully be shown in the course of this chapter.
7. See especially the introduction in the edited volume by Piazza, Bednarek and Rossi (2011) for a comparison of cinematic and television discourse.
8. In his description of this feature of advertising, Forceville (1996: 102) actually describes the multimodal character of advertisements, although they are to be found in different media, too.
9. The fourth aspect, 'ambiguity of the textual part of advertisements' (Forceville 1996: 102–4) entails the conscious use of ambiguous stimuli, which is not constrained to verbal modes but rather common for advertising in general (see, for example, Tanaka 1996; Cook 2006).
10. Latest models of mass communication show that this lack of feedback typical for a transmission model is not to be seen as absolute, but that media, including advertising, exist in a continuous feedback loop as they can be considered as embedded in contemporary culture (McQuail 2011: 70). What is probably rather

problematic is the possibility of short-term misunderstandings that arise if the potential customers are addressed in a way they do not approve of. This can be avoided by better knowledge of the prospective audience or target group.

11 This generic use is reminiscent of Grice's concept of 'utterance' (see Padilla Cruz 2016: 5; Yus 1998: 293) which referred 'not just to linguistic utterances but to any form of communicative behaviour' (Sperber and Wilson 1995: 21, see also Sperber and Wilson 1995: 29).

12 In this vein, using shot-detection tasks, Smith and Henderson (2008) have shown that match-action cuts are more likely to be missed than cuts between scenes. Also, the metastudy by Smith, Levin and Cutting (2012) presents the results of various empirical studies of film reception that suggest how films work 'by piggybacking on natural visual cognition' (108). More concretely, Schwan and Ildirar (2010) suggest that even film viewers without experience easily understand discontinuous film clips as long as they can perceive some line of action (975). These might be helpful results for estimating the rather low effort of understanding film trailers.

13 Note that the original designation of the trailer found on YouTube is misleading in this respect, being referred to as 'Lord of the Rings: The Fellowship of the Ring – Trailer', https://www.youtube.com/watch?v=z_WZxJpHzEE.

14 See also Shefrin (2004), Wasko and Shanadi (2006) and Thompson (2007) for further background on the marketing of *LotR*.

15 In their choice of target groups, Mikos at al. (2007) refer to the study by Jöckel (2005) and focus on gender, reading experience with *LotR* and fandom, adding affinity to media and technicity (211) as a fourth aspect.

16 For non-readers, the repeated mentioning of 'One Ring' can lead to a strengthening of the assumption that a ring plays a powerful role in the advertised film on the basis of diagrammatical iconicity. Also, if the power of the ring is taken literally, a fantasy genre might suggest itself.

17 The other two instances of speech differ in that they simultaneously belong to the narrative universe and can thus be also considered to be 'shown' as glimpses of the prospective film: Firstly, the same male off-screen narrator recites the Ring verse known from the beginning of the novels (0:08–0:24). Secondly, within the character-character level, Galadriel tells Frodo in a shot-reverse-shot: 'Even the smallest person can change the course of the future' (0:49–0:51).

18 Another case in point is the intertitle at the end of the trailer 'You will find adventure, or adventure will find you' (1:29–1:36).

19 www.goldentrailers.com

References

Bell, A. (1984), 'Language style as audience design', *Language and Society*, 13 (2): 145–204.
Bell, A. (1991), *The Language of News Media*, Oxford: Blackwell.
Clark, H. (1987), 'Relevance to what?' *Behavioural and Brain Sciences*, 10 (4): 714–15.
Clark, H. (1996), *Using Language*, Cambridge: Cambridge University Press.
Cook, G. (2006), *The Discourse of Advertising*, Abingdon: Routledge.
Díaz Pérez, F. J. (2000), 'Sperber and Wilson's relevance theory and its applicability to advertising discourse: Evidence from British press advertisements', *Atlantis*, 22 (2): 37–50.

Dynel, M. (2011), 'Stranger than fiction? A few methodological notes on linguistic research in film discourse', *Brno Studies in English*, 37 (1): 41–61.
Forceville, C. (1996), *Pictorial Metaphor in Advertising*, London: Routledge.
Forceville, C. (2014), 'Relevance Theory as model for analysing visual and multimodal communication', in D. Machin (ed.), *Visual Communication*, 51–70, Berlin: Walter deGruyter.
Golden Trailer Awards. Home Page, 1 March 2019. Available at: http://www.goldentrailer.com/.
Grainge, P. (2008), *Brand Hollywood: Selling Entertainment in a Global Media Age*, New York and London: Routledge.
Grice, H. P. (1989), *Studies in the Way of Words*, Cambridge, MA: Harvard University Press.
Hediger, V. (1999), 'Das vorläufige Gedächtnis des Films. Anmerkungen zu Morphologie und Wirkungsästhetik des Kinotrailers', *montage/av*, 8 (2): 111–32.
Hediger, V. (2001), *Verführung zum Film. Der amerikanische Kinotrailer seit 1912*, Marburg: Schüren.
Janney, R. (2012), 'Pragmatics and Cinematic Discourse', *Lodz Papers in Pragmatics*, 8 (1): 85–115.
Jöckel, S. (2005), *'Der Herr der Ringe' im Film, Event-Movie – postmoderne Ästhetik – aktive Rezeption*, München: Reinhard Fischer.
Johnston, K. (2009), *Coming Soon: Film Trailers and the Selling of Hollywood Technology*, Jefferson: McFarland.
Kernan, L. (2004), *Coming Attractions: Reading American Movie Trailers*, Austin: University of Texas Press.
Kress, G. (2014), 'What is mode?', in C. Jewitt (ed.), *The Routledge Handbook of Multimodal Analysis*, 60–75, Abingdon: Routledge.
Maier, C. (2009), 'Visual evaluation in film trailers', *Visual Communication*, 8: 159–81.
Maier, C. (2011), 'Structure and function in the generic staging of film trailers: A multimodal analysis', in R. Piazza, M. Bednarek and F. Rossi (eds), *Telecinematic Discourse*, 141–60, Amsterdam: John Benjamins.
McQuail, D. (2011), *McQuail's Mass Communication Theory*, London: Sage.
Mikos, L., Eichner, S., Prommer, E. and Wedel, M. (2007), *Die 'Herr der Ringe'-Trilogie. Attraktion und Faszination eines populärkulturellen Phänomens*, Konstanz: UVK.
Padilla Cruz, M. (2016), 'Introduction: Three decades of relevance theory', in M. Padilla Cruz (ed.), *Relevance Theory: Recent Developments, Current Challenges and Future Directions*, 1–29, Amsterdam: John Benjamins.
Piazza, R., Bednarek, M. and Rossi, F., eds. (2011), *Telecinematic Discourse: Approaches to the Language of Films and Television Series*, Amsterdam: John Benjamins.
Piazza, R. and Haarman, L. (2015), 'A pragmatic cognitive model for the interpretation of verbal-visual communication in television news programmes', *Visual Communication*, 15 (4): 461–86.
Pinar Sanz, M. J. (2013), 'Relevance Theory and political advertising: A case study', *European Journal of Humour Research*, 1 (2): 10–23.
Pollaroli, C. (2014), 'The argumentative relevance of rhetorical strategies in movie trailers', in B. Garssen, D. Godden, G. Mitchell and A. F. Snoeck Henkemans (eds), *Proceedings of the 8th International Conference of the International Society for the Study of Argumentation*, 1–4 July 2014, Amsterdam: SicSat.
Sacks, H., Schegloff, E. A. and Jefferson, G. (1974), 'A simplest systematics for the organization of turn taking for conversation', *Language*, 50 (4): 696–735.

Schwan, S. and Ildirar, S. (2010), 'Watching film for the first time: How adult viewers interpret perceptual discontinuities in film', *Psychological Science*, 21 (7): 970–6.

Shefrin, E. (2004), 'Lord of the rings, star wars, and participatory fandom: Mapping new congruencies between the internet and media entertainment culture', *Critical Studies in Media Communication*, 21 (3): 261–81.

Smith, T. J. and Henderson, J. M. (2008), 'Edit blindess: The relationship between attention and global change blindness in dynamic scenes', *Journal of Eye Movement Research*, 2 (2): 1–17.

Smith, T. J., Levin, D. and Cutting, J. E. (2012), 'A window on reality: Perceiving edited moving images', *Current Directions in Psychological Science*, 21 (2): 107–13.

Sperber, D. and Wilson, D. (1986), *Relevance Theory: Communication and Cognition*, Oxford: Blackwell.

Sperber, D. and Wilson, D. (1995), *Relevance Theory: Communication and Cognition*, 2nd edn, Oxford: Blackwell.

Taillard, M.-O. (2000), 'Persuasive communication: The case of marketing', *Working Papers in Linguistics*, 12: 145–74. [online]. Available at: https://www.phon.ucl.ac.uk/home/PUB/WPL/00papers/taillard.pdf (accessed 27 February 2019).

Tanaka, K. (1996), *Advertising Language: A Pragmatic Approach to Advertisements in Britain and Japan*, London: Routledge.

The Guardian (2000), 'Lord of the rings trailer sets internet record' [online]. Available at: https://www.theguardian.com/film/2000/apr/11/lordoftherings.news (accessed 1 March 2019).

Thompson, K. (2007), *The Frodo Franchise: The Lord of the Rings and Modern Hollywood*, Berkeley: University of California Press.

Tolkien, J. R. R. (1954), *The Lord of the Rings*, New York: Ballantine.

Wasko, J. and Shanadi, G. (2006), 'More than just rings: Merchandise for them all', in E. Mathijs (ed.), *The Lord of the Rings: Popular Culture in Global Context*, 23–42, London: Wallflower.

Wildfeuer, J. and Pollaroli, C. (2017), 'Seeing the untold: Multimodal argumentation in movie trailers', in A. Tseronis and C. Forceville (eds), *Multimodal Argumentation and Rhetoric in Media Genres*, 189–215, Amsterdam: John Benjamins.

Wilson, D. (2016), 'Relevance theory', in Y. Huang (ed.), *Oxford Handbook of Pragmatics*, Oxford: Oxford University Press. [online]. Available at: https://www.researchgate.net/publication/296332481_RELEVANCE_THEORY (accessed 27 February 2017).

YouTube. *Lord of the Rings: The Fellowship of the Ring – Trailer* [online]. Available at: https://www.youtube.com/watch?v=z_WZxJpHzEE (accessed 1 March 2019).

Yus Ramos, F. (1998), 'Relevance theory and media discourse: A verbal-visual model of communication', *Poetics*, 25: 293–309.

10

Adapting scripture to (trans)script

A cognitive-pragmatic approach to cinematic strategies of evoking pseudo-medieval frames

Monika Kirner-Ludwig

1 Introduction

Since the very beginnings of motion film making, medieval frames and motifs have been used to attract and fuel audiences' fascination worldwide. From the earliest English-speaking medieval films onwards (cf., for example, Curtiz et al.'s *The Adventures of Robin Hood*, USA, 1938; Fleischer's *The Vikings*, USA, 1958; Glenville's *Becket*, Britain, 1964), film makers working in and with this genre have had to face the challenges of creating an anachronistically medieval, illusionary frame pseudo-authentic enough to persuade their audience of letting themselves be deceived for the duration of the film. Besides suitable and proper shooting locations, flamboyant and expensive costumes, and usual prototypical motifs such as dragons, swords, kings, knights and damsels in distress, this chapter seeks to demonstrate to what extent particularly linguistic tools are strategically applied so to lend credence to medieval characters and their fictional worlds.

While this chapter will essentially contribute to already launched discussions of the much-disputed notion of 'medieval film' (cf., for example, Sauer and Lenker 2005; eds. Bernau and Bildhauer 2009; Pugh and Weisl 2013) and build upon earlier studies on adapting medieval motifs and frames to modern screen and recipients (cf., for example, Aronstein and Coiner 1994), my study shall do so by identifying pseudo-medieval linguistic features in selected specimens produced in the United States and brought to the screens since 1960. The corpus to be investigated comprises twelve movie transcripts, that is, written texts that were created by fans based on the cinematic/televisual production of a script, covering a period of forty-five years, that is, from 1960 through 2015.

2 Research background and objectives of this chapter

2.1 Medieval film, (New) Historicism, and the issue of metahistory

This chapter will use the notion *medieval film* in the sense of 'film about or concerning the Middle Ages', thus forming a subgenre to historical film (cf., for example, Rosenstone 2006). As a label, *medieval film* is thus understood as broadly as, for example, the much younger notion of *medieval blogs*, which is generally applied as an umbrella term for all kinds of blogs in any way concerned with the Middle Ages (cf., for example, Cohen 2010: 33ff.; Kirner-Ludwig 2018: 21). For the purposes of the present study, I will consider *medieval film* a genre in its own right, following, for example, Bildhauer (2011), who has convincingly promoted the idea that films about the Middle Ages must be viewed as an active, live interaction with the past. This idea ties in neatly with medieval film having come hand-in-glove with what has been called *New Historicism* (cf. Burt 2008) and the aim of 'reviving' the past through cinema. In this, New Historicism is 'engaged not only in reading the past but [...] also in attempting (and failing) to visualize it', as Burt aptly observes (2008: 178).

Most research on medieval films published since the break of the millennium has been contributed by historians and film historians (cf., for example, Harty 1999; Aberth 2003; Amy de la Bretèque 2004; Kiening and Adolf 2006; Bildhauer 2011). Recent studies have zeroed in on the relation between historiography and *historiophoty*, that is, 'the representation of history and our thought about it in visual images and filmic discourse' (White 1988: 1193; cf. Rosenstone 2006; Haydock 2008; Elliott 2011b). What is more, notions such as metahistory and practical past (cf. White 1973, 1987, 1988; Lindley 1998) have been taking center stage. Essentially, they promote the idea of historical consciousness and reflexivity in merging 'history proper' with 'speculative philosophy of history' (cf. Wilson 2014). In other words, they go from the assumption that medieval film makers will (ab)use the medieval frame as a platform or stage for discussing modern-day issues (cf. Sauer and Lenker 2005). This would presuppose that – while 'historians write narratives to explain the meaning of the past' (Munslow 2015: 158) script- and screenplay writers of medieval films may not only wish to entertain their audience, but also may be pursuing educational goals with their works at the same time.

It has been emphasized that medieval film will conventionally follow a set of relatively coherent criteria: If we, for instance, pick up the idea of medieval film symbolizing a modern world, this would mean that, 'despite their mythic overtones and romance coloring, films with medieval themes [...] are required by their audiences to deliver a convincing picture of life' (Wood 2014: 39). In addition to that, medieval films will have to employ certain features that are stereotypically associated with the Middle Ages – that is, particular kinds of clothes, gestures, and so on (cf., for example, Wood 2014: 47). Burkholder expands on this by claiming that

> [a]udiences enter historical film with certain expectations of what the past presumably should look like; films tend to deliver on those expectations, even at the expense of historical reality, and thus reinforce erroneous stereotypes for

the next cycle of films. Although there is no formal rulebook they must abide by, filmmakers who favor historical rigor over accepted (even if faulty) preconceptions of the past do so at their own peril. (2015: 20; also cf. Tashiro 2004; Finke and Shichtman 2010)

In a conciliatory vein and in agreement with Driver and Ray (2009: 20), who argue that even for the authentically medieval audience of an authentically medieval text, some loss of realism must have been acceptable. White stresses the same issue for written history accordingly, which is 'forced to represent some agents' or their roles in certain historical events in insufficiently general ways (1988: 1199). Rosenstone summarizes these arguments as follows:

> we always violate the past, even as we attempt to preserve its memory in whatever medium we use [...] Yet this violation is inevitable, part of the price of our attempts at understanding the vanished world of our forebears. (2006: 135)[1]

Therefore, the question as to what is to be deemed appropriately accurate in terms of historiographical details woven into a medieval film is probably the wrong question to ask. Rather, we may want to follow White in his tenet that both

> conventional films and conventional historiography [...] show us [...] that the criterion for determining what shall count as 'accuracy of detail' depends on the 'way' chosen to represent both 'the past' and our thought about its 'historical significance' alike.

In that vein, '[f]ilm critics and historians have by and large [been] arguing that it is better to treat [historical] films as films [rather] than to evaluate them in terms of how faithfully and how accurately they portray history' (Burt 2007: 217).

When taking the bird's view on these discussions just outlined, hardly any attention has been paid to how makers of medieval film systematically weave in linguistic clues or patterns that would enhance and maintain the 'medievalness' of their fictional world and narrative. As I have argued in another chapter and in relation to medieval blogs, the authenticity of any meant-to-be-medieval text is significantly enhanced by the employment of 'specific pseudo-medieval linguistic codes' (2018: 19). Thus, it is striking that no comprehensive discussion has been presented on the (in-)accuracies of such linguistic patterns, which is what the present chapter is setting out to provide.

2.2 Medieval, archaic and pseudo-archaic speech patterns

A medievalist has to make their peace with the fact that most of the research-relevant data possibly accessible and obtainable comes in written, sometimes in drawn, never, though, in audible form. The striving for fully reconstructing the latter is the historical linguist's quest for their very own Holy Grail: ever-ongoing and never to be fully grasped. While uncountable and extensive academic approaches have – based on the written records come down to us – been made to reconstruct diachronic varieties such as Old and Middle English on all their linguistically describable levels, this long tradition of linguistic research seems to have been mostly separate from what lay persons today tend to assume about 'how people spoke in the Middle Ages'.

With the birth of the medieval film genre, one could have certainly expected ample opportunities to open up for finally experimenting within the dimensions of 'spoken medieval speech'. However, it seems that hardly any attempts have been made in this direction until relatively recently: while code switching has been a well-established feature in telecinematic discourse for decades and across subgenres, few movies and TV series have dared to tread the shaky grounds of employing medieval varieties. One prominent exception is the Irish-Canadian series *Vikings* (2013–), which uses reconstructed and idealized stretches of Old Norse, Old English and medieval Latin speech. Further attempts to weave in Old English utterances have been made in the British TV series *Merlin* (2008–12) or, to a very small extent, in Zemeckis's British-American 3D computer-animated fantasy adventure film *Beowulf* (2007). Whereas the viewer of these productions will in most cases not have sufficient knowledge about medieval Latin or Old English to distinguish between what has been correctly reconstructed or not with regard to, for example, syntax and morphology, even medievalists themselves will not be able to fully assess the phonetic accuracy the actors will perform with. We are thus facing a highly complex build-up of intricate levels entailed in adding pseudo-medieval speech to screenplays.

While there has been a general discussion going on about to what extent screenplays represent spoken or written text, post-production transcripts of telecinematic discourse – that is, the kind the present chapter is using – may be available in written form, too, but are in fact, in some sense, spoken ones in written form.[2] At the same time, they can be so only partially, as actors will also have systematically embedded idiosyncratic features into their 'delivery' of the written screenplay text, including, for example, prosodic and paralinguistic features (not to mention particular accents of English). When 'lay' transcribers (i.e. fans with presumably no linguistic training) transcribe the spoken discourse back into a written form, though, they may not be taking these specific features into account at all. While these layers certainly deserve to be addressed when sketching out the process of (1) writing a screenplay > (2) acting the screenplay out > (3) transcribing that telecinematic discourse back into written text, the present study will only use the text level resulting from step (3) in the process just described. In ignoring prosodic and paralinguistic matters, the post-production fan transcripts adhered to in this study will merely be used as a means to an end and shall be considered faithful recoveries of the preproduction screenplays.

A closer look into the language used in medieval films will necessarily have to make that approach one that is based on what has been reconstructed and what has come to be conventionally believed about 'medieval speech' (cf. Vincendeau 2001; Davis 2000; Rosen 2001). Concretely, any assessment of marked linguistic features occurring in medieval films must inevitably be canvassed against 'rules' or conventionalities rather than have been established for the diachronic varieties of Old and Middle English so that one will be able to identify and discuss any pseudo-features to begin with. Several such attempts have been made in the course of the last fifteen years and a number

Adapting Scripture to (trans)script

of valuable linguistic studies have been produced, focusing on pseudo-archaisms and pseudo-medieval features in modern media including video games, computer mediated texts and, of course, film (cf. Harris 2004; Bryant 2010; Traxel 2008, 2012; Kirner-Ludwig 2018). Yet, not nearly enough attention has been paid to systematics and pragmatic implications pseudo-medieval linguistic features convey.

Archaisms may be defined as 'linguistic forms that used to be common but then went out of fashion' (Traxel 2012: 42), while pseudo-archaisms are such 'linguistic forms that never existed but [...] evoke the impression as if they could have' (Traxel 2012: 42f.). Traxel proposes a distinction of two subcategories of pseudo-archaisms, namely

(a) 'mock-archaisms [composed on the basis of] no or only limited knowledge of English language history [and] created mostly for humorous reasons'; and
(b) 'neo-Old or neo-Middle English by authors with an educated knowledge of English language history [and thus] intended as more serious recreations' (Traxel 2012: 43; cf., for example, Görlach 1981; Lenard and Walker 1991).

Traxel's type (a) overlaps with Eco's category of 'the Middle Ages as a pretext', a 'mythological stage on which to place contemporary characters', while 'there is no real interest in the historical background' (Eco 1973: 68).[3] It is certainly fair to assume that, in general, writers involved in producing screenplays (henceforth referred to as *pre-production screenplay scripts*), even if these are for medieval films, are not specifically educated or trained in any medieval or related discipline (e.g. linguistics, history). This is probably equally true for those individuals transcribing movie dialogues based on the produced screenplay and movie (henceforth referred to as *post-production fan transcripts*).[4] It can thus be hypothesized that respective transcripts and screenplays will hardly contain (m)any linguistic, anthropological or historical details of academically established depth or relevance. What is much rather to be expected, however, are visually and maybe less so auditively perceivable features that are to be classified as culturally shared knowledge and as such conventionally and saliently associated with the medieval period in general.

3 The corpus composed for this study

3.1 A corpus of post-production fan transcripts

The corpus used for the present study is composed of twelve film post-production fan transcripts (PPFTs) created and made available online by lay persons. These transcripts have – depending on the availability of each – been obtained from two websites: www.springfieldspringfield.co.uk and www.script-o-rama.com. The latter provides links to external sites hosting film transcripts, while the former hosts a database of several thousand TV and movie PPFTs itself. It has to be emphasized that the object material chosen for this study are in no case preproduction screenplay scripts (PPSSs), that is, such textual material produced by writers to be used mainly by directors and actors as a basis for cinematic/televisual production prior to any such production being generated.

While PPSSs would have certainly been considered the first and most authentic choice for a study such as this one, this option did not present itself as the most coherent as only one out of the twelve films chosen[5] could be retrieved in its actual screenplay or rather draft version thereof from the *Internet Movie Script Database* (the most comprehensive online database of screenplays, currently providing 1,198 screenplays for educational purposes).[6] Therefore, the corpus for this study is composed exclusively of screenplay transcripts – that is, fan-written texts created based on already existing cinematic/televisual productions. So to prevent any notional ambiguities that might arise from the quasi-synonymous use of terms *script* and *transcript* (even on the websites the object material has been collected from in the first place), the present study is henceforth referring to the object material as PPFTs as opposed to PPSSs, with the latter not being considered here.

While one might well question the reliability and accuracy of PPFTs produced and made available by mere film aficionados, the end will still justify the means, as these compilations are much more accessible than any original PPSSs. In fact, it has been maintained by a number of scholars that PPFTs of film and television series are in fact 'fairly accurate and very detailed, including several features that scripts [i.e. PPSSs] are not likely to present: hesitators, pauses, repeats, and contractions' (Quaglio 2008: 191–2; cf. Bednarek 2018). Table 10.1 displays all script titles featuring in this study.

All twelve movie samples fulfil such criteria or 'ground rules' as have been established and described for medieval films (Woods 2014: 4–9; also cf. Lindahl, McNamara and Lindow 2000), namely the geo-timely setting (cf. Section 3.2), the 'non-medievalist' background of the script writers (cf. Section 3.3),[7] and the topical frame (cf. Section 3.4). Based on these commonalities, the present study shall pursue a systematic identification and analysis of such linguistic features that can be classified as pseudo-characteristic of medieval English according to Traxel 2012 (cf. Chapter 4). Only type-(a)-pseudo-archaisms (cf. Traxel 2012) in these PPFTs will be taken into consideration in the following.

3.2 Geo-(ana)chronistic coherence on a timeline of fifty years

Lindley observed that film makers will generally seek to simplify the Middle Ages as much as possible, having an audience in mind that wishes to be entertained rather than educated: 'The notional Middle Ages supplants the historical one, being, after all, much simpler to deal with and easier to sell' (1998: no pagination; cf. Laity 2008: 147). This is certainly a case in point one has to take into consideration when levelling one's expectations of any authentic medieval (linguistic) features in a medieval film.

Burt established the notion 'Movie medievalism' as a broad term 'includ[ing] films set in the Middle Ages as well as films with contemporary settings that allude to the Middle Ages or are anchored in them' (2007: 219).[8] This study is going to be situated within this very broad frame, having composed a corpus that represents every decade

Table 10.1 The Medieval Film Corpus

	Year of release	Title of movie [acronym]	Genre	Directed by	Script/Screenplay by	Dialogue word count
1.	1963	Disney's *The Sword in the Stone* [DSS]	Animated comedy	Wolfgang Reitherman	Bill Peet [based on the book by T.H. White 1938]	7,615
2.	1965	*The War Lord* [WL]	Historical drama	Franklin J. Schaffner	John Collier, Millard Kaufman [The Lovers (play) by Leslie Stevens]	5,475
3.	1973	Disney's *Robin Hood* [DRH]	Animated comedy	Wolfgang Reitherman	Ken Anderson, Larry Clemmons	6,035
4.	1976	*Robin and Marian* [RM]	Historical drama	Richard Lester	James Goldman	5,576
5.	1981	*Dragonslayer* [DrSl]	Fantasy adventure	Matthew Robbins	Matthew Robbins, Hal Barwood	4,023
6.	1985	*Ladyhawke* [L]	Drama, comedy	Richard Donner	Edward Khmara, Michael Thomas, Tom Mankiewicz, David Peoples	5,255
7.	1993	*Robin Hood: Men in Tights* [RHMT]	Comedy adventure (parody)	Mel Brooks	Mel Brooks, Evan Chandler, J. David Shapiro	6,673
8.	1996	*Dragonheart* [Drh]	Fantasy adventure	Rob Cohen	Charles E. Pogue, Patrick R. Johnson	5,549
9.	2001	*A Knight's Tale* [KT]	Comedy adventure (parody)	Brian Helgeland	Brian Helgeland	6,906
10.	2005	*Kingdom of Heaven* [KH]	Drama adventure	Ridley Scott	William Monahan	7,530
11.	2010	*Robin Hood* [RH]	Drama adventure	Ridley Scott	Brian Helgeland	8,380
12.	2015	*Dragonheart 3: The Sorcerer's Curse* [Drh3]	Fantasy adventure	Colin Teague	Matthew Feitshans	4,782

Note that the word and token counts deviate slightly: the latter has been calculated with #LancsBox v 2.0.0 (Brezina et al. 2018) and shall be the number all further statistics are going to be based on.

Corpus word count total	73,799
Token count total	72,563
Type count total	6,902

since 1960 with one script each, with all of these having been produced in the United States.

In eight of the samples selected the plot is set in England, while the remaining four scripts have chosen Italy, Normandy, Jerusalem and Urland, a fictional place, as their geographical settings. While the film release dates range over five decades, the timely setting of the films themselves stretch over the whole of the Middle Ages, that is, from the fifth century AD through the fifteenth century. Nothing is further from my mind than suggesting a coherence of the Middle Ages over these 1,000 years, but as we shall see, such a coherence is in fact what is being suggested by the film makers themselves for simplifying reasons, which makes it feasible for this study to stick to such an overgeneralizing range of samples (cf. Table 10.2).

I have sought to not confine myself to already established and eagerly studied classes of medieval film, such as samples from what Harty (1987) referred to as 'Cinema Arthuriana', that is such films that address King Arthur, his knights, Merlin and so on (also cf. Elliott 2011a; Schwam-Baird 1999; Laity 2008), or the group of movies pertaining to the frame of Robin Hood and his merry men. Still, my medieval film corpus does contain samples from either of these two frames.

I have excluded the genre of Viking movies and the Nordic Middle Ages altogether as these form a rather coherent genre of their own (cf., for example, Aberth 2003; Harty 2011), mostly ignoring features characteristic of the feudal system, courtly love and the age of knighthood and chivalry itself, which are so prototypical for 'the Middle Ages' (cf., for example, Sturtevant 2010). In addition, I exclude *Beowulf* film renditions, as scholars have treated those as a distinct and homogenous group (cf., for example, Nokes 2015; Ambrisco 2016; Traidl 2016). I have also excluded medieval-framed TV series, despite their rich potential for pseudo-archaic investigations.[9]

The genres represented in the corpus are as varied as possible, including three fantasy adventures, two historical dramas, two drama adventures and two animated comedies. Some of the movies I selected had attracted multifaceted academic interest

Table 10.2 Time and Setting of Movies in the Film Corpus Sample

Time (all AD)	Title of movie	Setting	Year of release
Fifth/Sixth century	Disney's *The Sword in the Stone*	England	1963
Sixth century	*Dragonslayer*	Fictional kingdom of Urland	1981
Ninth century	*Dragonheart 3: The Sorcerer's Curse*	North England	2015
Tenth century	*Dragonheart*	England	1996
Eleventh century	*The War Lord*	Normandy	1965
Twelfth century	*Kingdom of Heaven*	Jerusalem	2005
Thirteenth century	*Ladyhawke*	Aquila, Italy	1985
Fourteenth century	*A Knight's Tale*	England	2001
Mid-fifteenth century	Disney's *Robin Hood*	England	1973
Mid-fifteenth century	*Robin and Marian*	England	1976
Mid-fifteenth century	*Robin Hood: Men in Tights*	England	1993
Mid-fifteenth century	*Robin Hood*	England	2010

before I did, for example, Helgeland's *A Knight's Tale* (cf. Haydock 2002; Dell 2008; Walker 2009) and *Kingdom of Heaven* (Scott 2005), the latter of which featured in an extended study of 'the Public Understanding of the Middle Ages' (Sturtevant 2010; also cf. Burt 2007, 2008). In addition, I have included two specific samples of 'historical film parody' – in contrast to 'serious historical film' (Burt 2007: 220) – the former of which appears to be 'a genre hitherto entirely neglected both by historians and film critics' (Burt 2007; but cf. Gorgievski 2000): *A Knight's Tale* (2001) and *Men in Tights* (Brooks, Chandler and Shapiro 1993). Indeed, I have not found any literature specifically dealing with the very latter.

3.3 A homogenous community of practice and their effective insertion of medieval stereotypes

Telecinematic discourse emerges at the interface of those who create it (directors, screenwriters), those who enact it (actors) and those who watch it (audience). This study sets out to investigate the density and quality of pseudo-medieval linguistic features in the medieval film corpus gathered for this study. The audience will only implicitly be taken into account insofar as the focus shall be put on the pragmatic strategies implemented on the linguistic level in response to the vague historio-cultural knowledge the screenwriters would presuppose to be shared with the audience of their later works on the movie screen.

As mentioned earlier and shown in Table 10.3, none of the script and screenplay writers of the movies selected for this study completed any academic studies into medieval history, anthropology or linguistics, let alone into medieval film.[10] Years and details on the written scripts were extracted from wikipedia.com and imdb.com.

It is certainly true that

> [t]he trouble with medievalism is that it doesn't belong anywhere in the academic world, and people interested in it might come from almost any field – except perhaps microbiology. (Workman, printed in Verduin 2009: 7–8.)

As such, the pre- (and mis-)conceptions a screenwriter would weave into their script would hardly exceed the (pseudo-)knowledge the majority of the audience would possess. Non-specialists of Old and Middle English that they would all be, they would have coherently vague ideas about the Middle Ages in general and 'medieval speech' in particular, beginning with the assumption that the Middle Ages were a relatively homogenous stretch of several hundred years, featuring the usual dragons, knights in shining armour, damsels in distress, swords, bows and arrows and so on.

3.4 Topical coherence

The selected movies all feature at least one out of four major medieval topical components, as displayed in Table 10.4:

Table 10.3 Script and Screenplay Writers of the Samples

Script/Screenplay by	Nationality	Professional background	Title of movie	Select filmography with focus on written screenplays/scripts
Anderson, Ken (1976–)	American	Animator, art director, writer at Walt Disney	Disney's Robin Hood (1973)	1950: Cinderella 1966: Winnie the Pooh and the Honey Tree 1967: The Jungle Book 1970: The AristoCats 1977: The Many Adventures of Winnie the Pooh 1977: The Rescuers
Barwood, Hal (? –)	American	Screenwriter, film producer, game designer, producer	Dragonslayer (1981)	1974: The Sugarland Express 1977: MacArthur; Close Encounters of the Third Kind 1978: Corvette Summer 1985: Warning Sign
Brooks, Mel (1926–)	American	Actor, comedian, filmmaker, composer, songwriter	Robin Hood: Men in Tights (1993)	1963: The Critic 1977: High Anxiety 1981: History of the World, Part I
Chandler, Evan (1944–2009)	American	Screenwriter, dentist	Robin Hood: Men in Tights (1993)	–
Clemmons, Larry (1906–1988)	American	Animator, screenwriter, voice actor	Disney's Robin Hood (1973)	1966: Winnie the Pooh and the Honey Tree 1967: The Jungle Book 1970: The AristoCats 1977: The Many Adventures of Winnie the Pooh 1977: The Rescuers
Collier, John (1901–1980)	British	Author, screenplay writer	The War Lord (1965)	1935: Sylvia Scarlett 1937: Elephant Boy 1942: Her Cardboard Lover 1946: Deception 1949: Roseanna McCoy 1955: I Am A Camera

Feitshans, Matthew (? –)	American	Screenwriter, assistant director	*Dragonheart 3: The Sorcerer's Curse* (2015) 2016: *Dragonheart 4*
Goldman, James (1927–1998)	American	Screenwriter, playwright	*Robin and Marian* (1976) 1968: *The Lion in Winter* 1971: *They Might Be Giants*; 1985: *White Nights*
Helgeland, Brian (1961–)	American	Screenwriter, film producer, director.	*A Knight's Tale* (2001); *Robin Hood* (2010) 1988: *A Nightmare on Elm Street 4: The Dream Master; 976-EVIL* 1992: *Highway to Hell* 1995: *Assassins* 1997: *L.A. Confidential* 1999: *Payback* 2002: *Blood Work* 2003: *Mystic River* 2003: *The Order* 2004: *Man on Fire* 2009: *The Taking of Pelham 123* 2010: *Green Zone* 2013: *42* 2015: *Legend*
Johnson, Patrick R. (1962–)	American	Director, actor	*Dragonheart* (1996) 1990: *Spaced Invaders* 2000: *Dragonheart – A new Beginning* 2001: *When Good Ghouls Go Bad* 2007: *77*
Kaufman, Millard (1917–2009)	American	Screenwriter, novelist	*The War Lord* (1965) 1951: *Unknown World* 1955: *Bad Day at Black Rock* 1957: *Raintree County* 1959: *Never so few* 1962: *Convicts 4* 1972: *Living Free* 1974: *Klansman*

(Continued)

Table 10.3 (Continued)

Script/Screenplay by	Nationality	Professional background	Title of movie	Select filmography with focus on written screenplays/scripts
Khmara, Edward (? –)	American	Writer, actor, producer	Ladyhawke (1985)	1985: *Enemy Mine* 1993: *Dragon – The Bruce Lee Story* 1998: *Merlin* [TV miniseries]
Mankiewicz, Tom (1942–2010)	American	Screenwriter, director, producer of motion pictures and television	Ladyhawke (1985)	1968: *The Sweet Ride* 1971: *Diamonds are Forever* 1973: *Live and let die* 1974: *The Man with the Golden Gun* 1976: *Mother, Jugs and Speed* 1978: *Superman: The Movie* 1987: *Dragnet*
Monahan, William (1960–)	American	Screenwriter, novelist	Kingdom of Heaven (2005)	2006: *The Departed* 2008: *Body of Lies* 2010: *Edge of Darkness* 2013: *Oblivion* 2014: *Sin City: A Dame to Kill for* 2015: *Mojave*
Peet, Bill (? –)	American	Children's book author	Disney's *The Sword in the Stone* (1963)	1940: *Fantasia* 1941: *Dumbo* 1946: *Song of the South* 1950: *Cinderella* 1951: *Alice in Wonderland* 1952: *Lambert the Sheepish Lion* 1953: *Peter Pan* 1959: *Sleeping Beauty* 1961: *101 Dalmatians*

Peoples, David Webb (1940–)	American	Screenwriter	Ladyhawke (1985)	1980: *The Day after Trinity* 1982: *Blade Runner* 1989: *Leviathan; The Blood of Heroes* 1990: *Fatal Sky* 1992: *Unforgiven* 1995: *12 Monkeys* 1998: *Soldier*
Pogue, Charles E. (1950–)	American	Screenwriter, playwright, stage actor.	Dragonheart (1996)	1983: *The Hound of the Baskervilles* 1983: *The Sign of Four* 1986: *Psycho III; The Fly* 1988: *D.O.A.* 1997: *Kull the Conqueror* 2001: *Hercules*
Robbins, Matthew (1945–)	American	Screenwriter, film producer, film director	Dragonslayer (1981)	1974: *The Sugarland Express* 1977: *MacArthur* 1985: *The Legend of Billie Jean* 1987: *Batteries not included* 2011: *Don't be afraid of the Dark* 2015: *Crimson Peak*
Shapiro, J. David (1969–)	American	Film maker, stand-up comedian	Robin Hood: Men in Tights (1993)	–
Thomas, Michael (?–)	?American	Writer, producer	Ladyhawke (1985)	–

Table 10.4 Medieval Topical Components Featured in the Movie Samples

Medieval topical features	Movie corpus		Further references
Castles, weapons and armour, nobility	12	100.0%	Cf. Traxel (2008: 130); Sturtevant (2010: ch. 5)
Sorcery, curses and magic	8	66.7%	Cf. Rider 2012; Marrone 2015
Dragons	4	30.0%	Cf. Lionarons 1998; Rose 2000; Lakowski 2015; McConnell 2015; Sturtevant (2010: ch. 5)
Romance	11	91.7%	Cf. Hasty 2016

Table 10.5 Wordlist of Most Frequent Types and Tokens in the Corpus

Types	Absolute frequency of tokens	Relative frequency of tokens within the complete corpus
King(s)	271	0.40%
Sir	216	0.30%
Lord(s)	207	0.29%
Knight(s)	134	0.18%
Love	119	0.16%
Dragon(s)	105	0.14%
Sword(s)	86	0.12%
Total	**1,138**	**1.6%**

The saliency of these topics can for one thing be affirmed by the fact that six of the film titles included in the corpus explicitly refer to one of the topics (i.e. *Dragonslayer* (1981), *Dragonheart* (1996), *Dragonheart 3* (2015), *The War Lord* (1965), Disney's *The Sword in the Stone* (1963), *A Knight's Tale* (2001)), or do so implicitly by calling upon the recipient's shared cultural knowledge triggered by the mentioning of personal names such as Robin (Hood) (i.e. Disney's *Robin Hood* (1973), *Robin and Marian* (1976), *Robin Hood: Men in Tights* (1993), *Robin Hood* (2010)) or of markedly non-salient phrases that still convey a reference to medieval frames (i.e. *Ladyhawke* (1985), *Kingdom of Heaven* (2005)). What is more, a word frequency list, created with AntConc, confirms their inert consistency with these topics (cf. Table 10.5). The topic of romantic love is certainly none particularly associated with the Middle Ages, but much more so a plotline running like a thread through the vast majority of movies in general. It therefore features in all my samples, with the exception of Disney's *The Sword in the Stone*.

4 Assessment of pseudo-archaic linguistic features in the corpus

While acknowledging as a given that visual effects and the different kinds of paratext (cf., for example, Burt 2007)[11] featuring in any medieval film as a whole will enhance if not determine the pragmatic effects of that movie in an inherently complementary, cumulative, even symbiotic manner,[12] this study is going to zero in on spoken and written language alone so to assess to what extent this level is in fact determining the authenticity of the medieval frame per se.

4.1 Common (mis)conceptions about 'Medieval English'

Semi-knowledge about the Middle Ages is widespread and spreading. Prototypical presuppositions and generalizations about 'medieval English' nowadays tend to be shared and picked up in, for example, fora and blogs and include misconceptions such as Old English being Shakespeare's English (cf. (1)) or, generally, the language of the Middle Ages (cf. (2), (3), (4)) altogether.[13]

(1) [blog title] Old English Terms for Understanding Shakespeare (http://translation-blog.trustedtranslations.com/7-old-english-terms-for-understanding-shakespeare-2016-05-09.html)

(2) What language did they speak in medieval England? – Something simple, like Latin or Old English. Thanks! (https://answers.yahoo.com/question/index?qid=20091116213137AA6JwhO)

(3)

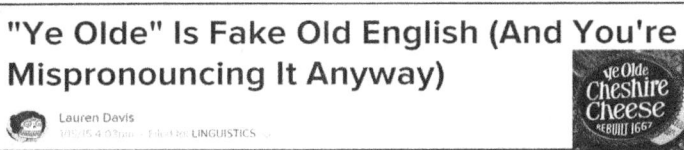

Figure 10.1 (http://io9.gizmodo.com/ye-olde-is-fake-old-english-and-youre-mispronouncing-1679780566)

(4)

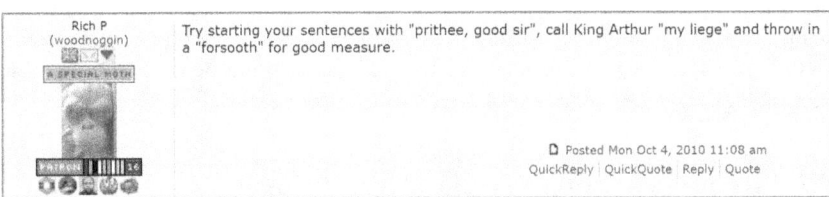

Figure 10.2 (https://boardgamegeek.com/thread/570408/how-speak-knights-worthy-sitting-round-table)

(5) What I've found in medieval [role play sims] is usually (I tell a lie – always) a funny mix of modern and old versions of English. Medieval English is what's known as Old English. (posted by Carole Franizzi on https://community.secondlife.com/t5/Role-Play/Language-for-medieval-roleplay/td-p/822601, 04-18-2011 04:37 AM).

(6) [response to a thread started with the question 'How do i make my story sound medieval?'] You can also make changes to your characters' speech, if you want to get super-accurate. Many words we use today did not exist five hundred years ago; for example, 'okay' is out. So are 'sayonara' and 'ciao' as salutations. ('Adieu' is probably still all right, if your story is set after the Norman Invasion in 1066.) While you want to keep your dialogue readable by a modern audience, a few minor changes may do you good. However, don't go overboard on your 'thee's and 'thou's unless you know how to use them. A misplaced 'thy' will be a continual annoyance to anyone who understands how the word should really be applied. The same goes for 'thence' (from there), 'whence' (from where), 'hence' (from here), etcetera.
(https://answers.yahoo.com/question/index?qid=20101026164700AA0S7En)

Examples of non-expertise comments on 'Old' or generally 'medieval English' such as these are numerous and yet few academic studies have sought to systematically identify the linguistic components they repeatedly feature.[14] Traxel produced one of those studies that look specifically at linguistic elements in online or computer role-playing games (2008), confirming that pseudo-archaic English composed today is largely influenced by the Early Modern English from the *King James Bible* (1611) and Shakespeare's works (cf. again (1)). In regard to the pseudo-archaic language used in three specific medieval computer games, Traxel continues that language is a '[c]hief element [...] among [...] pseudo-medieval elements' (2008: 132) – at the same time he only mentions few Latin examples that are all personal names or referring terms for objects carrying specific powers and so on and comes to the agreeable conclusion that 'most of the [...] verbal components of the games are given in modern languages that have been merely sprinkled with deliberate archaisms' (2008: 132). He explains the lack of any medieval varieties in the game by the fact that 'large passages of Old or Middle English [...] would be incomprehensible to many [if not most] players' (2008: 132).

I will hypothesize that medieval films will convey a similar picture, including merely (pseudo-)archaic bits in dialogues between characters, e.g. keywords, (the misuse of) archaic personal pronouns of the second-person singular and plural, lack of inversion in questions, archaic discourse markers and interjections, but much more so in the surrounding co-text (e.g. pseudo- and archaic inflectional endings, archaic morphology) to mark the speech of their characters as 'medieval'.

4.2 Pseudo-archaisms in medieval film dialogue

Table 10.6 is a checklist of the pseudo-archaic features manually and systematically retrieved from the corpus. Checkmarks indicate the presence of the pseudo-feature in the sample within characters' dialogues, blanks indicate a pseudo-feature's absence in the sample within characters' dialogues, and checkmarks in brackets indicate a feature's absence within characters' dialogues, but the presence of the pseudo-feature in the narrator's monologue framing the characters' dialogues. The latter, as can be seen from Table 10.6, is highly rare, occurring only in three of twelve scripts.

Table 10.6 Checklist of Pseudo-Archaic Features in the Movie Corpus

Timeline	1963											2015
Pseudo-features	DSS	WL	DRH	RM	DrSl	L	RHMT	Drh	KT	KH	RH	Drh3
Homonymy (4.2.1)							✓					
(Misuse of) personal pronouns (4.2.2)	✓	✓	✓		✓			(✓)	✓	✓		
Word formation (4.2.3.1)		✓					✓			✓		✓
Inflectional morphology (4.2.3.2)	(✓)	✓	(✓)				✓				✓	
Flexible syntax (4.2.3.3)		✓			✓		✓	✓	✓			✓
Modal verbs (4.2.3.5)	✓	✓			✓	✓	✓	✓	✓	✓		✓
Contractions (4.2.3.8)					✓	✓	✓		✓	✓		
Anachronistic lexico-semantic choices (4.3.1)	✓	✓			✓	✓	✓		✓	✓		
Archaic lexico-semantic choices (4.3.2)	✓	✓	✓	✓	✓	✓	✓	✓	✓	✓	✓	✓
Medieval code switching (4.4)	✓	✓			✓	✓	✓		✓	✓		
Count of pseudo-features	5	8	2	1	7	5	9	3	7	7	2	4

Overall, we may already deduce from the distribution of pseudo-features across the corpus and across five decades that there is no systematic diachronic increase or decrease in pseudo-features. Except for three PPFTs in the corpus – that is, Disney's *Robin Hood*, *Robin and Marian* and Scott's *Robin Hood* – all others contain four or more different pseudo-medieval linguistic features regardless of their situation on the timeline. The fact that the three exceptions are all Robin Hood films implies a certain coherence across this particular topical film frame. The one feature type all samples in the corpus share is archaic lexico-semantic vocabulary. Pseudo-features shall be discussed in Subsections 4.2.1 through 4.4.

4.2.1 *Homonymy and the spelling-pronunciation gap*

The only film in the corpus that actually ridicules the challenges of homonymic conflict and the then-versus-now spelling-pronunciation shift due to, for example, the Great Vowel Shift (ca. 1500–1800), is Brooks's comedy *Men in Tights*. Multiple examples suggest that Brooks and/or his co-PPSS-writers were in fact aware of the comical potential of the many homophonous items in the English, including, for example, *bore* and *boar* BritE /bəʊ/, AmE /bɔər/ (cf. (8)).[15] Such homophony games do, in my opinion, exemplify pseudo-archaisms: the two words on which homophony jokes rely used to have different pronunciations from one another in the olden days. Admittedly, contemporary audiences might presumably enjoy the jokes even if they had absolutely no knowledge of these phonological developments, but I will argue that the high frequency in which these homophony jokes are featured in this particular PPSS/PPST suggests that this is indeed systematically embedded.

Another example refers to the vowel /iː/ and its manifold graphemic realizations in Modern English: ancestors of ModE /iː/ were the vowels [eː] (ModE often <ee>; cf. *feet*) or [ɛː] (ModE often <ea>; cf. *feat*, cf. (99) below). The fact that both vowels in ME are attested in various spellings ranging from <ee>, <ea> to simply <e> may be what the writers refer to in (8), where only a viewer knowledgeable in historical phonology would notice that Don Giovanni's spelling of *dead* would in fact not have been incorrect in the time of King Richard 'Cœur de Lion' I (1189–99).[16] In sample (9), Brooks et al. seem to point to a similar phenomenon of potential confusion, namely the fact that BritE *dare* /deə/ and *deer* (as well as *dear*) /dɪə/ are rather close in their pronunciation and have been so in their highly variable forms in Middle English.

(7) [Robin:] A present for you and your guests.
[Sheriff of Rottingham:]: That's a wild boar!
[Robin:] No, no. That's a wild pig. That's a wild bore [pointing towards the King].

(8) [Don Giovanni to the Sheriff of Rottingham]: You want plain English? Robin is gonna be dead. **D-E-D** ... **dead.**

(9) [Sheriff of Rottingham:] He was poaching in the king's forest. He **deered** to kill a king's **dare** ... **Dared** to kill a king's **deer.**

(10) Sheriff of Rottingham: We have exotic foods from across the seas. Coconuts, bananas … and **dates**. Would you care for a **date**?
Marian: Yes, thank you.
Sheriff of Rottingham: How about next Thursday?

Sample (10) then is a well-chosen pair of total homonyms, seemingly reminding the recipient of the many instances of homonyms in Modern English and the need for context for the listener to understand which one is being used.[17]

4.2.2 (Mis)use of personal pronouns

The suggestion made in (6) above to use *thee* and *thou* with care, thereby implying that these pronouns are in fact features representative of 'medieval speech', has been picked up in seven of our transcripts. However, the numbers are highly unbalanced with *you* being the pronoun chosen in significantly high numbers throughout. The writers may have assumed that a consistent use of *thou* and *thee* could have been alienating the viewer in the sense that the markedness of these obsolete pronouns would have distracted the recipient from the actual storyline. As the numbers in Table 10.7 suggest, inserting but a small number of *thous* and *thees* seemed sufficient to set the tone.

In (18) and (19), *thou* and *thee* appear in the relatively salient reference to and quotes from the *Bible*, whereas in other scripts they are used 'naturally' by the characters in conversation. In *Dragonslayer*, for instance, *thee* occurs five times, *thou* six times (cf. (11)) and *ye* once (cf. (12)). *Ye* does also occur in (13) and (14), seemingly sounding 'medieval' to laymen's ears. All but one case are correct uses of singular *thou* and plural *ye* in the subject and *thee* in the object case: only (14) shows a use of *you* and *ye* that is seemingly incoherent with the historical development in use. However, it is likely that *ye* is in fact not meant to refer to the Old and early Middle English pronoun, but actually just picks it up as a feature of West Country dialect.

(11) Fear not, brethren.
There is no dragon.
Unclean beast! Get **thee** down!
Be **thou** consumed
by the fires that made **thee**! (*Dragonslayer*)

(12) **Ye** gods! (*Dragonslayer*)

(13) 'Hear **ye**, hear **ye**. For failure to pay taxes, all the lands and properties of the Loxley family shall be taken.' Signed, Prince John's Royal Accountant, H.M.R. Blockhead. (*Men in Tights*)

(14) [Mother Rabbit:] You poor old man. Do come in. Come in and rest yourself.
[Robin in disguise:] Thank **ye** kindly, Mother. Thank **ye**. (Disney's *Robin Hood*)

(15) Lord Philip of Aragon. Stand **ye** ready? Sir Ector. Stand **ye** ready? (*A Knight's Tale*)

(16) This one saved **thee**, man.
– This one can also hang **thee**. (*War Lord*)

Table 10.7 The Distribution of *Thou*, *Thee*, *Ye* and *You* in the Corpus

	DSS	WL	DRH	RM	DrSl	L	RHMT	Drh	KT	KH	RH	Drh3
Thou	0	0	0	0	3	0	0	1	0	0	0	0
Thee	0	3	0	0	5	0	2	0	1	2	0	0
Ye	0	0	2	0	1	0	2	0	2	0	0	0
You	312	191	208	275	173	214	267	268	307	294	298	196

(17) We thank **thee**. (*War Lord*)

(18) **Thou** … shalt … not … kill! (*Dragonheart*)

(19) Be brave and upright that God may love **thee**. (*Kingdom of Heaven*)

(20) Who calls?
 – It is I, Robin. We wish to get married. (*Men in Tights*)

In sample (20), Brooks et al. again demonstrate their historio-linguistic awareness by having Robin utter the grammatically correct but generally perceived-as-archaic sentence 'It is I' instead of the much more common and acceptable *It is me*.

4.2.3 Syntax, morphology and word-formational phenomena

4.2.3.1 Pseudo-archaic inflectional morphemes

Relatively few transcripts in the corpus contain archaic inflectional affixes, which is why all of these shall be quoted here. A fairly salient or 'typically archaic' (Traxel 2008: 53) morpheme is the third-person singular {-eth} (cf. (21), (22)), which, as Traxel maintains, tends to be generally employed by 'mock-archaic amateur[s]', i.e. non-specialists in historical linguistics (Traxel 2008: 53), even if the subject in a clause would not grammatically require it. While I would have expected the comedies in the corpus to misuse this ending, it occurs only once in Scott's *Robin Hood* (cf. (23)), where it simply should have been an infinitive, not an inflected form following the modal *shall*. The second-person singular suffix {-(e)st}, which would be another commonly known inflectional ending from Old and Middle English, is not used in any of the twelve scripts. The fixed second-person singular present indicative form *art* (< *bēon, bēn*) is also used once only within the complete corpus (cf. (24)).

(21) Pride **goeth** before the fall (*Dragonheart*)

(22) Whoso **pulleth** out this sword of this stone and anvil … is rightwise king born of England [part of a song to set the frame] (Disney's *The Sword in the Stone*)

(23) 'The Lord taketh … ' And we shall **giveth** back. (*Robin Hood*)

(24) Thou **art** baptised in the name of the Father, the Son, the Holy Ghost. (*Dragonslayer*)

Few more inflectional affixes are spread throughout the corpus in small numbers: the homonymic adjective and noun endings {-en} in (25) as well as in (26), and {a-} in (27) and (28).

(25) In **olden** times, they sanctified a marriage by giving the bride on her wedding night to … (*War Lord*)

(26) Now be it known throughout the kingdom that this **maiden**, having lawfully been chosen by a deed of fortune and destiny, shall hereby give up her life for the greater good of Urland … (*Dragonslayer*)

(27) [Narrator:] Never dreamin' that a schemin' sheriff and his posse was **a-watchin'** them (Disney's *Robin Hood*)

(28) But they will go **awantoning**. (*War Lord*)

4.2.3.2 Unconventional word formation processes

The different scripts give a highly multifaceted and creative display of rather unconventional word forms. The fact that almost all of them do so suggests that scriptwriters in general must have been in silent and (un)conscious agreement over the impression that such marked word forms would be perceived as archaic or even 'medieval'.

(29) These people here have ancient customs in which he may have **unthinkingly** have joined. (*War Lord*)

(30) I ask myself … 'Would Jesus do it. We need all these horses **shod thusly**?' (*Kingdom of Heaven*)

(31) But I also know, that you know, what a **weak-willed** person I am. (*Ladyhawke*)

(32) This is a **knotty problem** not easily solved. (*Men in Tights*)

(33) All right, you puking **foot-lickers**! Tomorrow, the squires who have pleased me will be knighted and earn a Silver Sword. (*Dragonheart 3*)

(34) For this **discombooberation**
It's a most **hodge-podgical**
Most **illogical** […]
Most **bamboozling**
Most **bemuddling**
Most **befuddling**
Thing (Disney's *Sword in the Stone*)

The adverb *unthinkingly* (cf. (29)) is an early eighteenth-century coinage and *thusly* (cf. (30)) is attested only rarely in the nineteenth century (OED). In (31) we have a parasynthetic adjective *weak-willed* (compare *weak-hearted, weak-sighted* etc.), which is only attested for ca. 1900, thus sets an archaic (if anachronistic) tone, too. *Knotty problem* in (32) is a very rare collocation with the adjective *knotty* being in fact attested since the early thirteenth century (OED).

The compound *foot-licker* in (33), premodified by the participle *puking* (attested since the sixteenth century), seems to be a creative combination by Peet, although the compound alone is attested twice around 1900 (OED, *foot* n.). Disney's *Sword in the Stone* certainly offers the richest range of creative word formation: a number of words are not even attested in the OED: *discombooberation* may be a (deliberate?) malapropism of *discombobulation* n. (mid-nineteenth century) 'confusion'; *hodge-podgical* is an otherwise unattested derivation from *hodge-podge* (< *hotchpotch*, early fifteenth century); *befuddling* is per se not attested in the OED (but cf. *be-*, prefix, 4.); *bamboozling* is only listed as a noun, that is, a gerund formed from the verb (OED), not, however, as a participle, which we find premodifying 'Thing' in (34); the adjective *illogical* is rare, but attested by the OED from the late sixteenth century onwards.

4.2.3.3 Variable syntax

A number of examples display what would be perceived as cases of non-inversion from a modern speaker's point of view, as *do* tends to not be used so to mark a negated syntactical structure or a question as archaic (cf. (35) – (39)):

(35) Worry not, Your Highness. (*Men in Tights*)

(36) I know. Your business is urgent. It doesn't matter. He sees no one. […] You who knows so much, answer me that. Hear me, you who dwell in Cragganmore. (*Dragonslayer*)

(37) [Priest:] Oh, Avalon, bright Avalon …
think me not a fool.
My quest is not for vanity,
my quest is spiritual. (*Dragonheart*)

(38) No bright souls glitter in this darkness. (*Dragonheart*)

(39) Why took he a virgin? (*War Lord*)

In some more instances the scriptwriters employ variable or flexible syntax, which would have indeed been possible in Old, less so in Middle English due to inflectional endings then already being dropped (which resulted in the need for fixed syntactic patterns). Brooks et al. carry this idea to its extremes in (44):

(40) [Priest:] Avalon, oh, Avalon.
For you I quest each day …
the resting place of Arthur …
and the Old Code of his way.
And when I find
those holy stones …
I'll pray, I'll pray, I'll pray. (*Dragonheart*)

(41) Indicate in which events shall your Lord Ulrich [shall] compete (*A Knight's Tale*)

(42) I have no objections, but I haven't yet kissed the bride [yet]. (*Men in Tights*)

(43) All cannot [not all can] survive this journey. Sacrifice what you must. (*Dragonheart 3*)

(44) [Sheriff of Rottingham:] King illegal forest to pig wild kill in it a is! [It is illegal to kill a wild pig in *the King*'s forest] (*Men in Tights*)

4.2.3.4 Pseudo-archaic use of modal verbs

From an American English speaker's point of view, *shall* instead of *must* or *will* has an archaic and solemn tone. That is why several of our scriptwriters employ that modal in a seemingly synonymous manner to *will* (cf. (45) – (49)). Brooks et al. overuse it for comic effect (cf. (49)).

(45) 'One day, he who is destined for me **shall** be endowed with the magical key that will bring an end to my virginity.' (*Men in Tights*)

(46) I **shall** dispose of this feathered upstart. (*Men in Tights*)

(47) Sire, I **shall** count to five. (*War Lord*)

(48) My blade **shall** defend the helpless. (*Dragonheart 3*)

(49) If we stand up to them all together as one, we can win the day! We **shall** go on to the end. We **shall** not flag or fail. We shall fight on the seas and oceans. We **shall** defend our isle, whatever the cost may be. We shall never surrender. Then they shall say of us: 'Never have so many owed so much to so few.' (*Men in Tights*)

Another archaizing move taken by some of our scripts is to use the Modern English modal *will* as the lexical verb it once was, which will certainly be understood by modern recipients, but evoke a strong archaic tone:

(50) Call when you need of me. Ask what you **will** of me. My sword, my service are yours. (*Dragonheart*)

(51) All is as God **wills** it. (*Kingdom of Heaven*)

4.2.3.5 Pseudo-archaic contractions

Another pseudo-archaic feature employed in three of our scripts are contractions of [*it* + inflected form of *be*]:

(52) At any rate, Your Grace, **'tis** only one insignificant petty thief. (*Ladyhawke*)

(53) Robin: … if only **t'were** me.
Marian: Oh, if it **t'were** you, t'would be … t'werrific. (*Men in Tights*)

(54) I passed along the River Thames
Its waters did they reek
'Twas there I met a pretty lass
She said her name was Nell (*A Knight's Tale*)

(55) Geoff, **'tis** my lady. (*A Knight's Tale*)

4.2.3.6 Alia

A good number of archaizing components or structures is hardly classifiable. This group of *alia* includes, for example, archaic formulae (cf. (56)), archaic conjunctions (cf. (57)), odd verbal forms (cf. (58)), or valency shifts (cf. (59)).

(56) What would you have of us? (*Dragonheart*)

(57) She died of pneumonia whilst … Oh, you were away. (*Men in Tights*)

(58) There's a great task needing to be done. (*Dragonslayer*)

(59) They'd think me infirm. (*Dragonslayer*)

4.3 Lexico-semantic choices

As Traxel notes, vocabulary is '[o]ne of the largest and most productive categories in the field of pseudo-archaic English' (2008: 51). He refers specifically to such words that are perceived as highly archaic today and thus add that 'medieval' sound to speech in medieval movies. The two main groups of vocabulary identified in the corpus are those that are archaic ones on the one hand, and such that are in fact anachronistic, on the other hand.

4.3.1 Archaic lexico-semantic choices

AntConc calculated the frequencies for typically medieval terms (excluding personal names such as Robin Hood, Merlin, Marian etc.) as shown in Table 10.8. Based on the reference corpus, that is the *Cornell Movie Dialogs Corpus* (Danescu-Niculescu-Mizi 2012), which contains 220,579 conversational exchanges between 10,292 pairs of movie characters from 617 movies and in total 304,713 utterances, the keywords and their keyness (log likelihood) were identified and calculated (cf. Table 10.8).

Two address nouns appearing to be highly frequent in the corpus and thus likely to function as medieval markers are *sir* and the more archaic form *sire*, which is why Table 10.9 itemizes their token numbers for each of the films. As shown, only Scott's *Robin Hood* and Disney's *Robin Hood* employ a comparably high number of *sire*, while another 50 per cent of the scripts do not contain it at all. The ModE continuation of (or reduction from) *sire, sir*, is used much more consistently throughout the corpus and by all scripts with the only exception being *Kingdom of Heaven*.

Apart from the keywords in Table 10.8, there is a high number of types, including nouns, verbs, adverbs, interjections and formulaic utterances, that are not used frequently at all, but still convey an archaic tone. Samples (60) through (75) provide just a selection of such instances, reflecting the versatility of lexical archaic devices employed by the script writers:

(60) My bots! (*Ladyhawke*)

(61) Joyful forevermore (*Men in Tights*)

(62) Good morrow, abbot. (*Men in Tights*)

(63) Just say nay! (*Men in Tights*)

(64) Nay! I will win for you. (*A Knight's Tale*)

Table 10.8 Keywords in the Corpus

Types	Absolute frequency	Keyness[18]	Keyness rank out of 5290
King(s)	271	1102.755	1.
Lord(s)	207	908.008	2.
Knight(s)	134	543.493	5.
Jerusalem	60	483.725	9.
Dragon(s)	105	432.286	11.
Sword(s)	86	374.808	12.
Sire	63	360.389	13.
Sir	216	291.199	19.
Crown	33	194.841	38.
Kingdom	34	182.792	41.
Prince	42	173.291	45.
Tournament	25	172.400	49.
England	44	167.514	51.
Lady, ladies	85	145.265	60.
Sorcerer	15	107.353	86.
Valor	15	107.353	87.
Arrows	8	107.165	88.
Castle	28	103.627	97.
Horse(s)	62	102.610	99.
France	28	98.834	102.
Dragonslayer	12	98.779	104.
Master	36	91.991	110.
Archer(s), archery	27	91.667	111.
Squire	19	90.103	118.
Curse(d)	27	78.355	130.
Joust	10	75.647	134.
Alms	9	67.616	151.
Druid(s)	15	65.853	158.
Holy	29	63.455	166.
Honor, honour	34	62.177	172.
Nobility, noble	6	60.616	175.
Bow	15	60.335	177.
Magic	23	60.193	179.
Saracen(s)	14	59.607	180.
Baron(s)	25	59.512	181.
Muslims	10	57.849	184.
Love	119	57.304	190.
Crusade(s)	17	56.000	192.
Mercy	16	55.452	194.
Kneel	9	54.092	201.
Throne	12	53.740	204.
Abbey	7	51.626	209.
Church	27	50.818	210.
Armor	12	50.161	212.

Table 10.9 Distribution of *Sir* and *Sire* across the Corpus

Title of movie	Tokens of *sir*	Tokens of *sire*	Sum of tokens
Robin Hood	56	22	78
A Knight's Tale	54	0	54
Disney's *Robin Hood*	14	25	39
Disney's *The Sword in the Stone*	26	0	26
Ladyhawke	23	0	23
The War Lord	8	7	15
Robin Hood: Men in Tights	10	4	14
Dragonheart 3: The Sorcerer's Curse	11	0	11
Dragonheart	9	0	9
Robin and Marian	4	4	8
Dragonslayer	2	2	4
Kingdom of Heaven	0	0	0

(65) My humble life is in debt to your exalted prowess … (*Dragonheart*)

(66) Well, by Jove. Hey, he's gone.
– Hm-mmm. Good riddance. (Disney's *Sword in the Stone*)

(67) These young folks here think of nothing but frolicking. 'Desist!' I tell them. (*War Lord*)

(68) [Prince John:] Stop the coach.
[Hiss:] Sire. Sire. They may be bandits.
[Prince John:] Oh, poppycock. (Disney's *Robin Hood*)

(69) Am I in the wrong? (*Robin and Marian*)

Men in Tights is filled with examples such as the following:

(70) my solemn oath on my father's honour

(71) How dare you talk to me in that fashion!

(72) He seeks to regain his family's honour.

(73) Greetings, Your Highness.

(74) Good grief!

(75) There's a foul plot afoot.

4.3.2 (Absence of) anachronistic lexico-semantic choices

The words and word forms gathered in Table 10.10 have been calculated by AntConc as the ones in the medieval film corpus possessing negative keyness in relation to the *Cornell Movie Dialogs Corpus*; that is, these types occur less often than would be expected by chance in comparison with the reference corpus. This is noteworthy

Table 10.10 Words with Negative Keyness in the Corpus

Types	Frequency	Negative keyness
Okay	8	−100.072
Yeah	40	−65.986
Shit	2	−64.860
Kid	3	−26.071
Gonna	33	−25.761
Ass	1	−24.908
Hi	1	−24.754
Mom	3	−22.519
Guys	6	−20.674
Daddy	1	−20.151
Wanna	3	−15.628
Crazy	4	−15.472
Buddy	2	−13.283
Thanks	10	−12.270
Gotta	13	−12.080
Cop	1	−11.205
Stuff	7	−10.235
Sex	1	−9.299
Coffee	1	−7.936
Kidding	1	−7.488
Bullshit	2	−7.470
Bitch	2	−6.667
Cash	1	−5.890
Huh	20	−5.478
Kinda	1	−5.378
Babe	1	−4.715
Cool	3	−4.407
Wow	1	−3.862
Fun	4	−3.184
Sorry	42	−3.103
Crap	1	−2.582
Funny	7	−2.494
Tough	2	−2.454
Amazing	1	−2.209
Cute	1	−2.209
Relax	2	−2.101
Business	16	−1.931
Television	1	−1.441
Private	3	−1.247
Outta	4	−1.164

because these are mostly words associated with ModE colloquial language (e.g. *shit, ass, guys, cop*), conversational linguistic forms (e.g. *gonna, gotta, wanna, thanks*) and discourse markers (e.g. *okay, yeah, wow*). Some words are simply underused because the medieval frame does not allow for the concepts they refer to (e.g. *coffee, cash, television*). We can thus infer that the scripts tend to be coherent in underusing such devices that would seem strongly anachronistic, presumably because this would put the integrity of the medieval film's authenticity at risk.

Yet, there are still instances of youth language employed for individual characters such as Wart in Disney's *Sword in the Stone*, Philippe Gaston in *Ladyhawke*, Little John and Robin in Disney's *Robin Hood*, and Ahchoo – an anachronistic character as a whole, being African American and thus stereotypically bound to use marked American English – so to have them appear as young and likeable and to mark them as the male protagonists of the film. This is particularly true in Disney movies where the male hero is frequently indicated as such by being equipped with (or rather marked by) an American accent and ductus (cf., for example, Lippi-Green 2012; Hodson 2014).

(76) [Wart:] I'm **tryin'** to be. […] I'm not even **movin'**. (Disney's *Sword in the Stone*)

(77) [Philippe:] It looks like a big one, Captain. We're **gonna** get soaked. (*Ladyhawke*)

(78) [Little John:] You know **somethin'**, Robin, I was just **wonderin'**. Are we good **guys** or bad **guys**? (*Robin Hood*)

(79) [Robin:] You don't just **walk up** to a girl, hand her a bouquet and say …'**Hey**, remember me? We were **kids** together. Will you marry me?' (*Robin Hood*)

(80) [Ahchoo:] He's **gonna** deflower her in the tower! (*Men in Tights*)

Apart from the scripts' coherent underuse of anachronistic terms and forms, few of the scripts stand out in that they employ a curious strategy of anachronicity: they explicitly point out to the recipient that the film is one set in the Middle Ages. Table 10.11 displays the three samples that have been found to do that by employing one or more of four phrases deemed particularly marked in that way: *medieval* (attested since the early nineteenth century; OED; also cf. Matthews 2011: 695), the Middle Ages (attested since ca. 1600; cf. OED *middle age, n.* and *adj., A.2*), *dark age* (attested since 1730; cf. OED *dark* adj., S3) and the youngest of them, *futuristic* (attested since the mid-twentieth century; cf. OED).

Disney's *Sword in the Stone* is the one most prolific in 'setting the setting', namely by featuring the adjectives *medieval* and *futuristic* as well as the noun phrases *dark age* and *Christendom*. Brooks's *Men in Tights* features *medieval* in dialogue, too, whereas it is the narrator in *A Knight's Tale* (and in Disney's *Sword in the Stone*) who sets the scene by using it.

(81) [Sheriff of Rottingham:] What will you do about Robin Hood?
[Prince John:] Listen, I've got an idea. Tomorrow, you're going to have your **medieval** fun and games. (*Men in Tights*)

(82) [Merlin:] One big **medieval** mess. […] Even in these bungling, backward medieval times … you have got to know where you're going, don't you? […] What a mess! What a **medieval muddle**. […] we've got to get all these **medieval** ideas out of your head. (Disney's *Sword in the Stone*)

(83) [narrator:] This was a **dark age** … without law and without order. Men lived in fear of one another … for the strong preyed upon the weak.
[Merlin:] A **dark age** indeed! Age of inconvenience. (Disney's *Sword in the Stone*)

Table 10.11 Anachronistic Reference Types

Anachronistic reference types	DSS	WL	DRH	RM	DrSl	L	RHMT	Drh	KT	KH	RH	Drh3
Medieval	✓					✓		(✓)				
Middle Ages												
Dark age	✓											
Futuristic	✓											

(84) [Archimedes:] I have nothing to do with your **futuristic** fiddle-faddle, you know that. (Disney's *Sword in the Stone*)

(85) [narrator:] In **medieval** times a sport arose (*A Knight's Tale*)

Disney's *Sword in the Stone* is the script containing most of the anachronistic references in the corpus, which is due to Merlin being able to travel through time and thus knowledgeable of future concepts, such as the 'steam locomotive', the *London Times* and *monkey suits*:

(86) [Merlin:] A fine **monkey suit** for polishing boots.
[Wart:] It's-It's what all the squires wear. (Disney's *Sword in the Stone*)

(87) You're supposed to be the **knight in shining armor.** (*Dragonheart 3*)

(88) What's the big idea of **gallivanting** off in the woods … (Disney's *Sword in the Stone*)

Samples (87) and (88) are further instances of anachronistic phrasings: the noun phrase *knight in shining armor* 'in informal or ironic use' is referring to 'a person regarded as a medieval knight in respect of his chivalrous spirit, especially towards women' (OED, *knight*, n., 4.e.) and as such is first attested in 1965.

The choice of 'gallivanting' in Disney's *Sword in the Stone* is a puzzling one: the major part of the audience (i.e. children) would most likely not be acquainted with the term at that point. The OED even indicates that the verb *gallivant* (<? 'perhaps a humorous perversion of' *gallant* v. < *gallant* adj. < F *galant* adj.; cf. OED *gallivant* v.) tends to come with a sexual connotation: 'To gad about in a showy fashion, esp. with persons of the other sex. Also merely = FLIRT *v.*' (OED).[19]

4.3.3 'Medieval' code switching

Six of the twelve scripts under investigation opt for occasional code switching into Latin or pseudo-Latin, which is noteworthy as this implies that Latin tends to be perceived as *the* medieval variety and believed to have been spoken far and wide. The scriptwriters mostly chose basic 'Latin for beginners' utterances (cf. (89) through (93)) – with only (90) and (92) being grammatically correct – as well as fixed notions commonly associated with medieval conventions (e.g. *ius primae noctis* 'the right to the first night [with an inferior's newlywed bride]', cf. (93)).

(89) Open up, I say! Caela orrida aperere [lit. 'the horrible skies to open']! (*Dragonslayer*)

(90) Mortem confundit magus. ([The wizard confounds death] *Dragonslayer*)

(91) Salve, magister juvenilis. I studied Latin. Greek, too. Me apellant Elspeth[am], filiam Regis. (*Dragonslayer*)

(92) Who are you?
Lilium inter spinas. The lily among the thorns. (*A Knight's Tale*)

(93) What do they say in Rome? *Jus primae noctis.* That being the Roman for it. (*War Lord*)

Particularly curious choices which seem to ridicule the fact that the majority of recipients would neither be capable of translating any Latin nor know what the original source of the Latin dictum would have been, are Robbins and Barwood's sample (94), which turns out to be a quote from a sex-related ritual in Aleister Crowley's *Book of Lies* (1913),[20] and sample (95), which seems to be a quote from a Roman gravesite.[21]

(94) Unus in nihil ...   One in nothing
     Omnia in duos ...   All in two
     Duo in unum ...   Two in one
     Unum in nihil.   One in nothing.
     Nec quattuor ...   They are neither four,
     nec omnia, nec unus, nec nihil sunt.   nor all, nor one, nor nothing.
     (*Dragonslayer*)

(95) adeptus minor, get yourself a handful of that sulphurous ash over there. Nunc habeamus lucem ... et calorem. (*Dragonslayer*)

Sample (95) may have been inspired by Matthias Untzer's *De sulphure tractatus medico-chymicus nunc noviter in lucem emissus* (1620), which would attest Robbins and/or Barwood quite some insights into Latin writings – this is in addition to the fact that they use the present optative (or hortative) form *habeamus* 'let us have, may we now have'.

The comedies within the corpus are expectedly prone to apply non-English features in a more humorous and playful manner. This is definitely true for Disney's *Sword in the Stone*, where Merlin re-latinizes highly complex English words such as *prestidigitation* by adding {-onium} to the stem. None of the four 'words' in (96) – *higitus, figitus, migitus* or *mum* make any sense – they thus must be classified as nonsense language, just like 'Hockety pockety wockety' and so on. In (97), *aquarius* and *aquaticus* are in fact attested adjectives, whereas *aqualitus* and *aquadigitarium* are not. Since they all contain *aqua* 'water', the meaning of which was certainly supposed to be known by recipients, the word-formational creativity is in fact motivated and meaningful to a certain extent.

(96) [Merlin singing:] Higitus figitus migitus mum / Prestidigitonium / Alika fez, balika zez / Malaca mez meripedes / Hockety pockety wockety ... (Disney's *Sword in the Stone*)

(97) [Merlin:] Archimedes, what, what is that fish formula?
[Archimedes:] Who? Who? What? What? What?
[Merlin:] You know, that, that, that Latin business.
[Archimedes:] Hmm? Fish? Latin? Oh, uh. Aquarius aquaticus aqualitus. […]
Aquarius aquaticus aqualitus quum. Aqua digi tarium. (Disney's *Sword in the Stone*)

Brooks's script does not actually have any of its characters switch codes, but only pretends to do so, when the abbot announces his prayer in what he refers to as 'new Latin':

(98) I will conduct the opening prayer in the new Latin: 'Oh, ordl-**ay** ... iveusg-**ay** oury-**ay** essingsbl-**ay**. Amen-**ay**.' (*Men in Tights*)

Once more, the historically versed linguist will notice that these are humorous references to the feminine inflectional suffix {-ae}, here represented as 'ay' /ei/, which is added to any word in this sentence regardless of its class. At the same time, the linear sequence of a meaningful utterance is confused by deliberate phonemic reversal or misplacement of consonants (i.e. 'ordl' instead of *lord*, 'essingsbl' instead of *blessings*).

Again, it is Brooks et al.'s script that does justice to historical linguistics more so than the others in that they pick up that French used to be spoken widely in Middle English times. Apart from the fact that Brooks et al. seem to point out the high potentials of homonymic conflict in Middle and Modern English in this sample (also cf. Section 4.2.1), it will only be noticed by a learned viewer that Asneeze's switching into French ('*Au contraire!*') may even have been an implicit reference to *feat* being a French borrowing (OF *fait*, attested 1326, cf. OED).

(99) [Robin:] What we need is a great feat of strength.
[Asneeze:] **Feat** of strength? *Au contraire!* Now that you're here with me, what we have is great strength of **feet**! (*Men in Tights*)

5 Conclusion

This chapter has made a comprehensive and systematic attempt to carve out such pseudo-linguistic components systematically applied by movie screenplay writers in order to render their works linguistically 'medieval'.

It has been shown that the film dialogues per se do in no case consistently employ pseudo-archaic features to establish a medieval frame. This suggests that the linguistic layer seems to not have been regarded as primarily essential in any of those twelve scripts this study has taken into account. Apparently, the focus for creating credibility and pseudo-authenticity has been placed within the visual dimensions of medieval film making, even though Elliott maintains that 'viewers are increasingly interested in the historical accuracy of films about the past' (2012: 8).

Also Grindley argues that

> [it] is […] important to draw a line between early films (and those leading up to the midpoint of last century) and those dating to the last 30 or so years. Audience

expectations have changed radically, to the point where holding Errol Flynn's Robin Hood to the same standards as Kevin Costner's does not make much sense. As well, in the early days of film, access to medieval scholarship was limited, as was the scholarship itself. Today, costume designers are Googling their way to information, whereas, sixty years ago, one would have to travel to a museum or research library, in many cases, far removed from the centers of film production. (2006: 15)

While Grindley may certainly be right with regard to film makers having to put much more effort in to living up to rising viewers' expectations with regard to props and sets, the corpus under investigation in this chapter has not revealed that this is also true for pseudo-medieval linguistic features. That is despite the fact that particularly today's pre-production screenplay writers would undoubtedly have much easier access to medieval scholarship while composing their works.

And yet, the few scattered pseudo-linguistic aspects identified are exactly what helps us distinguish those scriptwriters Traxel would refer to as linguistic 'mock-amateurs' on the one hand and those that demonstrate 'an educated knowledge of English language history' and thus their intention to create 'more serious' pieces with regard to language (Traxel 2012: 43). This supposed linguistic 'seriousness' in intent may appear irreconcilable with the fact that, for example, *Men in Tights* is inherently non-serious, but in fact Brooks et al.'s script has proven to be the most knowledgeable with regard to Middle English conventions within the small corpus composed.[22]

All in all, blogger Carole Franizzi (cf., (5)), despite obviously not being aware of the established terminology, is certainly right when she states in a tongue-in-cheek-manner that '[s]ticking "eth" on the end of words and calling one another "sire" and "lady" does not Old English make ... '.[23] However, the fact that all of our scriptwriters have been trying in one way or another to employ certain pseudo-archaic components in order to enhance the authenticity of their pieces, suggests that most of the authors must have expected their audience to expect and be responsive to 'medieval language'. In fact, as Elliott remarks, even though

> most of the [...] features [applied in adaptions of medieval stuff for new media] are, in fact, anachronistic, misleading or else wholly unfounded, by charging a historical space with credible and recognisable historical meaning (however stereotypical), these spaces create visual support for the narrator's claim to be recounting the untold truth. (2012: 4)

Notes

1 See Fitzpatrick (2015) for a discussion of the notions *medievalism, medieval studies* and *Middle Ages* as well as *neomedievalism*, and Utz (2011) for a chronological description of the emergence of medievalism as an academic discipline and a polysemous semantic notion. Also cf. Matthews (2011) for a discussion of the relationship between medieval studies and medievalism.

2. This impression is affirmed by transcribers' references to, for example, hesitations, pauses, repeats and contractions.
3. See Aronstein and Coiner (1994) for their insightful paper on how popular culture sites such as Disneyland and Las Vegas pick up and refunctionalize pseudo-medieval pretexts to attract visitors.
4. An intriguing exception may be E. Khmara, writer of both *Ladyhawke* (1985) and, more than ten years later, the TV miniseries *Merlin* (1998).
5. That is, *Dragonslayer* (1981); screenplay written by Hal Barwood and Matthew Robbins.
6. Compare https://www.imsdb.com/all%20scripts/ (last accessed 15 December 2018).
7. The corpus therefore also excludes Tolkien's fantasy stories (e.g. *The Lord of the Rings* and *The Hobbit*), since these are, for one thing, not explicitly set in the European Middle Ages (although certain medieval features are aimfully included). For another thing, Professor Tolkien actually knew Old English and Middle English well and built his legends and mythologies around the languages he actually created or adjusted.
8. Compare Pugh and Weisl's list of medieval films bundled according to the nature of anachronisms they employ (2013: ch. 6). Also cf. Lindley (2007).
9. Elliott (2011) established that 'television series based on the medieval period in fact differ from films in several aspects', namely for one thing in that 'unlike their cinematic counterparts which create a 'disposable' Middle Ages, serializations must invoke a believable medieval world to which they will return on a weekly basis' (2011: 53).
10. Few prestigious universities have been offering Bachelor's and Master's degrees in, for example, English and Film Studies (cf. Cambridge, King's College London, KU Leuven, Drury) for some years now.
11. Genette and McIntosh (1988) define 'paratext' as 'all of the marginal or supplementary data around the text. It comprises what one could call various thresholds: authorial and editorial (i.e. titles, insertions, dedications, epigraphs, prefaces and notes); media related (i.e. interviews with the author, official summaries) and private (i.e. correspondence, calculated or noncalculated disclosures), as well as those related to the material means of production and reception, such as groupings, segments, etc.' (1988: 63).
12. On medieval film music see, for example, Walker (2009).
13. Also cf., for example, http://www.shakespeare-online.com/biography/shakespeare language.html.
14. Curiously, neither has the OED dedicated a subentry on the anachronistic use of *Old English* despite its widespreadness.
15. The former is a noun that has been attested only well after the end of the Middle Ages (OED: 1766, *bore* n.2 <? French), while the latter has been in use since the Old English days as *bār* > ME *bōr* (also <bore>), with its modern spelling indicating its ME [ɔ:] sound.
16. Don Giovanni (aka Don Juan) is anachronistically included in this Robin Hood version, while generally situated in seventeenth-century Seville (at least if Brooks et al. had Mozart's opera in mind).
17. Whether Brooks et al. actually knew this or not cannot be said, but it is certainly curious that both *date* n.1 and *date* n.2 were first attested around 1300, both borrowed from French (cf. OED). The sense 'a social activity or meeting with a person in whom one has a romantic interest' of *date* n.2, however, is a late-nineteenth-century AmE coinage, thus used anachronistically in *Men in Tights*.

18 Only keyness above 50.000 was taken into account.
19 This word choice may stand in relation with numerous suggestions about 'hidden sexual messages' in Disney movies; cf. for example, http://www.huffingtonpost.com/2015/01/14/disney-sexual-messages_n_6452666.html; http://www.dorkly.com/post/73337/dirty-jokes-you-never-realized-were-hiding-in-disney-movies
20 Compare http://www.thelemapedia.org/index.php/The_Star_Sapphire
21 Compare https://de.wikipedia.org/wiki/Die_drei_Lebenden_und_die_drei_Toten)
22 Bizarrely, other medieval comedies have been shown to apply surprisingly high levels of accuracy in other regards, for example, Herek's American science fiction comedy film *Bill and Ted's Excellent Adventure* (1989) features 'some of best representations of authentically medieval arms and armor in contemporary film', as Grindley (2006: 17) observes.
23 https://community.secondlife.com/t5/Role-Play/Language-for-medieval-roleplay/td-p/822601, 04-18-2011 04:37 AM.

References

Aberth, J. (2003), *Knight at the Movies: Medieval History on Film*, New York: Routledge.
Ambrisco, A. S. (2016), 'Battling Monstrosity in Beowulf and Grendel (2005): Using a film adaptation to teach Beowulf', *Studies in Medieval and Renaissance Teaching [SMART]*, 23 (1): 29–40.
Amy de la Bretèque, F. (2004), *L'Imaginaire médiéval dans le cinéma occidental*, Paris: Honoré Champion.
Aronstein, S. and Coiner, N. (1994), 'Twice knightly: Democratizing the middle ages for middle class America', in K. Verduin (ed.), *Medievalism in North America*, 212–31, Cambridge: Brewer.
Bednarek, M. (2018), *Language and Television Series. A Linguistic Approach to TV Dialogue*. Cambridge: Cambridge University Press.
Bernau, A. and Bildhauer, B. (2009), *Medieval Film*, Manchester: Manchester University Press.
Bildhauer, B. (2011), *Filming the Middle Ages*, London: Reaktion Books Ltd.
Brezina, V., Timperley, M. and McEnery, T. (2018), #LancsBox v. 4.x [software]. Available at: http://corpora.lancs.ac.uk/lancsbox.
Bryant, B. L. (2010), *Geoffrey Chaucer Hath a Blog*, New York: Palgrave Macmillan.
Burkholder, P. (2015), 'X marks the plot: Crossbows in medieval film', *Studies in Popular Culture*, 38 (1): 19–40.
Burt, R. (2007), 'Getting schmedieval: Of manuscript and film prologues, paratexts, and parodies', *Exemplaria*, 19 (2): 217–42.
Burt, R. (2008), *Medieval and Early Modern Film and Media*, New York: Palgrave Macmillan.
Cohen, J. J. (2010), 'Blogging the middle ages', in Brantley L. Bryant (ed.), *Geoffrey Chaucer Hath a Blog* (Medieval Studies and New Media), New York: Palgrave Macmillan.
Danescu-Niculescu-Mizil, C. (2012), *Cornell Movie Dialogs Corpus*. Available at: http://www.cs.cornell.edu/~cristian/Cornell_Movie-Dialogs_Corpus.html (accessed 28 June 2017).
Davis, N. Z. (2000), 'The author's response', in V. Schwartz (ed.), *Film and Media: Natalie Zemon Davis's Slaves on Screen: A Review Forum*. Available at: http://www.historians.org/Perspectives/Issues/2001/0109/index.cfm (accessed 28 June 2017).

Dell, H. (2008), 'Past, present, future perfect: Paradigms of history in medievalism studies', *Parergon*, 25 (2): 58–79.
Driver, M. W. and Ray, S. (2009), *Shakespeare and the Middle Ages: Essays on the Performance and Adaptation of the Plays with Medieval Sources or Settings*, Jefferson: McFarland and Company.
Eco, U. (1973), *Faith in Fakes: Travels in Hyperreality*, San Diego: Harcourt Brace and Company.
Elliott, A. B. R. (2011a), 'The charm of the (re)making: Problems of arthurian television serialization', *Arthuriana*, 21 (4): 53–67.
Elliott, A. B. R. (2011b), *Remaking the Middle Ages: The Methods of Cinema and History in Portraying the Medieval World*, Jefferson: McFarland.
Elliott, A. B. R. (2012), 'Historical spaces as narrative: Mapping collective memory onto cinematic space', *Media Fields Journal*, 5: 1–15. Available at: http://eprints.lincoln.ac.uk/6015/1/Elliott.pdf (accessed 28 June 2017).
Ertl, T. (2009), 'Neue Synthesen zur Rettung des Mittelalters', *Zeitschrift für Historische Forschung*, 36 (4): 629–49. doi: 10.3790/zhf.36.4.629.
Finke, L. and Shichtman, M. (2010), *Cinematic Illuminations: The Middle Ages on Film*, Baltimore: Johns Hopkins Press.
Genette, G. and McIntosh, A. G. (1988), 'The proustian paratexte', *SubStance*, 56: 63–77.
Gorgievski, S. (2000), 'Réalisme, stylization et parodie dans le film à sujet médiéval des années 1970', in X. Kawa-Topor (ed.), *Le Moyen Âge vu par le cinema européen*, 199–220, Conques: Centre européen d'art et de civilisation médiévales.
Görlach, M., ed. (1981), *The Gestes of Mac and Morris: Presented to Hans Kurath on the Occasion of His 90th Birthday*, Heidelberg: Winter.
Grindley, C. J. (2006), 'Arms and the man: The curious inaccuracy of medieval arms and armor in contemporary film', *Film and History: An Interdisciplinary Journal of Film and Television Studies*, 36 (1): 14–19.
Harris, R. (2004), *The Linguistics of History*, Edinburgh: Edinburgh University Press.
Harty, K. J. (1987), 'Cinema Arthuriana: Translations of the Arthurian legend to the screen', *Arthurian Interpretations*, 2: 95–11.
Harty, K. J. (1999), *The Reel Middle Ages: American, Western and Eastern European, Middle Eastern and Asian Films about Medieval Europe*, Jefferson, NC: McFarland.
Harty, K. J., ed. (2011), *The Vikings on Film: Essays on Depictions of the Nordic Middle Ages*, Jefferson and London: McFarland and Company.
Hasty, W. (2016), *The Medieval Risk-Reward Society: Courts, Adventure, and Love in the European Middle Ages*, Columbus: Ohio State University Press.
Haydock, N. (2002), 'Arthurian melodrama, chaucerian spectacle and the waywardness of cinematic pastiche in first knight and a knight's tale', *Studies in Medievalism*, 12: 5–38.
Haydock, N. (2008), *Movie Medievalism: The Imaginary Middle Ages*, Jefferson: McFarland.
Hodson, J. (2014), *Dialect in Film and Literature*, Basingstoke: Palgrave Macmillan.
Kiening, C. and Adolf, H., eds (2006), *Mittlelter im Film*. [Trends in Medieval Philology 6]. Berlin: Walter de Gruyter.
Kirner-Ludwig, M. (2018), 'Great pretenders: The phenomenon of impersonating (pseudo-)historical personae in medieval blogs, or: Blogging for someone else's fame?', in B. Bös, S. Kleinke, S. Mollin and N. Hernández (eds), *The Discursive Construction of Identities On- and Offline. Personal – Group – Collective*, 15–55, Amsterdam and New York: John Benjamins.
Laity, K. A. (2008), 'Medieval community: Lessons from the film *Black Knight*', *LATCH: A Journal for the Study of the Literary Artifact in Theory, Culture, or History*, 1: 147–57.

Lakowski, R. I. (2015), '"A wilderness of Dragons": Tolkien's treatment of dragons in Roverandom and Farmer Giles of Ham', *Mythlore*, 34 (1): 83–103.
Lenard, A. and Walker, I. (1991), *Winnie ille Pu. A. A. Milne's Winnie-the-Pooh in Latin*, New York: Penguin Books.
Lindahl, C., McNamara, J. and Lindow, J., eds (2000), *Medieval Folklore: An Encyclopedia of Myths, Legends, Tales, Beliefs, and Customs*, Santa Barbara: ABC-CLIO.
Lindley, A. (1998), *The Ahistoricism of Medieval Film: Screening the Past 3*. Available at: http://www.latrobe.edu.au/screeningthepast/firstrelease/fir598/ALfr3a.htm (accessed 28 October 2017).
Lindley, A. (2007), 'Once, present and future kings: Kingdom of heaven and the multitemporality of medieval film', in L. T. Ramey and T. Pugh (eds), *Race, Class, and Gender in 'Medieval' Cinema*, 15–30, New York: Palgrave Macmillan.
Lionarons, J. T. (1998), *The Medieval Dragon: The Nature of the Beast in Germanic Literature*, Enfield Lock: Hisarlik Press.
Lippi-Green, R. (2012), *English with an Accent- Language, Ideology, and Discrimination in the United States*, London: Routledge.
Marrone, S. P. (2015), *A History of Science, Magic, and Belief: From Medieval to Early Modern Europe*, New York: Palgrave.
Matthews, D. (2011), 'From mediaeval to mediaevalism: A new semantic history', *The Review of English Studies, New Series*, 62 (257): 695–715.
McConnell, W. (2015), 'The Dragon in medieval literature of Europe', *Zeitschrift für Deutsches Altertum und deutsche Literatur*, 144 (1): 127–32.
Munslow, A. (2015), 'Genre and history/historying', *Rethinking History*, 19 (2): 158–76. doi: http://dx.doi.org/10.1080/13642529.2014.973711.
Nokes, R. S. (2015), 'Beowulf on film: Adaptations and variations', *Speculum: A Journal of Medieval Studies*, 90 (4): 1119–21.
Pugh, T. and Weisl, A. J. (2013), *Medievalisms: Making the Past in the Present*, New York: Routledge.
Quaglio, P. (2008), 'Television dialogue and natural conversation', in A. Ädel and R. Reppen (eds), *Corpora and Discourse: The Challenges of Different Settings*, 189–210, Amsterdam: Benjamins.
Rider, C. (2012), *Magic and Religion in Medieval England*, London: Reaktion Books.
Rose, C. (2000), *Giants, Monsters, and Dragons: An Encyclopedia of Folkore, Legend, and Myth*, New York: Norton.
Rosen, P. (2001), *Change Mummified: Cinema, Historicity, Theory*, Minneapolis: University of Minnesota Press.
Rosenstone, R. (2006), *History on Film/Film on History*, London: Longman Pearson.
Sauer, H. and Lenker, U. (2005), 'Das englische Mittelalter im Film – Perspektiven und Probleme: ein Bericht', in G. Knappe (ed.), *English Linguistics and Medieval Studies: Positions – Perspectives – New Approaches. Proceedings of the Conference in Bamberg, 21-22 May 2004*, 95–117, Frankfurt am Main: Lang.
Schwam-Baird, S. (1999), 'King Arthur in hollywood: The subversion of tragedy in first knight', *Medieval Perspectives*, 14: 202–13.
Scott, R. (2005), *Kingdom of Heaven*, USA: 20th Century Fox.
Stevens, L. (1956), *The Lovers*, New York: Samuel French.
Sturtevant, P. B. (2010), 'Based on a true history? The impact of popular "medieval film" on the public understanding of the middle ages', Doctoral dissertation, The University of Leeds, Institute for Medieval Studies and Centre for World Cinemas. Available

at: http://etheses.whiterose.ac.uk/1117/1/Paul_B_Sturtevant_PhD_Thesis_2010.pdf (accessed 28 October 2017).

Tashiro, C. (2004), 'Passing for the past: Production design and the historical film', *Cineaste*, 29 (2): 40–4.

Traidl, V. (2016), *Telling Tales about Beowulf: The Poem and the Film*, Munich: Utz.

Traxel, O. M. (2008), 'Medieval and pseudo-medieval elements in computer role-playing games: Use and interactivity', *Studies in Medievalism*, 16: 125–42.

Traxel, O. M. (2012), 'Pseudo-Archaic English: The modern perception and interpretation of the linguistic past', *Studia Anglica Posnaniensia*, 47 (2–3): 41–58.

Utz, R. (2011), 'Coming to terms with medievalism', *European Journal of English Studies*, 15 (2): 101–13.

Verduin, K. (2009), 'The founding and the founder: Medievalism and the legacy of Leslie J. Workman', *Studies in Medievalism*, 17: 1–27.

Vincendeau, G. (2001), 'Let films be films', in V. Schwartz (ed.), *Film and Media: Natalie Zemon Davis's Slaves on Screen: A Review Forum*. Available at: https://www.historians.org/publications-and-directories/perspectives-on-history/september-2001/natalie-zemon-daviss-slaves-on-screen-a-review-forum/let-films-be-films (accessed 28 October 2017).

Walker, A. T. (2009), 'Towards a theory of medieval film music', in A. Bernau and N. Bildhauer (eds), *Medieval Film*, 137–57, Manchester: Manchester University Press.

White, H. (1973), *Metahistory: The Historical Imagination in Nineteenth Century Europe*, Baltimore, et al.: Johns Hopkins University Press.

White, H. (1987), *The Content of the Form: Narrative Discourse and Historical Representation*, Baltimore, et al.: Johns Hopkins University Press.

White, H. (1988), 'Historiography and historiophoty', *The American Historical Review*, 93 (5): 1193–9.

White, T. H. (1938), *The Once and Future King Book 1: The Sword in the Stone*, Glasgow: Collins.

Wilson, A. (2014), 'The reflexive test of Hayden White's *Metahistory*', *History and Theory*, 53: 1–23.

Woods, W. F. (2014), *The Medieval Filmscape: Reflections of Fear and Desire in a Cinematic Mirror*, Jefferson: McFarland and Company.

Workman, L. J. (1999), 'The future of medievalism', *The Year's Work in Medievalism*, 10: 7–18.

Movie transcripts (PPTSs)

Anderson, K. and Clemmons, L. (script/screenplay), (1973), *Disney's Robin Hood*, USA: Buena Vista. Available at: http://www.springfieldspringfield.co.uk/movie_script.php?movie=robin-hood-1973 (accessed 28 June 2017).

Brooks, M., Chandler, E. and Shapiro, J. D. (script/screenplay), (1993), *Robin Hood: Men in Tights*, USA: 20th Century Fox, et al. Available at: http://www.script-o-rama.com/movie_scripts/r/robin-hood-men-in-tights-script.html (accessed 28 June 2017).

Collier, J. and Kaufman, M. (script/screenplay), (1965), *The War Lord*. USA: Universal Pictures. Available at: http://www.springfieldspringfield.co.uk/movie_script.php?movie=war-lord-the (accessed 28 June 2017).

Feitshans, M. (script/screenplay), (2015), *Dragonheart 3: The Sorcerer's Curse*, USA: Universal Studios Home Entertainment. Available at: http://www.springfieldspringfi

eld.co.uk/movie_script.php?movie=dragonheart-3-the-sorcerers-curse (accessed 28 June 2017).

Goldman, J. (script/screenplay), (1976), *Robin and Marian*, USA: Columbia Pictures. Available at: http://www.script-o-rama.com/movie_scripts/r/robin-and-marian-script-transcript.html (accessed 28 June 2017).

Helgeland, B. (script/screenplay), (2001), *A Knight's Tale*, Columbia. Available at: http://www.springfieldspringfield.co.uk/movie_script.php?movie=a-knights-tale (accessed 28 June 2017).

Helgeland, B. (script/screenplay), (2010), *Robin Hood*, USA: Universal. Available at: https://de.wikipedia.org/wiki/Brian_Helgelandhttp://www.springfieldspringfield.co.uk/movie_script.php?movie=robin-hood-2010 (accessed 28 June 2017).

Khmara, E., Thomas, M., Mankiewicz, T. and Peoples, D. (script/screenplay), (1985), *Ladyhawke*, USA: Warner Bros. and 20th Century Fox. Available at: http://www.script-o-rama.com/movie_scripts/l/ladyhawke-script-transcript-michelle-pfeiffer.html (accessed 28 June 2017).

Monahan, W. (script/screenplay), (2005), *Kingdom of Heaven*, USA: 20th Century Fox. Available at: http://www.springfieldspringfield.co.uk/movie_script.php?movie=kingdom-of-heaven (accessed 28 June 2017).

Peet, B. (script/screenplay), (1963), Disney's *The Sword in the Stone*, USA: Buena Vista. Available at: http://www.springfieldspringfield.co.uk/movie_script.php?movie=sword-in-the-stone-the (accessed 28 June 2017).

Pogue, C. E. and Johnson, P. R. (script/screenplay), (1996), *Dragonheart*, USA: Universal. Available at: http://www.springfieldspringfield.co.uk/movie_script.php?movie=dragonheart (accessed 28 June 2017).

Robbins, M. and Barwood, H. (script/screenplay), (1981), *Dragonslayer*, USA: Paramount. Available at: http://www.springfieldspringfield.co.uk/movie_script.php?movie=dragonslayer (accessed 28 June 2017).

11

How comics communicate on the screen

Telecinematic discourse in comic-to-film adaptations

Christina Sanchez-Stockhammer

1 Introduction

Recent years have seen a large number of commercially successful screen adaptations of printed comic books, such as Kenneth Branagh's *Thor* (2011) or the award-winning series of *Batman* films (e.g. Christopher Nolan's 2008 *The Dark Knight*).[1] Most of these screen adaptations of comics, like most studies of 'graphic cinema' (e.g. Booker 2007; Gordon, Jancovich and McAllister 2007; Rauscher 2010), focus on relatively dark superheroes.[2] Against this background, one box-office success stands out due to its friendly and positive hero for all audiences: Steven Spielberg's *The Adventures of Tintin* (2011), which is based on the comic book series *Tintin* by the Belgian artist Hergé (a pseudonym for Georges Rémi; cf. Peeters 1990: 9). In Hergé's comics, the young journalist Tintin experiences exciting adventures all over the world in the company of his dog Snowy. This chapter pays tribute to Hergé's popular comic book universe by investigating the relation between Spielberg's film adaptation and Hergé's comics from a linguistic perspective. It sets out to fill an important research gap by exploring how language use in the *scriptovisual*[3] medium of the comic (which combines still images and printed text) is rendered in the *audiovisual* medium of film (which combines moving images and spoken language). After discussing general linguistic similarities between comics and films and the use of language in each of the two media, this chapter compares the representation of voice, accent, thoughts, talking animals, sounds and written language in Spielberg's screen adaptation of *Tintin* to the original printed comic books. It analyses to what extent the language from comic books can be directly transferred to the filmic medium and investigates possible causes underlying any modifications in the above-mentioned domains.

2 Linguistic similarities and differences between comics and films

The juxtaposition of comics and films as such is no entirely new idea: Ecke (2010: 7–8) points out that comics have frequently been compared to films in the literature, with some researchers qualifying them as 'frozen film' (Berninger, Ecke and Haberkorn 2010: 1). It is therefore not surprising that director Steven Spielberg should also have used this analogy to describe Hergé's *Tintin* comics: 'Every single panel ... it told a story in cinematic terms. ... That was, I think, the genius of Hergé: it was a movie' (*The Journey to Tintin*, DVD special feature). Most studies on comic-to-film adaptations (e.g. Leitch 2007; Lefèvre 2007; Ofenloch 2007) share this quotation's focus on both media's prevalent use of images, which constitutes a particularly salient common feature of comics and films. Previous research often concentrates on analysing how the look of individual comics is captured by their screen adaptations, for example regarding the use of colour or concerning parallels between panels and shots.[4] However, even if both comics and films are characterized by the use of images, one should not overlook that they still rely very strongly on the use of language to transmit messages (with very few exceptions like silent films[5] or silent comic strips, for example Lewis Trondheim's *La Mouche*). Since the analysis of language in comic-to-film adaptations has been almost completely disregarded so far (e.g. in Fick 2004 or in Cohen 2007), the present study fills an important gap in research.

On a very general level, a crucial linguistic difference between comics and films is that the former are by necessity restricted to the written medium, whereas sound film has the technical means to render both spoken and written language. Lefèvre (2007: 4) therefore speaks of 'the importance of sound in film compared to the "silence" of comics'.[6]

In spite of this difference, comics and films share two other important language-related aspects, namely that they largely rely on dialogue in order to advance their narratives and that they attempt to simulate natural conversation. There even seems to be a common preconception that both comic and film dialogue are relatively naturalistic representations of actual spoken language: thus, students of linguistics frequently suggest studying language based on extracts from television series without being aware of the fact that 'TV film dialogue ... is an artfully-constructed selective simulation of natural realistic speech' (Toolan 2011: 181), scripted and thus different from the unplanned speech typical of natural conversation.

An important distinction for the comparison of comics to screen adaptations is made by Söll (1974: 16–17). He distinguishes between the medium of realization (in an auditory vs. visual code) and the characteristics of the conception of a text (spoken vs. written style).

For example, negative contractions such as *don't* are characteristic of spoken style in Standard English and will usually occur in the spoken code, but they may also occur in the written medium, for example in direct conversation in a novel. Conversely,

Table 11.1 Code parlé, écrit, phonique and orthographique

		Conception	
		spoken	written
Medium	Orthographic code	<don't>	<do not>
	Phonetic code	/dəʊnt/	/duː nɒt/

Source: adapted from Söll (1974: 16–18).

the full form *do not* is more characteristic of the written style and tends to occur in the written medium, but it may also be used in oral speech, for example when giving emphatic instructions or reading a newspaper article aloud. Usually, however, there is an affinity between spoken conception and phonetic code (e.g. in casual conversation) and written conception and orthographic code (e.g. in academic research articles).

If we apply Söll's distinctions to the language of comic books and the language of film dialogues, we find that both comic book and film dialogues can typically be classified as conceptionally spoken language (which makes them similar to spontaneous spoken language). For instance, the language used in the *Tintin* comic books' dialogues imitates spoken language in different ways. Thus Figure 11.1 contains contractions (***Didn't** you know that?*), hesitation phenomena (***I… er… I'm** Mr Bird's new secretary.*) and false starts (***I…no**, I hadn't heard*).

Similarities of the language used in comics and spoken language have been observed in several empirical studies: thus readability scores based on sentence length generally qualify the language employed in comics as simple (Sanchez-Stockhammer 2012: 68–9), and the increased use of question marks and exclamation marks in comics (Sanchez-Stockhammer 2016: 162–3) characterizes their language as conceptually oral following Söll (1974: 16–17). Nevertheless, the spatial limitations of the individual panels impose artificial restrictions on dialogues in comics (cf. also Sanchez-Stockhammer 2012), so that these cannot be considered identical with naturally occurring conversation.

The same is true of the language of screenplays, which are written in orthographic code supposed to be realized phonetically, that is 'to be spoken as if not written' (Söll 1974: 36): the literature on fictional dialogue (e.g. Bednarek 2010: 64–5; Toolan 2011: 161, 182) abounds with observations on the difference between natural conversation and televised dialogues, since the language used in films has a lower proportion of

1. background noise, unclear words and deficient syntax;
2. overlaps and interruptions;

Figure 11.1 Spoken-language features in *Tintin* (*The Secret of the Unicorn*: 45) © Hergé/Moulinsart 2019.

3. false starts, self-repairs and hesitation phenomena;
4. abrupt topic shifts, unresolved topics, incomplete exchanges and ignored or misheard turns;

in order to increase intelligibility and for a range of other purposes. Furthermore, dialogues on-screen have a lower proportion of fillers, redundancies and vague language (e.g. *kind of, stuff*), as these do not contribute to advancing the storyline. Narrative language is also used less in films than in natural conversation to avoid long and tedious monologues. Conversely, televised conversation has a larger proportion or degree of

1. coherence;
2. Gricean cooperativeness (to simplify the communicative process);
3. emotional and emphatic language (to entertain the audience);
4. informal language (to create more realistic characters);
5. stock lines (to attract a large audience) and
6. rhythmical arrangements (for aesthetic reasons).

Furthermore, there is less linguistic variation in fictional dialogue than in natural conversation (e.g. regarding the settings, types of interaction and topics), and short turns in constructed filmic dialogue are distributed relatively evenly (cf. Bednarek 2010: 64–5; Toolan 2011: 161, 182). It is very likely that many of these aspects also apply to the language of comics.

To conclude, neither the language of comics nor that of films is identical with naturally occurring conversation: while spontaneous conversation is shaped by the cognitive processing limitations of the speakers (cf., for example, Biber 1988: 131–2), dialogue in film rather focuses on the processing limitations of the hearers, whereas dialogue in comic books suffers less from such limitations, as speakers can 'choose their own reading speed', 'linger on a panel, scan the complete plate, and return to panels or whole sequences at free will' (Lefèvre 2007: 5).

3 Taxonomy of language use in comics and possible equivalents in film

Having discussed general linguistic similarities and differences between comic books and films, let us now consider the various ways in which language occurs in comic books and possible equivalents in film. The following overview represents a modification of the taxonomy in Sanchez-Stockhammer (2012: 58–9).

The very first instance of written language that readers usually encounter in a printed comic is the title of the book or the individual story as well as the name of the author. These can be subsumed with the preliminary matter comprising information about the publisher, the date of publication and so on as *metadata*. Since metadata involves the use of language outside the comic's narrative in the strictest sense, it will not be considered any further in the following.

By contrast, *boxes* containing narrative text constitute an important part of language use in comics. Usually, they are placed at the top-end inside a panel and can be attributed to a narrator that is not identical with the characters in the comic. In the *Tintin* comics, this special status of the brief narrative texts is emphasized by the fact that they use a script font rather than the print types used elsewhere. Most commonly, narrative boxes specify the time and/or location of the new panel in relation to the preceding one (e.g. 'A few minutes later...' in Hergé's *The Secret of the Unicorn*: 4). Occasionally, text boxes may be used to indicate that a character from the story is speaking from the off (cf. *Superman*: 64), but this tends to be signalled by additionally enclosing the text with quotation marks and by using introductory omission dots, since this communicative situation tends to involve the continuation of a turn begun in a previous panel (cf. Sanchez-Stockhammer 2016: 162).

The most characteristic use of language in comics is the direct speech of the characters depicted in a panel, generally integrated into *speech balloons*. The shape of the balloon represents the sound quality of a character's voice: thus spiky outlines signal screams; thin, broken lines signal whispers and curvy outlines represent internal speech – that is, thoughts (Fick 2004: 30–1). Occasionally, there is no balloon around direct speech, for example when a character produces a long monologue whose precise content is unimportant and on the gradient towards background noise (cf. Watterson 1987: 50). The type of lettering used may also convey a message, as when a wavy font in a speech balloon marks a sing-song intonation (cf. Fick 2004: 30–1).

This iconic lettering is particularly notorious in *onomatopoeia*, such as *graaaghh* or *wham*, which are usually superimposed on the picture and may employ spikes or red colour to indicate dynamics. These words, which are widely regarded as highly characteristic of the language of comics, represent sounds, such as the 'Peep!' of young birds (cf. *Uncle Scrooge*: 60). Onomatopoeia in comics often constitute the conventionalized combination of a particular linguistic form (i.e. a sequence of letters) with a particular meaning (cf. de Saussure 1916/1959: 66–7), such as the barking of a dog.

Written language constitutes the last linguistic feature in comics to be discussed here. It is typically neglected by other taxonomies which classify language use in comics (e.g. Fick 2004: 30–2). In comics, just like in the real world, written language may be encountered in the form of newspapers read by the protagonists, on traffic signs, number plates, billboards, shop signs and so on. Occasionally, these instances of written text in their different contexts of use in the linguistic landscape may be incomplete but can be filled in by the background knowledge of regular readers (e.g. the name of the newspaper *Daily Planet* in *Superman*: 10).

All these occurrences of written text in the comic interact with the drawings. According to McCloud (1993: 155), '[p]erhaps the most **common** type of word/picture combination is the **INTERDEPENDENT**, where words and pictures go **hand in hand** to convey an idea that neither could convey **alone**', for example when a man gestures with his hand and says: '**This** is all I need to **stop him!**' Alternatively, pictures may only have a supporting role as illustrations to a verbally told narration, or words may only have a supporting role as soundtrack to a visually told narration with the same message, for example the sound *mmm* made by kissing people (McCloud 1993: 153).[7]

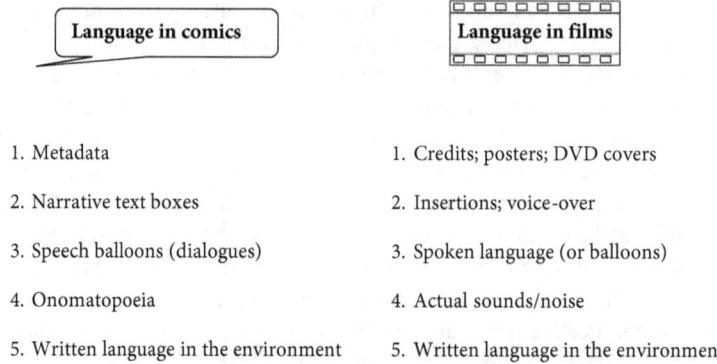

Figure 11.2 Correspondences between the use of language in comics versus films.

When comic books are adapted to the screen, one may expect their linguistic contents to be transferred in some way or another from the printed to the filmic medium. Figure 11.2 provides an overview of the possible correspondences between the occurrence of language in comic books (based on the taxonomy discussed above) and its equivalents on the screen.

As far as *metadata* is concerned, films contain orthographically coded information in their credits (which are part of the film) about the director, the author(s) of the script, the actors and so on. Such information is also printed on the covers of DVDs.

Insertions are equivalents to the *narrative boxes* of comic books in orthographic code, for example when the date of an event is superimposed on the moving images.[8] These can be replaced by voice-overs in phonetic code, for example when a narrator tells a story from the off (cf. also Fick 2004: 30). Alternatively, the shots in a film may be arranged in such a way that the change in place or time can be derived from non-verbal clues, such as the same landscape in another season.[9] In the Spielberg film under discussion here, a change in place is indicated without recourse to a narrating instance when the protagonists shake hands and exclaim: 'To Bagghar!' – after which they are shown riding through the desert in the next scene and then looking down on a city which is obviously Bagghar.

Whenever comic book *speech balloons* contain spoken dialogues, the most straightforward adaptation to the filmic medium is in the form of dialogue in phonetic code. This also allows for the natural representation of a trembling voice (sometimes indicated by a special type of line around the speech) or increasing loudness while talking (usually marked by the use of capital letters, for example when Tintin calls his dog: 'Snowy!... Where is the wretched animal? Snowy?... SNOWY?...' in *Red Rackham's Treasure*: 14). There have been experiments with speech balloons using orthographic code in films, but these 'do not function as well' and tend to look 'rather strange' (Lefèvre 2007: 11), because they do not conform to the expectations of the medium. The use of phonetic rather than orthographic code for dialogues in comic-to-film adaptations has one very important advantage for the reception process: the film's audience can watch the action and listen to the dialogues simultaneously, while printed comics – in which the visual channel is used for both action and dialogues – require their readers to compute both in alternation and in a certain, often linear, order.[10]

As *onomatopoeia* in comics are orthographic representations of sounds, using the actual sounds in screen adaptations may seem the most obvious solution (cf. the discussion in Section 4.6). Since the orthographic code in the comics merely serves as a crutch to conveying sounds, the medium of film thus has a very important advantage in that it can render sounds more realistically than the printed comics. Similarly, *written language* is most naturalistically rendered by using orthographic code in film, too – even if writing comes with its own, special requirements (cf. 4.7).

To conclude, all the various forms in which language occurs in printed comic books were found to have some possible correspondence in the filmic medium.

4 Qualitative study of speech (re-)presentation in *Tintin* comic-to-film adaptations

After these general observations, let us now consider one particular comic-to-film adaptation in more detail.

4.1 Corpus and method of analysis

Before his death in 1983, Hergé granted Steven Spielberg the rights to make a live-action film from his *Tintin* comic book series, believing that this particular director could best convey the atmosphere of his comic books in the filmic medium (cf. Bartlett 2012).[11] Spielberg's 2011 film *The Adventures of Tintin* is based on a script by Steven Moffat, Edgar Wright and Joe Cornish, which combines the storyline of a *Tintin* adventure extending over two albums, namely *The Secret of the Unicorn* (Hergé 1974a) and *Red Rackham's Treasure* (Hergé 1974b). However, the plot was modified considerably: while rarely alluding to the second of the two volumes, the screenplay of the film (which was approved by Hergé's widow) integrates large parts of yet another *Tintin* comic book, *The Crab with the Golden Claws* (Hergé 1974c), in which the character of Captain Haddock is first introduced (cf. *The World of Tintin*). Such modifications are not unusual for comic book adaptations, as few of the screen versions 'respect meticulously the storyline of a particular comic' due to the fact that each medium 'has its own laws and rules' and that 'some elements may work wonderfully in a comic, but cannot function in the context of a film' (Lefèvre 2007: 4). In view of the 'different narrative-length norms of the two media' (Lefèvre 2007: 4), script writers usually have to leave out some scenes and add others, so as to be more 'truthful to the spirit of the original work' (Lefèvre 2007: 5) in the other medium.

In the Spielberg film's modified plot, the young journalist Tintin buys a model of the ship *Unicorn* at a flea market and refuses to sell it to several men attempting to buy it from him immediately afterwards. Tintin's flat is broken into and the *Unicorn* model is stolen. Later, Tintin finds out that a parchment had been hidden in the ship's mast and had fallen out and rolled under a chest of drawers when the ship had been toppled by his dog Snowy prior to the burglary. The parchment with a mysterious message is one of three, which – placed together against the light – reveal the place where a treasure is hidden. Tintin is later abducted to a ship, where he gets to know Captain Haddock, the descendant of the captain of the *Unicorn*, who once sank the ship with the treasure. They live several adventures, eventually defeat the villain Ivan Ivanovitch Sakharine and unite the three pieces of parchment. It turns out that the treasure is hidden in Marlinspike Hall, the Haddock family's home, but a cliffhanger at the end of the film suggests that Tintin and his new friend Captain Haddock will soon embark on the hunt of an even larger part of the treasure.

For the empirical study presented here, the film was watched closely after a detailed reading of the three original comic books, and all passages that were similar enough to allow a comparison were transcribed manually. Furthermore, Spielberg's screen adaptation of the Red Rackham treasure hunt was occasionally contrasted with the use of language in Director Stephen Bernasconi's animated cartoon series from the 1990s.

Due to the dialogic nature of comics, one might generally have expected that most of the comic book dialogues could be directly copy-pasted into a film script. Spielberg's *Tintin* adaptation, however, has such a different storyline that there are hardly any of the original situations left – they are sometimes similar, but usually not identical (in Hergé's original, for instance, Tintin buys the model of the *Unicorn* for his friend Captain Haddock, whom he has not even met in the film yet). As the material does therefore not lend itself to a quantitative analysis, a qualitative approach was adopted in the following.

4.2 The modification of dialogues

Occasionally, however, scenes from the Spielberg film are similar enough to the original comic books to permit a comparison, even if the respective dialogues tend to differ in a more or less pronounced manner. This section explores possible reasons for such modifications when dialogues are adapted for the screen.

One scene which lends itself to such a comparison is when Tintin comes home to find that his flat was broken into once again. In the comic book, Tintin comments upon the situation, which is simultaneously depicted in several images, at length (1). He expresses his shock at finding his flat vandalized and wonders about the cause, as nothing is missing.

(1) My door's open! … What can be the matter now?
     My flat has been ransacked!…
     The gangsters! What have they done to my books?
     This one is completely ruined! … The vandals!
     Burgled twice in one day … Not bad at all!
     What have they taken this time?
     Very queer thieves: they haven't taken a thing.
     They've only searched the place … I wonder what they were looking for?
     (*The Secret of the Unicorn*: 9)

In Spielberg's film, by contrast, Tintin merely utters: 'Snowy! ... Great snakes! ... What is it, Snowy?' and the dog then shows him where to find the scroll (whereas the treasure map is only discovered much later in the comic book). While it is surprising that Tintin does not comment upon the fact that his door was opened or that someone has broken into his flat, it is understandable that this scene was shortened, since Tintin's search for stolen objects would have taken too long to show on the screen. Since the movement of the camera and the musical score already convey the atmosphere of mystery very well, it was also possible for the screenwriters to get rid of some of the text conveying this impression verbally in the comic book.

Another reason why the text from the comic books may not have been used word by word in the screen version is that the language in some scenes is slightly old-fashioned and thus unnatural for a present-day film audience; for example, Tintin's exclamation: 'we shall certainly have plenty of adventures on our treasure-hunt' (*The Secret of the Unicorn*: 62). This specific style is due to the early publication date of the comics in serial form in *Le Soir* from 1942 onwards (Peeters 1990: 73) and was preserved in the 1974 translations into English. While the film generally conserves the atmosphere of the 1940s regarding clothing, technology (e.g. cars and cameras) and so on, language use was modernized in some dialogues – presumably to increase identification.

A similar reason for the necessity to modify dialogues from comic books for screen adaptations is advanced by Lefèvre (2007: 11). According to him, '[t]he texts in speech balloons are generally not suited for film dialogue and they need some rewriting.' For instance, he argues that superhero comics 'often use very stylistic and bombastic dialogue', which does not work so well in the filmic medium, since it may come across as 'unintentional camp'. A similar reasoning may have led the screenwriters of the Spielberg film to modify the text in the fighting scene between the pirate Red Rackham and Sir Francis Haddock, Captain Haddock's predecessor. In the original comic book (*The Secret of the Unicorn*: 24), the two opponents exchange a considerable amount of speech. For instance, 'Retreat as you may, you cannot escape me!' is countered by 'I'll run you through, prattling porpoise!' This highly dramatic style, which is reminiscent of stage dialogue or early Hollywood swashbucklers, was replaced with relatively naturalistic occasional grunts in the film, presumably because it was expected that the typical present-day audience of a comic-to-screen adaptation would find such a conversation unusual. Furthermore, the original scene abounds with a characteristic of the Haddock family members, namely the use of very colourful (but infrequent and relatively harmless) swearwords, such as 'porcupine', 'squawking popinjay' and so on. The omission of these swearwords may have been a deliberate attempt at making the film more suitable for young viewers particularly in the United States.[12]

The last type of change in the dialogues can be observed very nicely in a scene whose original comic book text is contrasted with the transcription of the film dialogue in Table 11.2.

While the text is extremely similar in both columns, minor but revealing differences can be detected between the comic book dialogue and its film version: for instance, there is a change from the narrative verbs in the past tense (in bold print) to the present tense. As the action shown in moving images between the film's narrative sequences is thus evoked in an even livelier manner, this change is likely to have

Table 11.2 Comparison of the Dialogue in the Comic Book *The Secret of the Unicorn* (23) and the Spielberg Film *The Adventures of Tintin* (2011)

Original comic book text	Spielberg film dialogue
Haddock: *And* with these *words* he **hurled** himself ...	Haddock: With that he **hurls** himself *forward* ...
Tintin: On the pirates? ... Like that? ... Unarmed? ...	Tintin: On the pirates? Like that? Unarmed?
Haddock: No, on a bottle of rum, rolling on the deck! ... He **opened** it, **put** it to his lips, and ...	Haddock: No! <u>No</u>, on a bottle of rum, rolling on the deck, *and* he **opens** it *up*, *and* **puts** it to his lips, and ...
Tintin: And then he stops. 'This is no time for drinking,' he says, 'I need all my wits about me.' With that, he puts down the bottle ...	Tintin: And then he stops! 'This is no time for drinking,' he says. 'I need all my wits about me.' With that, he puts down the bottle *and* ...
Haddock: Yes, he puts down the bottle ... and seizes a cutlass.	Haddock: Yes, <u>yes</u>, *uh*, he puts down the bottle and ... *and* he seizes a cutlass.

been included deliberately in the screenplay by the screenwriters. The other changes, by contrast, are possibly unintentional: there are several instances where words are repeated (with underlining, for example, *yes*) or inserted additionally into the text (in italics, for example, *up* in *he opens it up*). It is highly plausible that these modifications were inserted spontaneously, unintentionally and subconsciously by the actor while attempting to play the scene as naturalistically as possible. This is particularly likely of the hesitation marker *uh* in the last turn (*Yes, yes, uh, ...*). Based on Quaglio's observation that the fan transcripts of television series are 'fairly accurate and very detailed, including several features that scripts are not likely to present: hesitators, pauses, repeats, and contractions' (2008: 191–2), we may conclude that such markers of natural conversation tend to be absent from written-to-be-spoken screenplays but are inserted by the actors spontaneously when performing the text in front of the camera.

4.3 The representation of voice

While the previous section has revolved around the modification of text from speech balloons, this section addresses how precisely the characters speak on the screen. One crucial aspect in this sense is the voice of the characters. Since all dialogues in the usual silent reading process of comics are read by the same person with their own internal voice, one might assume that all characters 'speak'[13] identically in a printed comic book. However, readers also form certain expectations regarding the sound of the individual characters' voices based on their sex, age, physical appearance and so on and may be 'shocked by the way an actor speaks when playing that character' in a film (Lefèvre 2007: 11). These expectations are presumably much stronger for comics with their graphical depiction of characters by comparison to novels, where the expectations regarding the voices of the protagonists are solely based on verbal information. The physical features ever-present in the drawings may incite readers to form certain expectations about the characters' voices, for example that that of Cuthbert Calculus is very soft, or that Captain Haddock has a deep, masculine voice. These imagined voices are, however, underspecified, so that readers are presumably unaware of their expectations, unless there is a large discrepancy between the imagined voice and the voice of a character in a screen adaptation of a comic book.

A particularly interesting character with regard to his way of speaking is Tintin, the protagonist, with whom readers will tend to identify. This identification process is aided by the simplicity of Tintin's features: according to McCloud (1993: 30–1), abstract images are more universal than realistic art, and '[t]he more cartoony a face is, … the more people it could be said to **describe**' (McCloud 1993: 31). Consequently, 'when you look at a photo or realistic drawing of a face … you see it as the face of **another**. But when you enter the world of the **cartoon** … you see **yourself**' (McCloud 1993: 36) – represented as a smiley by McCloud. When Tintin's features are compared to those of the other main characters in the series (cf. Figure 11.3), it becomes immediately obvious that the other men have more protruding and characteristic noses and often feature beards. Tintin's face, by contrast, consists of merely two dots for the eyes, a line for the mouth, a small curve for the nose and two larger ones for the eyebrows. An image of Tintin's face on its own is therefore very similar to a smiley, and it is his tuft of red hair, combined with his typical clothes (and the company of Snowy), that makes Tintin recognizable as a character.

In line with his physical appearance, Tintin in Spielberg's film has a friendly, youthful and comparatively high male voice. Since Tintin offers a blank slate for identification, one might expect his language and his way of speaking to be neutral as well. Indeed, his language in the comic books does not suggest itself as particularly remarkable (except in the sense that Tintin frequently uses pauses indicated by three consecutive dots). Tintin's sidekick Captain Haddock, by contrast, is clearly characterized by his use of colourful swearwords and – if we are to judge from his facial expressions in many panels, in which he seems to be shouting – loud, angry speech.

Figure 11.3 The main cast of *Tintin*.
Source: Moulinsart digital visual bank © Hergé/Moulinsart 2019.

4.4 The representation of accent

Another characteristic aspect of individual speakers' spoken language besides their voice is the type of accent that they use. According to George Bernard Shaw (1916: 5), 'it is impossible for an Englishman to open his mouth without making some other Englishman despise him', as hearers will automatically derive information about a speaker's regional, social and/or educational background from what they hear. While the use of a neutral stylistic level permits geographically relatively unspecified texts in the orthographic medium, any person speaking a language in phonetic code must necessarily use some kind of accent when producing text. Since accent is a very important criterion used in the determination of identity groups, the selection of accents for the protagonists in comic-to-film adaptations increases the identification of some groups of speakers with the heroes at the expense of others.

In view of Tintin's role as an identification figure (cf. above), one may assume that his accent in screen adaptations should ideally also be neutral – but this raises the question of which regional variety to choose: British or American English? An argument in favour of using a British English accent comes from the printed comic book, which employs the informal British English expression *quid* for a British Pound when referring to price of the ship model (*The Secret of the Unicorn*: 3). The British word *quid* is even used in the American comic book publication by Little Brown, despite the fact that American rather than British conventions are followed in the spelling (e.g. in the word *terrorized*; cf. *The Secret of the Unicorn*: 54). This is probably because Tintin lives on the European mainland in the original comic book series, so that the use of British English contributes to furthering the impression for an American audience that the *Tintin* adventures take place in a faraway Europe depicted as quaint. Furthermore, since the *Tintin* comic series was widely unknown in the United States, Spielberg's adaptation was released in Europe first, with the hope 'that favorable reviews would warm American audiences to the movie' (Internet Movie Database 2016). As a considerable proportion of European viewers are presumably taught at school to follow a British English model, yet another reason for choosing the British English accent may have been to increase European viewers' degree of identification with the main character.[14]

However, there are also good reasons to consider an American accent as a neutral equivalent for Tintin's original French: for instance, American English is the most commonly used accent in globally viewed films due to the Hollywood film industry. As a consequence, one might argue that an American English accent is the least marked accent in the filmic medium – and that may also be the reason why Bernasconi's animated series (1991–1992) gives Tintin an American accent and even changes the culturally marked currency term *quid* to *dollars*.

Captain Haddock, by contrast, has the same type of accent – a Scottish one – both in the film and the TV series. He also occasionally uses Scottish words – for example, *wee* in 'I lit a wee fire' in the film's lifeboat scene. Even for comic book readers who did not associate a specific kind of accent or dialect with Captain Haddock while reading the printed adventures, this decision is understandable. After all, Haddock's name is of English origin even in the French original (Wikipedia s.v. *Capitaine Haddock*), he is frequently associated with Scottish Loch Lomond Whiskey (Tintin Wiki s.v. *Loch Lomond*) and his 'hard drinking, foul mouthed' character 'with a propensity for violence [...] sounds just like an archaic Scottish stereotype' (Scotcampus). This reasoning is also supported by Andy Serkis, who plays Captain Haddock in the Spielberg film:

> We've decided to play Haddock with a Scot ... with a Scottish accent. ... It was ... seemed appropriate. You know, in the tests that we did, we sat round and talked about the character. That he should have, kind of, of the rawness and kind of emotional availability of a more Celtic kind of feel. (*The Who's Who of Tintin*)

While not Scottish himself (cf. Serkis 2016), Serkis manages to speak in the film with a Scottish accent that even satisfies Scottish film critics (cf. Scotcampus 2016).

4.5 The representation of thoughts and talking animals

Another language-related aspect to consider in the adaptation of comic books for the screen concerns two special instances of direct 'speech' usually printed in some type of bubble, namely thoughts and utterances by talking animals. These do not necessarily have a spoken equivalent in the filmic medium.

In the *Tintin* comic books under consideration, thoughts are not represented by the common means of thought bubbles, but the readers are still able to follow Tintin's thinking process, since he frequently talks to his dog Snowy about his plans, issues that puzzle him, and so on. It might be interesting to consider how other comic-to-film adaptations deal with the transfer of thought to the screen – with voice-over as a likely verbal option.

A feature of the *Tintin* comic books which works well in the orthographic medium but possibly less so in that of film is the occasional talking of the dog Snowy. For instance, when Snowy gets drunk, he utters: 'All right ... you ... you want a d-d-d-drink too?' (*Red Rackham's Treasure*: 19). However, only the readers can 'hear' him (Wikipedia s.v. *The Adventures of Tintin (TV series)*). While Tintin frequently reacts to Snowy, for example when Snowy helps him find the scroll under a chest of drawers (*The Secret of the Unicorn*: 11), this can be attributed to Snowy's barking and/or body language. The dog's verbal messages are actually ignored by his master. This becomes obvious when Snowy complains about an imminent submarine ride ('Weeds or no weeds, I don't set foot in that thing again!...'), but Tintin says: 'Fine. Get it ready. Snowy and I are setting out again immediately!', and in the next panel they can both be seen in the submarine (*Red Rackham's Treasure*: 33). Neither in the Spielberg film nor in the animated cartoon series does Snowy talk (cf. also Wikipedia s.v. *The Adventures of Tintin (TV series)*). This becomes most obvious when Tintin asks Snowy directly: 'How did you do that?' (i.e. get into the park) and Snowy only barks and shows Tintin a hole in the wall.

Spielberg explicitly comments on the representation of Snowy in the film (*The Who's Who of Tintin*), explaining that Snowy can express what he is thinking through his movements and does therefore not need to speak, whereas the comic book uses thought bubbles in order to overcome the limitations of its medium. The sounds made by Snowy do not come from a single real dog but are 'a mixture of probably twenty-five different dogs, some used in very small sections', for example 'just for a sniff', but 'for the most part, it's three or four key dogs' (*Snowy: From Beginning to End*). Justin Webster, the Snowy Vocals Editor, interprets Snowy's bark at the end of the film as the dog having the last word ('I was terrified that Snowy gets the last word in the film') and created five or six different versions of the bark in order to determine how much excitement to put into it, but still finds that 'it's bizarre to see so much in a bark' (*Snowy: From Beginning to End*).

4.6 The representation of sounds

Since comics 'do not have a soundtrack' (Lefèvre 2007: 11), they have to make use of *onomatopoeia* in order to represent sounds visually and verbally on paper.[15] The most obvious correspondence suggesting itself in a screen adaptation of onomatopoeia is to use the actual sounds and noises made by crashing objects, ringing doorbells and so on – and this is precisely what the Spielberg film does. Thus, the traditional onomatopoeic *BANG* in the shooting scene from the comic book (*The Secret of the Unicorn*: 31) is rendered with gun noise in the film. While it is a conceivable alternative to use printed onomatopoeia superimposed on the film or as hardware props, the small number of films making use of this effect presumably only do so in order to place particular emphasis on a specific sound or scene. Thus the *Batman* TV series from the 1960s (Dozier 1966–1968) uses onomatopoeia in this way when the protagonists fight, but still uses normal noises for other sounds. The reason for this is that even in an artificial comic-like world, the audience of a film is likely to expect some kind of background noise, for example of cars driving by.

For a computer-animated world like that in Spielberg's film, which was filmed in a studio with motion capture, this means that all sounds have to be inserted deliberately by the film makers. Comics, by contrast, are not forced to include any sounds except if these are important for the story. As a consequence, we find that many noises that one would expect in a real-life situation corresponding to the situation depicted in a comic book's drawings are not necessarily expressed explicitly by the use of onomatopoeia, but that they nonetheless need to be represented in a filmic adaptation. A good example is the kind of background noise that one would expect at a flea market, which is present in the film version, but not expressed verbally in the comic book. The readers of a comic book will presumably imagine prototypical background sounds to accompany the pictures, so that drinking pirates may be expected to laugh (cf. *The Secret of the Unicorn*: 22). Surprisingly, however, the *Tintin* comics only use onomatopoeia very sparingly even for sudden loud noises: thus the explosion and the firing of the cannons on pages 16 and 26 of *The Secret of the Unicorn* are not accompanied by any verbal sound markers, possibly because the accompanying sounds are so obvious. It seems that the majority of onomatopoeia in the comics under consideration represents sounds that are directly relevant to the action, such as ringing phones (which act as a summons to pick up the receiver) or off-panel noise that the characters react to or talk about (cf. *The Secret of the Unicorn*: 25, 40).

4.7 The use of written language on the screen

Let us now turn from the use of language superimposed on the image to the use of language in the image, that is, written text in the environment. Since film audiences are likely to consider a certain amount of written text in their own environment normal, there is no need to change the orthographic code of such text. However, comic-to-film adaptations need to take care of reducing the omnipresent writing on books, clocks, door-plates, shop windows and so on that are also found in the real world: thus, the comic aesthetics in Warren Beatty's (1990) live-action film *Dick Tracy* can be explained by a production design which is 'sparse and clean, devoid of realistic minutiae, to mimic the limitations of the comic strip, which cannot reproduce realistic details in a single panel' (Cohen 2007: 17). In the real world, writing is omnipresent (e.g. on wrappings or money), but comic-to-film adaptations may omit such written language in the environment where it is not necessary for understanding, or use generic labels in order to achieve the abstraction of props, for example, 'EXTRA' and 'Daily Paper' for the identification of newspapers, as in the film *Dick Tracy* (cf. Cohen 2007: 26). Since the whole environment in Spielberg's *Tintin* film was computer-generated, all writing in it must have been inserted deliberately – for example, the inscriptions on the bus, the signposts, the traffic signs and the newspaper articles on the wall of Tintin's flat. The font, colour, formatting and so on of the written texts plays an important role in conveying the authenticity of the writing. As a consequence, the text on the scroll with the location of the treasure in Figure 11.4 is handwritten.

Another important aspect to consider in this context is the language of the written text. While the *Tintin* adventures are set in a Francophone world, the film and the series were produced in English for a global audience, so that one of these languages had to be selected for orthographically represented text. While the translated English comic book uses English for the text of the scroll (cf. Figure 11.4), the two filmic adaptations of Hergé's *The Secret of the Unicorn* adventure differ in this respect: as Bernasconi's animated cartoon series uses French for 'all visuals (road signs, posters and settings)' (Wikipedia s.v. *The Adventures of Tintin (TV series)*), the non-English writing conveys an exotic flair for an educated English audience if they recognize some French words,

Figure 11.4 The scroll (*The Secret of the Unicorn*: 11) © Hergé/Moulinsart 2019.

such as the loan word *café*, or *boulangerie* ('baker's'). The Spielberg film's use of English, by contrast (even in inconspicuous shop signs like *butcher's*), makes it easier for an English-speaking audience to identify with the film's protagonists. Since the visuals are written in a language that is familiar to the audience, they understand everything, just like the protagonists of the film, and thereby experience the world shown in the film as more realistic than if the identification process were interrupted by non-understood foreign-language inscriptions that are understood by the film's protagonists.

When Tintin reads the text on the scroll in the Spielberg film, the audience can only read part of the text, since the remainder is outside the focus of his looking-glass or not shown in the scene. This marks an important difference between writing in comic-to-screen adaptations and printed comic books: while the audience of the comic books is usually able to read (because comic books are less commonly read to small children than picture books) and can thus be expected to manage reading not only the dialogues and narrative boxes but also the text in the environment, this is not necessarily the case of a film audience: since the Spielberg film was labelled suitable for viewers of six years and older, a certain proportion of the audience will presumably not have acquired sufficient reading skills yet to read such complex texts on their own, and at the required speed – a problem shared with visually challenged viewers. The restriction to writing in English also puts all non-English-speaking viewers of the dubbed film at a disadvantage.[16] As a consequence, all inscriptions whose understanding is absolutely necessary for the unfolding of the narrative are usually read out in some way or another. While the result in other films is sometimes slightly awkward and artificial, all relevant texts are verbalized very inconspicuously in Spielberg's film, since Tintin simply reads them aloud to his dog Snowy – not only in the case of the scroll but also when he deciphers the name on the model ship 'Unicorn' at the flea market.

Rendering all relevant orthographic code phonetically in films is crucial, because of an essential difference between the use of written language in comic books and in films: while the readers of a comic book read all text (including inscriptions) at their own pace and may reread it if they wish to do so, inscriptions in films are only shown for a certain amount of time (presumably that deemed necessary for the average audience to decipher the relevant text – whereas irrelevant inscriptions may simply swoosh by in the background). This makes the use of writing in films (and not just in comic-to-film adaptations) extremely unusual: while permanence is a defining characteristic of written compared to ephemeral oral language (cf. Biber 1988: 3), film audiences usually have no opportunity to turn back in order to reread texts.[17] As a consequence, texts in the filmic environment will presumably tend towards the orality end of the scale, with relatively short sentence length and reduced complexity. This is, however, less important when they are also read aloud, as in the Spielberg film, where the text on the scroll remains unmodified compared to the comic book original.

5 Conclusion

While it is tempting for film studies to consider comics as 'frozen film' (Berninger, Ecke and Haberkorn 2010: 1), comics actually represent a unique, hybrid medium that also overlaps with novels and graphic art. As '[f]ilms and comics are both media which tell stories by series of images: the spectator sees people act – while in a novel the actions must be verbally told', 'showing is already narrating in cinema and comics' (Lefèvre 2007: 2). Nonetheless, even though both types of media strongly rely on images, one should not overlook the important contribution of language to comics and films.

Comic-to-film adaptations are currently a thriving film genre. Interestingly, '[c]inema critics and comics fans seem to agree that it is hard to make a good movie of a comic', whereas '[t]he movie-going audience is less severe' (Lefèvre 2007: 1). This can, however, often be explained by the 'problem of primacy' (Lefèvre 2007: 2): 'usually people prefer the first version of a story they encounter', and '[a]ny filmic adaptation has to deal with these first personal interpretations and images', which are 'extremely hard to exorcise' – probably even more so for comics, which strongly shape the visual idea of a story by their drawings (compared to the purely verbal means made use of in novels). In comic-to-film adaptations, content is 'translated' not between languages but from one medium to another. Such a *transmedial translation* (cf. Mälzer 2015) from comic to film does not merely involve the consideration of language but of all content from the original that is inherent explicitly (i.e. verbally or in the drawings) or implicitly (e.g. in the so-called *gutter* between the panels; cf. McCloud 1993: 66). However, not all content is necessarily conserved, and modifications that are required by or salutary to the medium may be added.

We have seen earlier that all the forms of language that we find in printed comic books (cf. Sanchez-Stockhammer 2012: 58–9) have some correspondence in the filmic medium. For example, narrative boxes in comic books may be represented verbally by voice-over or insertions. At the same time, comics convey very nicely that language is always embedded into an extralinguistic context, as there is a strong interplay between the verbal and the visual semiotic systems within the panels. The adaptation to the filmic medium shows that a different visual semiotic system may also require changes in the verbal semiotic system – otherwise, we would expect more absolute coincidences between the text in the comic book original and the *Tintin* film by Steven Spielberg in parallel scenes: thus long quasi-monologues (e.g. the searching scene in the flat) are reduced intentionally, the actors insert fillers or repetitions spontaneously and possibly even unintentionally (as in the scene where Captain Haddock narrates the fight against the pirates), and relevant orthographically coded language in the environment is usually accompanied by an oral reading of the text (e.g. in the case of the text on the scroll of parchment). Language in comic-to-film adaptations is thus not only tied to the original context of occurrence in the printed comic book but furthermore filtered by the exigencies of the filmic medium.

6 Acknowledgement

I am very grateful to Moulinsart SA for granting me the permission to reproduce the three *Tintin* visuals contained in this article.

Notes

1 Compare Booker (2007: ix–xl) and Moscati (1988) for a historical account of comic-to-screen adaptations.
2 This strong interest in superheroes is sometimes linked to the post-09/11 situation (cf. Fick 2004: 35).
3 Since words are used in both comic books and films, Leitch's (2007: 194) term *lexicovisual* was replaced with the term *scriptovisual*, which emphasizes the use of writing in the printed medium.
4 Spielberg's film *The Adventures of Tintin* (which is analysed in this chapter) uses advanced digital technology to create such an effect of 'comic aesthetics' (Lefèvre 2007: 36) in order to transfer the atmosphere of the comic books into three moving dimensions. The success of this *Tintin* film adaptation compared to its predecessors (cf. Lefèvre 2007: 9) may be explained by the fact that it was shot completely in motion capture (with the exception of the CGI-animated Snowy; cf. *The Journey to Tintin*), thereby achieving a compromise between a realistic depiction and a stylized caricature echoing Hergé's *ligne claire* style.
5 Even in these exceptional cases, text sequences may occasionally be inserted in order to permit more complex narratives. For instance, Michel Hazanavicious' 2011 modern silent film *The Artist* displays utterances such as 'Don't laugh, George! That's the future' in white print on a black background.
6 Not only comic book dialogues are limited to the orthographic medium. This is also true of film screenplays, but since these are read out in the production of the film at a later stage, the final film dialogues are situated in the phonetic medium.
7 Less commonly, words and pictures may deliberately 'follow very different courses' in parallel combinations (McCloud 1993: 154).
8 Alternatively, longer orthographic insertions comprising one or more sentences may occur at the end of a film, when the audience is informed about future developments in the protagonists' lives (e.g. in Robert Luketic's 2001 *Legally Blonde*, where a marriage proposal is announced for the heroine with the words: 'Emmett is proposing to Elle tonight.').
9 Compare the scene in Roger Michell's 1999 film *Notting Hill*, in which the protagonist walks along the same street market while the weather and the seasons are changing around him and a pregnant woman in the beginning of the sequence is shown with her baby at the end.
10 The speech balloons and the action depicted in the drawings are usually arranged in a conventional way on the page so as to simplify the reading process: Western models traditionally rely on 'the horizontal order of appearance, as a primary order' (cf. Briel 2010: 189), but this type of arrangement is reversed in mangas (cf. Briel 2010: 189; Kukkonen and Haberkorn 2010: 240). The so-called *saccadic lines*, that is the eyes' *'preferred lines of movement across a picture'*, are, however, *'not nearly as strictly imposed upon the eye as the reading order of written text'* (Berninger, Ecke and Haberkorn 2010: 1).
11 This is not the only screen adaptation of the *Tintin* comic book series: the first adaptation of *The Crab with the Golden Claws* was a 1947 stop-motion film shown only once, which was soon followed by various other adaptations (Brewmasters 2011).
12 Interestingly, only Haddock's abuse of alcohol is discussed in the interviews in the DVD's special features section as a rather unusual topic for children's entertainment,

whereas the fact that a decision was taken regarding his use of swearwords is not communicated anywhere. This is particularly surprising in view of the important role that swearwords play in Haddock's language in the comic book series. There are many opportunities in the film where Haddock would most certainly have used swearwords if the scene had occurred in the comic book. Only very occasionally does he utter his characteristic 'Billions of blue blistering barnacles!'.

13 McCloud (1993: 25) exposes this understood convention in the discussion of Magritte's painting *The Treachery of Images*, when the narrating cartoon character suddenly addresses the reader directly with the question: 'Do you hear what I'm saying?' and then proceeds to state that 'if you **do**, have your **ears** checked, because no one said a word'.

14 Note, however, that Tintin's exclamation 'Me? I haven't ordered anything' from the comic book version of *The Secret of the Unicorn* (35) is Americanized and becomes 'But I didn't order anything' in the Spielberg film. Compare Swan (2005: 39, 444) for the differing use of present perfect and simple past in the two varieties of English.

15 However, these can only be approximations. For instance, it is not possible to determine whether the *RRRING* or the *RRRRING* (*The Secret of the Unicorn*: 7) refer to the phone or the doorbell, respectively. Nonetheless, one may advance that even the sound of a real phone and a real doorbell may be confused out of context.

16 While it might be conceivable to have English inscriptions and to automatically modify them in the non-English versions of the film, the German version of *Tintin* features the scroll in English.

17 The growing importance of films viewed on DVD, Blu-ray or by streaming may possibly change this in the future, if the personalized viewing situation (which permits the freezing or reviewing of scenes with orthographic code in the film) should come to be regarded as the prototypical and intended way of viewing films instead of the traditional cinema experience.

References

Bartlett, M. (2012), '"The adventures of Tintin": Drawn into motion', *Screen Education*, 65: 8–17.
Bednarek, M. (2010), *The Language of Fictional Television: Drama and Identity*, London: Continuum.
Berninger, M., Ecke, J. and Haberkorn, G. (2010), 'Introduction', in M. Berninger, J. Ecke and G. Haberkorn (eds), *Comics as a Nexus of Cultures*, 1–4, Jefferson: McFarland.
Biber, D. (1988), *Variation across Speech and Writing*, Cambridge: Cambridge University Press.
Booker, K. M. (2007), *'May Contain Graphic Material': Comic Books, Graphic Novels, and Film*, Westport: Praeger.
Briel, H. (2010), 'The roving eye meets traveling pictures: The field of vision and the global rise of adult manga', in M. Berninger, J. Ecke and G. Haberkorn (eds), *Comics as a Nexus of Cultures*, 187–210, Jefferson: McFarland.
Cohen, M. (2007), 'Dick Tracy: In pursuit of a comic book aesthetic', in I. Gordon, M. Jancovich and M. P. McAllister (eds), *Film and Comic Books*, 13–36, Jackson: University Press of Mississippi.
Ecke, J. (2010), 'Spatializing the movie screen: How mainstream cinema is catching up on the formal potentialities of the comic book page', in M. Berninger, J. Ecke and G. Haberkorn (eds), *Comics as a Nexus of Cultures*, 7–20, Jefferson: McFarland.

Fick, T. (2004), 'Vom starren Panel zum bewegten Bild': Comicverfilmung am Beispiel von 'From Hell', Master's thesis, University of Erlangen-Nuremberg.

Gordon, I., Jancovich, M. and McAllister, M. P., eds (2007), *Film and Comic Books*, Jackson: University Press of Mississippi.

Kukkonen, K. and Haberkorn, G. (2010), 'Workshop I: Towards a toolbox of comic studies', in M. Berninger, J. Ecke and G. Haberkorn (eds), *Comics as a Nexus of Cultures*, 237–44, Jefferson: McFarland.

Lefèvre, P. (2007), 'Incompatible visual ontologies? The problematic adaptation of drawn images', in I. Gordon, M. Jancovich and M. P. McAllister (eds), *Film and Comic Books*, 1–12, Jackson: University Press of Mississippi.

Leitch, T. M. (2007), *Film Adaptation and Its Discontents: From Gone with the Wind to The Passion of the Christ*, Baltimore: Johns Hopkins University Press.

Mälzer, N., ed. (2015), *Comics: Übersetzungen und Adaptionen*, Berlin: Frank and Timme.

McCloud, S. (1993), *Understanding Comics: The Invisible Art*, New York: HarperCollins.

Moscati, M. (1988), *Comics und Film*, trans. A. Drexel and G. Seeßlen, Frankfurt am Main: Ullstein.

Ofenloch, S. (2007), *Mit der Kamera gezeichnet: Zur Ästhetik realer Comicverfilmungen*, Saarbrücken: VDM Verlag.

Peeters, B. (1990), *Tintin y el mundo de Hergé*, Barcelona: Editorial Juventud.

Quaglio, P. (2008), 'Television dialogue and natural conversation', in A. Ädel and R. Reppen (eds), *Corpora and Discourse*, 189–210, Amsterdam: Benjamins.

Rauscher, A. (2010), 'Workshop IV: Teaching comics and film studies: Ang Lee's The Hulk (USA 2003)', in M. Berninger, J. Ecke and G. Haberkorn (eds), *Comics as a Nexus of Cultures*, 265–73, Jefferson: McFarland.

Sanchez-Stockhammer, C. (2012), 'Comicsprache – leichte Sprache?', in D. Pietrini (ed.), *Die Sprache(n) der Comics*, 55–74, Munich: Meidenbauer.

Sanchez-Stockhammer, C. (2016), 'Punctuation as an indication of register', in C. Schubert and C. Sanchez-Stockhammer (eds), *Variational Text Linguistics: Revisiting Register in English*, 139–67, Berlin: de Gruyter.

Saussure, F. de (1916/1959), *Course in General Linguistics*, trans. W. Baskin, New York: Philosophical Library.

Shaw, G. B. (1916), *Pygmalion*, London: Penguin.

Söll, L. (1974), *Gesprochenes und geschriebenes Französisch*, Berlin: Erich Schmidt.

Swan, M. (2005), *Practical English Usage*, 3rd edn, Oxford: Oxford University Press.

Toolan, M. (2011), '"I don't know what they're saying half the time, but I'm hooked on the series." Incomprehensible dialogue and integrated multimodal characterisation in *The Wire*', in R. Piazza, M. Bednarek and F. Rossi (eds), *Telecinematic Discourse: Approaches to the Language of Films and Television Series*, 161–83, Amsterdam: John Benjamins.

Internet sources

Brewmasters (2011), *Every Tintin Adaptation–And How Spielberg Stacks Up* [online]. Available at: http://www.cartoonbrew.com/comics/every-tintin-adaptation%E2%80%94and-how-spielberg-matches-up-54565.html (accessed 19 December 2016).

Internet Movie Database (2016), *Die Abenteuer von Tim und Struppi: Das Geheimnis der Einhorn. Trivia* [online]. Available at: http://www.imdb.com/title/tt0983193/trivia (accessed 19 December 2016).

Scotcampus (2016), *Film: Seriously, Is He Supposed to Be Scottish?* [online]. Available at: http://www.scotcampus.com/film-seriously-is-he-supposed-to-be-scottish (accessed 19 December 2016).

Serkis, A. (2016), *Biography* [online]. Available at: http://www.serkis.com/andy-serkis-biography.htm (accessed 19 December 2016).

Tintin Wiki (2016), *Loch Lomond* [online]. Available at: http://tintin.wikia.com/wiki/Loch_Lomond (accessed 19 December 2016).

Wikipedia (2016a), *The Adventures of Tintin* (TV Series) [online]. Available at: https://en.wikipedia.org/wiki/The_Adventures_of_Tintin_%28TV_series%29 (accessed 19 December 2016).

Wikipedia (2016b), *Capitaine Haddock* [online]. Available at: https://fr.wikipedia.org/wiki/Capitaine_Haddock (accessed 19 December 2016).

Comics

Berlitz (2007a), *Englisch lernen mit Batman: Bad Guys Gallery*, Munich: Berlitz.
Berlitz (2007b), *Englisch lernen mit Superman: Up, Up and Away!*, Munich: Berlitz.
Hergé (1974a/1946), *The Secret of the Unicorn*, trans. L. Lonsdale-Cooper and M. Turner, New York: Little, Brown and Company.
Hergé (1974b/1945), *Red Rackham's Treasure*, trans. L. Lonsdale-Cooper and M. Turner, New York: Little, Brown and Company.
Hergé (1974c/1953), *The Crab with the Golden Claws*, trans. L. Lonsdale-Cooper and M. Turner, New York: Little, Brown and Company.
Trondheim, L. (1995), *La mouche*, Paris: Seuil.
Walt Disney Company (2008), *Walt Disney's Uncle $crooge 376*, York: Gemstone.
Watterson, B. (1987), *Calvin and Hobbes*, London: Sphere Books.

Films

Beatty, W. (1990), *Dick Tracy*, Touchstone Pictures, Silver Screen Partners, and Mulholland Productions.
Bernasconi, S. (1991–1992), *The Adventures of Tintin*, Ellipse Programmé and Nelvana Limited.
Branagh, K. (2011), *Thor*, Marvel Studios.
Dozier, W. (1966–1968), *Batman*, TV Series, Greenway Productions and 20th Century Fox Television.
Hazanavicious, M. (2011), *The Artist*, La Petite Reine et al.
Luketic, R. (2001), *Legally Blonde*, Type A Films and Marc Platt Productions.
Michell, R. (1999), *Notting Hill*, PolyGram and Working Title.
Nolan, C. (2008), *The Dark Knight*, Warner Bros.
Snowy: From Beginning to End (2011), Special feature of *The Adventures of Tintin*. Directed by S. Spielberg, Columbia Pictures and Paramount Pictures. DVD by Sony Pictures Home Entertainment.
Spielberg, S. (2011), *The Adventures of Tintin*, Columbia Pictures and Paramount Pictures.
The Journey to Tintin (2011), Special feature of *The Adventures of Tintin*. Directed by S. Spielberg, Columbia Pictures and Paramount Pictures. DVD by Sony Pictures Home Entertainment.

The Who's Who of Tintin (2011), Special feature of *The Adventures of Tintin*. Directed by S. Spielberg, Columbia Pictures and Paramount Pictures. DVD by Sony Pictures Home Entertainment.

The World of Tintin (2011), Special feature of *The Adventures of Tintin*. Directed by S. Spielberg, Columbia Pictures and Paramount Pictures. DVD by Sony Pictures Home Entertainment.

12

'Subtitles have to become my ears not my eyes'

Pragmatic-stylistic choices behind Closed Captions for the deaf and hard of hearing: the example of *Breaking Bad*

Annie Dahne and Roberta Piazza

1 Introduction

Creating subtitles for deaf people or Closed Captions (henceforth CC) involves making active decisions on how best to represent a television programme's sound to give equal access to a deaf and hard of hearing audience.[1] Given the size of the deaf population in the UK (11 million according to a 2015 *Hearing Matters* report), a big responsibility is laid on subtitle producers. Although in the past the focus was on the quantity of subtitles available, there is now a growing demand for better quality. This study explores both the process and effects of creating 'good quality' subtitles.

People can be variously defined deaf depending on the audiological degree of their deafness (mild, moderate, severe or profound), the age of deafness onset (whether pre- or post-lingual, post-puberty or old age) and whether they can lip-read. It is extremely difficult to establish communalities among deaf people as everyone's deafness is shaped differently. Some deaf people see themselves as users of a minority language (the British/Irish/American etc. Sign Language) rather than individuals unable to hear, hence disabled; however, the legislation still refers to them by this term. As a result of the increasing demands for equality, new laws and regulations within the media are constantly being implemented (Ellcessor 2012: 335). For example, on 16 March 2015, the Federal Communication Commission (FCC) regulating media in the United States implemented the Closed Caption Quality Report and Order. The FCC Order includes guidelines of what they consider to be 'accurate' CC: among other instructions, CC must 'not rewrite dialogue' (FCC 2014: 22) but must make any sound in the programme beyond the dialogue audible. How this can be achieved is not clarified and this is one of the concerns of the present study.

The 2015 law also acknowledges the consequences for a deaf audience if close captions are not accurate. It states that paraphrasing should be avoided because omitted dialogue will result in a loss of the programme's 'impact' and 'nuances' (FCC 2014: 22). Furthermore, CC should 'replicate the hearing listener's aural experience' and 'be functionally equivalent' to that (FCC 2014: 22). Although it is not clear what is meant by the adverb 'functionally' or the nouns 'impact' and 'nuances', this study understands CC to be expected to assist the programme's moving images in creating characters and a narrative the audience can comprehend. This study therefore investigates the plausible reasons behind the choices made by captioners and the degree to which they impact the narrative and the character formation in it. The study is framed within translation studies, as outlined in the background section. In the analysis of the television drama *Breaking Bad*, a degree of triangulation is present in that, besides the data analysis, the project relies on: (1) an interview with a professional captioner who provides insight on established practice and (2) a conversation with a deaf university tutor of British Sign language who was asked to comment on the authors' interpretation. In general, the study hypothesized a difference between the two texts, the original and the CC for deaf and hard of hearing people, responsible for a different character impression formation between the two audiences. The findings show that in general captioners overcome the challenge of deciding how best to represent the form of audio into CC text by considering the relevance of the sound in its context.

2 Background of the study

The process of creating CC can be viewed as a type of 'audiovisual translation' (Neves 2005) in which the visual image and audio portion of a programme are the 'source text', or the text to translate, while the 'target text' or the resulting text, is the same audiovisual text with the addition of the CC. CC are also a mediation between 'intralingual' translation, if the language used in the source text is the same as the target text, and 'interlingual' translation (Wurm 2007), if one considers the audio as one code to be translated in to the writing code with the images having an impact on the choices of the final script.

Within translation studies, scholars still debate whether priority should be given to the form or content/function of the source text (Munday 2012: 30). Such a concern that started with the translation of Greek and Latin classical authors addressed the question of whether writers should opt for either 'word-for-word' or 'sense-for-sense' translations (Munday 2012: 30). In their audience reception survey, Szarkowska, Krejtz and Wieczorek (2011: 365) found that some deaf audiences wanted to know every single word because they viewed anything other than this as censorship. This desire for textual equivalence resonates with the demands that have led to the new FCC law in the United States. Other researchers such as Neves (2008: 136) and our deaf interviewee, as will be discussed, champion the use of edited captions and argue that the function of CC to be readable and enjoyable should triumph over prioritizing a verbatim text. Conversely, Bassnett (2014: 87) and Munday (2012: 274) advocate abandoning this old debate in favour of a more flexible and pragmatic way of understanding translation. Gutt (1989), whose study is referred to later, similarly argues a translation is not successful according to specific criteria of faithfulness but according to 'the causal interaction between stimulus, context and interpretation' (p. 2). The issue of translatability and textual accuracy in translation is relevant to the topic of CC. However, as a translation product close captioning is unique as it is multimodal in nature, being aided in its form by accompanying visuals. CC must also fit within a specified amount of characters and be presented at a certain speed within the spatio-temporal constraints that are absent in traditional translation cases. In light of this, this study will not discuss whether CC text can or should represent either the form *or* the function of programme audio, but will instead explore both of these aspects together.

Research within the field of CC mainly focuses on the eye-tracking measure of the deaf and hard of hearing, emphasizing the role of stylistic features on comprehension and making recommendation for the optimum amount of characters of text per caption line (Szarkowska, Krejtz and Wieczorek 2011; De Linde and Kay 1999: 12). However, whereas most of these studies focus on deaf audience reception in terms of readability, there is a large research gap in exploring the possible implications of meaning in CC text. The few studies that do attempt this lack a holistic approach. Observing CC in a number of Hollywood films and television series, Zdenek (2011), for example, considers close captioning as a 'rhetorical and interpretative practice' that 'recasts quality in terms of how genre, audience, context, and purpose shape the captioning act' (p. 74) and discusses instances where the form of CC may have brought confusion to a deaf audience. Similarly, McIntyre and Lugea (2015) posit the impact of dialogue omission within CC in the opening scenes of *The Wire*. These studies try to understand the general issue of CC, yet they do not consider the impact of CC on character impression throughout the space of an entire series. Furthermore, both of them concentrate on the effects of omitted dialogue, but not on other aspects of programme audio such as the representation of simultaneous speech or various sound effects. The present study fills this research gap by looking at a variety of elements that may impact reception of deaf audiences. The study refers to two cognitive models: Gutt's (2000) 'translation as an act of communication' determined by an intention to inform from the perspective of Relevance Theory (RT) (Sperber and Wilson 1986), and Culpeper's (2001: 35) 'comprehending character' that stresses the role of prior knowledge in the understanding of a character and the function of textual cues that trigger the particular idea audiences develop of a character. The following section offers a brief summary of the theoretical framework informing our study.

3 The study's cognitive approach

Communication relies on human ability to 'draw inferences from people's behaviour' (Gutt 2000: 23, whose study is informed by RT, Sperber and Wilson 1986). A 'communicator' is expected to be optimally *relevant* by producing a stimulus from which the 'receiver' may understand their intended message with *minimal effort*. The receiver assumes all transmitted information holds some relevance to the context and will infer it if it doesn't immediately show that relevance. Therefore, any necessary processing effort will be weighed against the cognitive reward of understanding the communicator's intentions; in other words, more accurate and context-relevant the

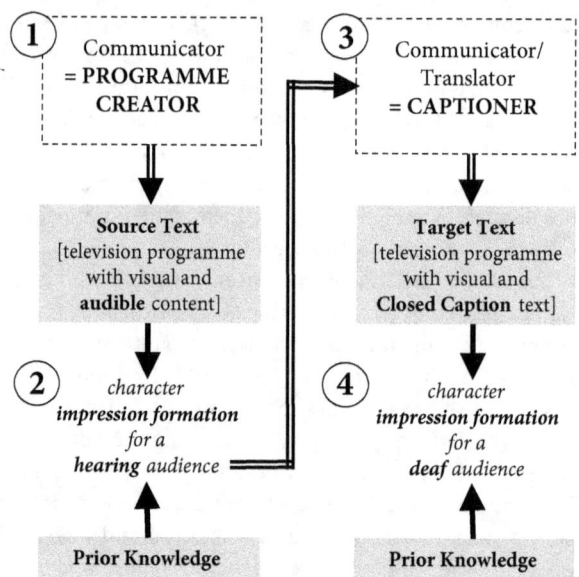

Figure 12.1 A relevance model of character impression formation for both hearing and deaf audiences.

message is, the less cognitive effort is needed by the receiver of that message and vice versa. The model (Figure 12.1) named Closed Caption Relevance Model (CCRM) depicts a four-stage successive process whereby a deaf audience may gain meaning from a television programme with Closed Captions. This model is inspired both by Gutt (2000) and Culpeper (2001: 35).

Stage 1 of the CCRM reflects Culpeper's (2001) model of characterization, which is based around the cognitive process, based on prior knowledge, which readers/viewers follow when forming an overall idea of a character. Partly borrowed from social psychology, the concept of impression formation refers to how we adapt the process by which we 'form impressions of people in the real world' to fictional characters (Culpeper 2001: 2). It is a two-way cognitive process: prior associations determine the inferences about a character's appearance and behaviour, and are combined with character's features and 'textual cues' (Culpeper 2001: 163) which he divides into explicit, implicit and authorial. Borrowing from Relevance-theoretical terminology, the producers of texts (in this context the programme creators) are viewed as the 'communicators' and the audience as the 'receivers'. Within Culpeper's (2001) two-way impression formation model, audiences will assume that all character traits or cues are relevant because the appearance and behaviour of fictional characters are purposefully created by a communicator/producer. If character cues confirm initial impressions, they are processed with relative ease by the viewer who would operate understanding along a pre-existing 'schema' or model of comprehension. Contrariwise, cues that disrupt expectations take more effort to process and require the construction of a new 'schema' that replaces the previous one the viewer automatically activated at the beginning of the impression formation or character comprehension. Following Gutt's (2000) RT-informed translation model, Stage 2 highlights the fact that captioners are simultaneously receivers situated within the hearing audience demographic, and communicators. As translators, captioners make choices that communicate the impression they inferred from the original characterization cues in the audible content of the programme. They are understood to have the responsibility of creating a target text that is optimally relevant and easy to process, which allows the audience to interpret the intended message of the source audio with the least cognitive effort.

This study gives equal consideration to the sound properties and the dialogue in the television programme studied. Instead of looking at a selection of unrelated scenes as in previous studies, it analyses a combination of impressions that follows one character's narrative development. Following Bassnett (2014: 87), the present study does not discuss whether formal *or* functional equivalence should be achieved. As will be explained in the analysis section, Gutt's (2000: 100–22) model goes beyond this debate and interprets translation as communication; by so doing, it recognizes to both the translator and the viewer the ability to understand that the information being conveyed needs to be relevant to make the communication accessible.

4 *Breaking Bad*

A short summary of the Netflix series may be useful at this point. '*Breaking Bad* tells the story of Walter White, a high school chemistry teacher, trying to make ends meet in post-Recession suburban Albuquerque' (Ledwon 2017: 400). Walt has two conflicting identities: the chemistry teacher and the clandestine drug dealer Heisenberg. In the series' first episode Walt is diagnosed with inoperable lung cancer. Soon after he partners up with his former chemistry student Jesse, Walt is impressed by the huge amount of easy money he can make in illegal methamphetamine production and, in consideration of his medical condition, plans to use it to pay for his treatment and to secure financial security for his pregnant wife and son, after his death. He then turns into a drug dealer and meth manufacturer, with his former student Jess. He will contribute the knowledge to produce the drug while Jess will deal with its distribution. As a result, the 'family man' character identity is born. 'Subsequently, the series traces Walt's transformation from Walter White, mild-mannered teacher, to Heisenberg, ruthless drug lord. Walt transforms by taking on a selfish, hyperaggressive form of masculinity' (Lodwon, 2017: 401). When Walt continues to manufacture drugs for money though, his honourable motivations are thrown into question. While Walt's 'Heisenberg' identity is developed, he descends into a criminal underworld, as the tension between the character's two identities gradually unfolds. According to Poe (2015: 10), Walt's Heisenberg identity is an act of resistance to an oppressive society and his wife's authoritative figure from whom he hides his Heisenberg identity. Presenting himself as a 'family man' and his actions as unavoidable 'sacrifices' for the family ('everything I do, I do for the family' Pettis 2015: 166), Walt insists on his identity even when his wife Skyler discovers the truth. However, in the final episode, Walt admits to her: 'I did it for me … I was good at it, I was alive.' Thus, he realizes that the 'family man' identity has been a disguise all along, and allows his Heisenberg identity to be exposed, both to himself and to Skyler.

5 The study's methodological approach

The CC text and corresponding audiovisual programme were the principal data for the present study. They were taken from pre-recorded television programming where the CC text has had the opportunity to be proofed and edited. This is opposed to live captioning where there is more opportunity for human error, which is beyond the remit of this study. As one of this study's aims is to examine how captioners are meeting US FCC guidelines, the data were obtained from the online American platform *Netflix*.

In order to identify elements that could lead to different 'character impression formations' (Culpeper, 2001) for hearing and deaf audiences, this study chose a fictional television series containing a changing character and a complex narrative. According to Culpeper (2001), readers/viewers develop and impression of a character based on their previous knowledge (top-down process) and the cues contained in the text (bottom-up process). The protagonist Walter White (henceforth Walt) from the five-season-drama *Breaking Bad* was of particular interest to this study. At the time of the study, *Breaking Bad* was a very popular and frequently streamed programme on *Netflix*, and in response to the public engagement with the show through social media, the creators went as far as allowing the audience to have a say in the development of the narrative (Blevins 2015: 1). We identified ten scenes[2] selected from the series as vital to an understanding of the character Walt in that they first introduce him in his context as a man who receives a dramatic diagnosis, which probably confirms viewers' schema about a married man who worries about himself and his family, and then systematically present his development to a problematic central character that contradicts viewers' expectations. It is important to bear in mind that the aim of the chapter is to highlight the difficulties of CC production and the responsibilities of captioners, rather than producing a comprehensive discussion of the whole series. On this basis, we believe that the selection of scenes from *Breaking Bad* suffices to illustrate the problem inherent to CC.

With the aim of exploring captioners' choices and establishing whether some elements in the CC could encourage a different character impression formation for the hearing and deaf audiences, a comparative analysis of programme's audio track and the CC text of the ten scenes of *Breaking Bad* was carried out using the proposed CCRM. Three different sets of data from *Breaking Bad* were collected: (1) ten fully transcribed scenes of the audio programme; (2) the fully transcribed Closed Caption text; (3) the visual level. With regard to the visuals where relevant to the discussion, film grabs that accompany the audio/CC texts were included.

To answer the question of how captioners decide to represent sound into the CC, isolated aspects of audio and corresponding CC text are analysed. Besides insight from audiovisual translation studies (Neves 2005), the analysis is informed by Conversation Analysis (CA). Input from CA is crucial to the analysis as the practice of producing captions can be thought of as a process of *transcribing* conversations if it includes pauses, false starts, breath intake and any suprasegmental features. The plausible interpretations of the texts were discussed in an interview with professional captioner Sally Nevrkla. Another interview was carried out with John Walker, teaching fellow at the University of Sussex and convenor of British Sign Language and Deaf culture programmes (also a regular user of subtitles) with the help of his interpreter Marco Nardi. The purpose of the two interviews was to ascertain the following questions:

a) What responsibility do captioners feel they have vis-à-vis a deaf audience?
b) What skills and training are needed to carry out the task of creating CC?
c) According to what parameters is the final CC product considered successful?
d) How are the captioners' choices perceived by a deaf user?

We are aware of course that two isolated conversations, albeit with key individuals, cannot substitute for a thorough investigation of what is behind the production of CC in one case or for a full-fledged test of the CC receptions in the other. Despite this caveat, we wish to propose a workable and reliable methodology for future studies.

The second question concerning whether CC allows for the same character impressions as the original text is tackled primarily through an implementation of Culpeper's (2001) model of characterization. The discussion identifies aspects of the audio text deemed highly relevant to the character of Walt and his dichotomous identity that, it is claimed, are not realized in the same fashion in the CC text.

6 Discussing the data from *Breaking Bad*

The discussion concentrates on three distinct components of the programme's audio track: the first section examines non-verbal sounds in Scenes 1–4; the next explores how the interactional dynamics of interlocutors are represented in Scenes 5–7, while the last section examines representations of the characters' emotional stance or attitude in Scenes 8–10.

6.1 Non-verbal sounds

A fundamental property of CC is its representation of written information in a programme in which that information is otherwise only originally obtained through sound. This section investigates representation of the audible non-verbal vocalizations made by people, as well as the sound effects both within the world of the characters and edited on top of the footage.

i. Non-verbal vocalizations

The FCC Order suggests that accurate captions should display characters' audible noises although these cannot be described as words:

> Although we recognize that utterances such as 'um' … may not be as critical to a program's content, accuracy also requires that these be captioned if needed for the viewer to understand the program. (FCC 2014: 22)

The significance of non-verbal vocalizations is recognized by CA, and Powers (2005: 50) in particular advises transcribers to include all hesitation signals in CC. Thus, in line 1 of Scene 3 (see Appendix for the transcription of the dialogue in 3A and the CC in 3B) the captioner decides to keep the noises 'hmm' and 'um' (Walt: Hmm um what. what about the: side effects?), albeit in a slightly altered form from the original (Walt: Hmm. Um, w-what about the side effects?[3]) as they are significant in signalling the character feeling uncomfortable about the question. Although such linguists as Ten Have (2007: 99) note that vocal sounds such as audible exhalations and inhalations carry importance for 'interactional meaning', not all these vocalizations are captioned. In Scene 4A, for example, Walt's exhalation '.Hh!', which could be otherwise described as a 'gasp', was not kept in the CC, perhaps as the audience could deduce the character's surprise from his expression on screen.

Furthermore, there may be an additional challenge of deciding how to transcribe non-verbal vocalizations. The exhalations and inhalations in Scene 4A, although similar in their formal properties, have been interpreted variously as shown in Table 12.1 instead of being transcribed in the CC. Such a choice that focuses on the purpose and function of a speaker's sound may encourage a particular character's impression.

Nevrkla confirms the interpretation of the earlier hesitations and explains that when captioners face particularly unusual human sounds, the method is to 'put yourself in the mind-set of the producer'. If a captioner supposes a sound was used to 'scare' the audience, s/he will aim to be equally 'terrifying'. In line 23 of Scene 2A, the sequence 'eh uh eh uh you' was particularly difficult to transcribe, and is translated as '[GRUNTING]' in line 26 of Scene 2B (see Appendix). Therefore, it is plausible to hypothesize that before transferring a sound to the CC, captioners consider its relevance within the interactional context and in relation to the character to whom the sounds belong. Rather than engaging with issues of faithfulness to the original text, therefore, captioners aim to convey to the deaf viewers a message about the character that is consistent with the context and hence relevant to make their process of character formation as easy as possible. Yet, the earlier translations of exhalation and inhalation suggest that captioners interpret the character of Walt rather than leaving that to the viewers. John Walker, with whom a sample of the data was discussed, confirmed the usefulness of reproducing hesitation markers in Scene 3A; in spite of this, he insists on the role of visuals in making the verbal message explicit to the right degree. For him therefore 'grunting' in Scene 2B as an interpretation of 'eh uh eh uh you' is acceptable only in the case in which a deaf audience cannot surmise the character's disposition from the visual level of his facial expression.

Table 12.1 Exhalations and Inhalations in Scene 4

Scene 4	CA transcription	Corresponding CC text
Line 48	Hh	[SIGHS]
Line 50	.hh hh .hh	[SOBBING]
Line 52	.hh hh .hh hh .hh	BREATHING HEAVILY
Line 53	.hh hh	[LAUGHS]

ii. Diegetic sounds

Sounds accompanying the narrative or diegetic, both internal (i.e. intra-diegetic) or external (i.e. extra-diegetic) to the story development are only occasionally captioned. In line 1 of Scene 2B the CC text the notation '[EASY-LISTENING MUSIC PLAYING]' may have been inserted by captioners to 'set the scene' of the calm before the storm of Walt's rage. On the other hand, in Scene 3A line 17 the intradiegetic 'phone ringing' sound in the doctor's office, while Walt receives the diagnosis and the list of possible forthcoming symptoms, was not included in the corresponding CC: (Doctor: You may lose weight due to reduced appetite and certain intestinal issues ((Phone ringing)) Doctor: Muscle aches and pains (.) Gums will get sore and bleed). It is of course difficult to establish the impact this decision may have on the viewers' perception of Walt; however, we want to draw the readers' attention to the choice captioners make in the name of relevance. As 'phone ringing' was judged 'uninformative' and hence 'irrelevant' (Sperber and Wilson 1986) it was omitted in CC.

According to Zdenek (2011: 81), diegetic sounds can be unnecessarily translated into CC text, a process he terms 'over-captioning'. For example, the television audio in Scene 4 functions only as background noise, but has been represented as full dialogue in the CC text. Zdenek (2011) would possibly view this as an unsuccessful translation as the television sound now becomes as meaningful as the character lines, thus causing distraction and confusion for the deaf viewers that hearing audiences do not experience. Walker confirmed this view and praised the captioners in Scene 2B for not reproducing verbally one character tapping his fingers on the table. He believes that if sounds can be understood from the visuals, words are useless and exaggerated because 'subtitles –he says – have to become my ears not my eyes'. As deaf viewers can see the tapping, it is therefore 'irrelevant' to include that information about that sound in the narrative (intradiegetic) in the CC.

iii. Extra-diegetic sounds

The programme's audio track of Scenes 1–4 contains an identical high-pitched ringing sound effect demonstrating that Walt is blocking out all noise and choosing not to hear what is being said to him. Speech is distorted or 'reverbed'[4] but not completely unintelligible, and this effect is represented in transcripts of Scenes 1A–4A. Knowledge of the sound effect is equally relevant in explaining Walt's actions and reactions across all four scenes, although the form differs in CC, as shown in Table 12.2.

The high-pitched ringing sound effect associates the four scenes described earlier as instances where Walt refuses to be engaged with those around him. When the audience encounters this behaviour on the part of Walt, they will plausibly assume it holds relevance as a characterization cue (Culpeper 2001). On the contrary, if the extra-diegetic sounds are not included in the CC, only a hearing audience will be able to make the link between these scenes as an emergence of the 'Heisenberg' identity in Walt who from mild-mannered family man has transformed into an unruly clandestine figure despising authority and law. This crucially includes Walt's wife, Skyler, whom he ignores. Walt's resistance could be interpreted as a consequence of his newly found medical condition (his terminal cancer), which he has not shared with Skyler; however,

Table 12.2 Properties of the High-Pitched Sound Effect in Scenes 1–4

	Scene 1: Cancer diagnosis	Scene 2: Quitting job	Scene 3: Chemotherapy side effects	Scene 4: Skyler trying to get Walt's attention
Sound effect acknowledged	No	Yes: [high-pitched buzzing]	No	No
Signal of reverbed dialogue	[MUFFLED SPEECH]	[DISTORTED]	[FADING]	No
Authority that Walt is ignoring	Doctor	Employer	Doctor	Wife

it can also hint at an emerging crisis in his 'family man' identity if we consider that Walt is resisting his wife in the same way as he resisting his doctors and his boss. Without the inclusion of these extra-diegetic sounds therefore deaf audiences may be missing out on this subtle but crucial component of Walt's character that includes a shift from a 'family man' to his alias 'Heisenberg'. Their character impression may therefore be different.

6.2 Conversation structure

The representation of speech and dialogue is just as important to CC as that of sound effects. To this end, this section explores how captioners represent what is being said, as well as who is speaking and when.

6.2.1 *Identifying the speaker*

The FCC Order states that CC text should mark each speaker through either 'caption identification or caption placement' (FCC 2014: 23). Generally, in CC (as well as in picture stories or comics) placing a line next to a character generally suffices to associate the dialogue with the person producing it. This however is not always the case. In Scene 5, first frame (12.3) for instance identification is needed for Walt's utterance as it cannot be lip-read (lip-reading in any case is a generally unreliable technique for deaf people and does not substitute captions, see Walker 2016 p.c.). In the second frame the close-up on the police officer makes it clear who the utterance producer is as Walker confirms in the interview (Table 12.3).

Overt speaker identification takes up valuable text space and so is only used when the dialogue is not supplemented by a visual frame of the speakers, as in Scene 6 in Table 12.4.

Turn-taking

The FCC Order states that accurate CC text should 'reflect natural linguistic breaks and the flow of the dialogue' (FCC 2014: 22). This 'flow' is analysed from a CA perspective within Sacks, Schegloff and Jefferson's (1974) model of 'turn-taking'. A participant is said to 'own' or 'hold' the floor for the duration of the conversational 'turn' they are uttering.

Table 12.3 Identifying Speakers 1

Visual frame with CC text	Corresponding programme audio (CA transcription)
	Walt: At least have the common de:cency to hear me out
	PO: I need you to step back right now= Walt: =Did you even (0.1) hear what I said=

Table 12.4 Identifying Speakers 2

Visual frame with CC text	Corresponding programme audio (CA transcription)
	Walt: Ted Beneke (.) you cannot be serious

CC has limited success in representing the frequency and extent of violations of turn-taking rules and simultaneous speech most often expressing adversarial behaviour. In Scene 5A (see Appendix) as the two characters persist in holding the floor despite their interlocutor starting a turn (in lines 6–7, 13, 19 and 23 for the officer and in lines 17, 20 and 25 for Walt), their interruptions are clearly a token of antagonism (Sidnell 2010: 54). Walt's continuous attempt to terminate the police officer's turns is marked, and signals resistance to authority that is reminiscent of his Heisenberg identity. Instances of overlap perhaps may at times be inferred through lip-reading but in general, the interjections and determination to gain the floor cannot be easily translated across to a deaf audience.

Similarly, when analysing a conversation, it is important to indicate when turns are *not* taken up. In Scene 7A, for example, although up until line 37 the conversation is characterized by speakers talking nearly simultaneously or 'latching' and some overlap, the second half of the conversation contains various kinds of 'silence' (Sacks, Schegloff and Jefferson 1974: 715). At one point, Walt allows an extended silence, or 'lapse', and a marked use of 'intra-turn pauses' which Skyler does not use as an opportunity to speak. These long pauses or silences demonstrate that in this context Walt has the power to hold the floor even through not speaking, which contributes to his strong character and adds meaning to his utterances when he does produce them (Stenström 1994: 77). Overall, as Gottlieb (1994: 105–6) discusses, the written 'sub-code' is not compatible with the oral code in its ability to transmit the timings of speaker's utterances. Thus, the functional meaning behind pauses, latching, interjections and successful interruptions is unavailable for interpretation to a deaf audience, who without such features or cues (Culpeper 2001) may form a different idea of Walt as a character.

6.2.2 Dialogue

According to the FCC Order captions should always 'contain all words in the order spoken, without paraphrasing' (FCC 2014: 22). Yet, due to the spatio-temporal constraints of captioning not all dialogue can always be included. De Linde and Kay (1999: 12) cite 'you know' as one example of a supposedly not relevant discourse marker that is often omitted, and in Scene 6A in Table 12.5 all instances of this phrase are indeed missing in the corresponding CC text.

Additionally, in Scene 5 only two of the seven instances in which the officer addresses Walt as 'sir' are captioned; and only one of the eight instances of Walt saying 'no' are included. Thus the relative extent to which the officer is attempting to be polite and Walt is disagreeing with him may be misrepresented in the captions with possible consequent effect on the character's perception by the audience. Commenting on the missing term of address, Walker points out how this captioners' choice has in fact a good degree of relevance to the context. 'Sir' has of course a crucial function as a face-saver and a token of politeness (Brown and Levinson 1987). In the specific context in which it is used, the deletion of this term of address may impact on the audience who will perceive the police officer as harsher and less respectful than he is in the original text. Additionally, the officer's utterances are transformed from declarative statements ('I need you to step back') to direct imperatives in the corresponding CC text in

Table 12.5 Missed '*You Know*'

Programme audio (CA transcription)	CC
Walt: Ted Beneke (.) you cannot be serious that guy is a *you know* is a jo:ke=	WALT [ON RECORDING]: Ted Beneke? You cannot be serious. That guy is a joke.
Skyler: =*You know what* (.) you called my bluff=	SKYLER: You called my bluff.
Walt: =I called your what does that even mean=	WALT: What does that mean?
Skyler: =You dared me to tell the police and I couldn't do it so you win.	SKYLER: You dared me to tell the police and I couldn't do it, so you win.

lines 16 and 27 (Table 12.6). By missing his polite attempt to establish some distance from Walt and emphasize his authority, the deaf viewers may miss out on a feature of this character. This may have possible consequences on the interpretation of other characters including Walt, who may be justified in his abruptness in consideration of the policeman's lack of politeness.

Similarly, line 21 of Scene 5A presents an omission of a relevant element. The copula and antecedent (PO: [Sir (0.1) this is your last warning) are deleted in the corresponding CC (PO: Last warning); by only captioning the predicate complement of the utterance, this has the consequence of making the officer appear much blunter than he actually is portrayed in the original screenplay. A deaf audience may therefore have the impression that Walt was provoked by an uncivil police officer who bluntly tells him to step back, may tend to justify him and develop a different impression of him in this instance.

Omissions of this kind also have important implications for the power dynamic between Walt and Skyler. In line 14 of Scene 7A a hearing audience will know that Skyler is quoting Walt in asserting that they are in danger, but the corresponding CC text in line 15 of Scene 7B gives the impression that she is declaring this herself. The CC text further fails to recreate the cooperative interaction within the couple by not reproducing the latching between Walt's and Skyler's turns following Walt's admission of responsibility and his supportive interruption (Sidnell 2010: 54; Ten Have 2007: 103) in the last line (Table 12.7).

Thus, in the above case, choices were made probably for economic reasons that alter the original text and plausibly impact the deaf audience's perception of the characters at hand. When asked to comment on the difference between the two scripts, Walker judged the absence of Skyler's reported speech as an important loss as it is a worry that originally comes from Walt and not her and because it reflects the relationship between Walt and Skyler who remembers the words her husband once used. Nevrkla reflects on

Table 12.6 From Embedded to Explicit Directives

CC text (with added speaker identification)	Corresponding programme audio (CA transcription)
Police Officer: Step back now.	PO: *I need you to* step back *right* now=
Police Officer: Step back now.	PO: *Sir I need you to step back* (0.1) *I need you to* step back [right no::w]

Table 12.7 Omissions in the CC Text

CC text (with added speaker identification)	Corresponding programme audio (CA transcription)
Skyler: We're in danger.	Skyler: =*But you said* we're in danger
Walt: Yes, that's true. Because of me	(0.1)
Skyler: It doesn't matter.	Walt: Yes that's true because of me=
Walt: All that matters is that the rest of you are safe.	Skyler: =*No* it doesn't matter *now all that ma[tters*
	Walt: [All that matters is that the rest of you are safe

the delicate issue of the captioners' responsibility when she comments in the interview 'who am I to choose which part is important?' Choices concerning the representation of the conversation structure are important characterization cues (Culpeper 2001: 172–3). A deaf audience relying on the CC text may not form the same impression of the family man versus Heisenberg power struggles that Walt is engaged in. Only a hearing audience will have knowledge of the officer's polite mitigation strategies and the extent to which Walt disregards these by producing interruptions. Only a hearing audience is given the opportunity to experience the extent of the power grabbing in the audio recorded squabble as Skyler does not accept Walt's justification for his actions, thereby challenging his 'family man' identity. Finally, only a hearing audience will be aware that in Scene 7 the power dynamic of the couple dramatically shifts as Skyler allows Walt to hold the floor, and arguably *does* accept his family man performance by forgiving him momentarily. The above features all have relevance and not only contribute to creating a particular impression of a character but ease the cognitive process of comprehension of what that particular character is saying. This is of course crucial as the different representations of talk structure in the programme's audio track and the CC text induce different character impression formations in deaf and hearing audiences.

6.3 Attitude

In Scenes 8–11, Walt's switches from 'family man' to 'Heisenberg' are signalled by a number of intonation features that have an 'attitudinal function' (Roach 2000: 183) and work as character's cues, for example visual or paralinguistic features of facial expression, body movements, prosodic features of pitch, loudness, speed and voice quality (Roach 2000: 187). In view of these paralinguistic facets of speech, the FCC Order recommends that 'where necessary to understand a program's content, accurate captions also convey the manner and tone of the speaker's voice' (FCC 2014: 22). Therefore to ensure that intonation is appropriately represented, captioners may overtly mark aspects of prosody instead of simply relying on the visuals. They may choose to signal prosodic features of a character's utterance: Scene 8 provides an example of where this has been used with success. As Walt is with his family, he attempts to hide his illegal Heisenberg activity and so is markedly quiet when speaking to Jesse who has rung, pretending to be a sales person. The decreased volume is translated in line 42 of Scene 8B as '[WHISPERING]'. As frame 2 in Table 12.8 shows, the camera shows the perspective of Skyler's character and so does not allow the audience to see Walt's facial expression. Therefore the image does not reliably convey the exact point at which Walt begins to perform a different identity. Furthermore, in frame 3 Skyler is very close to Walt when he is being overtly angry. So the information about him whispering is crucially relevant for the viewers to avoid potential confusion for an audience which is deaf or hard of hearing.

Note that prosodic features are generally not included if the dialogue and/or the image containing paralinguistic features are deemed sufficiently clear by the captioners to suggest a character's stance. Such exclusions are not instantiated because of space and time constraints rather they are chosen because making explicit in writing what is clear, hence not necessarily context-relevant, *can* be perceived to be 'patronizing' (Nevrkla) and thus 'offensive' (Walker, p.c. 2016). Scene 9 provides an example of where this type of choice to omit prosodic features is successful. In line 21 of Scene 9A Walt switches promptly from a cooperative to an insulting register. This change allows the audience to identify the exact point in which Walt switches his 'family man' to a 'Heisenberg' identity. The alteration becomes particularly tangible when it is combined with Walt's concurrent facial expression, turning from a smile to a grimace (see frames 4–5 in table 12.9).

Table 12.8 Identifying Point of Identity Change 1

	Visual frame with CC text	Corresponding programme audio (CA transcription)
1		Walt: And I I really don't appreciate these sa:les calls
2		Walt: >°Calm down damn it°<
3		Walt: °Calm down (0.2)
4		Walt: <u>Listen</u> uh: that is just <u>not</u> gonna work for me: ((smile voice))

Table 12.9 Identifying Point of Identity Change 2

	Visual frame with CC text	Corresponding programme audio (CA transcription)
1	So you heard, huh? Yes, yes.	Walt: So you heard huh? ((smile voice)) Yes: yes
2	Good news. Oh, she's just so beautiful. Heh.	Walt: good news oh she's just so beautiful heh (.) ((smile voice))
3		
4		
5	You junkie imbecile.	Walt: °↓You junkie imbecile

Table 12.9 (Continued)

	Visual frame with CC text	Corresponding programme audio (CA transcription)
6	You junkie imbecile.	

Whenever visuals are not reliable indicators of a character's attitude, information is added to the CC text as recommended by the FCC:

> If the speaker is not visible onscreen, or visual cues that denote the emotional state are not shown, indicate the speaker's emotion. (FCC 2014: 22)

Take a look at Scene 10, which is more complex. Walt calls Skyler at home following the abduction of their daughter and, being aware that police are listening in, he decides to strategically behave as an 'abusive husband' (Pettis 2015: 185) to alleviate Skyler of any potential blame from the police. His heightened angry tone and facial expressions are shown in frames 1 and 2 in Table 12.10. Later there appears to be an identity switch following the point in which Walt mentions 'Hank' in frame 3. The visual image depicts Walt's changing facial expression from anger to despair in frames 4–6. While Walt begins to weep, his weeping is silent. In the CC, there is no mention of '[WEEPING]' or even '[UPSET]' to mark his voice quality, so a deaf audience cannot be aware of it. His break down can be seen by the audience, but not heard by Skyler and the police at the other end of the line since it does not affect the prosodic features of Walt's voice. Although it *seems*, as suggested by the visuals, that Walt's interlocutors know he is actually upset by what he has done (because of his family man identity), both a deaf and hearing audience has no way of knowing that he does successfully maintain an angry abusive husband act throughout the phone call.

Representing emotions in the CC therefore is a challenging exercise, as Nevrkla explains:

> We can hear a lot in people's voices about the emotion that they have, but I don't want to put something on an actor that they're not actually conveying, I might be wrong.

Due to this complexity, the CC text of *Breaking Bad* avoids the explicit articulation of objective prosodic features as 'faint echoes' of emotion (Gottlieb 1994: 102) or leaves to the characters' facial expression the task of conveying emotions.

Table 12.10 Clear Visuals

	Visual frame with CC text	Corresponding programme audio (CA transcription)
1		Walt: You were never grateful for <u>anything</u> I did for this family
2		Walt: You you have no right
3		Walt: You're never gonna see Hank again
4		
5		Skyler: Walt (0.1) I just want Holly back

Table 12.10 (Continued)

Visual frame with CC text	Corresponding programme audio (CA transcription)
6 — *I just want Holly back.*	Skyler: Walt (0.1) I just want Holly back

7 Discussion

The analysis has pointed out the broad challenges that captioners face when representing programme audio/source text in the CC:

1. Deciding *how* to represent certain formal sound properties. Aspects of the audio such as noises characters make overlaps or silences in conversation or prosodic vocal features all prove difficult to transfer between the semiotic medium of sound and writing.
2. As they work within spatio-temporal constraints, captioners simply cannot include all audio, and need to be selective with overt speaker identification, sound effects, noises and dialogue content in fast paced scenes.

The interview with Nevrkla was invaluable in informing the study about how these challenges are overcome. Captioners in general come from an editorial background, and so trust their 'editorial instinct' in the choices they make when producing CC text. The overall message Nevrkla gave was that captioners' motivations are centred on granting accessibility to a deaf audience that is communicating relevant audio information to retain the programme 'flavour'. However, she warns against captioning so much that it would cause the deaf audience to 'switch off, like a hearing viewer would if there was someone babbling to them'. Her final comment aptly summarizes the essence of the CC text:

> Although your subtitles are very important, don't assume they are the most important thing and block out everything else. They may as well go read a book – they are watching a programme for the special effects, and facial expressions, not just to read subtitles … [Closed captions] should almost feel invisible if they're doing their job properly.

It seems that captioners interpret the audio track not in the name of faithfulness to the form or function to the original text but in virtue of what they perceive is the relevance of a particular message. Once identified the relevance of a particular message, captioners determine whether it is worth the cognitive effort required to process it in a caption, and subsequently what form it should take. In spite of this, as we hope to have demonstrated, there are instances in which their interpretive choices transform a character's cues, which may impact on the viewers' impression of that character.

Walt's story focuses on a 'family man' disguising his 'Heisenberg' identity. It is plausible to think that due to the textual differences between original audio track and CC, different audiences may form different impressions of this narrative development. The character of Walt is initially presented as a 'nerdy chemistry teacher who can't take care of his family' (Poe 2015: 120). Audiences may have prior experience of similar characters, and so in accordance with Culpeper's (2001) characterization model, they may form a first impression of Walt as a conforming 'nerd'. When the 'Heisenberg' identity emerges, however, such initial impressions may be challenged. It is possible that the characterization cues that allow these challenges to be inferred are not presented to the exact same extent for a deaf audience. In the CC text, the link may be missed between Walt turned criminal and Walt viewing Skyler as an authority figure that is resisted in the exact same way as his doctors and employer. As the narrative develops, Walt's strive for power as 'Heisenberg' hiding behind the mask of the 'family man' proves successful. Once more this is perhaps not presented in the same way to a deaf audience relying on the CC text. Only a hearing audience will be aware of his ability to silence a police officer and the fact that Skyler finally accepts his 'family man' justification. Thus, audiences who are getting meaning from the source text audio and audiences who are getting meaning from the target CC text may not have the same access to Walt performing the 'family man' to hide his 'Heisenberg' self. These audiences may therefore be in different positions in the final stage of the CCRM.

8 Conclusion

This study has followed Bassett's (2014: 87) call to move beyond the old debate of whether form or function should be prioritized in translation. A translation approach to CC as combined with cognitive stylistics (Culpeper 2001) was implemented to reflect on the decisions captioners possibly make to create the CC text, and whether as a consequence a deaf and hearing audience form different impressions about the characters and the narrative. Exploring the CC text from a cognitive stylistics perspective has proved useful in informing further captioning practice especially now that the FCC Order has been officially implemented. Importantly, this study has shown that reading times are not the only aspect that should be questioned: the narrative implications that captions hold need to be investigated further if a deaf audience are truly to get equal access. Finally, following on from Neves (2005), our reflection on the role of images has highlighted what is necessary to include and what can be left out in subtitles that as Walker recites 'have to become [a deaf person's] ears not [their] eyes'. This study is a small investigation into the complex issue of CC and its reliability would be much increased by proper surveys or interviews into genuine audience impressions and a comparison of the responses of deaf and hearing demographics. However, it has made an attempt to bring together two different dimensions accompanying the data analysis. By interviewing a professional captioner, it has been informed by the criteria they follow when representing in writing the audio source; similarly, by testing the analysis on a deaf person, it has made an initial attempt to stretch the analysis into the TV series' actual reception.

Acknowledgements

We wish to sincerely thank Sally Nevrkla for sharing her professional knowledge and insight with us and John Walker (University of Sussex) and his interpreter Marco Nardi for generously agreeing to respond to our analysis thus making our reading of the data much more reliable.

Notes

1 This chapter has appeared in Language and Literature and is reprinted here with permission.
2 Season 1 Episode 1 18:12-19:21.
   Season 1 Episode 1 20:23-21:24.
   Season 1 Episode 4 39:08-39:59.
   Season 2 Episode 1 10:58-14:22.
   Season 3 Episode 2 03:18-04:08.
   Season 3 Episode 4 04:46-05:37.
   Season 4 Episode 12 00:25-03:05.
   Season 1 Episode 2 07:30-08:44.
   Season 2 Episode 12 10:02-11:09.
   Season 5 Episode 14 41:15-44:25.
3 See legend of symbols.
4 A reverberation is perceived when the reflected sound wave reaches your ear in less than 0.1 second after the original sound wave. Reverbed therefore indicates an altered sound.

References

Bassnett, S. (2014), *Translation Studies*, 4th edn, Abingdon: Taylor and Francis.
Blevins, J. (2015), 'Introduction', in J. Blevins and D. Wood (eds), *The Methods of Breaking Bad*, 1–10, Jefferson: McFarland and Company.
Brown, P. and Levinson, S. C. (1987), *Politeness: Some Universals in Language Usage*, Cambridge: Cambridge University Press. (First published 1978 as part of Esther N. Goody (ed.), *Questions and Politeness*. Cambridge University Press.)
Culpeper, J. (2001), *Language and Characterisation: People in Plays and Other Texts*, London: Longman.

De Linde, Z. and Kay, N. (1999), 'Processing subtitles and film images: Hearing vs deaf viewers', *The Translator*, 5 (1): 45–60.

Ellcessor, E. (2012), 'Captions on, off, on TV, online: Accessibility and search engine optimization in online closed captioning', *Television and New Media*, 13 (4): 329–52.

Federal Communication Commission (FCC) (2014), *Closed Captioning Quality Report and Order, Declaratory Ruling, FNPRM* (accessed 20 May 2015).

Gottlieb, H. (1994), 'Subtitling: Diagonal translation', *Perspectives: Studies in Translatology*, 2 (1): 101–21.

Gutt, E.-A. (1989), *Translation and Relevance*, PhD thesis, Department of Phonetics and Linguistics, University College London.

Gutt, E.-A. (2000), *Translation and Relevance: Cognition and Context*, Abingdon: Taylor and Francis.

Ledwon, L. (2017), '"Breaking bad" contracts: Bargaining for masculinity in popular culture', *William and Mary Journal of Women and the Law*, 23 (3): 397–431.

McIntyre, D. and Lugea, J. (2015), 'The effects of deaf and hard-of-hearing subtitles on the characterisation process: A cognitive stylistic study of The Wire', *Perspectives: Studies in Translatology*, 23 (1): 62–88.

Munday, J. (2012), *Introducing Translation Studies: Theories and Applications*, 3rd edn, Abingdon: Taylor and Francis.

Neves, J. (2005), *Audiovisual Translation: Subtitling for the Deaf and Hard-of-Hearing*, PhD thesis, University of Roeampton, http://roehampton.openrepository.com/roehampton/bitstream/10142/12580/1/neves%20audiovisual.pdf (accessed 01 January 2016).

Neves, J. (2008), '10 fallacies about Subtitling for the d/Deaf and the hard of hearing', *The Journal of Specialised Translation*, 10: 128–43.

Pettis, J. (2015), 'Men in control: Panopticism and performance', in B. Roussell Cowlishaw (ed.), *Masculinity in Breaking Bad: Critical Perspectives*, Jefferson: McFarland and Company.

Poe, P. (2015), 'Patriarchy and the "Heisenberg principle"', in J. Blevins and D. Wood (eds), *The Methods of Breaking Bad*, 109–11, Jefferson: McFarland and Company.

Powers, W. R. (2005), 'Creating the verbatim transcript', in *Transcription Techniques for the Spoken Word*, 39–60, Oxford: AltaMira Press.

Roach, P. (2000), *English Phonetics and Phonology: A Practical Course*, 3rd edn, Cambridge: Cambridge University Press.

Sacks, H., Schegloff, E. A. and Jefferson, G. (1974), 'A simplest systematics for the organization of turn-taking for conversation', *Language*, 50 (4): 696–735.

Sidnell, J. (2010), 'Turn taking', in *Conversation Analysis: An Introduction*, Chichester: Wiley-Blackwell.

Sperber, D. and Wilson, D. (1986), *Relevance: Communication and Cognition*, Oxford: Blackwell.

Stenström, A.-B. (1994), *An Introduction to Spoken Interaction*, Abingdon: Routledge.

Szarkowska, A., Krejtz, I., Klyszejko, Z. and Wieczorek, A. (2011), 'Verbatim, standard, or edited?: Reading patterns of different captioning styles among deaf, hard of hearing, and hearing viewers', *American Annals of the Deaf*, 156 (4): 363–78.

Ten Have, P. (2007), *Doing Conversation Analysis: A Practical Guide*, 2nd edn, London: Sage.

Wurm, S. (2007), 'Intralingual and interlingual subtitling: A discussion of the mode and medium in film translation', *The Sign Language Translator and Interpreter*, 1 (1): 115–41.

Zdenek, S. (2011), 'Which sounds are significant? Towards a rhetoric of closed captioning', *Disability Studies Quarterly*, 31 (3): 74–97.

Legend of symbols

grey text	Reverbed audio
((text))	Comments/audio description
(.)	Just noticeable pause
(.3), (2.6)	Examples of timed pauses
word= =word	No pause between speakers – latching speech
word [word [word	The point where overlapping speech begins
:	Sound elongation
wor-	Word has been cut off
hh	Audible aspiration
.hh	Audible inspiration
underline text	Audio is emphasized – slight increased volume
CAPITALS	Shouting/loud voice
°text°	Whispering/low voice
>text<	Accelerated speech
?	Rising intonation
.	Descending intonation
↑word,↓word	Higher pitch, lower pitch

Appendices

Scenes 2A and 2B
Scenes 3A and 3B
Scene 5A and 5B

13

Metapragmatic awareness in cinematic discourse

Cohesive devices in *Notorious* (Hitchcock, 1946)

Adriana Gordejuela

1 Introduction

Since its origins, film theory has pondered on the nature and the multiple dimensions of the cinematic medium from diverse perspectives: as early as 1916, Münsterberg, for instance, considered the cognitive functioning of film; Soviet film-makers like Eisenstein (1949) theorized about film montage; and Bazin (1971) reflected upon the ontology of the film image. An issue addressed by different film-makers and thinkers was that of the 'language' of film (e.g. Metz 1974): Does cinema constitute a coded system? How does cinema convey meaning, and how do viewers make sense of it? A variety of explanations have been put forth from different theoretical fields that apply cognitive (e.g. Bordwell 1985), structuralist, semiotic (e.g. Stam, Burgoyne and Flitterman-Lewis 1996), narratological (e.g. Gaudreault 2009) and other approaches to the study of cinema. Within this multidisciplinary study of film, pragmatic considerations of cinematic discourse have not been an exception, but they have mostly been centred on the pragmatic workings of film dialogue (e.g. Dynel 2011; Piazza 2011; Rossi 2011). More recently, some studies have addressed the pragmatic dimension of cinematic discourse as a whole (i.e. taking into account all its levels of expression: visual, auditory and verbal) (e.g. Janney 2012). Certainly, the film medium is fundamentally audiovisual, and a pragmatic analysis of its functioning should take that into consideration.

The present study takes the concept of 'metapragmatic awareness' (Verschueren 2000) as a point of departure to analyse how certain devices in cinematic discourse call attention upon their own shape and how those mechanisms take part in the process of meaning construction and negotiation in film. Particularly, indicators of metapragmatic awareness will be analysed in Hitchcock's *Notorious* (1946), while parallelisms with other films of the director will be shown, namely *Suspicion* (1941), *Shadow of a Doubt* (1943), *North by Northwest* (1959) and *Marnie* (1964). The reason to look at the functioning of metapragmatic awareness specifically in Hitchcock's work is that a conscious author imprint can be traced throughout his filmography (e.g. Walker 2005). The motifs and patterns characteristic of his creative world are intentionally designed as author marks whose salience allows them to be examined from a metapragmatic standpoint. On the other hand, the selected motifs that will be analysed ('tunnel shots', staircases and drinks) are constructed to a great extent at a purely visual level, without the support of verbal and auditory resources. They reveal Hitchcock's preference for 'pure cinema': one that relies primarily on visual means and does not just consist of 'photographs of people talking' (Truffaut 1985: 61; Gottlieb 1995: 290). The analysis of such visual mechanisms will show how metapragmatic awareness, which plays a central role in any kind of language use (Verschueren 2000), is also a fundamental feature of cinematic discourse both at the level of construction and interpretation.

The first part of the chapter presents the concept of metapragmatic awareness and discusses its relevance for the generation of meaning in cinematic discourse. The second part deals with indicators of metapragmatic awareness in Hitchcock's *Notorious*: specifically, it pays attention to the reiteration of specific motifs ('tunnel shots', staircases and drinks) as a source of cohesion, and also discusses some intertextual links established between *Notorious* and other films of the director. The pragmatic concept of 'adaptability' (Verschueren and Brisard 2009) is also introduced as an important ingredient for the comprehension of the selected motifs.

2 Metapragmatic awareness in cinematic discourse

Considered in its entirety, as a unitary whole made up of visual, auditory and verbal elements, it can be said that cinematic discourse

> is not the use of language in film (film dialogue, scripted conversation, fictional interaction) but the audiovisual discourse of film narration itself: the discourse of mise-en-scène, cinematography, montage, and sound editing used in narrating cinematic stories to viewers. ... [I]t is the filmmaker's main expressive vehicle and primary form of communication with, and influence over, the audience. (Janney 2012: 1–2)

Being a form of communication, cinematic discourse should follow many of the pragmatic principles found in other communicative media, and it could benefit as well from the pragmatic concepts and tools applied to the analysis of other kinds of media and of different types of human communication (e.g. verbal communication, co-speech gesture). In this sense, cinematic discourse can be discussed in terms of its metapragmatic dimension (Janney 2012). More specifically, as will be seen later, it is a kind of discourse that shows traces of 'metapragmatic awareness' or 'reflexive consciousness', a fundamental aspect of linguistic communication. As Verschueren (2000: 444) puts it, '[b]eing a crucial aspect of what goes on when language is used (whether in uttering or in interpreting), pragmatic analyses have to come to terms with the role of consciousness, awareness, or salience ... in order to understand linguistic behaviour'.

In the same way that verbal communication can be self-referential and reflect upon its own communicative choices (as is the case of metalanguage, for instance), cinematic discourse shows its own indicators of metapragmatic awareness which call attention to themselves, to the discourse itself.

This reflexivity of discourse is not merely aesthetic or accessory, but plays a central role in the process of constructing and negotiating meaning in communication:

> [s]tudying this type of awareness is crucial to an understanding of verbal *behavior* because, like any other form of social action, language use is always *interpreted*, in the sense that the actors involved attach meaning to it, so that the actors' interpretations become part and parcel of what needs to be described and explained. (Verschueren 2000: 445)

In order to clarify this idea of dynamic construction of meaning, it may be useful to look at Widdowson's (2004) distinction between two concepts: 'text' and 'discourse'. The main difference between them does not lie in their extension, where length or size would determine if a piece of verbal communication is classified as text or as discourse. Rather, a text is identified 'not by its linguistic extent but by its social intent. ... But identifying something as a text is not the same as interpreting it. ... This is where discourse comes in. ... Unless it is activated by ... [a] contextual connection, the text is inert' (Widdowson 2004: 8). Discourse is thus 'the acting of context on code, ... the pragmatic process of meaning negotiation. Text is its product' (Widdowson 2004: 8). It is in this sense that cinematic discourse should be understood in relation to metapragmatic awareness. The reflexive consciousness or salience that certain cinematic devices display (e.g. Hitchcock's 'tunnel shot' pattern, discussed later) plays an important role in the process of negotiating the meaning of those devices: on the one hand, they are intentionally designed by the film-maker to be self-referential, and on the other hand they are perceived as such by the viewer, who attaches meaning to them by means of contextual connections.

Metapragmatic awareness in cinematic discourse involves the activity of both author (Hitchcock, in this case) and viewer: even though the author may be fully intentional in the way he crafts certain cinematic devices to be distinctively salient, the reflexive consciousness manifested by those devices must be perceived by the spectator as well. However, not all viewers notice cinematic discourse's self-referentiality to the same degree. In the dynamic process of interpreting cinematic discourse, previous knowledge, expectations and other elements contribute to the viewer's understanding of motifs and patterns that take part in the unfolding story, and thus spectators achieve different levels of reading and, consequently, of interpretation (see Persson 2003).

In the following section, three specific motifs in Hitchcock's *Notorious* will be analysed in terms of their metapragmatic awareness: 'tunnel shots', staircases and drinks. In addition, intertextual links and parallelisms with other films of the director will be briefly explored to show the unitary quality of Hitchcock's creative world.

3 Hitchcock's *Notorious* (1946)

Film-maker François Truffaut (1985: 167) described *Notorious* as 'the very quintessence of Hitchcock'. Throughout the film, one finds several of the characteristic motifs of Hitchcock's universe (see Walker 2005). This study will zoom in on three of them: 'tunnel shots', staircases and drinks. The film tells the story of Alicia Huberman, the daughter of a Nazi spy who opposes her father's ideas. She is contacted by US agent T.R. Devlin to spy for them, and, later on, they fall in love. Alicia faces a dilemma when Nazi leader Alex Sebastian asks her to marry him, and she is pushed to accept in order to keep the mission going. The Sebastians' house constitutes the main scenario for the development of the staircase motif (the ascent and descent of the stairs in the house becomes significant in several scenes). On the other hand, the drinks motif appears in the mysterious bottles hidden by the Sebastians in the cellar, and also in the poisoned drinks given to Alicia in order to kill her. Finally, different scenes display what Rothman (1988, 2012) has called a 'tunnel shot', which, as explained in the following section, is characterized by its singular perspective and composition. These three Hitchcockian motifs work in a way that elicits metapragmatic awareness. More specifically, through their reiteration in the film and the intertextual links they establish, they function as indicators of that reflexive salience.

3.1 'Tunnel shots'

A 'tunnel shot' is a Hitchcockian shot or frame composition identified by a deep, marked perspective (see Figures 13.1–13.3).[1] William Rothman, who coined the term, states that this kind of shot 'occurs in every Hitchcock film and always announces a space of dream or nightmare, a space that is not quite or not exactly real' (1988: 179). Also, 'tunnel shots' are often linked to another recurrent Hitchcockian motif, namely what has been referred to as parallel vertical lines (////): 'at one level, the //// serves as a Hitchcock signature: it is his mark on the frame (…). It is also associated with sexual fear and the specific threat of loss of control or breakdown' (Rothman 2012: 34). This motif usually becomes visible in the distinctive vertical lines of walls, hallways and banisters (Figures 13.1 and 13.2), but it also leaves space for creativity, as in Figure 13.3, where the motif is shaped by the vertical figures of people standing in the room, spread in such a way as to create a deep perspective that reveals Alicia's figure in the background.

The 'tunnel shot' is repeated several times throughout *Notorious* (some instances are shown in Figures 13.1, 13.2, 13.3, 13.5 and 13.11), and thus cohesive ties are established between shots through reiteration of the same pattern (Halliday and Hasan 1976; Janney 2010).[2]

By highlighting their compositional structure (mainly deep perspective and parallel vertical lines) and by relating to each other through parallelism, 'tunnel shots' elicit metapragmatic awareness and work as cohesive devices. The key for their interpretation lies in the reiteration of the same structural pattern, which calls attention to itself and acquires meaning through contextual connections. Furthermore, those connections go beyond the internal ties created within a film (i.e. *Notorious*), and intertextual links with other Hitchcock films are developed. The first 'tunnel shot' in *Notorious*, for instance,

[01:10:38]   [01:40:50]

[01:03:35]

Figures 13.1–13.3 'Tunnel shots'. 'Notorious' directed by Alfred Hitchcock © RKO Radio Pictures. 1946. All rights reserved.

is intertextually linked with another one in *Marnie* (1964). In one of the scenes in the first part of *Notorious*, Alicia and Devlin go horse riding and try to provoke Alicia's encounter with the villain, Alex Sebastian, who was once in love with Alicia. Devlin causes Alicia's horse to flee, out of control, so that Sebastian can chase and rescue her. This key moment is shown in the shape of a 'tunnel shot' (Figure 13.5): a path flanked by trees and a fence (which recreate the //// motif) goes deep in the distance, and its end cannot be seen. In the middle of the path Alicia and Sebastian shake hands, while Devlin observes the scene from a distance (Figure 13.4). He does not seem happy with the situation, but he puts the mission entrusted to him above anything else.

A very similar scene is found in another Hitchcock movie, *Marnie* (1964). A newly-wed couple leaves the house in a car which disappears down the road, also flanked by trees and a fence (Figure 13.6).[3] One of the characters, the girl that has always been in love with the groom, observes the scene from the house and sees the car moving away (Figure 13.7). Referring to this 'tunnel shot' from the girl's point of view, Rothman suggests that 'the shot marks the death of her dream' (2012: 402). Devlin's 'tunnel shot' could be understood in a similar way, because he loves Alicia but is losing her to another man. The parallelism between both scenes confirms that 'tunnel shots' are used by Hitchcock in a very particular way: on the one hand, they serve as the author's signature; on the other hand, they function as units that elicit metapragmatic awareness by drawing attention to their own shape and, furthermore, develop cohesive

Figures 13.4 and 13.5 Devlin observes Alicia and Alex Sebastian's reencounter. 'Notorious' directed by Alfred Hitchcock © RKO Radio Pictures. 1946. All rights reserved.

Figures 13.6 and 13.7 'Tunnel shot'. 'Marnie' directed by Alfred Hitchcock © Universal Pictures. 1964. All rights reserved.

ties through their recurrence and through intertextual links. These connections are fundamental in the process of meaning negotiation that allows the viewer to interpret each 'tunnel shot' in the context of the narrative.

3.2 The stairs

One of Alfred Hitchcock's most frequent motifs, and one of the many influences he received from German Expressionism (Gottlieb 2002), is that of the house with different levels connected by a staircase which the characters ascend and descend. Zirnite speaks of a *main level* and an *upper level*. The first one is 'generally characterized by banality, complacency, and a shallow vigilance'; it is '[an] "earth-bound" plane' (1986: 4). The *upper level*, on the other hand, 'is the oppressive dominion of a malignant force, of human destructiveness; (…) [it] is incarnated by those who unleash the darkest human impulses' (1986: 4).[4] As a result, the ascent and descent of the stairs becomes significant as well. For the main-level characters, ascending to the 'malignant domain' is always associated with danger, and descending from it implies liberation. This is the case with Alicia, who is trapped by the Sebastians in the upper level of their house (Figure 13.8), but is eventually rescued by Devlin in the final scene, as Figure 13.9 shows (Zirnite 1986: 9; Walker 2005: 356). In contrast, the characters associated with the upper

[01:29:15] [01:39:30]

Figures 13.8 and 13.9 Alicia's ascent and descent. 'Notorious' directed by Alfred Hitchcock © RKO Radio Pictures. 1946. All rights reserved.

level – that is, the villains – always carry sinister connotations with them whenever they descend. For instance, when Madame Sebastian comes down to welcome Alicia (Figures 13.10 and 13.11), she brings down with her all the evil linked to the upper level, and that is reflected in Alicia's tense countenance (Zirnite 1986: 9; Walker 2005: 356). The sense of menace and danger that surrounds the scene is reinforced by a 'tunnel shot' composition from Alicia's point of view (Figure 13.11), which is shaped by a deep perspective (emphasized by Madame Sebastian's progressive approach to the foreground) and also by the //// motif visible on the banister of the staircase.

A character from the upper level going up the stairs has equally sinister undertones. After Alex discovers his wife's secret, he goes upstairs to his mother's room, and they shortly after decide to poison Alicia. A shot from the top of the staircase shows Alex's climb (Figure 13.12), one which, Zirnite (1986: 8) argues, is intertextually linked to that of Johnny carrying the glass of (poisoned?) milk in *Suspicion*, a 1941 Hitchcock film (Figure 13.13).

Referring to the stairs motif in Hitchcock, Walker concludes that 'ascending or descending a staircase in Hitchcock is rarely a neutral act (…). In other words, the expressionist notion of the staircase as a source of threat or menace is rarely far away' (2005: 362). The reiterative use of the motif in *Notorious* functions as a cohesive device and also as an indicator of metapragmatic awareness. The motif is shaped and repeated in such a way as to draw attention to its own form, and triggers contextual connections that lead the viewer to attach meaning to every occurrence of the staircase motif. The process of meaning negotiation on the part of the viewer is solidly based on the reflective quality of cinematic discourse.

3.3 Suspicious drinks

Drinks have a clear prominence in *Notorious*. They are already present in one of the first scenes, when Alicia meets Devlin and gets drunk. Then, in the following scene, Devlin gives her some beverage to relieve her inebriation, and the glass is shown in a close-up, slightly covering Alicia's face (Figure 13.14). This shot is connected to those at

[00:41:10]   [00:41:20]
[01:16:50]   [01:33:15]

Figures 13.10–13.13 Evil characters up and down the stairs in Notorious (1946) and Suspicion (1941). 'Notorious' directed by Alfred Hitchcock © RKO Radio Pictures. 1946. All rights reserved. 'Suspicion' directed by Alfred Hitchcock © RKO Radio Pictures. 1941. All rights reserved.

the end of the film which show the cup of coffee that is poisoning Alicia (Figures 13.15, 13.16 and 13.17): there is a contrastive parallelism between them, for the first drink has restorative purposes and the following ones are made to kill. Moreover, the way drinks are foregrounded in Figures 13.14 and 13.17 (while Alicia is left in the background) draws the viewer's attention to the object, not the protagonist. It is not just that the cups are shot in close-up but also, and most importantly, that they are deliberately given prominence over Alicia.

The Sebastians keep a few bottles of wine containing uranium in the cellar. This is the secret that Alicia and Devlin will eventually unveil. The bottles (also shown in close-up about ten times) and the cups all have a deceiving appearance in common, which hides the true nature of the object. Parallelism is set up, then, in multiple ways: between the different drinks shown in close-up, between the beneficial and the harmful drinks, and between the bottles of wine and the cups of coffee as containers of a mysterious, uncertain and menacing liquid. The visual salience of cups and bottles in close-up shots, as well as the reiteration of the drink motif throughout *Notorious* is a manifestation of metapragmatic awareness: cinematic discourse is consciously reflecting on and calling attention to its own shape and

Figures 13.14–13.17 Drinks of an uncertain nature. 'Notorious' directed by Alfred Hitchcock © RKO Radio Pictures. 1946. All rights reserved.

construction. Apart from functioning as a cohesive device, the recurrence and salience of the drink motif in the film sets up contextual connections that lead the viewer to interpret the narrative and symbolic meaning of each occurrence of the motif.

3.4 Cohesion beyond *Notorious*

Cinematic manifestations of metapragmatic awareness in Hitchcock's motifs and patterns ('tunnel shots', staircases and drinks) are not only found in *Notorious* but constitute recurring elements in Hitchcock's filmography. Such devices are distinguishing features of the film-maker as author and artist, and they function as cohesive ties which unify every film's cinematic discourse and the director's work as a whole.

The 'tunnel shot' pattern appears in multiple scenes of Hitchcock's filmography. Apart from the aforementioned scene in *Marnie*, other meaningful examples are found, for instance, in *Shadow of a Doubt* (1943) and *North by Northwest* (1959) (Figures 13.18 and 13.19). They all have in common the depth of the shot and the //// motif, but sometimes other components are added to the frame, such as the staircase motif. This is the case of a famous scene from *Shadow of a Doubt* in which the 'tunnel shot' is filmed from the top of the stairs, showing Charlotte from Uncle Charlie's point

[01:24:05]   [00:44:28]

Figures 13.18 and 13.19 'Tunnel shots' in Shadow of a Doubt (1943) and North by Northwest (1959). 'Shadow of a Doubt' directed by Alfred Hitchcock © Universal Pictures. 1943. All rights reserved. 'North by Northwest' directed by Alfred Hitchcock © Metro-Goldwyn-Mayer. 1959. All rights reserved.

of view (Figure 13.18). She has found out that he is guilty of murder, and even though the police are having trouble proving it, Uncle Charlie realizes that Charlotte knows the truth and he cannot escape that: '[t]he image of Uncle Charlie's point-of-view after turning renders his niece's appearance on the porch apparitional. ... [H]er seeming materialization on the plane below suggests a formidable countervailing decency' (Zirnite 1986: 10). Charlotte and the main level she occupies defeat the evil of the upper level, embodied by Uncle Charlie.

Likewise, the stairs motif is a recurrent one in Hitchcock's movies (Zirnite 1986; Walker 2005). This motif links the above-mentioned scene of Alex going up the stairs in *Notorious* (Figure 13.12) with a parallel one in *Suspicion* (Figure 13.13), and allows us to read one in light of the other. Interestingly, in *Notorious* Hitchcock included yet another reference to the poisoned milk in *Suspicion*. The scene in which Devlin gives Alicia a drink to restore her condition (Figure 13.20) shares many similarities with that of Johnny bringing a glass of milk to his wife, who, like Alicia, is sick in bed (Figure 13.21). In both scenes it is the same actor, Cary Grant, who brings a beverage to a woman lying in bed. Also, the drinks in both films have a bright, white colour which draws the viewer's attention to them. These correlations make these two scenes evoke each other in an intertextual manner, and it is possible to understand them in a dialogical way. However, although there is formal correspondence between them, deep down they are antithetical: Devlin and Johnny's purposes are opposed, because the latter wants to kill his wife, while the former cares for Alicia's recovery. In fact, Devlin will, in the end, rescue Alicia (in a scene crafted to parallel the one shown in Figure 13.20) from those who have been poisoning her.

As can be seen, the three Hitchcockian motifs discussed ('tunnel shots', staircases and drinks), recurrent throughout the director's filmography, are not rigid units which must be always interpreted in an invariable way. On the contrary, they are flexible resources which can be adapted to different expressive needs. Verschueren defines 'adaptability' as 'the property of language which enables human beings [either as utterers or interpreters] to make negotiable choices from the variable range of possibilities in such a way as to satisfy basic human communicative needs' (via Moyer 1996: 132; see also

Metapragmatic Awareness in Cinematic Discourse 319

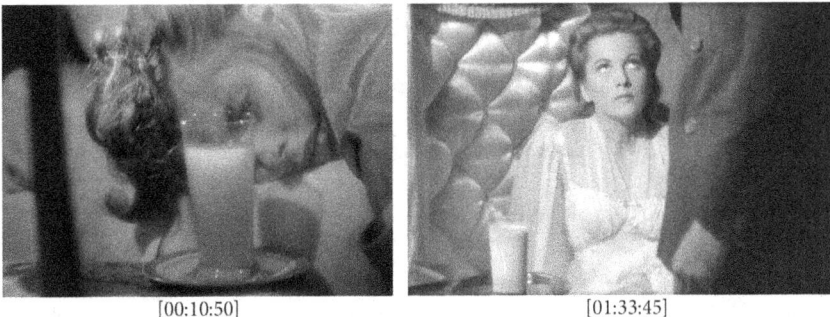

[00:10:50]   [01:33:45]

Figures 13.20 and 13.21 Parallelism between Notorious (1946) and Suspicion (1941). 'Notorious' directed by Alfred Hitchcock © RKO Radio Pictures. 1946. All rights reserved. 'Suspicion' directed by Alfred Hitchcock © RKO Radio Pictures. 1941. All rights reserved.

Verschueren and Brisard 2009). The concept, although initially defined as a property of verbal communication, can also be applied to the pragmatic analysis of cinematic discourse. For instance, the way Hitchcock employs the 'tunnel shot' is a good example of adaptability: it is a cinematic device which conveys a more or less fixed meaning, but plays with different nuances every time it is used. That is, there are a few rules which always operate in the interpretation of a 'tunnel shot', but ultimately each one of those shots has to be taken individually to be comprehended in relation to the narrative context, the preceding and following shots and so on. The formal salience of the 'tunnel shot' and the reiteration of the motif in Hitchcock's films highlight the metapragmatic dimension of the device – a dimension which is essential in the process of meaning construction and negotiation. Contextual connections are fundamental as well in that process, and vary for each occurrence of the 'tunnel shot': thus, the reading of the motif is not invariable and always identical, but it relies on adaptability as one of its central properties. Furthermore, the generation and negotiation of meaning in each case takes place in a dynamic ground of interpretation which depends, among other things, on the viewer's knowledge about Hitchcock's universe and its peculiarities (his themes, motifs, patterns etc.). In this sense, a regular spectator will not make such an elaborated interpretation as that of a critic or a Hitchcock scholar, but meaning will be negotiated at different levels in order to successfully comprehend the narrative in progress (see Persson 2003).

In short, the diverse metapragmatic devices employed in *Notorious* and in many other Hitchcock films make up 'a system of self-reference' (Rothman 2012: 246), which is an essential trait of the film-maker's creative universe. Those self-referential, metapragmatic motifs serve as cohesive devices in the Hitchcockian world, making it genuine and consistent. Speaking of the dialectical space created by the upper and main levels of the house in Hitchcock's films, Zirnite points out that its intricacy as a system was developed 'in both the sophistication of its form and in the abundance of meaning this form conveys' (1986: 3), an idea that can be extended to the entire creative cosmos of the film-maker.

4 Conclusions

The aim of this study has been to show the centrality of metapragmatic awareness in cinematic discourse, and more specifically in the works of Alfred Hitchcock. The cinematic motifs analysed, namely 'tunnel shots', staircases and drinks, function as imprints of the film-maker as author and as conscious marks of his unique and coherent creative universe. The formal salience of these devices and their reiterative appearance in *Notorious* (1946) and in other Hitchcock films are manifestations of their metapragmatic awareness (i.e. reflexive consciousness). Being self-referential, they contribute, on the one hand, to the process of construction and negotiation of narrative meaning in a given film. They elicit contextual connections and intertextual links which lead the viewer to interpret each cinematic motif in a particular way. On the other hand, the repetition of the analysed motifs in *Notorious* and other films, and the parallelisms created between them serve as cohesive devices that sustain links at different levels of Hitchcock's cinematic discourse. In short, just as it is claimed to be a fundamental property of verbal communication (Verschueren 2000), metapragmatic awareness is shown as an essential feature of cinematic discourse.

Notes

1 The reproduction of film stills in this chapter is strictly limited to academic purposes, following the principles of Fair Use of copyrighted materials.
2 Cohesive ties link two items (two shots, in the case of 'tunnel shots') in such a way that they are related to each other. Cohesion 'occurs where the interpretation of some element in the discourse is dependent on that of another. The one presupposes the other, in the sense that it cannot be effectively decoded except by recourse to it' (Halliday and Hasan 1976: 4).
3 The car is only shown disappearing in the distance, but auditory cues (e.g. the doors closing and the engine running) unequivocally indicate that the couple has left in a car.
4 Other authors, taking a Freudian approach to Hitchcock's creative world, project the iceberg metaphor of the human mind onto a three-level house, and as a result the following correspondences emerge: upper level-*superego*; main level-*ego*; sublevel-*id*. This last level of the human mind, the unconscious, is embodied by the house cellar or basement, and it is often related to the uncanny and secret (cf. Fiennes 2006; Pheasant-Kelly 2016). Even though it seems that Hitchcock never really agreed with Psychoanalysis as a theory (nor with its practice) (Sandis 2009), Sandis (2009: 58) argues that he found it appealing as a conceptual system because of its simplicity at a basic level and, more importantly, because of its aesthetic and artistic applicability. That the secrets in *Notorious* are hidden and revealed in the cellar is not, then, a pure coincidence, but something very much in tune with Hitchcock's artistic world.

References

Bazin, A. (1971), *What Is Cinema?*, trans. H. Gray, Berkeley: University of California Press.
Bordwell, D. (1985), *Narration in the Fiction Film*, London: Routledge.
Dynel, M. (2011), 'Stranger than fiction? A few methodological notes on linguistic research in film discourse', *Brno Studies in English*, 37: 41–61.
Eisenstein, S. (1949), *Film Form: Essays in Film Theory*, trans. J. Leyda, New York: Harcourt, Brace and Company.
Fiennes, S. (2006), *The Pervert's Guide to Cinema*, UK, Austria and Netherlands: Lone Star Productions.
Gaudreault, A. (2009), *From Plato to Lumière: Narration and Monstration in Literature and Cinema*, trans. T. Barnard, Toronto: University of Toronto Press.
Gottlieb, S., ed. (1995), *Hitchcock on Hitchcock: Selected Writings and Interviews*, Berkeley: University of California Press.
Gottlieb, S. (2002), 'Early Hitchcock: The German influence', in S. Gottlieb and C. Brookhouse (eds), *Framing Hitchcock: Selected Essays from the Hitchcock Annual*, 35–58, Detroit: Wayne State University Press.
Halliday, M. A. K. and Hasan, R. (1976), *Cohesion in English*, London: Longman.
Hitchcock, A. (1941), *Suspicion*, USA: RKO Radio Pictures.
Hitchcock, A. (1943), *Shadow of a Doubt*, USA: Universal Pictures.
Hitchcock, A. (1946), *Notorious*, USA: RKO Radio Pictures.
Hitchcock, A. (1959), *North by Northwest*, USA: Metro-Goldwyn-Mayer.
Hitchcock, A. (1964), *Marnie*, USA: Universal Pictures.
Janney, R. (2010), 'Film discourse cohesion', in C. Hoffmann (ed.), *Narrative Revisited*, 245–65, Amsterdam: Benjamins.
Janney, R. (2012), 'Pragmatics and cinematic discourse', *Lodz Papers in Pragmatics*, 8 (1): 1–18.
Metz, C. (1974), *Film Language: A Semiotics of the Cinema*, Chicago: University of Chicago Press.
Moyer, M. G. (1996), 'Pragmatics, the state of the art: A talk with Jef Verschueren', *Links and Letters*, 3: 127–40.
Münsterberg, H. (1916), *The Photoplay: A Psychological Study*, New York: Appleton.
Persson, P. (2003), *Understanding Cinema: A Psychological Theory of Moving Imagery*, Cambridge: Cambridge University Press.
Pheasant-Kelly, F. (2016), 'Secrets, memory and imagination: The psychic space of the cinematic attic', in *Spaces of the Cinematic Home: Behind the Screen Door*, London and New York: Routledge.
Piazza, R. (2011), *The Discourse of Italian Cinema and Beyond: Let Cinema Speak*, London and New York: Continuum.
Rossi, F. (2011), 'Discourse analysis of film dialogues: Italian comedy between linguistic realism and pragmatic non-realism', in R. Piazza, M. Bednarek and F. Rossi (eds), *Telecinematic Discourse: Approaches to the Language of Films and Television Series*, 21–46, Amsterdam: Benjamins.
Rothman, W. (1988), *The 'I' of the Camera: Essays in Film Criticism, History, and Aesthetics*, Cambridge: Cambridge University Press.
Rothman, W. (2012), *Hitchcock: The Murderous Gaze*, Albany: State University of New York Press.

Sandis, C. (2009), 'Hitchcock's conscious use of Freud's unconscious', *Europe's Journal of Psychology*, 3: 56–81.

Stam, R., Burgoyne, R. and Flitterman-Lewis, S. (1996), *New Vocabularies in Film Semiotics: Structuralism, Post-structuralism and Beyond*, London: Routledge.

Truffaut, F. (1985), *Hitchcock*, New York: Simon and Schuster.

Verschueren, J. (2000), 'Notes on the role of metapragmatic awareness in language use', *Pragmatics*, 10 (4): 439–56.

Verschueren, J. and Brisard, F. (2009), 'Adaptability', in J. Verschueren and J.-O. Östman (eds), *Key Notions for Pragmatics*, Amsterdam: John Benjamins.

Walker, M. (2005), *Hitchcock's Motifs*, Amsterdam: Amsterdam University Press.

Widdowson, H. G. (2004), *Text, Context, Pretext: Critical Issues in Discourse Analysis*, Malden: Blackwell.

Zirnite, D. (1986), 'Hitchcock, on the level: The heights of spatial tension', *Film Criticism*, 10 (3): 2–21.

Index

accent 8, 42, 129, 145, 226, 251, 259, 263, 274–5
  English (*see* English)
accessibility 7, 303
action 46, 65, 83, 89, 90, 97, 99–100, 109, 117, 126, 143, 149–50, 158–60, 188, 197, 201, 211, 214, 220 n.12, 268–9, 271, 276–7, 279, 280 n.10, 289, 293, 298, 311
  on-screen 150
adaptability 310, 318–19
adaptation 12–13, 189, 210, 212, 214, 216, 263–4, 268–71, 273–80, 282
  screen (*see* screen)
addressee 21–2, 28, 30, 34, 72–80, 82–3, 153, 170, 183, 185, 208, 210, 214, 218
adjective 31, 56 n.7, 104, 150, 171, 243–5, 251, 253
  parasynthetic (*see* parasynthetic)
adventure 214, 220 n.18, 226, 229–30, 257 n.22, 263, 269–71, 274, 277
  fantasy 230
Adventures of Robin Hood, The [movie], *see* Robin Hood
advertising 205–6, 208–9, 211–12, 214, 216–18, 219 nn.1, 3, 8, 9, 10
ain't 32, 34, 49–54
anachronistic 239, 244, 247, 249–52, 255, 256 n.14
analysis, *see* conversation; discourse; scene
Androutsopoulos, Jannis 3–4, 9, 14, 40, 42, 55, 64, 72, 165, 169, 174
animal 132, 198, 268, 275
  talking 263, 275
animated, animation 43, 226, 229–30, 270, 274–7, 280 n.4
  comedies 229–30
annotation 94
archaic, archaism 12, 225, 227–8, 230, 236, 238–40, 243–7, 254–5, 275

conjunctions (*see* conjunction)
formulae (*see* formulae)
pseudo- 12, 225, 227–8, 230, 236, 238, 240, 243, 246–7, 254–5
articulation 8, 127, 301
  dual, double 8, 127
attention 1–2, 12, 19–22, 24–6, 29–30, 35, 36 n.4, 43, 66, 71, 73, 80, 82, 87, 115, 119, 121, 141, 184, 188, 193–4, 201, 210, 215, 218, 225, 227, 293–4, 309–13, 315–16, 318
  joint focus of 21
audience 1–2, 5, 7–10, 12–13, 25, 27–8, 35, 39, 41–2, 65–6, 82–3, 89–90, 92–8, 101, 103–4, 107–9, 114, 116, 118, 144, 146–9, 152, 155, 158–9, 166–7, 173, 175, 179–80, 183–6, 189–90, 192–3, 195–6, 198, 200–2, 205–6, 208–15, 216–17, 219 n.3, 220 n.10, 223–5, 228, 231, 238, 240, 252, 254–5, 263, 266, 268, 271, 274, 276–9, 280 n.8, 285–99, 301, 303–4, 310
  design (*see* recipient design)
  film 1, 8, 10, 196, 200, 271, 277–8
authenticity, authentic 3, 12, 42, 70, 117, 143, 161 n.3, 165, 195, 198, 223, 225, 228, 237, 250, 254–5, 277
  non- 143
  pseudo- 223
  real 143
autism spectrum disorder 12, 165–6
awareness 8, 19, 70, 179–80, 212, 243, 309–13, 315–17, 319–20
  historio-linguistic 243
  metapragmatic 309–13, 315–17, 319–20
  pragmatic (*see* pragmatic)

Baker, Paul 10, 40, 43, 122
Bateman, John 3–4, 9, 12–13, 185

Bednarek, Monika   1–5, 7, 9–10, 13 n.2, 14 n.4, 6, 33, 35, 39–46, 48–9, 54, 56 n.6, 8, 64, 68–9, 72, 83, 89, 100, 113, 115–16, 118, 127, 136, 141, 143, 166–7, 169, 184–5, 219 n.7, 228, 265–6
Bend It Like Beckham [movie]   26–7, 29, 31, 33
Beowulf [movie]   226, 230, 257
Berninger, Mark   264, 278, 280 n.10
Big Bang Theory, The [tv series]   41–2, 48, 100, 166, see also Cooper, Sheldon
blog   42, 224–5, 237
  medieval   224–5
body, *see* language
bonding   153, 161 n.5
Bram Stoker's Dracula [movie]   187–8, 193–4, 197–8, 202, see also Dracula
Braverman, Crosby   12, 167, see also Parenthood
Breaking Bad [tv series]   13, 285–6, 289–91, 301, see also Heisenberg; White, Skyler; White, Walter
broadcast   44, 64, 71–2, 93–4, 113–14, 136, 141, 160 n.1, 161 n.3, 167, 195
  sports   9
  talk (*see* talk)
Brock, Timothy C.   8, 35, 87, 89–90, 161 n.3
Brooks, Mel   229, 231–2, 240, 243, 245–6, 251, 254–5, 256 n.16, 17
Brown, Penelope   83, 183, 194, 196, 296

call-back   98, 107
camera   6–7, 23, 25–6, 66, 92–3, 101, 118, 120–2, 127, 129, 132–4, 137 n.4, 142–3, 146, 152, 155–7, 159, 161 n.3, 175, 179–80, 184, 186–8, 191–3, 195–201, 207, 214, 232, 271–2, 298
  angle   66, 201
  handheld   188, 191, 193, 195, 198, 200
  subjective   186, 195–6, 201
Candlin, Christopher   116–17, 125
Captain Haddock   269–70, 271–5, 279, see also Hergé
captions   13, 237, 285–6, 288, 290–1, 294, 296, 298, 303–4
  closed   285, 288, 303

Carter, Ronald   20–1
cartoon   270, 273, 275, 277, 281 n.13
catchphrase   42, 63
categorization   91, 94–5, 102, 106, 116–19, 121–2, 125–7, 135–6
'cause   50, 52
celebrity   141, 144–5
  narrator (*see* narrator)
Channel 4   114, 116, 118, 120, 122, 125, 133–4, 143, 148
Chapman, Siobhan   10, 134, 184, 189
character   2, 5–8, 10–12, 19, 25–6, 28–9, 31, 33, 35, 40–1, 44, 46–9, 54, 56 n.1, 6, 63–8, 71–2, 74–6, 83–4, 88–90, 92–4, 97–105, 107–8, 114, 133, 142–3, 145, 154, 165–9, 172–5, 179–81, 184–9, 191–201, 207–8, 210, 212, 214–17, 219 n.8, 223, 227, 238, 241, 247, 251, 254, 266–7, 269, 272–6, 281, 286–98, 301, 303–4, 313–16
  analysis   165, 167, 169, 172, 174, 180
  communication (*see* communication)
  cue   166, 288
  gesture   88, 90, 94, 99, 101–2
  impression formation   286, 288, 290, 298
characterization   9, 47, 49, 55, 100, 102, 107, 143, 166–7, 169, 174, 179–81, 184, 288–9, 291, 293, 298, 304
Chovanec, Jan   5, 9, 11–12, 14 n.7, 141–2, 144, 153, 161 n.3
Cinema Arthuriana   230
cinematic   1–6, 9–12, 13 n.1, 25, 142–3, 183–6, 188–97, 200, 206–8, 219 n.5, 7, 223, 228, 256 n.9, 264, 309–11, 315–17, 319–20
  art   143
  discourse (*see* discourse)
  fiction   143
  implicature   184, 190–91, 193, 195, 200
  narrator   143
cinematography   2, 5, 9, 169, 183–4, 186, 188–90, 197–8, 200–1, 207, 310
Clark, Billy   10, 184, 189
Clark, Herbert H.   207, 220
close-up   129, 132–5, 175, 184, 186, 191–2, 198, 200, 294, 315–16

co-construction 154
code 8, 12–13, 29, 31, 94, 225–6, 239, 245, 252, 254, 264–5, 268–9, 274, 277–8, 281 n.17, 286, 296, 311
  orthographic 264
  phonetic 264–5, 268, 274
  switching 8, 226, 239, 252
coding 7, 73, 94, 101, 168, see also annotation
  trans 12–13
cognition, cognitive 13, 21, 27, 30, 88–90, 185, 191, 208–10, 212–15, 218, 220 n.12, 223, 266, 287–9, 298, 304, 309
  effect 191, 210, 212–15
  environment 209–10, 214, 218
coherence 6, 9–10, 12, 106, 117–18, 158, 228, 230–1, 240, 266
  topical 9–10, 231
cohesion 9, 88, 97, 100–2, 106, 108, 148, 152, 160, 191, 196, 310, 317, 320 n.2
collective, see sender
Collier, John 229, 232, 260
collocation 9, 244
comedy 5, 8, 11, 40, 44, 69, 90, 106, 186, 229–30, 240, 243, 253, 257 n.22
  animated 229
  film 257 n.22
comics, comic books 13, 263–73, 275–9, 280 nn.3, 4, 6, 11, 281 nn.12, 14, 294
commentary 41, 141, 147, 150, 158, 167
  running 150
communication, communicative 5, 8, 12, 14 n.7, 20, 30, 35, 54, 64, 68, 87, 89, 92, 98, 103, 108–9, 141–3, 146, 153, 155, 159–60, 166, 171, 173–4, 180, 183–4, 188–91, 196, 200–1, 205, 207–18, 219 n.10, 220 n.11, 266–7, 285, 287, 289, 310–11, 318–20
  character 208
  frame (see frame)
  harmony 153
  intention (see intention)
  levels 89, 92, 103, 160, 190
  maxim (see maxim)
  setting 30, 89
  spectator 208

community of practice 231
competence 165–6, 168–9, 171–4, 179–80
  pragmatic (see pragmatic)
complexity 5–6, 8, 136, 143, 206, 278, 301, see also problem
computer mediated texts 227
conception 231, 237, 264, 265
  spoken 265
  written 265
concordance 9–10, 31–4, 121
conflict, see talk
conjunction 104, 121, 246
  archaic 246
connotation 186, 252, 315
  negative 31–2, 34
  sexual 252
context 4, 8, 19–29, 31, 35, 36 n.2, 40, 43, 52, 88, 90, 92, 95–8, 101, 109, 113, 115, 117, 127, 130, 134–6, 138, 149, 165, 169–73, 180, 184–5, 188–9, 191–2, 205, 210–11, 213, 216–17, 219 n.3, 241, 267, 269, 277, 279, 281 n.15, 286–90, 292, 296, 298, 311–12, 314–15, 317, 319–20
contractions 44, 54, 228, 239, 246 n.2, 256, 264–5, 272
conversation 2–3, 9, 20, 36 n.4, 41–2, 52, 64–79, 82–3, 85, 92, 98, 101, 108, 133, 142, 153, 159, 170–2, 180, 183, 185, 196, 241, 264–6, 271–2, 286, 290–1, 294, 296, 298, 303, 310, see also talk
  analysis 3, 9, 142, 290
  naturally-occurring 70, 265–6
Cooper, Sheldon 48–9, 166, see also Big Bang Theory, The
cooperative principle 12, 183, 188–9
corpus, corpora 3, 7–11, 13, 20, 22–4, 30, 36, 39–40, 43–50, 52–5, 56 n.6, 57 n.11, 64, 66–70, 72–4, 81–2, 109, 167–8, 170–2, 174, 181, 212, 223, 227–31, 236, 238–40, 242–3, 247–50, 252–3, 255, 256 n.7, 269
  -based 10, 20, 22–3
  of Contemporary American English 67, 72
  design 8, 44
  linguistics (see linguistics)

reference   10–11, 46–8, 55, 247, 249
SOAP   43, 70, 72–4, 81–2 (*see also* soap opera)
Sydney of Television dialogue   9–10, 39–40, 44, 54
cue, *see* metacommunicative
Culpeper, Jonathan   43, 100, 142, 166, 287–8, 290–1, 293, 296, 298, 304
cut (edit)   4, 66, 87, 149–50, 157–8, 175, 183–4, 188, 191, 193, 196–8, 200–2, 212, 220 n.12
  jump   191
  straight   191, 196–7, 201
cutting   152, 157, *see also* editing; montage

Dahne, Annie   10, 13, 285
deaf   13, 285–8, 290–8, 301, 303–5
deixis, deictic   19–25, 27, 31, 34–5, 134
demonstratives   10, 19–26, 28–31, 34–5
  endophoric   19
  exophoric   20, 23–4, 29
  gestural   25–6
  symbolic   22, 26, 28–9, 35
descriptive   94, 206, 211–13, 216–17
dialect   8, 10, 42, 49, 169, 185, 241, 274, 319
dialogue   1–10, 12–13, 14 n.6, 19–20, 22–4, 26–7, 31, 33, 35, 36 n.2, 39–49, 51, 54–5, 56 n.1, 63–71, 74, 79, 89–90, 92, 103, 127, 143, 160, 166–7, 174, 179–80, 185, 188–201, 227, 229, 238, 251, 254, 264–6, 268–72, 278, 280 n.6, 285–7, 289, 292–4, 296, 298, 303, 309–10
  diegetic   143
  film (*see* film)
  trope (*see* formulaic language; trope)
  TV   39–40, 42–6, 54–5, 56 n.1, 68
diegesis, diegetic   2, 5, 8, 12, 19, 22, 25, 92, 94, 118, 141–3, 145–6, 148, 150–4, 156–9, 160–61 n.1, 180, 198, 200, 293–4
  dialogue (*see* dialogue)
  hetero (*see* narration)
  narrator, narration (*see* narrator, narration)
  non (*see* non-diegetic)
  world   92, 143, 145

director, *see* film; screen
disconnection   148
  temporal   148
discourse   1–12, 13 n.1, 14 n.5, 6, 19–20, 22–4, 26, 30–1, 35, 36 n.4, 39, 42, 44–6, 48, 54, 64–5, 67–74, 82, 87, 89, 113, 116–19, 122, 135, 137 n.1, 138, 141–3, 145, 147, 152, 158–9, 169, 171–3, 179–81, 183–6, 188–91, 193, 196, 200, 205–9, 213–14, 219 n.1, 5, 7, 224, 226, 231, 238, 250, 263, 296, 309–11, 315–17, 319, 320 n.2
  analysis   11, 13, 39, 113, 137 n.1, 11, 13, 39, 113, 137 n.1
  cinematic   2–5, 9–12, 13 n.1, 183–5, 188–9, 196, 206–7, 219, 309–11, 315–17, 319–20
  critical   3, 11, 113
  film   2, 4–5, 9–10, 13 n.1, 183–5, 189, 191, 196, 219
  layered   207
  marker   44, 48, 152, 169, 171–2, 238, 250, 296
  multimodal   113, 137, 185, 190
  narrative (*see* narrative)
  studies   3
  telecinematic   3–6, 8, 10–11, 13–14, 20, 39, 64–5, 67–9, 71–3, 87, 89, 141–3, 173, 179–81, 226, 231, 263
discovery quest   141
Disney, Walt   229–30, 232, 234, 236, 240–1, 243–4, 247, 249, 251–4, 257 n.19
displacement   148
  humorous   148
documentary   2, 4–5, 11–12, 113–28, 132–7, 141–53, 155–6, 158–9, 160 n.1, 161 nn.2, 3, 6, 186, 195, 201
  expository   142, 144
  hybrid   144
  TV   141–4, 159
dominance   119, 145–6
Dracula   187–8, 193–5, 197–8, *see also Bram Stoker's Dracula*
Dragonheart [movie]   229, 230, 233, 235–6, 243–7, 249, 252

drama, dramatic   11–12, 41, 43–4, 46, 49, 64–6, 68–9, 73, 76, 82–3, 114, 123, 129, 145, 161 n.6, 167, 174, 185, 229–30, 271, 286, 290
   adventures   229–30
   pause   145
Dynel, Marta   8–9, 14 n.7, 39, 87, 89, 94, 142, 184–5, 207–8, 213, 219 n.5, 309

editing   3–4, 127, 142, 152, 158–9, 184–5, 188–9, 191, 196, 207, 211, 214–17, 310, *see also* cutting; montage
   technique   3, 196
effect-size   46–7, 54
emphasis   3, 21, 24, 30, 69, 78, 102–3, 108, 116, 126, 134, 164, 185, 207–8, 276
endophoric, *see* demonstratives
English   11, 20–3, 29, 35, 36 n.4, 40, 46, 49–50, 52–5, 57, 67, 70, 72, 115, 135, 145, 149, 155, 216, 223, 226–8, 231, 237–8, 240–1, 243, 245–7, 251, 253–5, 256 nn.7, 10, 14, 15, 264, 271, 274, 277–8, 281 nn.14, 16
   accent   274
   medieval   228, 237–8
   Middle   226–7, 231, 238, 240–1, 243, 245, 254–5, 256 n.7
   Old   226, 237, 255, 256 n.7, 14, 15
entertainment   116, 120, 137, 144, 190, 280 n.12
episode, *see* narrative episode
ethnomethodology, *see* methodology
evaluation, evaluative   12, 31, 103, 130–2, 144, 147, 149, 152, 159–60, 167, 173, 210, 213
exegesis   143
exophoric, *see* demonstratives
experience   1, 3–7, 11, 13, 20, 30, 65, 68, 83, 104, 116–18, 143–4, 147, 155, 160, 195, 200, 210, 215, 217, 220 nn.12, 15, 263, 278, 281 n.17, 286, 293, 298, 304
expertise   116, 118, 144, 150, 153, 159, 162, 238, *see also* knowledge
expository   65–6, 113, 142, 144–5, 150–1, 153–7, 159
   documentary (*see* documentary)
   mode (*see* mode)

facial expression   4, 90, 92–3, 96, 100–1, 105, 107–9, 192–3, 273, 292, 298–9, 301, 303
   repetition of (*see* repetition)
Fahey, Palma M.   70–1
fan   7–8, 39, 42, 44, 56 n.6, 63, 167, 216, 223, 226–8, 272, 279
   communities   39, 42
   transcripts (*see* transcripts)
fantasy adventure   226, 229–30
fiction, fictional   2–5, 10, 14 n.5, 19–20, 35, 36 n.4, 39, 41–4, 52, 56 n.1, 67–9, 72, 87, 89, 92, 97, 101, 106, 117, 141–3, 152, 165–7, 180, 184–7, 189–91, 196, 207, 212, 217, 223, 225, 230, 257 n.22, 265–6, 288, 290, 310
   cinematic   143
   film   4–5, 143, 186
   genres   142, 186 (*see also* genre)
   non-   4–5, 14 n.5, 36 n.4, 141–3, 186 (*see also* narrative)
fictionalization, fictionalized   152
   narrative (*see* narrative)
   voice   152
film   1–12, 13 n.1, 2, 14 n.7, 19–20, 22–36, 41, 63, 68–9, 72, 74, 87, 113–19, 121–2, 124, 126–8, 132–3, 135–8, 141–3, 147, 183–97, 199–202, 205–18, 219 n.3, 5, 320 n.12, 16, 17, 223–33, 235–6, 238, 240, 247, 249–51, 254–5, 256 n.10, 12, 257 n.22, 263–6, 268–9, 280–1 nn.4, 5, 6, 8, 9, 11, 14, 16, 17, 290, 309–12, 315–20, 320 n.1, *see also* motion picture
   audience (*see* audience)
   comedy (*see* comedy)
   dialogue   3, 5–6, 10, 12–13, 19, 22–4, 31, 33, 69, 74, 185, 238, 254, 264–5, 271–2, 280 n.6, 309–10
   director   1, 5, 7–8, 11–12, 127, 132, 183, 185, 187, 200, 207, 218, 227, 231–5, 264, 268–70, 309–11, 317–18
   discourse (*see* discourse)
   fictional (*see* fiction)
   genre (*see* genre)
   historical   224, 231

horror 11–12, 183–4, 186–7, 190–2, 195–6, 200–2
medieval 223–31, 236, 238, 249, 250, 254, 256 n.12
motion 223, 280 n.11
parody of (*see* parody)
scene (*see* scene)
shot (*see* shot)
sound (*see* sound)
trailer (*see* trailer)
transcripts 7, 43–4, 52, 56–7, 72, 74, 167–8, 223, 226–8, 241, 243, 260, 272, 293
flashback 159, 194, 197
flash-forward 148
flouting 188, 190–1, 193, 198, 201
focus 3, 5–6, 8, 10, 12, 21–2, 26, 30, 35, 40, 45, 47, 64–5, 72–4, 80, 83, 87–9, 108, 114, 117–20, 126, 144, 165, 167, 169, 175, 180, 185–8, 191, 194–5, 198, 201, 205–6, 208, 211–13, 215, 220 n.15, 231–2, 234, 254, 263–4, 278, 285, 287
footage 188, 195, 197, 201
formulaicity, formulaic language, formulae, formula 63–4, 67–70, 72, 74, 98, 246, *see also* language
archaic 246–7
frame, framing 4, 6–8, 11, 13, 44, 89–91, 96–8, 101–3, 106–10, 116, 118–22, 124, 126–7, 135–6, 142–3, 145–6, 148–50, 152, 156, 159–60, 161 n.3, 175, 180, 190–1, 193, 197, 215, 223–4, 228, 230, 236–8, 240, 25, 254, 294–25, 298–303, 312, 317
communicative 8, 142–3, 146, 159
dual 142
medieval 223–4, 236–7, 250, 254
play 90–1, 109
semantic (*see* semantic)
framework 8, 12–13, 14 n.7, 21, 55, 71, 89, 113, 119, 149–50, 153, 165, 169, 184, 188, 205–6, 208, 212–13, 216, 218, 219 n.1, 287, *see also* model
frontstage, performance 143

Garcés-Conejos Blitvich, Pilar 9, 143–4
gaze 25–6, 174–5, 180, 205
genre 2, 4, 6, 8, 10–12, 23, 25, 40, 43–6, 49, 53, 65–6, 68–9, 71–3, 88, 90, 106, 113, 116, 127, 141–4, 159, 160 n.1, 184–7, 195, 199–202, 206, 207, 214, 216–17, 220 n.16, 223–4, 226, 229–31, 279, 287
cinematic 142, 186
film 2, 12, 185–6, 226, 279
hybrid 2
non-fictional 143, 186
sub 2, 11, 68, 82, 187, 195, 224, 226
television 2, 4, 6, 8, 11
Gilmore, Lorelai 48–9, *see also Gilmore Girls*
Gilmore Girls [tv series] 40–1, 43, 46–8, 56 n.6, *see also* Gilmore, Lorelai
gonna 32, 44, 49–51, 66, 75, 96, 154, 156–7, 171, 177–9, 240, 250–1, 299, 302
gotta 50, 53, 56–7 n.10, 66, 250
grammar 9, 40, 67, 87, 100, 183
visual 9
Green, Melanie C. 35
Grice, H. Paul 12, 65, 183, 188–9, 191, 194–6, 198–9, 200, 208, 220 n.11, 266
gypsies 113–16, 120, 122–3, 126, 128–9

hashtag 42, 77
hearer 20, 21, 26, 35, 73, 127, 266, 274
over- (*see* overhearer)
hedge 32, 79, 171–3, 174, 181
Heisenberg 289–90, 293–5, 298–9, 304, *see also Breaking Bad*
Hergé 263–5, 263–4, 267, 269–70, 273, 277, 280 n.4, *see also* Captain Haddock; Tintin
Hess, Graham 192–3, 197–8, *see also Signs*
Historicism 224
New 224
historiography 224–5
historiophoty 224
history, historical 12–13, 89, 122, 144, 147, 152–3, 157, 160, 186–7, 205–6, 219 n.3, 224–5, 227–32, 240–1, 243, 254–5, 280 n.1
drama 12, 229–30
film (*see* film)
meta- 224
Hitchcock, Alfred 13, 187, 309, 310–20, 320 n.4

Hoffmann, Christian   1, 36 n.4, 39, 92, 142, 219 n.5
Hollywood   5, 13, 219 n.3, 271, 274, 287
homonymy   239–41, 243, 254
horror   11–12, 183–4, 186–8, 190–2, 195–6, 198–202
   film (*see* film)
How Britain Worked [documentary series]   12, 143, 145–6, 148–9, 151, 154, 156, *see also* Guy Martin, Guy; *How Britain Worked*
humour, humourous   8–9, 11, 87–91, 93–5, 97–110, 147–8, 189, 197, 201, 227, 252–4
   displacement (*see* displacement)
   telecinematic   11, 87–8, 94, 106
   turn (*see* turn)
hybrid   2, 113, 144, 278
   documentary (*see* documentary)
   genre (*see* genre)

iconicity   20, 24, 35, 220 n.16
ideology, ideological   3, 9, 11, 42, 113–14, 116–19, 121, 127–8, 130, 137
idiosyncratic   68, 200–1, 226
   features   226
imitation   98, 143
   poetic   143
impersonal   143
   style (*see* style)
implicature   10, 12, 125, 128, 130, 134, 184, 188–9, 190–1, 193, 195–8, 200–1, *see also* maxims of conversation
   conversational   10, 188
implicit   4, 122, 125, 157, 166–7, 171, 180, 183, 231, 236, 254, 279, 288
incongruity   11, 88–91, 95–9, 104–9
   resolution (*see* model)
indexicality   169
Industrial Revolution   144
inference, inferential   127, 157, 170, 172, 188, 207, 209, 217, 287–8
inflection, inflectional   238–9, 243, 245, 254
   morphology   239
informal   49–51, 54–5, 70, 252, 266, 274
   language (*see* language)

information   7, 21, 23–4, 31, 36 n.3, 43, 46, 55, 66–7, 70, 72, 75, 78, 90, 117, 119, 125, 127, 150–1, 153–5, 157–9, 192–4, 199–200, 209–11, 214–15, 219 n.3, 255, 266, 268, 272, 274, 287, 289, 291, 293, 298, 301, 303
   factual   150
intention   88, 92, 94, 96, 109, 183, 200, 209, 211, 215, 218, 255, 287
   communicative   209, 211
   informative   209, 218
interaction   2, 9, 12, 19–22, 26, 30, 35, 42, 56 n.1, 65, 71, 89–90, 92–4, 97, 99, 100–1, 107–9, 126, 142, 145, 148, 150, 153, 154, 156, 159, 165, 170–2, 174, 183, 185, 188–9, 191, 211, 215, 224, 266, 286, 291–2, 297, 310
   dialogical   145, 148
   embedded (conversational)   148
inter-character   143, 184–5, 189, 207
   diegetic dialogue (*see* dialogue)
intermediality   10, 12–13
interruption   147, 265, 295–8
intertextuality, intertextual   10, 12–13, 45, 89, 92, 185, 310–12, 318, 320
   link   310–14, 320
interturn   94–7, 99–101, 104–9
   repetition (*see* repetition)
intraturn   94–6, 101–3, 105–09
   repetition (*see* repetition)

Janney, Richard W.   2, 4, 9, 183, 185, 189, 191, 196, 205–7, 219 n.5, 309–10, 312
Jefferson, Gail   109, 213, 296
joint   20–1, 144–5, 150, 153–4, 156, 158, 160
   focus of attention (*see* attention)
   narration (*see* narration)
   negotiation (*see* negotiation)
   telling (*see* telling)
Jurassic Park [movie]   187, 192, 196, 200

Kaufman, Geoff F.   35
Kaufman, Millard   229, 233
keyness   4, 46, 48, 59, 247–50, 257 n.18
keywords   9, 11, 48–9, 56 n.5, 166, 238, 247–8

Kirner-Ludwig, Monika   12, 39, 219 n.5, 223–4, 227, 230
knowledge   6, 19, 24, 27, 30, 39, 75, 87, 89, 97–8, 103, 107, 116, 118, 126–7, 137, 144, 159–60, 170, 172, 180, 183, 185, 189, 210, 213–16, 218, 220 n.10, 226–7, 231, 236–7, 240, 255, 267, 287–90, 293, 298, 305, 311, 319, *see also* expertise
　culturally shared   227
Krebs, Heike   11–12, 205
Kubrick, Stanley   187, 190, 196, 199, *see also Shining, The* [movie]

Ladyhawke [movie]   229–30, 234–6, 244–7, 249, 251, 256 n.4
language
　body   3, 174–5, 193–4, 197, 200, 205, 275, 298
　colloquial   50–1, 54, 250
　formulaic   11, 64, 67–70, 72–3, 79, 86, 107
　informal   70, 266
　non-standard   11, 50–1, 54, 56
　spoken   185, 206, 212, 217, 263–5, 268
　telecinematic (*see* telecinematic discourse)
　written   1–6, 212, 237, 264, 266–9, 277–8
　youth   251
Latin
　medieval   226
　relatinization   253
laughter   18, 23, 26–8, 60, 90, 93–4, 107, 110, 112, 144, 147, 162, 164
layer, layering   6, 20, 211, 217, 254, 261, *see also* discourse
Leeuwen, Theo van   9, 16, 117, 124, 134, 139–40
Levinson, Stephen C.   8, 16, 21, 24–5, 30, 37, 83–4, 297, 305
lighting, low-key   186, 191, 193–4, 198
linguistics
　corpus   3, 11, 39–40, 43
　socio   3, 10, 15, 40, 60, 85, 181–2
　systemic functional   3, 17
log likelihood, *see* keyness

logocentrism, logocentric   6
Lord of the Rings, The [movie]   205–6, 220, 222, 256
low-key, *see* lighting

McCarthy, Michael   16, 20–1, 36, 59
McIntyre, Dan   2, 4, 9–10, 15–16, 43, 59, 100–11, 186, 189, 203, 287, 306
malapropism   244
manner, *see* maxim of
Martin, Guy   144–5, 147, 149–50, 152, 155, 158, 161
maxims of conversation, maxim   12, 183–4, 190–1, 196, 200, *see also* implicature
　of manner   198
　of quality   195
　of quantity   65, 191
　of relation   196–8, 200–01
medieval, medievalism
　blog (*see* blog)
　English (*see* English)
　film   223–31, 236, 238, 249–50, 254, 256–7, 259–60
　frame (*see* frame)
　Latin (*see* Latin)
　motif   223
　movie (*see* film)
　pseudo-   223, 225–7, 231, 238, 240, 255, 256, 260
　stereotype (*see* stereotype)
medium, media   ix, x, 3–6, 10, 12–18, 20, 24–5, 37–43, 52–60, 64, 85, 110, 116–17, 119, 125, 138–42, 152, 161–3, 166, 169, 180–1, 185, 190, 203, 208, 219 nn.1, 8, 10, 220 n.15, 221–2, 227, 255–60, 264, 269, 273, 279, 285, 290, 306, 310
meme   42
Merlin [tv series]   226, 230, 234, 256
Messerli, Thomas C.   11, 36–7, 87, 89, 93, 111
metacommunicative cue   11–12, 25, 44, 66, 90, 94, 101, 166–7, 169, 172–83, 180, 287–90, 293, 296, 298, 301, 304, 320 n.3
method, methodology   3, 5, 8–13, 18, 37, 59, 72, 74, 89, 93–4, 106, 107, 142, 156, 165, 167, 180, 181, 191, 203,

212, 219, 221, 258, 269, 290, 291, 292, 305–6
ethno   3, 9
mixed   10, 12, 165, 180
Metro-Goldwyn-Mayer   318
Middle English, *see* English
mimetic art   143
mind, *see* style
misalignment, of verbal and visual tracks   155, 160
mixed method approach, *see* methodology
modalities   2, 4, 8, 119
modes, *see also* modalities; resources
   expository   145, 150–1, 153–5, 159
model, *see also* framework
   incongruity-resolution   11, 88–9, 108
monologue   2, 4–5, 9, 56, 148, 152–3, 155–7, 159–60, 183, 185, 238, 266–7, 279
montage   2, 4, 221, *see also* cutting; editing
Montgomery, Martin   2, 5, 9, 16, 117–18, 139, 147, 163
motif   223, 310–30
   medieval   10
motion film, *see* film
movie, *see* film
   transcripts (*see* transcripts)
multimodality, multimodal
   analysis   16–17, 206, 213, 216, 221
   discourse (*see* discourse)
   environment   31, 120, 268, 277–9
   film discourse (*see* discourse)
   recipient design (*see* recipient design)
multiple tellership, *see* narration; tellership
music   2–6, 16, 63, 135, 141, 146, 148, 152, 161, 170, 180, 183, 193, 202, 206–8, 213–17, 293
   track   141, 148, 152

narration, narrative, *see also* tellership
   box   267–8, 278–9
   co-construction   154
   (non-)diegetic   158
   discourse   147
   episode   6, 42–5, 47–51, 54, 56, 66, 71–2, 76, 88, 92–101, 103, 105–6, 108–9, 149, 167–8, 174, 180, 191, 289, 305

heterodiegetic   143–5, 153, 158, 160
joint   154, 156
non-fiction   142
presenter (*see* presenter)
self-enclosed   144, 160
structure   64, 154
technique   146–7, 155, 157, 160, 187, 191, 194–5, 200–1, 295
visual   2
voice (*see* voice)
voice-over   142, 146–9, 152, 157, 163
narrator
   celebrity   141
   diegetic   141, 143, 146, 150
   external   142
   extradiegetic   19, 29, 94, 111, 142–3, 180, 293–4
   invisible   121, 142
   non-diegetic   145, 148, 152, 159, 160
   off-screen   2, 5, 142, 147, 216–17, 220
   omniscient   143, 150, 153, 155, 159
   on-screen   2, 36 n.2
   presenter (*see* presenter)
   voice (*see* voice)
   voice-over   142, 144, 146–2, 154–5, 157–61, 217
negotiation, joint   150
New Historicism, *see* Historicism
n-grams   viii, 11, 46–8, 56 n.8, 73
non-authenticity, *see* authenticity
non-diegetic   147
   sound (*see* sound)
   voice (*see* voice)
non-eliteness, non-elite   145
non-verbal (modes, signs, communication)   19, 24, 31, 164, 174, 180, 183, 205, 212, 214, 268, 291–2

off-screen   2, 5, 142, 147, 216–17, 220
   narrator (*see* narrator)
Old English, *see* English
Old Norse   226
onomatopoeia   267–9, 276
on-screen
   action (*see* action; narrator)
ordinariness, ordinary   18, 68, 125, 144, 216–17
   people   144

ostension, ostensive 19, 185, 195, 209–11, 215
overhearer 153, 179, 185

panel, comic 264–7, 273, 275–7, 279, 282
paralinguistic
    features 31, 105, 226, 298
parallelism
    structural 88, 93, 96, 99, 100, 103, 105, 107, 108
parasynthetic
    adjective 244
Parenthood [tv series] 165, 167–8, 170–2, 180, 182, *see also* Braverman, Crosby
parody 229, 231
participant, participation
    complex 6, 8
    non-elite (*see* non-eliteness)
    structure 37, 89–90, 111
Pavesi, Maria 10, 17, 19, 22–3, 37–8
personalization
    synthetic 152, 157
Piazza, Roberta 3–5, 9–11, 13, 15, 17–18, 40, 57–60, 89, 112–13, 115, 127, 136–7, 139, 142, 163, 184–6, 204, 219, 221, 282, 286, 309
play frame, *see* frame
poetic 131, 143, 186
    imitation (*see* imitation)
point-of-view
    shot (*see* shot)
post-production 93, 142, 146, 157, 159, 207, 226–7
    fan transcripts (*see* transcripts)
practical past 224
pragmastylistics, *see* stylistics
pragmatics, (meta) pragmatic
    awareness 309–13, 315–17, 319–20
    competence 165–6, 168–9, 171–2, 174, 180
    failure 169, 182
    implications 227
    marker 166–7, 169–73, 181
    meta 309–13, 315–17, 319–20
pre-production
    screenplay (*see* screenplay)
presenter
    narrator, narration 142, 144–7, 150–2, 154, 156, 159–60

privilege, privileged
    voice (*see* voice)
problem
    complexity 6, 8
    oriented talk (*see* talk)
    -solution pattern 149
pronoun
    personal 170, 238–9, 241
pronunciation 11, 44, 49, 145, 240
prosody, prosodic
    repetition (*see* repetition)
    semantic 31, 38
pseudo-
    archaism (*see* archaic)
    authentic (*see* authenticity)
    medieval (*see* medieval)

reaction
    shot (*see* shot)
real, reality
    authenticity (*see* authenticity)
    TV (*see* TV)
recipient design 8–9, 200, 213, *see also* audience design
    multimodal 213, 217
recontextualization 95, 98
Red Rackham [movie] 268–71, 275, 283
Reichelt, Susan 9–12, 17, 40, 60, 166
relatinization, *see* Latin
relevance, relevant
    optimal, optimally 208, 210
    principle of 208, 213
    theory, theoretical 205, 220–2, 287
repetition
    of facial expressions 93, 100–1, 105, 108 (*see also* facial expressions)
    functions of 98, 108, 111
    interturn 95, 100–1, 104, 106–7
    intraturn 95–6, 101–2, 105–09
    lexical 92, 95–9, 102–3, 106–9
    prosodic 93–4, 96, 99–100, 103–5, 107, 109
    telecinematic 93, 96, 101, 107, 108
representation 4, 12, 16, 18–20, 23, 35, 36, 43, 59, 90, 92, 100, 110, 114–19, 121, 124, 127, 136–7, 139
requests 77, 79–80, 82–3
resolution, *see also* model
    incongruity 11, 88–9, 105, 108

resources   3–6, 8, 11–13, 35, 115, 206–7, 310, 318, *see also* modes
Robbins, Matthew   230, 235, 253, 256, 261
Robin Hood, *see Adventures of Robin Hood, The* [movie]
Rossi, Fabio   3–5, 15, 17–18, 39, 57–60, 89, 112, 113–14, 127, 139, 142, 163, 184, 204, 219, 221, 282, 310

Sacks, Harvey   125, 140, 213, 221, 294, 296, 306
salience, saliency   6, 189, 310–12, 316–17, 319–20
Sanchez-Stockhammer, Christina   10, 13, 256–7, 263, 279, 282
Sarangi, Srikant   116–17, 125, 127, 140
scene
  analysis   165, 167, 169, 174, 180
  film   12, 211–12
  scripted   143
Schegloff, Emanuel A.   213, 221, 294, 296, 306
Schmidt, Karl-Heinrich   4, 9, 14, 185, 204, 282
Schubert, Christoph   9–12, 17, 183–4, 187, 189, 204, 282
screen
  adaptation   263–4, 269–71, 273–4, 276, 280
  directions   7, 56
  play (*see* screenplay)
  split   194, 201
  writer   8, 10, 63, 231–3, 272–3
screenplay
  pre-production   7, 225, 227
script
  writer   37, 71, 111, 183–5, 200, 207, 228, 244–7, 252, 255, 269
scripted, scriptedness
  scene (*see* scene)
  talk (*see* talk)
scriptovisual medium   264, 280
segment
  narrative (*see* narrative)
semantics, semantic
  frame   89, 96, 98
  prosody (*see* prosody)

semiotic   4–7, 11–13, 16–18, 29, 37, 45, 60, 85, 112, 183, 185, 201, 203, 206–7, 211–12, 279, 303, 309
sender
  collective   8, 14 n.4, 89, 92, 94, 98, 100, 103, 106–9, 185, 207–9, 211, 213, 217–18
series, *see* TV
setting
  geo-timely   228
sexual
  connotation (*see* connotation)
Shining, The [movie]   187–8, 190–1, 197, 199, 202, 231, 252, *see also* Kubrick, Stanley
shot
  film   1, 6, 8, 87, 184
  point-of-view   191, 196–7, 200, 318
  reaction   191–2, 201
Signs [movie]   161, 187, 197–8, 200, 202, *see also* Hess, Graham
sitcom   11, 15, 17, 18, 38, 41–2, 48, 60, 70, 85, 87, 89–90, 92–5, 97, 100–2, 105–10
soap opera   7, 11, 43, 52–4, 63–5, 67–74, 84–5, 144
social media   15, 57–8, 61, 110, 161–2, 163, 290
sociolinguistic, sociolinguistics, *see* linguistics
software   48, 55–6, 60, 181, 257
solution
  problem-pattern (*see* problem)
sound
  film   9
  non-diegetic   2, 146, 160
  track   4, 13, 18, 141, 146–8, 159, 161, 201, 207, 267, 276
space   19, 26, 37, 76, 90, 102, 115, 120, 122–3, 131, 136, 184, 187, 194, 201, 233, 255, 258, 287, 294, 298, 312, 319
speech bubbles, speech balloons   271–2, 275–6, 276–8, 280
Sperber, Dan   12, 18, 126, 140, 205–18, 220, 222, 287, 293, 306, 333
Spielberg, Steven   8, 13, 187, 192, 196–7, 202–3, 264, 267–76, 278–84
stand-up comedy   15, 106, 110, 161, 235
Star Trek [movie]   17, 40, 43, 59, 60

stereotype
   medieval   231
stimulus, stimuli   10–11, 89–91, 108, 210, 214–15, 218, 219 n.9, 287
story, *see also* narrative; style
   line   64–5, 67, 83, 144, 167, 241, 266, 269–70
   telling   1, 15, 36, 149, 159–61, 163, 183–4, 189
structure
   narrative (*see* narrative)
   participation (*see* participation)
style
   conversational   71
   detached   143
   impersonal   143
   mind   169
   storytelling   131
stylistics   2, 8–10, 13, 15–16, 18, 37, 39, 41, 45, 55, 85, 87, 111–12, 142, 163, 184, 189, 190, 202–4, 206, 304
   pragma   10–13, 15, 160, 185, 201
   pragmatic literary   9, 15
   telecinematic   2, 8–10, 13
stylization, styled   13, 143, 172–3, 174, 180–1, 258
subgenre, *see* genre
subnarrative, *see* narrative
subtitle   205, 285
Syd-TV   55, 58, *see also* Corpus; Sydney Corpus of Television dialogue
synonymy   38
syntax   16, 37–8, 40, 72, 85, 184, 202, 226, 239, 243, 245, 265
synthetic, *see* personalization

talk, *see also* conversation
   broadcast   141, 160
   conflict   8, 11, 33, 35–6, 46, 71, 73, 91, 195, 240, 254
   problem-oriented   11, 63, 73–4, 76, 82–3
   scripted   11
   spontaneous   158
technique
   narrative (*see* narrative)
telecinematic
   discourse (*see* discourse)
   humor (*see* humor)
   language (*see* language)
   repetition (*see* repetition)
   stylistics (*see* stylistics)
television, *see* TV
   genre (*see* genre)
tellership, *see also* narrative
   multiple   157
telling
   joint   156
tense (verbal)   148, 271
texture   10–11
third-person account   143
thought bubbles   275–6
Tintin, *see* Hergé
Toolan, Michael   1–2, 9, 39, 87, 104, 106, 184, 264–6
track   13, 141, 147–8, 152, 185, 201, 290–1, 293, 298, 303–4
   alignment of   160
   laugh   88, 93, 105
   verbal   141, 148, 152, 158, 160
   visual   141–3, 146–50, 152, 155, 158–60
trailer   12, 115–16, 132–5, 205–19, 219 nn.2, 3, 5, 220 nn.12, 13, 18
   film   11–12, 119, 147, 205–9, 211–12, 216, 218–20
transactional, *see* communication
transcoding, *see* coding
transcriber   7, 226, 256 n.2, 292
transcription   7, 44, 56n n.8, 9, 94, 109, 110 n.3, 145, 164, 167–8, 271, 292, 295–7, 299–303
   issue   6, 8
transcripts, *see also* post-production
   fan   44, 56, 226–7, 272
   movie   223, 260
translation   12–13, 142, 271, 279, 286–7, 289–90, 292–3, 304
transmedia, *see* media
traveller   11, 113–37, 137 n.2, 138 n.5
travelogue   141
Traxel, Oliver M.   227–8, 236, 238, 243, 247, 255
trope   63
   dialogue   63, 67 (*see also* formulaic language)
turn
   humorous   94, 97, 105, 109

inter (*see* repetition)
intra (*see* repetition)
taking   171, 180, 294
TV (television)
  broadcast (*see* broadcast)
  dialogue (*see* dialogue)
  documentary (*see* documentary)
  reality   144
  series   39–47, 49–50, 54, 56 nn.1, 2, 6, 72, 226, 230, 274–7, 305

valency shifts   246
variation   39, 49, 54, 70, 71, 83, 91, 93, 95, 104, 106, 169, 213, 266
  regional   10
  social   10
ventriloquizing   98, 152
verbal, *see also* non-verbal
  forms, odd forms   246
  track (*see* track)
video game   227
visual
  grammar (*see* grammar)

narrative (*see* narrative)
track (*see* track)
vocatives   24, 64, 71–2, 82
voice
  accessed   141, 146
  authoritative   116, 118, 143, 145, 159
  narrative   141, 144–6, 155–8, 160
  non-diegetic   12, 142, 143
  over (*see* narration, narrator)
  privileged   143
  superimposed narrator   146

wanna   50, 52, 250
White, Skyler   289–90, 293–4, 296–8, 301, 303–4, *see also Breaking Bad*
White, Walter   289–90, *see also Breaking Bad*
Wildfeuer, Janina   9–10, 12, 13 n.13, 183, 185, 219 n.4
Wodak, Ruth   40–1, 124
word formation   239, 244

zoom   191–2, 199

www.ingramcontent.com/pod-product-compliance
Lightning Source LLC
Chambersburg PA
CBHW072120290426
44111CB00012B/1728